# ZAGATSURVEY®

# 2000

# AMERICA'S TOP
# RESTAURANTS

Published and distributed by
ZAGAT SURVEY, LLC
4 Columbus Circle
New York, New York 10019
Tel: 212 977 6000
E-mail: zagat@zagatsurvey.com
Web site: www.zagat.com

# Acknowledgments

Our special thanks to the thousands of surveyors who have shared their views with us and made this nationwide *Survey* possible. We would also like to thank our editors in each city: Nichole Bernier Ahern, Andrew Berk, Karen Berk, Marlene Berlow, Anthony Dias Blue, Arlene Blut, Olga Boikess, Mark Brown, Nikki Buchanan, Teresa Byrne-Dodge, Jon Christensen, Providence Cicero, Chris Cook, Andrea Clurfeld, Pat Denechaud, Victoria Pesce Elliott, Carrie Floyd, Hal Foster, Jeanette Foster, William Fox, Connie Frost, David Gadd, Norma Gottlieb, Barbara Herring, Suzanne Hough, Bobbye Hughes, Ed Jonna, Marty Katz, Joan Keane, Michael Klein, Sandy Kupfer, Gretchen Kurz, Nancy Leson, Sharon Litwin, John Long, Myrna Marston, John Martellaro, John McDermott, Carolyn McGuire, Maryanne Muller, Kelley Nakamura, David Nelson, Kristine Nickel, Ann Orton, Ann Lemons Pollack, Joe Pollack, June Naylor Rodriguez, Susan Safronoff, Shelley Skiles Sawyer, John Schell, Carol Seibert, Merrill Shindler, Mary Stagaman, Muriel Stevens, Bill St. John, Steve Stover, Paul Uhlmann III, Jill Van Cleave, Ann Verme, Phil Vettel, Carla Waldemar, Sue Zelickson and Nancy Zimmerman.

Fourth Printing
© 1999 Zagat Survey, LLC
ISBN 1-57006-199-8

# Contents

# Introduction

Here are the results of our *2000 Zagat Survey of America's Top Restaurants,* covering over 1,130 restaurants in 42 US cities and states. This book represents a compilation of the best restaurants selected by thousands of local *Survey* participants. For each area, we have included a list of the top restaurants (based on the results of our most recent *Surveys* in that area) as well as a list of other "important places" chosen by our local editors.

The cities covered were chosen mainly because they are leading culinary centers. However, this is still a "work in progress." Each year we add more areas of the country, but we still have more to cover.

By regularly surveying large numbers of local restaurant-goers across the country, we think we have achieved a uniquely reliable guide. We hope you agree. On the assumption that most people want a "quick fix" on the places at which they are considering eating, we've tried to be concise, and have provided a handy cuisine index.

Knowing that the quality of this *Survey* is the direct result of their voting and commentary, we sincerely thank each participant. They include numerous professionals, business executives and just plain folks – food lovers all. We also thank our local editors. It was they who helped us choose the restaurants to be surveyed and edited the *Survey* results.

**We invite you to be a reviewer in our city *Restaurant Surveys* or in our nationwide *Hotel Survey.*** So that we can contact you at the time of the next *Survey*, send a stamped, self-addressed, business-size envelope to ZAGAT SURVEY, 4 Columbus Circle, New York, NY 10019 indicating the *Survey* in which you would like to participate, e.g. "LA" or "Hotel." Each participant will receive a free copy of the resulting *Survey* when it's published.

Your comments, suggestions and criticisms of this *Survey* are also solicited. There is always room for improvement – with your help.

New York, New York                    Nina and Tim Zagat
November 5, 1999

# Foreword

As millennial madness gathers momentum, it seems an appropriate time to reflect on the culinary state of America. Over the last 20 years, the growth of fine dining has been nothing less than astonishing; one need look no further than the cities surveyed in this guide to see the variety of gastronomic riches our country has to offer.

A number of factors lie behind this development: the rise of women in the workplace, for one thing, has translated into more meals being taken outside the home, and thus an entire generation has become accustomed to dining out with more frequency than in the past. Generous expense accounts and a robust economy further fuel the trend, while improved global transportation has educated and elevated America's palate when it comes to foreign flavors. And those eager to revisit these ethnic tastes back home have little difficulty finding them. We are, after all, a land of immigrants, and our latest settlers have arrived eager to share their own native recipes.

In addition, culinary schools, which scarcely existed here in the 1960s, have sprung up as the role of chef has been elevated to a profession of some cachet. The apogee of this development is the celebrity chef, reflecting America's ever-growing fascination with icons of all kinds. Today's star chefs not only supervise kitchens, but are also minicorporations with publishing contracts, product lines, TV shows, web sites and merchandising deals. Their success helps raise the food bar throughout the restaurant community as others aspire to follow in their footsteps. And the fact that so many of these top toques are under the age of 40 suggests that we are only midway into the culinary revolution.

Thus, the new century promises even more dining pleasures to look forward to. We celebrate our country's current culinary derring-do with this *2000 Zagat Survey of America's Top Restaurants,* and we hope you'll visit us at our gustatory laboratory – zagat.com – to give us your feedback and vote for your own favorites in over 40 cities, both in America and abroad.

New York, New York                    Nina and Tim Zagat
November 5, 1999

# Key to Ratings/Symbols

**This sample entry identifies the various types of information contained in your Zagat Survey.**

**(1) Restaurant Name, Address & Phone Number**

**(2) Hours & Credit Cards**

**(3) ZAGAT Ratings**

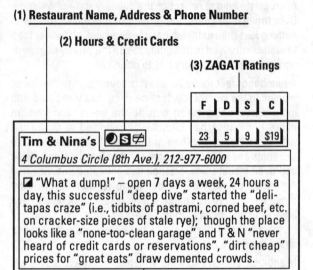

| F | D | S | C |
|----|----|----|-----|
| 23 | 5 | 9 | $19 |

**Tim & Nina's**  ◑ⓢ⌿

*4 Columbus Circle (8th Ave.), 212-977-6000*

■ "What a dump!" – open 7 days a week, 24 hours a day, this successful "deep dive" started the "deli-tapas craze" (i.e., tidbits of pastrami, corned beef, etc. on cracker-size pieces of stale rye); though the place looks like a "none-too-clean garage" and T & N "never heard of credit cards or reservations", "dirt cheap" prices for "great eats" draw demented crowds.

**(4) Surveyors' Commentary**

## (2) Hours & Credit Cards

After each restaurant name you will find the following courtesy information:

◑ ............................ *serving after 11 PM*

ⓢ ............................ *open on Sunday*

⌿ ............................ *no credit cards accepted*

## (3) ZAGAT Ratings

**Food**, **Decor** and **Service** are each rated on a scale of **0** to **30**:

| F | D | S | C |
|---|---|---|---|

F ........................ *Food*
D ........................ *Decor*
S ........................ *Service*
C ........................ *Cost*

| 23 | 5 | 9 | $19 |
|----|---|---|-----|

| 0 - 9 | ................. *poor to fair* |
| 10 - 15 | ................. *fair to good* |
| 16 - 19 | ................. *good to very good* |
| 20 - 25 | ................. *very good to excellent* |
| 26 - 30 | ................. *extraordinary to perfection* |

| ▽ 23 | 5 | 9 | $19 |
|------|---|---|-----|

▽ ........................ *Low number of votes/less reliable*

The **Cost (C)** column reflects the estimated price of a dinner with one drink and tip. Lunch usually costs 25% less.

A restaurant listed without ratings is either an important **newcomer** or a popular **write-in**. The estimated cost, with one drink and tip, is indicated by the following symbols.

| – | – | – | VE |
|---|---|---|----|

I ........................ *$15 and below*
M ........................ *$16 to $30*
E ........................ *$31 to $50*
VE ........................ *$51 or more*

## (4) Surveyors' Commentary

Surveyors' comments are summarized, with literal comments shown in quotation marks. The following symbols indicate whether responses were mixed or uniform.

◪ ........................ *mixed*
◼ ........................ *uniform*

7

# Top Five Food Rankings by Area

**Atlanta**
1. Bacchanalia
2. Ritz-Carlton Din. Rm.
3. Soto
4. Pano's & Paul's
5. Chops

**Atlantic City**
1. Le Palais
2. White House
3. Savaradio
4. Tre Figlio
5. Chef Vola's

**Baltimore/Annapolis**
1. Prime Rib
2. Hampton's
3. Linwood's
4. 208 Talbot
5. Charleston

**Boston**
1. L'Espalier
2. Aujourd'hui
3. Olives
4. Hamersley's Bistro
5. Caffe Bella

**Chicago**
1. Le Français
2. Ambria
3. Carlos'
4. Tallgrass
5. Le Titi de Paris

**Cincinnati**
1. Maisonette
2. Palace
3. Precinct
4. BonBonerie
5. Phoenix

**Cleveland**
1. Johnny's Bar
2. Sans Souci
3. Chez François
4. Hyde Park Grill
5. Baricelli Inn

**Columbus**
1. L'Antibes
2. Handke's
3. Refectory
4. Rigsby's
5. Rotolo's Pizza

**Dallas**
1. French Room
2. Riviera
3. Mansion on Turtle Creek
4. Pyramid Room
5. Cafe Pacific

**Denver/Mountain Resorts**
1. Papillon Café
2. Highlands Garden Cafe
3. Sweet Basil
4. Renaissance
5. Keystone Ranch

**Detroit**
1. Lark
2. Golden Mushroom
3. Opus One
4. Zingerman's Deli
5. Cafe Bon Homme

**Fort Lauderdale**
1. Eduardo de San Angel
2. Darrel & Oliver's Cafe
3. Armadillo Cafe
4. Mark's Las Olas
5. Black Orchid Cafe

**Fort Worth**
1. Cacharel
2. Del Frisco's
3. Saint-Emilion
4. Bistro Louise
5. Railhead Smokehouse

**Honolulu**
1. Alan Wong's
2. La Mer
3. Roy's
4. Hoku's
5. Hy's Steak House

8

## Houston
1. DeVille
2. Rotisserie/Beef & Bird
3. Chez Nous
4. Cafe Annie
5. La Réserve

## Kansas City
1. Cafe Allegro
2. American Rest.
3. Tatsu's
4. Ruth's Chris
5. Metropolis

## Las Vegas
1. Andre's
2. Michael's
3. Portofino
4. Steak Hse. (Circus Circus)
5. Emeril's New Orleans

## Los Angeles
1. Matsuhisa
2. Sushi Nozawa
3. Chinois on Main
4. Patina
5. L'Orangerie

## Miami/Miami Beach
1. Norman's
2. Osteria del Teatro
3. Chef Allen's
4. Tropical Chinese
5. Palm

## Minneapolis/St. Paul
1. Goodfellow's
2. D'Amico Cucina
3. Bayport Cookery
4. Manny's
5. Lucia's

## New Jersey
1. Jeffrey's
2. Saddle River Inn
3. Sagami
4. Scalini Fedeli
5. Ryland Inn

## New Orleans
1. Grill Room
2. Peristyle
3. Gabrielle
4. Brigtsen's
5. Ruth's Chris

## New York City
1. Le Bernardin
2. Daniel
3. Peter Luger
4. Nobu
5. Chanterelle

## Orange County
1. Pascal
2. Troquet
3. Ramos Hse. Cafe
4. Gustaf Anders
5. Ritz, The

## Orlando
1. Victoria & Albert's
2. La Coquina
3. Del Frisco's
4. Le Coq au Vin
5. California Grill

## Palm Beach
1. Four Seasons
2. Maison Janiero
3. La Vieille Maison
4. Kathy's Gazebo
5. Morton's of Chicago

## Philadelphia
1. Le Bec-Fin
2. Fountain
3. Le Bar Lyonnais
4. Brasserie Perrier
5. Susanna Foo

## Phoenix/Scottsdale
1. Pizzeria Bianco
2. Vincent Guerithault
3. Mary Elaine's
4. Los Dos Molinos
5. Ruth's Chris

## Portland
1. Genoa
2. Paley's Place
3. Couvron
4. Heathman
5. Tina's

## Salt Lake City
1. Fresco
2. Grapevine
3. Mariposa
4. New Yorker Club
5. Glitretind

## San Diego
1. El Bizcocho
2. WineSellar/Brasserie
3. Mille Fleurs
4. Sushi Ota
5. Azzura Point

## San Francisco
1. French Laundry
2. Sent Sovi
3. Masa's
4. Ritz-Carlton Din. Rm.
5. La Folie

## Santa Fe
1. Santacafe
2. Cafe Pasqual's
3. Coyote Cafe
4. Carlos' Gospel Cafe
5. India Palace

## Seattle
1. Rover's
2. Campagne
3. Tosoni
4. Fullers
5. Shiro's Sushi

## St. Louis
1. Fio's La Fourchette
2. Tony's
3. Trattoria Marcella
4. Dominic's
5. Café de France

## Tampa Bay/Sarasota
1. Mise en Place
2. Beach Bistro
3. Bern's Steak House
4. Blue Heron
5. Euphemia Haye

## Tucson
1. Ventana Room
2. Janos
3. Vivace
4. Le Rendez-Vous
5. Gold Room

## Washington, D.C.
1. Inn at Little Washington
2. Kinkead's
3. Makoto
4. L'Auberge Chez François
5. Obelisk

# Most Popular by Area

**Atlanta**
1. Bacchanalia
2. Brasserie Le Coze
3. Nava
4. Canoe
5. Bone's

**Atlantic City**
1. Ram's Head Inn
2. Le Palais
3. Chef Vola's
4. White House
5. Girasole

**Baltimore/Annapolis**
1. Tio Pepe
2. Prime Rib
3. Linwood's
4. Ruth's Chris
5. Cheesecake Factory

**Boston**
1. Aujourd'hui
2. Olives
3. Hamersley's Bistro
4. Elephant Walk
5. Rialto

**Chicago**
1. Charlie Trotter's
2. Le Français
3. Ambria
4. Everest
5. Frontera Grill

**Cincinnati**
1. Maisonette
2. Precinct
3. Montgomery Inn
4. Palace
5. Grand Finale

**Cleveland**
1. Johnny's Bar
2. Baricelli Inn
3. Sans Souci
4. Giovanni's
5. Johnny's Downtown

**Columbus**
1. Refectory
2. Lindey's
3. Rigsby's
4. Handke's
5. Cameron's

**Dallas**
1. Mansion on Turtle Creek
2. Cafe Pacific
3. Riviera
4. Star Canyon
5. French Room

**Denver/Mountain Resorts**
1. Papillon Café
2. Barolo Grill
3. Aubergine Cafe
4. Flagstaff House
5. Highlands Garden Cafe

**Detroit**
1. Lark
2. Golden Mushroom
3. Opus One
4. Rattlesnake Club
5. Whitney

**Fort Lauderdale**
1. Mark's Las Olas
2. Darrel & Oliver's Cafe
3. Brooks
4. Darrel & Oliver's/Grill
5. Armadillo Cafe

**Fort Worth**
1. Bistro Louise
2. Del Frisco's
3. Reata
4. La Piazza
5. Saint-Emilion

**Honolulu**
1. Alan Wong's
2. Roy's
3. Sam Choy's Diamond
4. 3660 on the Rise
5. Hy's Steak House

## Houston
1. Cafe Annie
2. Brennan's
3. Anthony's
4. Rotisserie/Beef & Bird
5. Ruggles Grill

## Kansas City
1. Cafe Allegro
2. American Rest.
3. Grand St. Cafe
4. Garozzo's
5. JJ's

## Las Vegas
1. Andre's
2. Spago
3. Emeril's New Orleans
4. P.F. Chang's
5. Palm Rest.

## Los Angeles
1. Patina
2. Cafe Bizou
3. Spago Beverly Hills
4. Bel-Air Hotel
5. Campanile

## Miami/Miami Beach
1. Norman's
2. Joe's Stone Crab
3. Chef Allen's
4. Forge, The
5. Pacific Time

## Minneapolis/St. Paul
1. Goodfellow's
2. D'Amico Cucina
3. Kincaid's
4. Palomino
5. Manny's

## New Jersey
1. Ryland Inn
2. Saddle River Inn
3. Scalini Fedeli
4. Chez Madeleine
5. Cafe Panache

## New Orleans
1. Commander's Palace
2. Galatoire's
3. Emeril's
4. Bayona
5. Brennan's

## New York City
1. Union Square Cafe
2. Gramercy Tavern
3. Gotham Bar & Grill
4. Aureole
5. Le Bernadin

## Orange County
1. Ritz, The
2. Pascal
3. Troquet
4. Gustaf Anders
5. Five Crowns

## Orlando
1. California Grill
2. Le Coq au Vin
3. Pebbles
4. Maison et Jardin
5. Enzo's on the Lake

## Palm Beach
1. La Vieille Maison
2. Cafe L'Europe
3. Four Seasons
4. Cafe Chardonnay
5. Max's Grille

## Philadelphia
1. Le Bec-Fin
2. Fountain
3. Susanna Foo
4. Brasserie Perrier
5. Striped Bass

## Phoenix/Scottsdale
1. Vincent Guerithault
2. Ruth's Chris
3. RoxSand
4. Lon's at the Hermosa
5. Christo's

## Portland

1. Genoa
2. Higgins
3. Paley's Place
4. Wildwood
5. Cafe des Amis

## Salt Lake City

1. New Yorker Club
2. Fresco Italian Cafe
3. Log Haven
4. Tuscany
5. Metropolitan

## San Diego

1. George's at the Cove
2. Mille Fleurs
3. Laurel
4. Pamplemousse Grille
5. WineSellar/Brasserie

## San Francisco

1. Boulevard
2. Aqua
3. French Laundry
4. Fleur de Lys
5. Postrio

## Sante Fe

1. Coyote Cafe
2. Santacafe
3. Inn of the Anasazi
4. Geronimo
5. La Casa Sena

## Seattle

1. Wild Ginger
2. Dahlia Lounge
3. Campagne
4. Rover's
5. Canlis

## St. Louis

1. Fio's La Fourchette
2. Tony's
3. Sidney Street Cafe
4. Trattoria Marcella
5. Harvest

## Tampa Bay/Sarasota

1. Michael's on East
2. Bern's Steak House
3. Bijou Café
4. Mise en Place
5. Café L'Europe

## Tucson

1. Janos
2. Vivace
3. Arizona Inn
4. Anthony's
5. Ventana Room

## Washington, D.C.

1. L'Auberge Chez François
2. Kinkead's
3. Inn at Little Washington
4. Galileo
5. Vidalia

# Alphabetical
# Directory of
# Restaurants

# Atlanta

## TOP 20 FOOD RANKING

| Restaurant | Cuisine Type |
|---|---|
| *28* Bacchanalia | New American |
| Ritz-Carlton Buck. Din. Rm. | Mediterranean |
| *27* Soto | Japanese |
| Pano's & Paul's | Continental/New Amer. |
| Chops | Steakhouse |
| *26* Bone's | Steakhouse |
| Brasserie Le Coze | French Bistro |
| Seeger's | New American |
| Sushi Huku | Japanese |
| La Grotta | N/S Italian |
| Ritz-Carlton Buck. Cafe | Continental/French |
| Bread Garden | Bakery/Sandwiches |
| Nikolai's Roof | Continental/Russian |
| *25* Hedgerose | New American |
| Morton's of Chicago | Steakhouse |
| Nava | Southwestern |
| 103 West | Continental/French |
| Van Gogh's | New American |
| dick and harry's | New American |
| Kamogawa | Japanese |

## OTHER IMPORTANT PLACES

| | |
|---|---|
| Abruzzi | N/S Italian |
| Babette's Cafe | French Bistro |
| Buckhead Diner | New American |
| Canoe | Continental/New Amer. |
| Chopstix | Chinese |
| Floataway Cafe | French/Italian |
| Flying Biscuit Cafe | Southern/Vegetarian |
| Food Studio | American |
| Fusebox | Asian |
| Mumbo Jumbo | New American |
| Palm Restaurant | Seafood/Steakhouse |
| Park 75 | New American |
| Prime | Seafood/Steakhouse |
| South City Kitchen | Southern |
| Tamarind | Thai |
| Tierra | Latin American |
| Veni Vidi Vici | Northern Italian |
| Watershed | Regional Amer. |

### Abruzzi
| 24 | 20 | 24 | $41 |

*Peachtree Battle Shopping Ctr., 2355 Peachtree Rd. (Peachtree Battle Ave.),*
*404-261-8186*

▇ You'll find "a bit of New York" at this "upscale Italian" "favorite" in Buckhead where the "well-heeled retired set" goes for "timeless" food and "personal attention" by "old-school waiters"; but even admirers admit the interior "needs to be renovated" and a miffed minority maintains that "service can be snobby if you're not a regular."

### Babette's Cafe ⑤
| 24 | 20 | 22 | $26 |

*471 N. Highland Ave. (bet. Colquitt Ave. & Freedom Pkwy.),*
*404-523-9121*

■ "Success has not spoiled anything" at this "charming country French" that adds a "European touch to Poncey-Highlands" with its "romantic", "cozy" atmosphere and "affordable" "creative" cuisine, including "theme meals" like the re-creation of *Babette's Feast*; its "very loyal following" laments "if only they would take reservations."

### Bacchanalia
| 28 | 25 | 27 | $51 |

*3125 Piedmont Rd. (Martina Dr.), 404-365-0410*

■ Anne Quatrano and Clifford Harrison's "intimate" prix fixe New American in a "beautiful Victorian home" "continues to hit all the notes", delivering a "flawless", "unparalleled", "A++" experience "without the Buckhead attitude" and earning the No. 1 score for both Food and Popularity in the *Atlanta Survey* once again; no wonder it's "difficult to get a reservation on weekends."

### Bone's ⑤
| 26 | 23 | 25 | $45 |

*3130 Piedmont Rd. (Peachtree Rd.), 404-237-2663*

■ Make "no bones about it" – this "pricey" Buckhead beef "bastion" is a "man's delight" with its "great drinks", "major league steaks", "cigar chomping" and "clubby" ambiance that "make you want to do a deal"; naturally, a few nonmembers feel that "regulars get the best service."

### Brasserie Le Coze
| 26 | 24 | 23 | $34 |

*Lenox Sq., 3393 Peachtree Rd. (Lenox Rd.), 404-266-1440*

■ "Close my eyes and I'm in France" gush devotees of this "sophisticated" "Country French bistro" in Buckhead with "Le Bernardin [NYC] lineage" where they turn out "fabulous" seafood dishes" and "soups that are good to the last drop"; only the "Neiman Marcus shopping bags" remind you that "you're eating in a mall" – the "only drawback" for some, but others add "deafening" "noise" levels to the list.

### Bread Garden ⑦
| 26 | 11 | 16 | $8 |

*549 Amsterdam Ave. (Monroe Dr.), 404-875-1166*

■ Everyone agrees this Va-Highlands darling doles out the "best bread available in the city"; chef-owner Catherine Krasnow's creations are "too good to be true", with the "best sandwiches" and "amazing desserts" flying out the door of this takeout-only, no-frills bakery.

**Buckhead Diner ◐[S]** 24 | 23 | 21 | $26

*3073 Piedmont Rd. NE (Pharr Rd.), 404-262-3336*

◪ When it comes to "innovative", "upscale diner" food, "nobody does it better" than this "gleaming and glitzy", "see and be seen" Buckhead American (the most highly trafficked restaurant in the *Atlanta Survey*) where locals, out-of-towners and celebrities go for veal meat loaf, homemade potato chips with Maytag blue cheese and white chocolate banana cream pie; not everyone is willing to endure "extremely long waits", however, especially those who find it "the original Snobs R Us."

**Canoe [S]** 23 | 26 | 22 | $34

*Vinings on the River, 4199 Paces Ferry Rd. (I-75), 770-432-2663*

◪ "How sublime!" gush enthusiasts of this New American–Continental boasting "beautiful architecture and design" and a "wonderful terrace" overlooking the Chattahoochee River where "beautiful people" flock to "see and be seen" while dining on "fabulous creative cuisine"; for most, this "stunning" spot "hits all the senses" ("earplugs necessary"), but a boatload of patrons gripe "unless you're the mayor, expect a wait, even with reservations."

**Chops [S]** 27 | 25 | 25 | $42

*Buckhead Plaza, 70 W. Paces Ferry Rd. (Peachtree Rd.), 404-262-2675*

■ For "melt in your mouth steaks" or a "lobster feast with finesse" at the "excellent" lobster bar downstairs, this Buckhead "boys' club" is the "best in Atlanta, bar none"; a few beef about "haughty service", but for most the "masculine decor" and "comfortable", "relaxing" atmosphere bolster this "pricey but worth it" power scene; after all, "sometimes it's ok to pay a lot for meat."

**Chopstix [S]** 24 | 20 | 22 | $29

*Chastain Sq., 4279 Roswell Rd. (Wieuca Rd.), 404-255-4868*

■ The No. 1 Chinese in the *Atlanta Survey* is a "gourmet" operation in Buckhead offering candlelight, white tablecloths, a "relaxing pianist" and "outstanding" "upscale Hong Kong–style" fare to a "dressed-up clientele"; it's "expensive but worth it" – owner "Philip Chan really knows what he's doing."

**dick and harry's** 25 | 20 | 22 | $33

*Holcomb Woods Village, 1570 Holcomb Bridge Rd. (½ mi. east of GA 400), Roswell, 770-641-8757*

■ There's "well-deserved praise" for this New American with "innovative", "excellent food" that's "the best thing to happen to the suburbs" in a long time; it's a "very loud", "fun, 'in' place" for locals and Intowners who think this "treat by any standard" is "worth every minute of the long drive to Roswell."

**Floataway Cafe** – | – | – | M

*1123 Zonolite Rd. (bet. Briarcliff & Johnson Rds.), 404-892-1414*

Little sister to Bacchanalia, Atlanta's highest-rated darling (No. 1 for Food and Popularity), this lively Country French–Italian near Emory is blossoming into a prized peach on the ever-growing family tree of chef-owners Annie Quatrano and Clifford Harrison; her phenomenal fare is uplifting, the eclectic wine list buoys the spirits, and fresh, sheer fabrics and airy cloud paintings set a casually chic scene.

## Flying Biscuit Cafe 🖥

| 23 | 19 | 19 | $15 |

*1655 McLendon Ave. (Clifton Rd.), 404-687-8888*

■ Breakfast lovers unite over this "warm and fuzzy" "bohemian delight" in Candler Park offering "homemade everything" on a "healthy, creative" Southern-Vegetarian menu; while the weekend "wait can be unbearable", most are willing to line up because the "sage turkey sausage and biscuits are as good as champagne and caviar."

## Food Studio 🖥

| 23 | 27 | 22 | $34 |

*887 W. Marietta St. (Howell Mill Rd.), 404-815-6677*

■ Dinner at this "stunning" New American in an "out-of-the-way" 1902 farm equipment factory west of Georgia Tech is "like sitting in a feature article of *Architectural Digest*"; while a few cynics snipe "beauty is only skin deep" and "the food can't live up to the great decor", the majority maintains the "creative" menu and "hip, warm and artsy" atmosphere are "way ahead of the Atlanta scene."

## Fusebox 🖥

| – | – | – | E |

*3085 Piedmont Rd. (Phair Rd.), 404-233-3383*

Those Zeit Guys (Mumbo Jumbo) have done it again at their beautiful, tragically chic Buckhead bar/restaurant, which boasts Eastern artifacts, cashmere-covered banquettes and more than 80,000 silver-leaf ceiling squares; scenesters gather to gaze and graze, sample flights of outstanding sakes and partake of chef Troy Thompson's rendition of Asian fusion; whether for lunch, dinner or Sunday dim-sum brunch, the creations of Guenter Seeger's protégé make for some happy chopsticks-wielders.

## Hedgerose

| 25 | 26 | 26 | $52 |

*490 E. Paces Ferry Rd. (Maple Dr.), 404-233-7673*

☑ This Buckhead New American is a "top to bottom" remake (from decor and owners to chef and cuisine) of the former Hedgerose Heights Inn and some who have paid a visit to this "romantic" prix fixe affair praise it as "a rose in Atlanta's culinary garden" thanks to "beautiful food" and "attentive" service in "elegantly comfortable" surroundings; others, however, complain of "overpriced" fare that's a "mixed success" and an atmosphere a "little stiff"; still, no one can deny that it "shows a lot of promise."

## Kamogawa 🖥

| 25 | 24 | 23 | $39 |

*Grand Hyatt Atlanta, 3300 Peachtree Rd. NE (Piedmont Rd.), 404-841-0314*

■ One of the top Japanese restaurants in our *Survey*, an "expense-account" affair in the Grand Hyatt, is praised for "beautifully served food" ("sushi to die for") that would "satisfy" any "Japanese client" and a "serene" setting complete with "traditional tatami rooms"; "sometimes you have to wait for your check", but it's "worth" it.

## La Grotta

| 26 | 23 | 25 | $40 |

*2637 Peachtree Rd. (bet. Lindbergh Dr. & W. Wesley Rd.), 404-231-1368*
*Crowne Plaza Ravinia Hotel, 4355 Ashford Dunwoody Rd. (I-285), 770-395-9925*

■ The No. 1 Italian in the *Atlanta Survey*, presided over by "primo padrone" Sergio Favalli, is "what fancy Italian restaurants used to be" with its "dark" and "romantic" setting, "very attentive service" and "beautiful food"; the original Buckhead location "hidden in the basement of a condo" is dinner only, while the newer branch in the Crowne Plaza Ravinia also serves lunch to a largely business crowd.

## Morton's of Chicago 🖪
25 | 22 | 23 | $42

*3379 Peachtree Rd. (Lenox Rd.), 404-816-6535*
*303 Peachtree Ctr. Ave. (Baker St.), 404-577-4366*

☑ "If you want lots of beef", put on your "power suit" and head to one of these "deluxe" "carnivore feeding grounds" that supporters swear "can compete with any steakhouse in town"; both the Downtown and Buckhead branches are "very good" for business lunches and dinners, but some grumble about the practice of peddling the cuts tableside – "the servers need to be told this is food, not Broadway."

## Mumbo Jumbo 🖪
22 | 25 | 20 | $32

*89 Park Pl. NE (Auburn Ave.), 404-523-0330*

☑ This "sexy, sassy" Downtown New American is "a delicious feast for the senses" with its "global menu" featuring "cutting-edge food" courtesy of "genius" chef Shawn Doty, "incredible" "eccentric" decor and "glitzy, preening" servers; but it can be more than "a bit of a scene" for the fainthearted who find "too much attitude" and "overpriced" "small portions."

## Nava 🖪
25 | 27 | 22 | $33

*Buckhead Plaza, 3060 Peachtree Rd. NW (W. Paces Ferry Rd.), 404-240-1984*

■ The No. 1 Southwestern in the *Atlanta Survey* is an "awesome experience" with "one of the more innovative kitchens in town" steered by Kevin Rathbun, "stunning" decor that matches the "food as art" and "awesome" margaritas that make the "great people-watching" even better; aside from the occasional "Santa Fe on steroids" slam of the interior, the main complaint from the few grumblers is "snooty hostesses"; everyone else "can't get enough of Nava."

## Nikolai's Roof 🖪
26 | 26 | 26 | $59

*Atlanta Hilton, 255 Courtland St., 30th fl. (bet. Baker & Harris Sts.), 404-221-6362*

■ After more than 20 years, this Russian-Continental is "still one of Atlanta's best" for "special" "romantic" evenings, "superb" expense-account dining or just a "unique night out"; an "elegant" prix fixe is "beautifully presented" by old-world waiters in costume in front of an "awesome view" of Downtown, but even the vista can't make a few forget how "expensive" it is.

## 103 West
25 | 23 | 25 | $45

*103 W. Paces Ferry Rd. (Peachtree St.), 404-233-5993*

☑ Surveyors in search of "excellent" cuisine, "attentive service" and an "opulent" setting frequent this Buckhead Life Group French-Continental "landmark" "best known for fried lobster tails"; a few find the "menu stale", the service "stuffy" and the "red velvet" "New Orleans brothel" decor "dated", but many more swear it's "expensive but worth it" for "special-occasion dining."

## Palm Restaurant 🖪
23 | 20 | 22 | $45

*Swissôtel Atlanta, 3391 Peachtree Rd. NE (Lenox Rd.), 404-814-1955*

☑ For "an infusion of cholesterol", devotees of "tasty" steaks, "gargantuan" lobsters and basically "big everything" mosey on over to this "classy, sassy" à la carte steakhouse/seafooder "hidden" in Buckhead's Swissôtel; "at these prices it better be perfect", but foes feel it's not, beefing "too loud", "overrated" and "doesn't measure up to the original" in New York.

### Pano's & Paul's — 27 | 23 | 26 | $45

*W. Paces Ferry Shopping Ctr., 1232 W. Paces Ferry Rd. (Northside Pkwy.), 404-261-3662*

■ The original "star" in the Buckhead Life Group's ever-expanding universe, this "sumptuous" and "scrumptious" Continental–New American is still a shining example of special-occasion dining; "as soon as you step inside, you're in a different century" with piano music, "private, cozy booths" and "ornate" decor as the backdrop to "divine" fried lobster tail and other "marvelous" creations; while a few fuss about "rushed" service and "house of ill repute" decor, most say it "lives up to its reputation"; N.B. namesake chef Paul has left to open his own venture in Florida.

### Park 75 — – | – | – | E

(fka Four Seasons Cafe)

*Four Seasons Atlanta, 75 14th St. (Peachtree St.), 404-881-9898*

Bright and lofty American in the Four Seasons that sports dual personalities as the only restaurant on the property: breakfast and lunch are casually elegant, with clean, wood-topped tables, but evening ushers in white linen, candlelight and crisp service; chef Brooke Vosika makes the most of regional specialty items from purveyors around the country in à la carte or prix fixe menus (including a vegetarian option); the terrace and lounge are ideal for a rendezvous or an après-theater drink (try a glass of their signature Cask 75 merlot).

### Prime [S] — 24 | 24 | 23 | $39

*Lenox Sq., 3393 Peachtree Rd. (Lenox Rd.), 404-812-0555*

■ What a "great concept" – a "stylish mix" of "excellent steaks" and "flawless sushi" ensures there's "something for everyone" who's willing to pay "high prices"; it's "too bad it's in a mall", but this "extremely enjoyable" "oasis" "overcomes" its Lenox location with a "pampering" staff, "hip" clientele and "cool" maple and metalwork decor.

### Ritz-Carlton Buckhead Cafe [S] — 26 | 26 | 26 | $41

*Ritz-Carlton Buckhead, 3434 Peachtree Rd. NE (Lenox Rd.), 404-237-2700*

■ Admirers of this "thoroughly civilized" Buckhead French-Continental consider it "a real treat for special occasions", an afternoon "tea date", Saturday night dancing or for "a brilliant Sunday buffet" – all done in the "extraordinary" style (and at the "incredible prices") of the Ritz; "unwind, relax and let the luxury begin."

### Ritz-Carlton Buckhead Dining Room — 28 | 27 | 28 | $68

*Ritz-Carlton Buckhead, 3434 Peachtree Rd. NE (Lenox Rd.), 404-237-2700*

■ "Yes, yes and oh yes!" moan enthusiasts about the "most exquisite taste sensations ever" created by chef Joel Antunes in this "inspired" Mediterranean in the Buckhead Ritz; while a few sniff "stuffy" and warn "bring your wallet", an "excellent wine list", the "best sommelier in the city", "polished service" and an "elegant atmosphere" all add up to one of Atlanta's "crème de la crème dining" experiences.

## Seeger's

26 | 26 | 26 | $72

*111 W. Paces Ferry Rd. (E. Andrews Dr.), 404-846-9779*
■ Guenter Seeger (ex Ritz-Carlton Buckhead Dining Room), a "genius" who's "in a class by himself", created this New American "hot spot" in Buckhead where "food as art" is only a part of the "visual feast"; the "beautiful contemporary" decor and "best service we have ever seen" complete a "sophisticated" picture; but fans and foes alike are hungry for "more, more, more", claiming the portions are "way too small" and the prices are "astronomical."

## Soto ❶

27 | 14 | 14 | $29

*Kroger Shopping Ctr., 3330 Piedmont Rd. (Peachtree Rd.), 404-233-2005*
■ "There is no better sushi and there is only one Soto!" declare zealots of the No. 1 Japanese in the *Atlanta Survey* and its eponymous "genius" who creates "amazingly fresh and inventive" fare that "makes others pale in comparison"; yet even the most ardent boosters acknowledge that the "quirky strip mall" spot in Buckhead has "no ambiance" and service is "painfully slow"; but once you get your food, it's "just heaven."

## South City Kitchen 🆂

23 | 22 | 20 | $28

*1144 Crescent Ave. (bet. 14th & Peachtree Sts.), 404-873-7358*
■ "Upscale twist" on Southern cuisine ("mama don't cook like this") that comes "highly recommended" for its "snazzy" fare, "terrific" and "reasonable" wine list and "urban chic" setting in a renovated Midtown house fronted by a "very well done" patio; it's an "in vogue" place for people-watching and, as a result, often "oooh so loud", "crowded" and loaded with "attitude."

## Sushi Huku 🆂

26 | 19 | 20 | $28

*Powers Ferry Landing, 6300 Powers Ferry Rd. (Northside Dr.), 770-956-9559*
■ The "best sushi on the Northside" and "in Atlanta" declare devotees of this highly rated "authentic" Japanese where you can "sit at the bar and watch the show" starring "entertaining sushi chefs" who "consistently" turn out "high-quality" fare to a "largely Japanese clientele"; it's "smoky" and certainly "not cheap", but the "great hospitality" and "marvelous" cuisine make it a "favorite."

## Tamarind 🆂

– | – | – | M

*80 14th St. (bet. Spring & Williams Sts.), 404-873-4888*
New, sophisticated Thai in Midtown near Georgia Tech, where a Pedicab parked by the front door is the first sign of a truly authentic experience; owners Charlie and Nan Nikomkul, who owned a restaurant in New York, have everything running smoothly – from bite-sized appetizers served on banana leaves to unbelievably good dishes beyond the traditional curries and pad Thai; don't let the unassuming exterior and inconvenient parking deter you.

## Tierra 🆂

– | – | – | M

*1425 Piedmont Ave. (Westminster Dr.), 404-874-5951*
Latin Fusion finally merengues onto the Atlanta dining scene, and tongues tango around mole lasagnas and pupusa (Salvadoran cheese-stuffed corn cakes) that are turned out by the skillful hands of Dan and Ticha Krinsky at this Latin American in Ansley; the tiny terra-cotta dining room is hung with tasteful black-and-white photos featuring typical Latin American scenes; parking (around back) is a challenge, but eating here is worth the effort.

---

**Van Gogh's [S]** 25 | 23 | 22 | $31

*70 W. Crossville Rd. (Crabapple Rd.), Roswell, 770-993-1156*

■ "Consistently excellent", "carefully prepared food" that's "clearly a work of art" is the draw at this Roswell New American, which is the *Atlanta Survey*'s top-rated spot in the city's northern environs; a "great wine list" and "prime" paintings on the walls enhance the "upscale" atmo; P.S. for those who say they "need to take reservations" – they do now.

**Veni Vidi Vici [S]** 24 | 24 | 22 | $33

*41 14th St. (bet. Spring & W. Peachtree Sts.), 404-875-8424*

◪ Formerly the brainchild of Marcella Hazan, the diva of Italian cuisine, this "fabulous", "upscale" Midtown Northern Italian has been under the aegis of the Buckhead Life kingdom for a while; chef Jamie Adams' "brilliant" cooking, the "sexy" postmodern interior and "smooth" service keep it a "favorite for business lunches" and "sophisticated" dinners; even dissenters who dub it "inconsistent" and "noisy" admit it's still "enjoyable."

**Watershed** – | – | – | I

*406 W. Ponce de Leon Ave. (bet. Clairmont Rd. & Water St.), Decatur, 404-378-4900*

Indeed, it is a watershed – this Downtown Decatur garage turned gourmet heaven is unlike anything else around here: it's a retail space for everything from candles to condiments, a wine shop/bar where the vino is poured into tony Reidel glasses, and a top-notch take-out/eat-in emporium for salads, to-die-for desserts and other Americana; the combined project of the Indigo Girls' Emily Saliers, chef Annie Quatrano (Bacchanalia, Floataway Cafe) and Southern toque Scott Peacock, this polished gem is sure to please.

# Atlantic City

## TOP 10 FOOD RANKING

| Restaurant | Cuisine Type |
|---|---|
| **27** Le Palais | New French |
| **26** White House | Deli/Sandwich Shop |
| Savaradio | Eclectic |
| **25** Tre Figlio | N/S Italian |
| **24** Chef Vola's | N/S Italian |
| Brighton Steak House | Steakhouse |
| Little Saigon* | Vietnamese |
| Ram's Head Inn, The* | Traditional American |
| **23** Cousin's | N/S Italian |
| Girasole | N/S Italian |

| F | D | S | C |
|---|---|---|---|

### Brighton Steak House 🅂

| 24 | 23 | 23 | $44 |
|---|---|---|---|

*Sands Hotel & Casino, Indiana Ave. (Brighton Park), 609-441-4300*

■ "Succulent steaks, nicely served" is the MO at this AC beef parlor in the Sands, with live piano music and "one of the best brunches around"; those enviously eyeing all the comped diners remark that it's a "typical, pricey meat place"; N.B. a recent renovation is not yet reflected in its decor score.

### Chef Vola's 🅂🖘

| 24 | 11 | 22 | $37 |
|---|---|---|---|

*111 S. Albion Pl. (Pacific Ave.), 609-345-2022*

☑ Enthusiasts of this AC "hideaway" in a "cramped" basement say it's like "dining with the perfect Italian family you never had" and undergo reservations boot camp for entry: leave a message for owner Louise Esposito, wait several months or secure a last-minute cancellation, grab cash and vino, then hightail it over for "plentiful portions" of "excellent" food; truly a "one-of-a-kind" experience.

### Cousin's 🅂

| 23 | 15 | 21 | $28 |
|---|---|---|---|

*104 Asbury Ave. (1st Ave.), Ocean City, 609-399-9462*

■ "No trip to the Shore is complete without a meal" at this "great little Italian restaurant in the basement of an old house", serving "home-cooked gourmet meals with flair"; Ocean City is a dry town, so don't expect vino with your lusty Mediterranean-accented supper, but you can take home the newly published *Cousin's Cookbook* to keep you warm in the off-season.

### Girasole 🅂

| 23 | 21 | 20 | $35 |
|---|---|---|---|

*Ocean Club Condos, 3108 Pacific Ave. (bet. Chelsea & Montpeller Aves.), 609-345-5554*

■ "Beautiful people like to be seen" and "see the clothes" of other "chic" patrons at this "trendy" AC Italian at the Ocean Club Condos, an "always hopping" setting for "yummy food" such as pizzas, pastas and "tuna carpaccio to die for"; a few puff about "attitude", though even casino employees tout this nongambling option.

---

\* Tied with the restaurant listed directly above.

| F | D | S | C |
|---|---|---|---|

**Le Palais** [S] — 27 | 27 | 27 | $49

*Resorts Casino & Hotel, 1133 Boardwalk (North Carolina Ave.), 609-340-6400*

■ This "top-notch" New French in the Resorts Hotel showcases "outstanding cuisine" and "elegant decor" to create a casino restaurant that's "one of this gambling town's finest, most sophisticated dining experiences", and rated No. 1 for Food, Decor and Service in AC; the "utter indulgence" includes a pianist and singer that help fuel the "romantic" atmosphere.

**Little Saigon** [S]≠ — 24 | 10 | 20 | $20

*2801 Arctic Ave. (Iowa Ave.), 609-347-9119*

■ "Excellent Vietnamese" that's "the real deal" according to "NY friends" is the skinny on this AC BYO where "attentive service" and a "delightful, caring" chef enhance an eatery that's unusual for South Jersey; N.B. vegetarians will find plenty to munch on.

**Ram's Head Inn, The** [S] — 24 | 26 | 24 | $42

*9 W. White Horse Pike (bet. Garden State Pkwy S. & Rte. 30), Absecon, 609-652-1700*

■ The "stately, old-world aura" of this Absecon spot, voted Most Popular in AC, makes it a "destination" that diners feel they "must do once a year", especially around Christmas; expect "white-glove" service, fireplaces and candlelit tables that bring a glow to the seasonal Traditional American menu, even though a few glower that it's "living off its reputation."

**Savaradio** [S]≠ — 26 | 18 | 22 | $31

*5223 Ventnor Ave. (Little Rock Ave.), Ventnor, 609-823-2110*

■ Chef-owner Lisa Savage creates "sophisticated and unique" Eclectic dishes along with "great specials" at this Ventnor BYO, which recently moved to art-filled, slightly "larger quarters" with a "sparse, modern look"; the infatuated tout the "best coffee and desserts" around, as well as the $15.95 prix fixe dinner, available weekdays in the off-season.

**Tre Figlio** [S] — 25 | 20 | 22 | $35

*500 W. White Horse Pike (bet. Pomona Ave. & Tilton Rd.), Egg Harbor City, 609-965-3303*

■ "Be very hungry when you go" to "this little bit of South Philly" in Egg Harbor City, which offers "high-quality Italian food" (the "best veal chop ever", an "excellent" early-bird prix fixe) as well as "attentive", "friendly" service in a "warm" setting; N.B. don't miss the award-winning wine list.

**White House** [S]≠ — 26 | 9 | 16 | $12

*2301 Arctic Ave. (Mississippi Ave.), 609-345-1564*

■ Some of "the best subs in the USA" emerge from this AC sandwich landmark (since 1946) and are the "choice of a last meal" for many as well as No. 1 Bang for the Buck in AC; not only do "Hollywood stars have the subs shipped to them", but fans add that the "only thing better than the food and the prices are the aromas."

# Baltimore/Annapolis

## TOP 10 FOOD RANKING

| Restaurant | Cuisine Type |
|---|---|
| *28* Prime Rib | Steakhouse |
| *27* Hampton's | New American |
| Linwood's | Californian |
| 208 Talbot/A | New American |
| Charleston | American/Southern |
| Inn at Perry Cabin/A | Continental |
| *26* Milton Inn | Regional American |
| Lewnes' Steakhouse/A | Steakhouse |
| Boccaccio | Northern Italian |
| Rudys' 2900 | Continental/New Amer. |

## OTHER IMPORTANT PLACES

| | |
|---|---|
| Black Olive | Greek/Seafood |
| Cantler's Riverside Inn/A | Crab House/Seafood |
| Cheesecake Factory | Californian |
| Helmand, The | Afghan |
| Kennedyville Inn/A | BBQ/Regional American |
| Marconi's | Traditional American |
| McCormick & Schmick's | Seafood |
| Oregon Grille | Regional American |
| Pierpoint | New/Regional American |
| Polo Grill | Continental |
| Ruth's Chris Steak House | Steakhouse |
| Tio Pepe | Continental/Spanish |
| Vera's Bakery | Bakery/Brazilian |

| F | D | S | C |
|---|---|---|---|

### Black Olive 🖫

| 26 | 18 | 21 | $38 |
|---|---|---|---|

*814 S. Bond St. (Shakespeare St.), 410-276-7141*
■ "Great everything" – no wonder this young Greek scored high food ratings on its first try, proving that in Fells Point, as on the Aegean, classically "simple" preparations and hands-on "hospitality" impress; its white brick and wood decor "is like being in a Greek fishing village", yet a few feel entitled to more "for the price."

### Boccaccio 🖫

| 26 | 23 | 24 | $41 |
|---|---|---|---|

*925 Eastern Ave. (bet. Exeter & High Sts.), 410-234-1322*
■ The "chef receives in the kitchen" of this "high-end", "celebrity-filled", "real [Northern] Italian" where he shows Baltimore that there is more to Little Italy than "red sauce" pastas; perhaps "reservations are not always on time", but the "wonderful" veal chop is.

A = Annapolis/Eastern Shore

## Cantler's Riverside Inn ▣     22 | 15 | 18 | $20
*458 Forest Beach Rd. (Brown's Wood Rd.), Annapolis, 410-757-1311*
■ "It's worth getting lost to find" this "wonderful, on the river" site near Annapolis for "elbow-to-elbow crab picking"; the seafood arrives daily, and diners can enjoy a "great" open-air deck overlooking a wooded creek; maybe it's "not perfect" ("needs better parking"), but it's one of the "most relaxed crab places" in the vicinity; N.B. call for directions.

## Charleston ▣     27 | 25 | 26 | $40
*1000 Lancaster St. (bet. Central & Exeter Sts.), 410-332-7373*
■ Even though it only opened shortly before our *Baltimore Survey* was conducted, this "stunning" Southern American vaulted to No. 5 for Food, 3 for Service and 9 for Decor; chef-owner Cindy Wolf and her husband Tony Forman's stellar performance at the defunct Savannah continues here with "unique, delicious" takes on "Low Country delicacies" and one of the "best wine cellars in town"; even the harbor-view office building location is "smashing", if "totally un-Baltimore."

## Cheesecake Factory ▣     21 | 18 | 18 | $21
*Harborplace, Pratt St. Pavilion (Calvert St.), 410-234-3990*
☑ There are no just-in-time arrivals at this Big Food factory – with "no reservations", "humongous" servings and an "overwhelming" California menu (most of it "consistently good"), near "unbearable" noise and waits are routine; adherents avoid the "department store at Christmas" frenzy and bypass the "beeper hall" for the bar, where they "get served right away."

## Hampton's ▣     27 | 28 | 27 | $54
*Harbor Court Hotel, 550 Light St. (bet. Conway & Lee Sts.), 410-347-9744*
■ Voted No. 1 for Decor and Service in Baltimore, "first-class" formal dining "doesn't get any better" than at this premiere "event restaurant"; the breathtaking harbor views and "top-quality" New American menu leave patrons feeling "pampered"; P.S. "a drink in the Explorer's Lounge" starts the evening off in style.

## Helmand, The ▣     25 | 21 | 23 | $22
*806 N. Charles St. (bet. Madison & Read Sts.), 410-752-0311*
■ "Highly recommended" for serving some of Baltimore's "best ethnic food" at "fantastic prices", this Mt. Vernon Afghan is also esteemed for its "intimate atmosphere" and "quick service"; out-of-towners even plan excursions "for its rack of lamb – the best anywhere."

## Inn at Perry Cabin ▣     27 | 28 | 26 | $54
*Inn at Perry Cabin, 308 Watkins Ln. (Talbot St.), St. Michaels, 410-745-2200*
■ Join luminaries looking for privacy at this "elegant" Eastern Shore getaway; though the "dinner 'production'" strikes some as "pretentious", the modern Continental food, "great wine list" and "professional" service "befit the lovely surroundings" and do justice to the spectacular water view from the lovely patio; N.B. though no longer affiliated with the Ashley House hotels, nothing has visibly changed.

F D S C

## Kennedyville Inn 🅂
– – – M

*11986 Rte. 213 (5 mi. north of Chestertown), Kennedyville, 410-348-2400*
The laid-back charm, lively American cooking and pit barbecuing
that popularized Chestertown's Ironstone Cafe, once owned by
Kevin McKinney and Barbara Silcox, work just as well at this
vintage wooden house in Kennedyville; here they host dinner
Wednesdays–Saturdays, as well as an all-day, whim-of-the-chef
meal on Sundays.

## Lewnes' Steakhouse ❶🅂
26 19 21 $48

*401 Fourth St. (Severn Ave.), Annapolis, 410-263-1617*
■ For "great steaks in a seafood town", Annapolis carnivores
proudly point to this "classic", which boasts "humongous, bring
your appetite" portions of "outstanding meat" and men's-clubby
vibes; devotees swear it's every bit "as good as the Palm" and,
some say, just as "expensive."

## Linwood's 🅂
27 26 25 $41

*McDonough Crossroads, 25 Crossroads Dr. (McDonough &*
*Reisterstown Rds.), Owings Mills, 410-356-3030*
■ A "class act", this "elegant" bistro ("no need to board the QE2")
has fans dubbing it "amazingly consistent" for an "imaginative"
California-style menu; this is where Owings Mills goes "for a
celebration" overseen by a "well-trained staff", or to "watch all
the action" from the bar; there's never "too much table-hopping"
for its steady customers, who go to "eat well, see and be seen."

## Marconi's
23 18 24 $30

*106 W. Saratoga St. (bet. Cathedral St. & Park Ave.), 410-727-9522*
■ "Like Gibraltar, a sturdy Baltimore tradition"– this American's
"delicious signature dishes" ("great lobster cardinale" and hot
fudge sundaes) are still a "draw"; also compelling is the "old
Baltimore atmosphere", which harks back to "H. L. Mencken's
time", not to mention the servers ("average age only 65"); but,
yes, there are a couple of curmudgeons who "never did like
grainy chocolate sauce."

## McCormick & Schmick's 🅂
– – – M

*Harbor Inn Pier 5, 711 Eastern Ave. (President St.), 410-234-1300*
Floor-to-ceiling windows, sweeping waterfront views and a
dockside outdoor cafe distinguish Baltimore's link in this high-end,
Edwardian-feeling West Coast seafood chain; virtually a clubroom
for Downtown since day one, its open, yet workman-like, manners
are reflected in the clientele's loosened ties and rolled-up sleeves,
but tourists tout it too.

## Milton Inn 🅂
26 26 25 $48

*14833 York Rd. (2½ mi. north of Shawan Rd.), Sparks, 410-771-4366*
■ New owners (Brass Elephant, King's Contrivance) have
brightened this 18th-century destination without disturbing its
"country atmosphere" or its tradition of "excellent" Maryland
regional food and service; as "rustic and romantic" as ever, it's a
premier special-occasion place – the lovely "walk to the door",
the smell of woodsmoke from the hearth room and the glow of
candlelight are "only a hint of the wonderful things to come."

## Oregon Grille S

24 | 27 | 22 | $47

*1201 Shawan Rd. (Beaver Dam Rd.), Hunt Valley, 410-771-0505*

◪ This "classy, clubby" Hunt Country "high roller" showcasing chef Mark Henry's "genius" with Regional American cuisine is "fast becoming one of the best formal restaurants" in the area; though a minority feels it "still needs work", "when it's good, it's great"; the help may be "a bit young", but rest assured the "expensive" wines are not.

## Pierpoint S

25 | 17 | 21 | $35

*1822 Aliceanna St. (bet. Ann & Wolfe Sts.), 410-675-2080*

■ "Sophisticated and intimate" Fells Point boîte that showcases chef-owner Nancy Longo's "innovative Maryland cuisine"; her fans "love its smallness", which permits her to produce "tremendous food without the prices and atmosphere of a high-class restaurant"; while some regret the "tight quarters", virtually all agree that "when it's good, it's very, very good", especially at brunch.

## Polo Grill S

26 | 25 | 24 | $42

*Inn at the Colonnade, 4 W. University Pkwy. (bet. Canterbury & Charles Sts.), 410-235-8200*

■ A "really classy", "clubby", "truly professional operation" in a Homewood location, where Charm City's "big dogs" and "power players" come to nod and "be seen" (not heard – it's "too noisy"); the atmosphere is a bit "stuffy", but the "kitchen turns out well-done innovations on classic Continentals" that earn raves.

## Prime Rib ●S

28 | 25 | 25 | $46

*Horizon House, 1101 N. Calvert St. (Chase St.), 410-539-1804*

■ The town "never tires" of this "swank", "old-fashioned supper club" (our version of the "Stork Club"), with its "sexy bar", glass-topped baby grand and "retro-chic decor"; "butter-soft steak" and the "best crab imperial around" win it top ratings for Food (it's No. 2 for Popularity) in this year's *Baltimore Survey*; devotees say it "blows away the chains" by making each diner "feel special."

## Rudys' 2900 S

26 | 22 | 24 | $39

*2900 Baltimore Blvd. (Rte. 91), Finksburg, 410-833-5777*

■ At their "marvelous" Continental-American "classic" in Finksburg, the "two Rudys are always on their toes": Rudy Speckamp, a "champion" chef, keeps his "consistently fine food" fresh with regional and "Austrian innovations", while Rudy Paul and his "very knowledgeable staff" orchestrate a "special dining experience" for each table; though a few shrug "too far from town", most maintain it's "worth the trip."

## Ruth's Chris Steak House S

24 | 22 | 23 | $44

*600 Water St. (bet. Gay St. & Market Pl.), 410-783-0033*

■ "You get what you pay for" at this "solid" cow palace: butter-drenched beef, "fancy" New Orleans decor, and "extraordinary" courtesy; some say it ranks "at the lower end of the top tier" – possibly Ruth's "formula" is a little too "different tasting", "pricey" or "not personally engaging."

**Tio Pepe [S]** 25 22 22 $38

*10 E. Franklin St. (bet. Charles & St. Paul Sts.), 410-539-4675*

◪ An "institution" and voted the Most Popular Restaurant in Baltimore, this Downtown Spanish-Continental is one of those places people love to hate — they complain about having to "wait with reservations" in a "whitewashed dungeon"; however, loyalists like the "great garlic shrimp" and roast pig served in "cozy nooks."

**208 Talbot [S]** 27 23 24 $39

*208 N. Talbot St. (bet. Dodson Ave. & North St.), St. Michaels, 410-745-3838*

■ "Superb" is how surveyors summarize this St. Michaels New American whose "fine kitchen" exemplifies "culinary creativity at its best"; set in a "romantic" townhouse, diners feel like they're "eating in a private home", albeit one that's overseen by a "great" staff; overall, it's considered "the greatest treat", "très chic and worth every penny."

**Vera's Bakery [S]** – – – M

*548 Baltimore-Annapolis Blvd. (McKinsey Rd.), Severna Park, 410-647-3337*

"Amusing" ex-diplomats let the world come to their "tiny" bakery/cafe "hidden" in Severna Park, where fresh flowers and antique accents augur some of the area's "best", but least expensive, Brazilian and internationally inspired fare, wonderful breads and beautifully decorated special-occasion cakes; you can stuff yourself at their brunch buffet (under $10) or go for a romantic BYO dinner.

## TOP 20 FOOD RANKING

| Restaurant | Cuisine Type |
|---|---|
| **28** L'Espalier | New French |
| Aujourd'hui | New American |
| **27** Olives | Mediterranean |
| Hamersley's Bistro | French Bistro/New Amer. |
| **26** Caffe Bella | Mediterranean |
| Julien | New French |
| Il Capriccio | Northern Italian |
| Radius | New French |
| Saporito's | N/S Italian |
| Rialto | Mediterranean |
| Lumière | New French |
| Sage | Californian/Italian |
| Icarus | New American |
| Blue Ginger | Asian/Eclectic |
| Clio | New French |
| **25** Silks | New French |
| Maurizio's | Italian/Med. |
| Ginza | Japanese |
| Terramia | N/S Italian |
| La Campania | N/S Italian |

## OTHER IMPORTANT PLACES

| | |
|---|---|
| Ambrosia on Huntington | Asian/French Bistro |
| Anago | New American |
| Aquitaine | French Bistro |
| Biba | New American |
| Blue Room, The | Eclectic |
| Café Louis | Northern Italian |
| Chez Henri | French Bistro/Cuban |
| East Coast Grill & Raw Bar | BBQ/Seafood |
| Elephant Walk | Cambodian/New French |
| Grill 23 & Bar | Steakhouse |
| Harvest | Traditional American |
| La Bettola | New American |
| Legal Sea Foods | Seafood |
| Maison Robert | Classic French |
| Mistral | French |
| Ritz-Carlton Dining Room | French |
| Rowes Wharf | Regional American |
| Salamander | Asian/Eclectic |
| Tremont 647 | New American |
| Truc | French Bistro |

| F | D | S | C |
|---|---|---|---|

## Ambrosia on Huntington [S]

| 24 | 24 | 23 | $50 |
|---|---|---|---|

*116 Huntington Ave. (bet. Dartmouth & Newton Sts.), 617-247-2400*

◪ This "flashy" Back Bay spot "hits the mark" with "great eye appeal" and a "chic, sophisticated ambiance"; equally noteworthy is its "inventive" Franco-Asian cuisine that some call a "tasty but precious" example of "fusion intrusion"; still, the service is "attentive" (if "pretentious") and the "sexy bar" attracts a "glitzy" clientele; P.S. don't forget to "bring your platinum card."

## Anago [S]

| 24 | 23 | 22 | $49 |
|---|---|---|---|

*Lenox Hotel, 65 Exeter St. (Boylston St.), 617-266-6222*

◪ Since moving last year from Cambridge to the "trendy" Lenox Hotel in the Back Bay, this little red room has become quite the "happening scene" with a "young, professional crowd", which "feels regal" dining on "innovative" American cuisine in the "high-ceilinged" space; dissenters, however, find it "overrated", "overpriced" and "snooty", and wonder "what all the fuss is about."

## Aquitaine [S]

| 23 | 22 | 20 | $42 |
|---|---|---|---|

*569 Tremont St. (Clarendon St.), 617-424-8577*

◪ Bringing "France to the South End", this "beautiful" "find" appeals with "quintessential bistro fare" prepared with "flair", accompanied by an "excellent wine list"; while critics grumble that it's "overrated" and staffed by an unusually "loud" bunch, devotees insist it's "warm and welcoming, and we could stay all night."

## Aujourd'hui [S]

| 28 | 28 | 28 | $64 |
|---|---|---|---|

*Four Seasons Hotel, 200 Boylston St. (bet. Arlington & S. Charles Sts.), 617-351-2071*

■ "Heaven's main dining room", according to disciples, is in the "luxurious" Four Seasons Hotel where pampered diners are virtually guaranteed "an elegant", "world-class" evening; in a "magnificent" space with "regal decor" and a stellar view of the Public Garden, an "impeccable" staff proffers "glorious" New American cuisine layered with French and Asian accents; Boston's Most Popular Restaurant, it also ranks as the No. 1 restaurant overall in the city, with the top combined scores for Food (No. 2), Decor (No. 1) and Service (No. 1).

## Biba [S]

| 25 | 24 | 22 | $52 |
|---|---|---|---|

*272 Boylston St. (bet. Arlington & S. Charles Sts.), 617-426-7878*

◪ Among the city's premier "power dining spots", this "oh-so-chic" Back Bay New American boasts a "fantastic view of the Public Garden" from the "fabulous" Adam Tihany–designed room and "inspired", "innovative" dishes from chefs Lydia Shire and Susan Regis that are admittedly "sometimes weird"; but even if the "menu is too avant-garde, this is still one of Boston's best tables"; P.S. the "buzzing" bar is a "good place to eat and people-watch."

## Blue Ginger [S]

| 26 | 22 | 23 | $41 |
|---|---|---|---|

*583 Washington St. (Rte. 16), Wellesley, 781-283-5790*

■ "Good luck getting reservations" at "brilliant chef" Ming Tsai's "casually elegant" "gem" in Wellesley, "but if you do, you're in for a treat" because his "exciting East-meets-West fusion" cuisine is "uniquely" "exquisite" (don't miss his "awesome" signature sake-marinated Chilean sea bass); despite some negative marks for the "hard-edged decor", most "welcome" it as a "first-class" "oasis in the Western suburbs."

### Blue Room, The 🅂   24 | 20 | 22 | $36
*1 Kendall Sq. (bet. Broadway & Hampshire St.), Cambridge, 617-494-9034*
☑ In Kendall Square, this "upbeat", "always satisfying" experience seems to "get even better every year"; chef Steve Johnson's "fabulous" Eclectic menu (with "Asian touches") is "innovative and flavorful, based on unexpected combinations that work", and it's matched with a "killer wine list"; the "attractive, relaxing" surroundings make this an "all-around great hangout", and "you'll leave as happy" as Julia Child (this "jewel" is one of her favorites).

### Café Louis   23 | 19 | 21 | $44
*Louis, Boston, 234 Berkeley St. (Newbury St.), 617-266-4680*
☑ Fashionistas urge don't "spend all your money" while shopping at the Back Bay's Louis, Boston, because its "stylish" cafe boasts a "terrific" Northern Italian menu that spotlights "excellent" pizzas and "dynamite pastas"; the room is "frightfully loud", the ambiance is a bit "cold" and the prices are, well, "pricey", but "you'd never believe you could get food this good at a clothing store."

### Caffe Bella   26 | 19 | 22 | $34
*19 Warren St. (bet. Main St. & Rte. 139), Randolph, 781-961-7729*
■ Set in a strip mall in Randolph, this "unbelievable" Mediterranean gem is the "South Shore's culinary trophy"; revel in the "divine" creations of "genius" chef-owner Patrick Barnes Jr. – "perfectly prepared" dishes with "wonderful flavors" – accompanied by an "incredible wine list"; it's "too loud" and "crowded", with "squishy seating" and "ridiculous waits", but even so, devotees "could dine here nightly"; "don't miss this one."

### Chez Henri 🅂   23 | 20 | 20 | $35
*1 Shepard St. (Mass Ave.), Cambridge, 617-354-8980*
■ Devotees declare it's "so very Cambridge" of this "dynamic" bistro to spark "innovative French food with Cuban influences", resulting in "clever" combinations that "pack a flavor punch"; the room is "inviting" and "romantic", with an "unpretentious" ambiance, and it boasts the "perfect bar to eat at alone" because "you'll always meet interesting people there."

### Clio 🅂   26 | 26 | 24 | $57
*Eliot Suite Hotel, 370A Commonwealth Ave. (Mass Ave.), 617-536-7200*
■ "Swanky" and "romantic", this petite Eliot Suite Hotel dining room in the Back Bay is "where the chic eat", surrounded by "plush" appointments like cushy banquettes and a leopard-print carpet; "brilliant" chef Ken Oringer (ex SF's Silks) "gets it just right", turning out "divine" interpretations of New French cuisine that are "orgasmic taste sensations"; despite a few jabs about a "snooty" ambiance, admirers only wish they'd "consider serving lunch" – and lower the "astronomical" prices.

### East Coast Grill & Raw Bar 🅂   24 | 18 | 20 | $32
*1271 Cambridge St. (Prospect St.), Cambridge, 617-491-6568*
■ Chris Schlesinger's Inman Square "seafood thriller" continues to sizzle with "finger-licking 'cue" and "sensory-overload sides" delivered in an "exuberant" room with a "funky" vibe; heat-chasers urge "come on 'hotter-than-hell' nights" when the "spicy" food is notched up yet a few more degrees; despite a "jammed" site and "long waits", these masters of the grill "know their smoky stuff" – in fact, it was ranked the No. 1 BBQ in Boston.

**Elephant Walk [S]** | 23 | 21 | 20 | $30 |

*900 Beacon St. (Park Dr.), 617-247-1500*
*2067 Mass Ave. (bet. Hadley & Russell Sts.), Cambridge, 617-492-6900*
◪ Hordes "stampede" to Kenmore and Porter Squares for the "wonderful juxtaposition" of Cambodian and New French cuisines, which "deliciously" results in "eclectic" dishes such as *loc lac* (lime-cured beef) and "phenomenal" chile tuna; the "classy" ambiance is made "exotic" with elephant figurines along the ceiling, and despite "long waits" for "crowded seating", most urge "run, don't walk", to get in on this "unique" experience.

**Ginza [S]** | 25 | 17 | 18 | $29 |

*16 Hudson St. (bet. Beach & Kneeland Sts.), 617-338-2261* ◐
*1002 Beacon St. (St. Mary's St.), Brookline, 617-566-9688*
■ Rated the No. 1 Japanese in Boston, this "bit of Tokyo" in Chinatown and Brookline will "make you wonder why food should ever be cooked" after just one bite of its "amazing" sushi, "artistically presented"; the "late-night" Hudson Street flagship is "hip and crowded", despite somewhat "sterile" surroundings, so expect "long waits" because it "doesn't take reservations", except for parties of six or more.

**Grill 23 & Bar [S]** | 25 | 23 | 24 | $49 |

*161 Berkeley St. (Stuart St.), 617-542-2255*
■ "Movers and shakers" gather at this "manly" Back Bay steakhouse to "indulge" in new chef Jay Murray's "superb" menu, which goes "beyond beef" to "excellent" seafood as well; the historic building boasts a "beautiful", "soaring interior", and now after a recent design tune-up, the "gin-fueled din" is more muted.

**Hamersley's Bistro [S]** | 27 | 24 | 24 | $51 |

*553 Tremont St. (Clarendon St.), 617-423-2700*
■ Gordon Hamersley's South End namesake is a "stylish yet understated" New American–French "phenomenon", with a "versatile", "consistently excellent" seasonal menu offering the likes of bouillabaisse and "jaw-droppingly good" roast chicken to the city's power brokers; along with "impeccable decor", "attentive service" and an "interesting wine list", it "remains a classic" and "every visit reinforces" its rep.

**Harvest [S]** | 23 | 22 | 22 | $43 |

*44 Brattle St. (Church St.), Cambridge, 617-868-2255*
■ Now run by the Grill 23 & Bar management team, this revived "Cambridge relic" in Harvard Square is "clubbier and more mature" than before, with an "outstanding" American menu showcasing striped bass, grilled rack of lamb and "one mean chowder"; the "tasteful" layout features subdued wood with taupe tones, a "lovely courtyard" and the perfect bar for a "sophisticated drink"; the verdict: "reincarnation works."

**Icarus [S]** | 26 | 24 | 24 | $47 |

*3 Appleton St. (bet. Arlington & Berkeley Sts.), 617-426-1790*
■ When it's time for a "splurge", the well-heeled wing it to this "sophisticated" South Ender, a "class act" where "superb", "inventive" American fare is delivered by an "A+ staff" amid "stunning decor"; most agree it "lives up to its well-deserved reputation" as a "formal" standout where the extras include live jazz Friday nights and valet parking.

## Il Capriccio 26 | 21 | 23 | $45

*888 Main St. (Prospect St.), Waltham, 781-894-2234*

■ "Why go to Boston?" suburbanites wonder when there's a "first-class" Northern Italian right in Waltham serving "delicious, innovative" handmade pastas (and a "sublime" porcini soufflé), matched with a "great wine list"; devotees deem it "elegant", if "noisy", and its status as "Waltham's best" means it can be "difficult to get in."

## Julien 26 | 27 | 26 | $57

*Le Meridien Hotel, 250 Franklin St. (bet. Oliver & Pearl Sts.), 617-451-1900*

◪ "Civility" defines this "elegant", "formal" New French experience in Le Meridien Hotel where diners savor "perfection" in "every bite"; look forward to a "wonderful wine list", "great" "European-style" service and a "relaxing" ambiance; overall, it's an "awesome place" for a "quiet" "celebration" or a "power lunch", but then again, it "should be at these prices."

## La Bettola [S] 24 | 20 | 22 | $51

*480A Columbus Ave. (bet. Rutland Sq. & W. Newton St.), 617-236-5252*

◪ "So this is what the 'next level' means" gush admirers of "inspired" chef Rene Michelena's "adventurous" and "artistic" Asian-influenced New American cuisine, which is making waves beyond its "spare but attractive" South End locale; while dissenters nitpick about "overpriced" "small portions", more recognize it as a "great dining experience."

## La Campania 25 | 22 | 22 | $35

*504 Main St. (bet. Cross & Heard Sts.), Waltham, 781-894-4280*

■ Run by a "gracious", "hardworking" family that's "devoted to its food and customers", this "Waltham hot spot" with "charming country decor" wins raves for its "gourmet and traditional" Italian offerings, complemented by a 300-bottle wine list; the only complaint is that its 40 seats are clearly "not enough."

## Legal Sea Foods [S] 21 | 15 | 18 | $30

*Long Wharf, 255 State St. (Court St.), 617-227-3115*
*Prudential Ctr., 800 Boylston St. (bet. Fairfield & Gloucester Sts.), 617-266-6800*
*Copley Pl., 100 Huntington Ave. (bet. Dartmouth & Exeter Sts.), 617-266-7775*
*Park Plaza Hotel, 35 Columbus Ave. (Arlington St.), 617-426-4444*
*South Shore Plaza, 250 Granite St., Braintree, 781-356-3070*
*Burlington Mall, 1131 Middlesex Tpke. (Rte. 128), Burlington, 781-270-9700*
*Kendall Sq., 5 Cambridge Ctr. (bet. Ames & Main Sts.), Cambridge, 617-864-3400*
*43 Boylston St. (Hammond Pond Pkwy.), Chestnut Hill, 617-277-7300*
*Miltons Plaza, 1400 Worcester Rd. (bet. Speen St. & Rte. 126), Natick, 508-820-1115*
*Northshore Mall, Rtes. 114 & 128, Peabody, 978-532-4500*
*Additional locations throughout the Boston area.*

◪ A "local legend" that's "gone national", Roger Berkowitz's ever-expanding fleet of fish houses owes its "hall-of-fame" status to "impeccably fresh" seafood, including the "best chowder" and steamed lobster; while detractors carp about "pricey" yet "boring" preparations, "plain" settings and "interminable waits", they're outvoted by many fin fans who are eagerly lured in.

### L'Espalier

| 28 | 27 | 27 | $69 |

*30 Gloucester St. (bet. Commonwealth Ave. & Newbury St.), 617-262-3023*

■ Count the accolades: Frank McClelland's "world-class" Back Bay New French ranks No. 1 for Food, No. 2 for Decor and No. 3 for Service; revel in "sheer bliss" with a "sumptuous" three-course prix fixe or seven-course degustation meal served in a "gorgeous" townhouse setting by an "outstandingly" "gracious" staff; the tab is definitely "not for the faint of heart", but this is a "perfect experience from coat check to goodbye."

### Lumière 🖸

| 26 | 24 | 25 | $44 |

*1293 Washington St. (Waltham St.), West Newton, 617-244-9199*

■ "The brightest new light" in the suburbs is this "small", cozy Contemporary French bistro in West Newton that turns out "straightforward", "absolutely delicious" cuisine ("try the sea scallops"), paired with a "dynamite" wine list and served by an "excellent" staff; the "upbeat" interior features whimsical light fixtures and an open kitchen that "radiates warmth."

### Maison Robert

| 24 | 24 | 24 | $48 |

*Old City Hall, 45 School St. (bet. Tremont & Washington Sts.), 617-227-3370*

☑ "*C'est magnifique!*" declare devotees of this Old City Hall Classic French where Jacky Robert crafts "top-notch" preparations, the "professional" staff "pampers" all and the "magnificent" peach-colored, crystal chandelier–graced "formal" room exudes pure "elegance"; dissenters, however, cite a "stodgy" ambiance, but they're far outvoted by those who relish it as a special-occasion "favorite."

### Maurizio's 🖸

| 25 | 16 | 21 | $30 |

*364 Hanover St. (Clark St.), 617-367-1123*

■ "Bring a date" to this "first-rate" North End Italian-Med where chef Maurizio Loddo is "actually at the stove", preparing the "world's best bruschetta" and appetizers "so huge you have to make room" for his "terrific Sardinian" specialties; it's "cramped", but the "attentive" staff helps compensate.

### Mistral 🖸

| 25 | 25 | 23 | $54 |

*223 Columbus Ave. (Berkeley St.), 617-867-9300*

☑ Straddling the Back Bay and the South End is this "electric" Provençal destination, often "filled at midnight on a Wednesday" with a "trendy" "power" crowd, thanks to a room that's "one of the most beautiful in Boston", as well as "excellent" cuisine prepared by "talented chef" Jamie Mammano; so "dress to impress", "bring $$$" and prepare for a major "people-watching" "scene."

### Olives

| 27 | 22 | 22 | $48 |

*10 City Sq. (bet. Main & Park Sts.), Charlestown, 617-242-1999*

☑ "Every bite introduces something new" at the Charlestown headquarters of chef Todd English, whose unique brand of Mediterranean involves an "enormous menu" of "complex combinations", resulting in "layers and layers of flavors" that most call "exquisite" but a few find "over the top"; the "casual", "beautiful" room is another crowd-pleaser, though even devotees are irked by the "no-reservations" policy (for parties fewer than six) that creates "mob-scene" waits.

## Radius
26 25 25 $57

*8 High St. (bet. Federal & Summer Sts.), 617-426-1234*

■ "The best new place in town" must be this Financial District "power scene" where chef-partner Michael Schlow (ex Café Louis) makes his mark with "daring", "indescribably delicious" Contemporary French fare, "magnificently presented" and served by one of "the best staffs in the city" in an "amazing space" with an "energized atmosphere"; even though it's "obscenely expensive", most rave that "everything is wonderful."

## Rialto [S]
26 25 24 $53

*Charles Hotel, 1 Bennett St. (Harvard Sq.), Cambridge, 617-661-5050*

■ Chef "Jody Adams' jewel", this Cambridge "heavyweight" boasts an "elegant setting that's a perfect foil for the bold flavors" of her "dynamite" Mediterranean interpretations; a "beautiful" venue that's as "high energy" as it is "formal" makes it "the ultimate" "special-event destination"; though it's "getting to be an expense-account type of restaurant", most insist this sheer "bliss" is "worth every penny."

## Ritz-Carlton Dining Room [S]
25 27 27 $59

*Ritz-Carlton, 15 Arlington St. (Newbury St.), 617-536-5700*

■ An "old Boston" legacy lives on at this "classic" bastion of Back Bay society dining, which reaches "the pinnacle" of French cuisine; the "world-class" fare, matched with an "outstanding" wine list, is proffered by an "extraordinary" staff in a "country-club setting" that provides a "great view of the Public Garden", as well as a glimpse into how "the other half lives"; in sum, most purr "it's the Ritz – what do you expect except the best?"

## Rowes Wharf [S]
24 27 24 $53

*Boston Harbor Hotel, 70 Rowes Wharf (Atlantic Ave.), 617-439-3995*

■ In a "beautiful" space with "magnificent waterfront views", this "fabulous" restaurant in the Boston Harbor Hotel showcases the works of "remarkable chef Daniel Bruce", "a great interpreter of New England–style cuisine" (don't miss the "awesome brunch"); yes, it's "very expensive, but what a treat!"

## Sage [S]
26 18 23 $35

*69 Prince St. (bet. Hanover & Salem Sts.), 617-248-8814*

■ An "adorable", "surprisingly sophisticated" "little place" in the North End offering a "limited menu" of "innovative" contemporary Californian-Italian specialties "cooked to order" ("homemade pastas are the way to go") and served by a "delightful staff"; seating is "limited" too and it's always "crowded", so "reservations are a must."

## Salamander
25 23 23 $47

*1 Athenaeum St. (1st St.), Cambridge, 617-225-2121*

◪ "Magical combinations" of "bold, assertive flavors" earn raves for chef-owner Stan Frankenthaler's "wildly creative" Cambridge Asian-Eclectic; the "complex" dishes are "a little too funky" for some, but the majority feels it's "fusion at its best" and insist the "peaceful" atmosphere and "professional panache" make this "class act" "perfect if you want to impress a date."

## Saporito's S

26 | 17 | 23 | $37

*11 Rockland Circle (George Washington Blvd.), Hull, 781-925-3023*
■ It's a "small, plain beach cottage" "far off the beaten path" in Hull, but reviewers report this "creative" Italian is "worth the drive from anywhere" for its "tasty, fresh, carefully prepared dishes" and "excellent daily specials" at "half the price of in-town restaurants"; enthusiasts insist it's an "institution in the making."

## Silks S

25 | 25 | 25 | $52

*Stonehedge Inn, 160 Pawtucket Blvd. (Rte. 113), Tyngsboro, 978-649-4400*
■ It's "worth the ride" to this "lavish country manor" in Tyngsboro, a "special" inn restaurant boasting a "superbly prepared" (if "limited") New French menu, "knockout wine list", "lovely decor" and "marvelous service"; a few feel it's "pretentious for the suburbs", but many more deem it "dining at its finest" – "Four Seasons North."

## Terramia S

25 | 16 | 20 | $38

*98 Salem St. (Parmenter St.), 617-523-3112*
■ "Put yourself in the hands of Mario Nocera" advise the many fans of this "intimate North End" Italian that's "as good as it gets", with "fresh, delicate, creative" fare and a staff "right out of central casting"; the sweet of tooth moan about the lack of desserts, but others "go out for cannoli" afterward and stretch their legs after sitting in a room that "walks a fine line between cozy and cramped."

## Tremont 647 S

22 | 19 | 20 | $37

*647 Tremont St. (W. Brookline St.), 617-266-4600*
■ The "grill is the centerpiece" of chef-owner Andy Husbands' New American in the South End where "imaginative", "cutting-edge" fare prepared "with zip" and accompanied by an outstanding wine list are served by an "accommodating staff"; a handful feels the fare is "uneven" and "overpriced", but the majority maintains it's a "real treat"; P.S. the "pajama brunch is the best scene in town on Sunday morning."

## Truc S

23 | 20 | 21 | $44

*560 Tremont St. (Clarendon St.), 617-338-8070*
◪ "Within the French bistro craze, Truc gets it right" rave Francophiles who flock to this subterranean "South End charmer" sporting a "small but well-executed" and "inventive" menu; reviewers also talk up the "romantic" "back-room greenhouse" – like a "winter garden" – but quite a few find the selection "entirely too limited."

## TOP 20 FOOD RANKING

| Restaurant | Cuisine Type |
|---|---|
| **29** Le Français | French |
| **28** Ambria | New French |
| Carlos' | New French |
| Tallgrass | New French |
| **27** Le Titi de Paris | French |
| Topolobampo | Mexican |
| Ritz-Carlton Dining Room | New French |
| Arun's | Thai |
| Charlie Trotter's | New American |
| Everest | New French |
| Trio | Eclectic |
| Seasons | New American |
| **26** Frontera Grill | Mexican |
| Morton's of Chicago | Steakhouse |
| Mesón Sabika | Spanish/Tapas |
| Bistro Banlieue | French Bistro |
| **25** Courtright's | New American |
| Fond de la Tour | Classic French |
| Gabriel's | French/Italian |
| Gordon | New American |

## OTHER IMPORTANT PLACES

| | |
|---|---|
| Aubriot | New French |
| Cafe 36 | French |
| Coco Pazzo | Northern Italian |
| Crofton on Wells | New American |
| Emilio's Tapas Bar | Spanish/Tapas |
| Entre Nous | Regional American |
| Fahrenheit | New American |
| Gibsons Steakhouse | Steakhouse |
| Grace | New American |
| Harvest on Huron | New American |
| Ixcapuzalco | Mexican |
| Le Bouchon | French Bistro |
| Les Nomades | French |
| Le Vichyssois | New French |
| Mia Francesca | Northern Italian |
| Montparnasse | French |
| one sixtyblue | New American |
| Park Avenue Cafe | New American |
| Pasteur | Vietnamese |
| Printer's Row | New American |
| Savarin | French |
| Spago | Californian |
| Spiaggia | N/S Italian |
| 302 West | New American |
| TRU | New American |
| Va Pensiero | N/S Italian |
| Vong | French/Thai |

| | F | D | S | C |
|---|---|---|---|---|
| **Ambria** | 28 | 27 | 28 | $62 |

*2300 N. Lincoln Park W. (Belden Ave.), 773-472-5959*

■ This Lincoln Park Contemporary French "special-occasion" jewel garnered the No. 2 spot across-the-board for Food, Decor and Service in the *Chicago Survey* and requires both jackets and (far in advance) reservations for entry; surveyors rave about chef Gabino Sotelino's "superb" cuisine, an art nouveau interior that's "classy but unpretentious" and service so attentive, one person testifies "I was afraid to scratch my nose for fear that three waiters would appear with Kleenex"; and romantics, listen up – this is *the* place "for a middle-aged man to propose marriage."

| | F | D | S | C |
|---|---|---|---|---|
| **Arun's [S]** | 27 | 24 | 25 | VE |

*4156 N. Kedzie Ave. (2 blocks north of Irving Park Rd.), 773-539-1909*

■ It's an "awesome culinary experience" that awaits those who trek to this North Side Thai where Arun Sampanthavivat offers "top-drawer" cuisine so beautifully presented that "you eat with your eyes first"; while at the time of our *Chicago Survey*, many respondents recommended the $75 tasting menu, raving that "there's nothing else like it in North America", it's now the only way to order, which will further disappoint the minority who already gripes about "astronomical prices" and "microscopic portions."

| | F | D | S | C |
|---|---|---|---|---|
| **Aubriot [S]** | – | – | – | E |

*1962 N. Halsted St. (Armitage Ave.), 773-281-4211*

Simplicity and clean flavors are the hallmarks of this ambitious Halsted Street Contemporary French from ex-Carlos' chef Eric Aubriot; the small dining room is unfussy and very attractive, as are the relatively friendly prices.

| | F | D | S | C |
|---|---|---|---|---|
| **Bistro Banlieue [S]** | 26 | 20 | 23 | $31 |

*44 Yorktown Convenience Ctr. (bet. Butterfield Rd. & Highland Ave.), Lombard, 630-629-6560*

■ For the third straight year, this "outpost of taste" in DuPage County is the highest-rated French bistro in the *Chicago Survey*, earning raves for "terrific food" with "well-layered flavors" and such customer-friendly touches as offering petite portions of some entrees; the "improbable" strip mall location aside, this "real suburban treasure" "could be a star even in the city"; N.B. a recent redo and expansion outdate the above decor score.

| | F | D | S | C |
|---|---|---|---|---|
| **Cafe 36 [S]** | 24 | 18 | 22 | $33 |

*36 S. La Grange Rd. (Harris St.), La Grange, 708-354-5722*

■ "A real sleeper" ("I don't know of a restaurant that tries harder"), this West Suburban French specializes in game and "extraordinary sauces"; it garners kudos for a menu that "runs with the big dogs in the city" and might even be "too great for its setting."

| | F | D | S | C |
|---|---|---|---|---|
| **Carlos' [S]** | 28 | 24 | 27 | $63 |

*429 Temple Ave. (bet. Green Bay & Half Day Rds.), Highland Park, 847-432-0770*

■ Despite the "ups and downs" of a "chef shuffle", this "small, romantic" North Shore New French still remains "a treasure" – "everyone is treated like royalty" by owners Carlos and Debbie Nieto and "every meal is a special occasion"; there are a few scattered quibbles about the high prices, but consistently high marks bear out the sentiment that it's "still one of the best" for "a memorable evening"; N.B. there's no corkage fee on Mondays.

## Charlie Trotter's
27 | 26 | 27 | $92

*816 W. Armitage Ave. (Halsted St.), 773-248-6228*

☑ Voted the *Chicago Survey*'s Most Popular restaurant, Charlie Trotter's Lincoln Park temple to New American dining wins raves for his "master of his own domain", never-repeat-a-dish approach and painstakingly presented courses that are "like going to an art show on plates"; while some find it all "too precious" and "stuffy", many others opine "we will never have a better meal."

## Coco Pazzo 🅂
24 | 22 | 22 | $38

*300 W. Hubbard St. (Franklin St.), 312-836-0900*

■ "It's a sure winner" say fans of this Manhattan import where "amazing", "sophisticated" Tuscan cuisine and a "classy but homey" atmosphere add up to a "topflight" dining experience Downtown; the food is "about as good as Italian gets in this town" and the "attentive", "well-informed" service makes it a "fine celebratory choice", though some wish it would "lose the New York prices."

## Courtright's 🅂
25 | 26 | 24 | $41

*8989 S. Archer Ave. (2 blocks west of Willow Springs Rd.),*
*Willow Springs, 708-839-8000*

■ "A perfect 10" "headed for four stars" enthuse supporters of this South Suburban New American that's a "high aspiration" operation with "wonderful food", a "top-notch" (600-label) wine list and a "unique" setting featuring double-height windows that showcase forest preserve vistas; "what one expects and doesn't always get Downtown" says one convert to this "gem in the 'burbs."

## Crofton on Wells
24 | 19 | 20 | $40

*535 N. Wells St. (bet. Grand Ave. & Ohio St.), 312-755-1790*

■ Pros praise this River North New American and its chef Suzy Crofton's "world-class", "nuanced cooking", even though her "very tasteful" dining room – which seats fewer than 75 – makes reservations mandatory and difficult to obtain; some suggest that the place "needs polish", particularly on the service end, but overall, this "jewel among newcomers" is a "keeper."

## Emilio's Tapas Bar & Restaurant 🅂
22 | 19 | 20 | $26

*444 W. Fullerton Ave. (Clark St.), 773-327-5100*
*4100 W. Roosevelt Rd. (Mannheim Rd.), Hillside, 708-547-7177*

■ These Lakeview and West Suburban flagships of Emilio Gervilla's empire inspire fierce loyalty among fans who laud the "superb", "always interesting menu choices" and swear that "no other tapas compare"; scattered complaints that "to get enough, it gets pretty expensive" are countered with "it's cheaper than a plane ticket to Spain."

## Entre Nous
25 | 26 | 25 | $51

*Fairmont Hotel, 200 N. Columbus Dr. (Wacker Dr.), 312-565-7997*

■ For "lovely hotel dining", it's hard to outdo this "elegant" Regional American room east of Michigan Avenue, whose lavish appointments and soft piano music make it "a place for a special dinner"; although "it looks like it needs people", the atmosphere is "so romantic, you can recharge your love here" (or slip over to the gift shop for new batteries).

## Everest
| 27 | 27 | 27 | $73 |

*One Financial Plaza, 440 S. LaSalle St., 40th fl. (Congress Pkwy.),*
*312-663-8920*

■ Scoring in the *Chicago Survey*'s Top 10 for Food and Service and No. 1 for Decor, this Downtown Contemporary French showcases "the most beautiful view in Chicago" from its 40th-floor aerie; chef Jean Joho's "attention to subtle detail shines through" a "wonderfully creative" menu that's tempered with a "touch of Alsace"; factor in "impeccable service", "superb wines" and it's "clearly at the top of the mountain"; the only question that remains: "how do you get a window table?"

## Fahrenheit S
| – | – | – | E |

*695 N. Milwaukee Ave. (bet. Chicago & Grand Aves.), 312-733-7400*
Miami-cool colors and an energetic open kitchen add heat to this sizzling River West Contemporary American whose menu is overseen by the increasingly visible Patrick Concannon; its offbeat location doesn't deter a steady stream of trendies from stopping by, many of whom take up residence in the cigar-friendly bar.

## Fond de la Tour
| 25 | 24 | 24 | $42 |

*40 N. Tower Rd. (bet. Butterfield & Meyers Rds.), Oak Brook,*
*630-620-1500*

■ West Suburbanites in the mood to play dress-up head to this jacket-required Classic French, an "elegant, special" place where the food "is rich and fattening but oh, so good"; though some observe that the "menu is in a time warp" and the "decor is lagging behind 20 years", where else can you count on "an experience" like this?

## Frontera Grill
| 26 | 21 | 22 | $29 |

*445 N. Clark St. (bet. Hubbard & Illinois Sts.), 312-661-1434*

■ "There aren't enough superlatives" to describe Rick Bayless' seminal, nationally renowned River North establishment, but that doesn't stop surveyors from trying; the praise rolls in for "the best Mexican restaurant in the US (take that, LA)", whose "imaginative", "scrumptious" food is "damn near perfect"; Bayless may indeed be "a sorcerer", but even he can't conjure up enough seating to meet the demand – "you could qualify for Social Security waiting for a table."

## Gabriel's
| 25 | 21 | 24 | $47 |

*310 Green Bay Rd. (Highwood Ave.), Highwood, 847-433-0031*

■ "As good as it gets" on the North Shore, this French-Italian hybrid marries a "first-class atmosphere" with "creative" food by "meticulous" chef-owner Gabriel Viti that "meets all expectations"; aesthetes add that the "open-kitchen concept works well here."

## Gibsons Steakhouse ●S
| 24 | 19 | 21 | $44 |

*1028 N. Rush St. (bet. Bellevue Pl. & Oak St.), 312-266-8999*

■ "Big steaks, tall martinis, long cigars and short skirts" make up the "good show" at this "loud", "glamorous" Rush Street steakhouse that draws a "colorful" mix of "who's who in Chicago" and conventioneers; those taking a break from the "top-notch people-watching" add that the food's "wonderful", especially dessert, which consists of the "largest pieces of cake in the city."

## Gordon S
25 | 25 | 24 | $48

*500 N. Clark St. (Illinois St.), 312-467-9780*

■ Gordon Sinclair's "cutting edge" River North New American continues to wow 'em after 23 years with an "elegant atmosphere" where an "oh so cool" crowd dons (required) jackets for dinner and the entrees are available in full and half-portions to encourage multi-course nibbling; it "gets better with age no matter who the chef is" (and there've been many over the years) and Gordon himself "still has the magic touch."

## Grace
– | – | – | E

*623 W. Randolph St. (2 blocks east of Halsted St.), 312-928-9200*

West-of-Loop newcomer on red-hot Randolph Street, whose chef Ted Cizma was foxy enough to make game an integral, all-year-round part of the Contemporary American menu; apparently the young and trendy don't balk at having a bite of Bambi, because they crowd the comfortable, candlelit dining room and bar most nights.

## Harvest on Huron ●S
24 | 21 | 20 | $40

*217 W. Huron St. (bet. Franklin & Wells Sts.), 312-587-9600*

◪ Chef Alan Sternweiler's "delicious", "interesting" Contemporary American fare and an interior that's "pure elegance" are why many dub this River North spot a "best newcomer"; however, the Harvest also yields more than a few complaints of "inattentive" service and "unacceptably loud" noise.

## Ixcapuzalco S
– | – | – | M

*2919 N. Milwaukee Ave. (W. Diversey Pkwy.), 773-486-7340*

Geno Bahena, a longtime chef at Rick Bayless' highly rated Frontera Grill and Topolobampo, is making a name for himself with his first solo effort, a cute little Mexican that's got foodies flocking to Logan Square for the first time in memory; after Bahena encloses his backyard patio, he'll have ample space to accommodate the crowds clamoring to eat here.

## Le Bouchon
24 | 18 | 21 | $33

*1958 N. Damen Ave. (Armitage Ave.), 773-862-6600*

■ "Pinch me, I'm in Paris" marvel those who secure a table in this "tiny", "cozy" Bucktown bistro, which the smitten promote as being home to "the best French food in the city", citing the "great" onion tart and "amazing" roast duck for two; though the noise level makes the "cramped" dining room "no place for conversation", fans shrug "who cares – I love this place."

## Le Français
29 | 27 | 28 | $77

*269 S. Milwaukee Ave. (bet. Dundee & Willow Rds.), Wheeling, 847-541-7470*

■ A perennial top scorer for Food and Service in the *Chicago Survey*, this Wheeling wonder went through a major upheaval in the summer of '99: gone are Roland and Mary Beth Liccioni, who leased and ran the establishment for 10 years, and back in is founding chef-owner Jean Banchet, an international culinary star; he's retained the front-room staff , but redone the dining room in a contemporary mix of light wood and neutral tones, with an open kitchen; the menu is a mix of French classics like duck consommé with more modern dishes such as crabmeat over celery root salad.

## Les Nomades

25 | 23 | 24 | $58

*222 E. Ontario St. (1½ blocks east of Michigan Ave.), 312-649-9010*

◪ Roland and Mary Beth Liccioni's 'other' restaurant, just off the Mag Mile, has become their principal business, now that Jean Banchet has resumed control of Chicago's top-rated Le Français in Wheeling; expect Roland's blend of Classic and Contemporary French cuisine to bring renewed attention to this quietly elegant two-story space, which pros pronounce "sophisticated" and critics call "stuffy" (jacket required and "hushed tones necessary here"), in the heart of tony Streeterville; N.B. dinner Tuesday–Saturday.

## Le Titi de Paris

27 | 25 | 26 | $55

*1015 W. Dundee Rd. (Kennicott St.), Arlington Heights, 847-506-0222*

■ "How does Pierre Pollin do it?" ask awestruck surveyors who find this more than 25-years-old Northwest Suburban French "still alive with new ideas" – well, let's give chef de cuisine Michael Maddox some credit; in addition, a "wonderful welcome at the door", a "warm", "attentive" staff and prices that are, relatively speaking, an "amazing bargain" contribute to the "fond memories."

## Le Vichyssois [S]

24 | 22 | 22 | $47

*220 W. Rte. 120 (2 mi. west of Rte. 12), Lakemoor, 815-385-8221*

■ Bernard Cretier's pioneering Far Northwest Suburban is "a long trip from anywhere", but acolytes happily fill up their gas tanks for "superb" Contemporary French in a charming country setting – a freestanding building that makes some proclaim "now *this* is a roadhouse!"; the atmosphere is "romantic" and it's "the best value in the area."

## Mesón Sabika [S]

26 | 25 | 23 | $28

(fka Emilio's Mesón Sabika)

*1025 Aurora Ave. (bet. Rte. 59 & Washington St.), Naperville, 630-983-3000*
*Northfield Village Ctr., 310 Happ Rd. (Willow Rd.), Northfield, 847-784-9300*

■ Though Emilio Gervilla has moved on from this Naperville Spaniard (he sold out to former partners), "the dining is still great", winning raves for "splendid tapas" and "wonderful sangria"; those with a taste for "elegant surroundings" particularly appreciate the setting – a "romantic", "old white mansion" with a "gorgeous patio in summer"; N.B. the Northfield branch opened post-*Chicago Survey* and is unrated.

## Mia Francesca [S]

24 | 16 | 19 | $26

*3311 N. Clark St. (School St.), 773-281-3310*

■ The restaurant that launched three sequels is a Wrigleyville phenomenon – a no-reservations Northern Italian where patrons "gladly line up or dine at 5 PM" to secure a precious table; skeptics wonder what "makes it the Microsoft" of the Chicago scene, while pros praise "always delicious" and "affordable" food, especially the "superb pastas", and, of course, the "great people-watching."

## Montparnasse

25 | 22 | 23 | $48

*200 E. Fifth Ave. (1½ blocks east of Washington Blvd.), Naperville, 630-961-8203*

■ "Special-occasion restaurant" that some nominate as the "top French in the Western Suburbs"; "the area's prettiest room" features "absolutely outstanding food and service", leading loyalists to add that this gem "deserves more weekday patronage."

## Morton's of Chicago S
26 | 20 | 23 | $49

*Newberry Plaza, 1050 N. State St., lower level (Maple St.), 312-266-4820*
*9525 W. Bryn Mawr Ave. (River Rd.), Rosemont, 847-678-5155*
*1 Westbrook Corporate Ctr. (22nd St. & Wolf Rd.), Westchester, 708-562-7000*
■ Suveryors once again have voted this trio "best steakhouse in
Chicago"; a "meat lover's paradise", it's built its reputation on
"quality, aged steaks", plus "very attentive" service that some
consider "the most consistent" around; there are those who feel
the decor "needs an update", but why mess with success?

## one sixtyblue
– | – | – | E

*160 N. Loomis St. (Randolph St.), 312-850-0303*
The worst-kept secret in town is that this West Side Contemporary
American (just blocks from the United Center) has Michael Jordan
as a silent partner; but don't look for basketball memorabilia here –
instead, there's an Adam Tihany design and dishes with culinary
and visual flash.

## Park Avenue Cafe S
25 | 21 | 22 | $46

*Doubletree Guest Suites Hotel, 199 E. Walton Pl. (Mies van der Rohe Way),*
*312-944-4414*
■ Fanciers of Contemporary American fare say Chicago's
Streeterville sibling of this NYC original is "superb", an "oasis of
class and service" with an "eclectic" menu offered amid collectible
Americana; the food is "exquisite", desserts are "too pretty to eat"
and the "spectacular dim sum–style brunch" is a "fresh change";
for those who need extra convincing, it's all complemented by a
"primo vino selection."

## Pasteur S
24 | 23 | 19 | $27

*5525 N. Broadway (Bryn Mawr Ave.), 773-878-1061*
■ Surveyors shout "welcome back!" to the top-rated Vietnamese
in the *Chicago Survey* that's "better than ever" thanks to a
"beautifully decorated", more spacious new Edgewater location
that's reminiscent of "old French Saigon"; look for "superb",
"perfectly prepared" cuisine that's so popular that regulars advise
going "late to avoid the noisy" crowds.

## Printer's Row
25 | 21 | 23 | $40

*550 S. Dearborn St. (Congress Pkwy.), 312-461-0780*
■ Surveyors have only "superlatives" for this "resilient" New
American located south of the Loop and near the Auditorium
Theater; it's "always a pleasure" to wade through Michael Foley's
"innovative menu", especially for one of his "superb game dishes"
("best venison in the US"); an "attentive staff" contributes to an
ambiance that's "perfect for pampering on that special occasion."

## Ritz-Carlton Dining Room S
27 | 27 | 27 | $59

*Ritz-Carlton Hotel, 160 E. Pearson St. (Michigan Ave.), 312-573-5223*
■ Chicago's highest-rated hotel restaurant (once again) showcases
chef Sarah Stegner's "perfect" Contemporary French food and a
cheese cart "so good it can't be legal"; factor in "outstanding
service" that "will make you feel like a millionaire" and "classy
yet unpretentious" decor, and it's no surprise that reviewers think
dinner is akin to "a three-hour vacation"; P.S. Sunday brunch
is "absolutely awesome."

## Savarin S
— — — E

*713 N. Wells St. (bet. Erie & Superior Sts.), 312-255-9520*
Fine-dining French in River North that's garnering near-universal praise for the outstanding Classic and Contemporary cuisine of chef-proprietor John Hogan (ex KiKi's Bistro, Park Avenue Café); visitors are advised to check out the second-floor lounge and its portrait gallery of famous Chicago-area chefs.

## Seasons S
27 26 27 $59

*Four Seasons Hotel, 120 E. Delaware Pl., 7th fl. (bet. Michigan Ave. & Rush St.), 312-649-2349*
■ "You feel you've arrived" when dining at this "lots of moolah" Michigan Avenue hotel dining room where "wonderful service", "beautiful decor" and Mark Baker's "delicious" New American cooking add up to a "first-class" experience; while it makes a "wonderful anniversary restaurant", surveyors say don't overlook the awe-inspiring brunch that's among "the best in Chicago."

## Spago
24 22 22 $42

*520 N. Dearborn St. (Grand Ave.), 312-527-3700*
☑ Chicagoans have embraced Wolfgang Puck's satellite operation and say it "actually deserves its hype", thanks to "puckishly delightful" (ouch) Californian cuisine and "excellent service with no attitude"; insiders advise "try the smoked salmon pizza" (it isn't always on the menu, but you can order it) and other "witty, wood-fired" pies, and check out the grill room, which has a less pricey menu, but offers Puck signatures such as meat loaf; the main dining room is "beautiful" and a "great show", but very "noisy."

## Spiaggia S
25 26 24 $52

*One Magnificent Mile Bldg., 980 N. Michigan Ave., 2nd fl. (Oak St.), 312-280-2750*
■ Scores are as high as the prices at this luxury Italian that's "by far the city's best"; Paul Bartolotta's pastas are "phenomenal" ("the tortellini can make you cry"), but you "can't get a bad meal" regardless of what you order; the "romantic", "vibrant dining room" is "beautiful", as are its "spectacular views" of the lake and Michigan Avenue; add "exquisite service" that is "dedicated to detail" and you have "a great place to impress whomever."

## Tallgrass S
28 23 26 $58

*1006 S. State St. (10th St.), Lockport, 815-838-5566*
■ "Charming period decor" and "service so unobtrusive it's almost scary" are two highlights of this far-flung New French, the sophisticated sibling of Public Landing in historic Lockport; while it's a "long drive", Robert Burcenski's "outstanding" cooking is "creativity personified" and so, as "the suburban [restaurant equivalent of] Everest", it's "worth the trip."

## 302 West
▽ 25 23 23 $46

*302 W. State St. (3rd St.), Geneva, 630 232-9302*
■ Located in a "lovely" refurbished Far West Suburban bank building, this "outstanding" New American offers a "sophisticated menu" of "innovative cooking", a massive choice of desserts made on premises and an award-winning wine list; live music and the "watchful eye of hostess/co-owner Catherine Findlay" add to the atmosphere; overall, "bank on good food and an empty piggy bank."

## Topolobampo    27 | 24 | 25 | $43 |
*445 N. Clark St. (bet. Hubbard & Illinois Sts.), 312-661-1434*
■ Rick Bayless' dressier, pricier sibling of the Frontera Grill (in the same River North building) is "reason enough to live in Chicago" say civic-boosting boasters who are proud to call this "best Mexican in the country" their own; a recent expansion has relieved the "cramped space" somewhat, but made it no easier to secure reservations for a "great experience" that "never disappoints" locals or their "out-of-town guests"; for those who "can't wait to go back", much of the menu changes bi-weekly.

## Trio 🅢    27 | 25 | 27 | $67 |
*1625 Hinman Ave. (Davis St.), Evanston, 847-733-8746*
■ This "amazing" North Shore Eclectic provides "one of the greatest culinary experiences you will ever have" thanks to "outstanding" service, "continually creative" cooking and artistic presentations so "visually striking" they look like "Cirque du Soleil on a plate"; a few claim that it's "fading from glory", but the majority thinks it's still a surefire "winner" "for special occasions", and if you can handle the "expensive" tab, try the "to-die-for" dégustation menu.

## TRU    – | – | – | VE |
*676 N. St. Clair St. (Huron St.), 312-202-0001*
Rick Tramonto and Gale Gand, the husband-and-wife chef team that opened Trio, are back in the luxury-dining business (teaming up with Lettuce Entertain You Enterprises' Rich Melman) with this splendid Streeterville Contemporary American whose minimalist look and fascinating artworks make patrons think they're eating in a museum; a host of prix fixe and tasting-menu options make ordering easy, freeing the culinary cognoscenti to lavish praise on this extraordinary newcomer.

## Va Pensiero 🅢    25 | 22 | 23 | $39 |
*Margarita Inn, 1566 Oak Ave. (Davis St.), Evanston, 847-475-7779*
■ "Yesterday's ambiance, tomorrow's food" is one way of summing up Peggy Ryan's highly rated North Shore Italian, an "exquisite gem" serving "innovative, delicious" cuisine in an "understated" and "romantic" environment; the low-key location may explain why "it's the least famous of the top-tier restaurants, yet one of the best" – it's "the place to take people you want to impress."

## Vong 🅢    – | – | – | VE |
*6 W. Hubbard St. (State St.), 312-644-8664*
Jean-Georges Vongerichten's French-Thai fusion phenomenon hits River North, via a partnership with Rich Melman; it's primarily a business crowd by day, but at dinner trendies and older patrons sit side-by-side in the dramatic David Rockwell–designed space; it's not a cheap night out by any means, though visiting New Yorkers will find the prices are lower than back home and there's a three-course prix fixe lunch for $22.

# Cincinnati

## TOP 15 FOOD RANKING

| | Restaurant | Cuisine Type |
|---|---|---|
| **28** | Maisonette | Classic French |
| **27** | Palace | New American |
| | Precinct | Steakhouse |
| | BonBonerie | Bakery/Tearoom |
| **26** | Phoenix | New American |
| **25** | Grand Finale | French/New American |
| | Germano's | N/S Italian |
| | Morton's of Chicago | Steakhouse |
| | Palm Court Grill | Regional American |
| **24** | J's Fresh Seafood | Seafood |
| | Barresi's | N/S Italian |
| | Plaza 600 | New American |
| | Boca | Eclectic/New American |
| | Primavista | N/S Italian |
| | La Petite France | Classic French |

## OTHER IMPORTANT PLACES

| | |
|---|---|
| Chez Alphonse | New French |
| Dee Felice Cafe | Cajun/Creole |
| Greyhound Tavern | Regional American |
| Iron Horse Inn | New American |
| JoAn | Japanese |
| Montgomery Inn | BBQ |
| Nicola's | Northern Italian |
| Pacific Moon | Asian |
| Scalea's | N/S Italian |
| Sturkey's | New American |
| Trio | New American |

| F | D | S | C |
|---|---|---|---|

**Barresi's**     | 24 | 19 | 22 | $28 |

*4111 Webster Ave. (Blue Ash Rd.), Deer Park, 513-793-2540*
■ This family-run "cozy neighborhood Italian bistro" with "attentive service" and a "long-standing reputation" is one of the city's "best-kept secrets"; surveyors like its "terrific value", "authentic" menu and "homey but classy" feel – plus the chance to rub shoulders with some of Cincinnati's most prominent citizens.

**Boca** S     | 24 | 18 | 17 | $20 |

*4034 Hamilton Ave. (Blue Rock Rd.), 513-542-2022*
☑ Funky Northside is the perfect home for this "hip" Eclectic–New American; local Birkenstockers in search of "imaginative" cooking pack the renovated storefront on weekends, unfazed by absentminded service and earsplitting din; modest prices are another reason why it's a neighborhood favorite.

## BonBonerie　　27 | 17 | 20 | $8

*2030 Madison Rd. (O'Bryon St.), 513-321-3399*

🔲 Upscale neighbors stand in line Saturday mornings for the "best pastries in town" and "fabulous scones" at this tony O'Bryonville bakery-cum-tearoom with plebeian prices; it's "the perfect place to bring your mother or best friend" for a "ladies' lunch" or afternoon tea.

## Chez Alphonse　　– | – | – | E

*654 Highland Ave. (Grand Ave.), Ft. Thomas, KY, 606-442-5488*

Former Maisonette maitre d' Alphonse Kaelbel offers Contemporary French cuisine to a loyal following in the quiet KY suburb of Fort Thomas; formal service, reasonable prices and a wine list strong on Alsatians offset the plain-Jane setting; dinner only.

## Dee Felice Cafe Ⓢ　　23 | 20 | 20 | $21

*529 Main St. (6th St.), Covington, KY, 606-261-2365*

■ You'll think you're in New Orleans at this "crowded", "dark" and "smoky" cafe on the edge of the Covington Main Strasse district that can get every bit as raucous as Bourbon Street; "jumpin'" Dixieland jazz, "spicy" food and "super" service provide a true "Cajun feeling in Kentucky."

## Germano's　　25 | 19 | 21 | $23

*9415 Montgomery Rd. (bet. Cooper & Remington Rds.), Montgomery, 513-794-1155*

■ "Carefully prepared, authentic Italian" fare is on the bill at this family-run suburban in the Montgomery shopping district; though waits can be "long" and some find it "way too pricey" (especially off-menu seafood specials), its sportswear-clad fans tout the "great" fish, desserts and "sidewalk action" visible from window tables, adding that its "nicer" new location makes it "even better."

## Grand Finale Ⓢ　　25 | 24 | 23 | $22

*3 E. Sharon Ave. (Congress Ave.), Glendale, 513-771-5925*

■ An "always busy", antiques-filled "Victorian-style house" in stately Glendale boasting the "best brunch", "excellent crêpes", "incredible desserts" and other "high-quality" American-French food; though some complain about "uncomfortable chairs" and "long waits for tables", it's a Cincinnati "institution."

## Greyhound Tavern Ⓢ　　– | – | – | I

*2500 Dixie Hwy. (Buttermilk Pike), Ft. Mitchell, KY, 606-331-3767*

There's more than a soupçon of Southern hospitality on display in the Colonial-style dining rooms of this Ft. Mitchell, KY American, justifiably renowned for fried chicken and other delish down-home dishes at more-than-fair prices; patrons of this venerable spot (since 1921) seem to have been around almost as long as the gracious, loyal staff.

## Iron Horse Inn Ⓢ　　– | – | – | M

*40 Village Sq. (Greenville Ave.), Glendale, 513-771-4787*

Hands-on owners (the Sawyer family) are much in evidence at this recently renovated and expanded historic tavern (circa 1858) set trackside in charming Glendale Square; the competent and occasionally inventive New American fare is cordially served in a gracious setting livened by jazz on weekends and by passing trains the rest of the week.

## JoAn
– – – VE

*3940 Olympic Blvd. (Mineola Pike), Erlanger, KY, 606-746-2634*

A Toyota exec hungry for the tastes of home is behind this austere Japanese in the shadow of Erlanger's Toyota plant; the offerings go beyond the expected sushi and sashimi, with Kotaro Nakamura gently guiding novices through the many courses of a kaiseki meal; the menu is seasonal, the presentation artful and the prices commensurate with the quality.

## J's Fresh Seafood Restaurant [S]
24 21 22 $26

*Regency Condos, 2444 Madison Rd. (Dana Ave.), 513-871-2888*

■ "Wonderful fresh seafood" and a "quiet atmosphere with excellent service" are hallmarks of this Hyde Park standby; though it can be "pricey", "mature" residents from the condos above consider it their private dining room.

## La Petite France
24 17 20 $22

*3177 Glendale-Milford Rd. (Reading Rd.), Evendale, 513-733-8383*

◪ A suburban strip mall location and theme-park interior mask an "authentic French restaurant"; the "comfortable" ambiance of this "undiscovered gem" makes it a "good place to visit with old friends"; P.S. leave the calorie counter at home – this is "rich" stuff.

## Maisonette
28 28 28 $48

*114 E. Sixth St. (bet. Main & Walnut Sts.), 513-721-2260*

■ Chef Jean-Robert de Cavel's Med touch has brought this Downtown Classic French into the '90s and earned it Cincinnati's No. 1 ratings for Food and Popularity; "meticulous" cuisine, "formal" rooms and "proper" service prompt well-heeled patrons to rave "best in America"; though a few say "overrated", "a Midwestern dream of deluxe", to most it's the ultimate for "special occasions."

## Montgomery Inn [S]
23 19 21 $20

*9440 Montgomery Rd. (Cooper Rd.), Montgomery, 513-791-3482*

## Montgomery Inn Boathouse

*925 Eastern Ave. (Eggleston Ave.), 513-721-7427*

◪ "World-class" ribs offset "rushed" service and "long waits" at these "crowd-pleasing" BBQ "meccas" that draw "people from miles around", especially to the Downtown Boathouse location with its river view; some find the sauce too sweet, but the fact that the ribs are shipped to fans nationwide says something.

## Morton's of Chicago [S]
25 23 23 $38

*Tower Place Mall, 28 W. Fourth St. (Race St.), 513-241-4104*

◪ "Portions are enormous and so is the bill" at this Downtown steakhouse with a "clubby", "very corporate" setting filled with high rollers and tourists; service is "prompt and sharp" and most have no beef with the beef at this "carnivore heaven"; critics want smaller portions with prices to match.

## Nicola's
– – – E

*1420 Sycamore St. (Liberty St.), 513-721-6200*

There's a Tuscan touch to this classy Over-the-Rhine Northern Italian with Uptown prices and polished service; just minutes by car from the Music Hall, it's a good choice for elegant dining before the opera or symphony and you can practice your Italian while supping on bruschetta, calamari, osso buco, panna cotta and more.

### Pacific Moon 🄢　　　　　　　23　17　19　$21

*Market Place Complex, 8300 Market Place Ln. (Montgomery Rd.),*
*Montgomery, 513-891-0091*
■ "East meets West" at this suburban "gourmet Asian" with an
upscale following that likes the "interesting" food, "knowledgeable"
service and "good jazz" on weekends.

### Palace, The 🄢　　　　　　　27　26　26　$41

*Cincinnatian Hotel, 601 Vine St. (6th St.), 513-381-6006*
■ "Excellent, innovative" cuisine (Cincinnati's "best hotel food")
and "ballet-like service" prompt return visits to this "intimate"
New American in a restored Downtown landmark; it's a "favorite
place to celebrate" or simply enjoy a very "elegant evening."

### Palm Court Grill 🄢　　　　　　25　27　24　$35
(fka Orchids)

*Omni Netherland Plaza, 35 W. Fifth St. (Race St.), 513-421-9100*
◪ "Elegant dining" with "unobtrusive service" in one of the
"prettiest" rooms in town keeps expense-accounters returning to
this Midwestern Regional in the soaring atrium of a "glamorous"
"art deco masterpiece"; dissenters suggest the food and service
aren't up to the highly rated decor, but a meal here "makes
you feel important."

### Phoenix, Restaurant at The　　　26　25　25　$30

*812 Race St. (9th St.), 513-721-8901*
■ What many call Cincinnati's "best value in fine dining" offers
a "classic club atmosphere" in a "beautiful old building" on
Downtown's Garfield Place; this "imaginative" New American
will "cater to vegetarians" and has an "excellent wine list" and
"competent" service; despite a few "inconsistent" reports, it
turns in a "terrific" performance.

### Plaza 600 🄢　　　　　　　24　21　22　$27

*600 Walnut St. (6th St.), 513-721-8600*
■ Slick and "trendy" Downtown New American with International
accents that bustles on performance nights at the adjacent Aronoff
Center; it's a "creative" "NY bistro right here in River City", offering
"beautiful presentations" and lots of "après-theater" appeal;
though some dislike the decibel level and smoke, "they get you to
the show on time" and satisfied.

### Precinct, The 🄢　　　　　　　27　22　24　$34

*311 Delta Ave. (Columbia Pkwy.), 513-321-5454*
■ "Meat rules" at this "hype"-heavy "jock hangout" in a former
police station in historic Columbia-Tusculum; visiting celebs and
wanna-bes overlook the "noisy", "crowded" rooms and sometimes
"rushed" service to enjoy "melt-in-your-mouth" steak that many
judge to be the "best this side of the Mississippi."

### Primavista 🄢　　　　　　　24　25　22　$28

*Queens Tower, 8100 Matson Pl. (bet. Price & W. 8th Aves.), 513-251-6467*
■ This "attractive", tavernlike Italian in a Price Hill high-rise is a top
choice for "romantic meals" or entertaining visitors, mostly for its
"magnificent view looking east to Downtown and the river"; opinion
on the food runs from "pretty good" to "superb", but the point is
"Cincy looks great from here."

**Scalea's** | – | – | – | E

*320 Greenup St. (Park Pl.), Covington, KY, 606-491-3334*
Foodies are flocking to Covington, KY for this contemporary Italian with a slick crew in the dining room; the pricey pastas, risottos and more are complemented by the instructive all-Italian wine list, and the tony crowd looks good in the understated decor; word to the wise: the adjacent deli sells the best Italian sausage in town.

**Sturkey's** [S] | – | – | – | M

*400 Wyoming Ave. (Grove Ave.), Wyoming, 513-821-9200*
Well-heeled suburbanites pack this former Wyoming firehouse on weekends to sample chef-owner Paul Sturkey's New American cuisine, and on weeknights, substantial salads and sandwiches make it just right for a reasonable bite; N.B. save room for the delectable desserts created by Paul's wife and partner, Pamela.

**Trio** [S] | 23 | 18 | 21 | $17

*Jos. A. Bank Plaza, 7565 Kenwood Rd. (Montgomery Rd.), Kenwood, 513-984-1905*
■ Seniors and families rule in the early evenings at this "classy, casual" New American bistro that's a frequent post-movie and shopping stop thanks to its Uptown decor, "interesting" food, "fresh fish" and extensive choice of wines by the glass; this may be the city's favorite midpriced table.

# Cleveland

## TOP 15 FOOD RANKING

| | Restaurant | Cuisine Type |
|---|---|---|
| 28 | Johnny's Bar on Fulton | Continental/N. Italian |
| 27 | Sans Souci | Mediterranean |
| | Chez François | Classic French |
| | Hyde Park Grille | Steakhouse |
| | Baricelli Inn | French/Italian |
| | Parker's | New French |
| | Shuhei | Japanese |
| 26 | Morton's of Chicago | Steakhouse |
| | Giovanni's | Northern Italian |
| | Hyde Park Chop House | Steakhouse |
| | Hyde Park Downtown | Steakhouse |
| | Riverview Room | New American |
| 25 | Luchita's | Mexican |
| | Sergio's | Brazilian |
| | Fratello's | N/S Italian |

## OTHER IMPORTANT PLACES

| | |
|---|---|
| Flying Fig | New American |
| Johnny's Downtown | Continental/N. Italian |
| Kosta's | New American |
| Lockkeeper's Inn | Eclectic |
| Lola | Regional American |
| Market Square Bistro | New American |
| Moxie | Traditional American |
| Phnom Penh | Asian |
| Ruth's Chris | Steakhouse |

| | F | D | S | C |
|---|---|---|---|---|
| **Baricelli Inn** | 27 | 27 | 26 | $43 |

*2203 Cornell Rd. (Murray Hill Rd.), 216-791-6500*

■ This "elegant", "romantic" old mansion in Little Italy has an "ambitious menu" of "sophisticated" French and Italian fare plus an extensive wine list; it's "expensive", but a much cheaper bistro menu has been introduced for more casual patio dining in season; some find service "slow", but that gives diners more reason to linger, sometimes late enough to make use of the seven-room inn.

| | F | D | S | C |
|---|---|---|---|---|
| **Chez François [S]** | 27 | 27 | 25 | $40 |

*555 Main St. (Liberty Ave.), Vermilion, 440-967-0630*

■ "Excellent" French food and a "lovely setting" on the river a stone's throw from Lake Erie make this "romantic" destination a "place to celebrate something special" and "worth the trip" from Cleveland or Toledo; book ahead because summer weekends are crowded and it closes for winter vacation from New Year's through early March.

F | D | S | C

**Flying Fig** — | — | — | M
*2523 Market St. (W. 25th St.), 216-241-4243*
This new Ohio City hot spot is flying high with a New American bistro menu courtesy of chef-owner Karen Small, who displays an assured touch starting with her freshmade breads; the lively, sophisticated room is already a popular meeting place.

**Fratello's** 25 | 18 | 22 | $21
*32085 Electric Blvd. (Lear Rd.), Avon Lake, 440-871-3054*
■ "Terrific", simply prepared Italian food draws crowds to this casual "neighborhood" winner where portions are large and the wine list was recently expanded; the decor is a bore and service can be slow, but most are too busy enjoying their meal to notice.

**Giovanni's** 26 | 24 | 26 | $43
*25550 Chagrin Blvd. (Richmond Rd.), Beachwood, 216-831-8625*
◩ A very "elegant" setting for "excellent" Northern Italian dining; devotees don't mind paying stiff prices for "top-notch" food that includes innovative twists on old standards, but while some revel in the ultra-"fancy" service, others find it "too much of a good thing."

**Hyde Park Chop House** 26 | 21 | 24 | $35
*34205 Chagrin Blvd. (S.O.M. Center Rd.), 216-464-0688*
■ Like its two siblings, this chophouse is always "busy" because it always provides "great steaks" that are a "good value" considering free side dishes like the tasty Greek salad; some find it "noisy and crowded", but that's what you'd expect from a "hot local spot."

**Hyde Park Downtown [S]** 26 | 25 | 25 | $35
*123 Prospect Ave. (W. 2nd St.), 216-344-2444*
■ The newest branch of the local steakhouse chain moved in right next to Morton's Downtown and is "sure to be a winner", thanks to steaks that are "reason to never become a vegetarian."

**Hyde Park Grille** 27 | 24 | 25 | $35
*1825 Coventry Rd. (bet. Hampshire & Lancashire Rds.), Cleveland Heights, 216-321-6444*
■ Here's the original and, by most accounts, best of Cleveland's Hyde Park steakhouse trio, offering "consistently excellent food and service" in a "very New York City" atmosphere; the dark paneled bar is where many regulars prefer to eat.

**Johnny's Bar on Fulton** 28 | 21 | 25 | $38
*3164 Fulton Rd. (Trent Ave.), 216-281-0055*
■ Rated No. 1 for Food in Cleveland, as well as Most Popular, this "lively" Continental–Northern Italian has long earned raves for its "superb" food and "nostalgic" art deco setting in a converted old tavern; it can be "quite expensive" but most rate it a "good buy" given the quality and unusually large portions; at lunch you can sample this "total class" act for a fraction of the dinner price.

**Johnny's Downtown [S]** 25 | 24 | 23 | $38
*1406 W. Sixth St. (bet. St. Clair & Superior Aves.), 216-623-0055*
◩ It's tough living up to its big brother on Fulton, and while everyone agrees that the Downtown Johnny's has "well-prepared and presented" Continental–Northern Italian food, many rate it "one small step below" the original; still, its "cool, comfortable" marbled setting scores higher and it's a lot easier to get to.

**Kosta's** | – | – | – | M |

*2179 W. 11th St. (Fairfield Ave.), 216-622-0011*
Though this upscale Contemporary American has undergone some growing pains, new chef Brandt Evans (ex Ward's Inn) has jump-started the menu with bold, experimental flavors and a particular emphasis on fresh seafood; chalk it up as another plus for the Tremont area, fast becoming Cleveland's most vibrant neighborhood for eating out.

**Lockkeeper's Inn** | 24 | 20 | 22 | $31 |

*6190 Canal Rd. (Rockside Rd.), Valley View, 216-524-9404*
■ The menu is typical upscale steakhouse fare, but the specials are "innovative" Franco-Californian cuisine at this Eclectic "up and comer" with an award-winning wine list; though "pricey", it's a pleasant "surprise" to find such "creative cuisine, warm ambiance and friendly service" in a "historic" setting in the southern suburbs.

**Lola** ◐ [S] | – | – | – | M |

*900 Literary Rd. (Professor Rd.), 216-771-5652*
After successfully putting Caxton Cafe on the map with his exotic menu and stacked-to-the-sky presentations, Michael Symon now offers his own Midwestern bistro with eclectic flair; utilizing the freshest foods from the Midwest and supplementing them with flavors from around the globe, this hip spot is usually booked weeks in advance.

**Luchita's** [S] | 25 | 13 | 21 | $15 |

*3456 W. 117th St. (Governor St.), 216-252-1169*
■ It may look like a "hole-in-the-wall" from outside, but the interior has been remodeled and locals think it has the "best", "most authentic" Mexican food in town: "the real McCoy", "great salsa", "good mole"; but it's "perhaps too real for the Chi-Chi's crowd."

**Market Square Bistro** [S] | 25 | 20 | 21 | $25 |

*16725 Chillicothe Rd. (E. Washington St.), Bainbridge Twp., 440-543-5115*
■ This American bistro has been drawing standing-room-only crowds in a strip mall outside of Chagrin Falls, where patrons watch chefs in the open kitchen turning out large portions of "inventive", "healthier-style" pizzas, pastas, fish, beef and more; the atmosphere is bright and "lively" if a bit "too loud" for some.

**Morton's of Chicago** [S] | 26 | 23 | 24 | $40 |

*The Avenue at Tower City Ctr., 1660 W. Second St. (Prospect Ave.), 216-621-6200*
■ "Portions are too large" insist some (ditto prices), but admirers of this upscale chain steakhouse say "big works here" thanks to "perfectly prepared" meat, lobsters and side dishes served in a "classy" room by "attentive" staff; even if you "feel like a glutton", don't forget dessert: "the Grand Marnier soufflé is to die for."

**Moxie** [S] | – | – | – | M |

*3355 Richmond Rd. (Chagrin Blvd.), 216-831-5599*
There's more than a touch of NYC–style brass at this lively, noisy Beechwood American that's frequented by scenemakers and wanna-bes; chef Doug Katz's open kitchen turns out topflight, camera-ready bistro fare, including a notable roasted chicken with wild mushrooms and jumbo, fall-off-the-bone lamb shanks.

## Parker's Restaurant and Bistro Bar S   27 | 23 | 24 | $42
*2801 Bridge Ave. (28th St.), Ohio City, 216-771-7130*
■ Chef Parker Bosley's big following is pleased that he's opened the doors of his "sophisticated" Ohio City New French for weekday dinner (previously served Friday and Saturday only); while it's slipped a tiny bit from its former No. 1 food ranking, most praise "imaginative" cuisine, made with mostly local ingredients, though a few balk at "small portions" for "very big prices."

## Phnom Penh Restaurant S⌷   ▽ 27 | 12 | 20 | $16
*13124 Lorain Ave. (W. 131st St.), 216-251-0210*
■ Considered the best value around for quality Asian fare, with such a "wide variety" of "spicy" Cambodian, Thai and Vietnamese offerings that it's "hard to choose" – just about everything is "excellent"; BYO and there's no corkage fee (or wine glasses).

## Riverview Room S   26 | 28 | 26 | $42
*Ritz-Carlton, 1515 W. Third St. (bet. Prospect Ave. & Huron Rd.), 216-623-1300*
■ One of the city's most "elegant" dining rooms draws raves for its "impressive views", "unobtrusive service" and "superior" Contemporary American fare that a new chef has made a bit more cutting edge and eclectic; it's "first class all the way" (price included) and Sunday brunch is widely considered the best around.

## Ruth's Chris Steak House S   – | – | – | E
*Eton Collection, 28699 Chagrin Blvd. (Brainard Rd.), Woodmere, 216-595-0809*
This national steakhouse chain with a big reputation and prices to match opened its doors in Woodmere Village post-*Survey;* since many surveyors were "looking forward" to this highly popular, tried-and-true operation, it's sure to be a hit.

## Sans Souci S   27 | 27 | 26 | $35
*Cleveland Renaissance Hotel, 24 Public Sq. (Superior Ave. & W. 3rd St.), 216-696-5600*
■ Earning Cleveland's No. 2 food rating, this Mediterranean hotel dining room is "not cheap, but it is a great value" given its "superb", "imaginative" cuisine, "beautiful", "warm" atmosphere and "excellent" service; its annual two-month fall lobster menu is one of the most popular promotions in town.

## Sergio's in University Circle   25 | 19 | 22 | $32
*1903 Ford Dr. (Bellflower Rd.), 216-231-1234*
■ Chef Sergio Abramof, who spent 10 years cooking Italian at Giovanni's, is tantalizing diners with "unique Brazilian food" in this "small", bright, "noisy" University Circle space where diners go nuts for his "creative" fare; many consider it one of Cleveland's best new additions.

## Shuhei, The Restaurant of Japan S   27 | 21 | 22 | $27
*23360 Chagrin Blvd. (Green Rd.), Beachwood, 216-464-1720*
■ Hiroshi Tsuji previously owned Shujiro, one of Cleveland's top-rated restaurants, and he's keeping up that tradition at this "stylish" Japanese serving "excellent sushi", seafood and "wonderful" traditional fare, all beautifully presented; be sure to book – most nights it's packed and "noisy."

# Columbus

## TOP 10 FOOD RANKING

| | Restaurant | Cuisine Type |
|---|---|---|
| *28* | L'Antibes | French |
| | Handke's | Eclectic/New American |
| *27* | Refectory | Classic French |
| | Rigsby's Cuisine Volatile | Eclectic/Mediterranean |
| *26* | Rotolo's Pizza | Pizza |
| | Lindey's | New American |
| | Hyde Park Grille | Steakhouse |
| | Restaurant Japan | Japanese |
| | Worthington Inn | Traditional American |
| | Morton's of Chicago | Steakhouse |

## OTHER IMPORTANT PLACES

| | |
|---|---|
| Bexley's Monk | Eclectic |
| Bombay Grille | Indian |
| Braddock's Grandview | Regional American |
| Cameron's | Regional American |
| Cap City Fine Diner | Traditional American |
| Figlio Wood-Fired Pizza | Pizza |
| Fishermans Wharf | Seafood |
| Giuseppe's Ritrovo | Southern Italian |
| Harold's Cajun Glory | Cajun/Creole |
| Hunan Lion | Chinese |
| La Tavola | Italian |
| Latin Rooster Rotisserie | Latin American |
| Sapporo Wind | Japanese |
| Shaw's | Traditional American |
| Taj Palace | Indian |
| Trattoria Roma | N/S Italian |

F | D | S | C

**Bexley's Monk** [S] 25 | 23 | 23 | $24

*2232 E. Main St. (College Ave.), 614-239-6665*

■ "Good seafood", "excellent pastas", "imaginative pizzas" – "it all comes together" at this inventive Eclectic that has "kept Bexley from starving for years"; apart from an undercurrent of griping about service ("too friendly" vs. "snooty") and a few claims that it's "overrated", most enjoy this "lively neighborhood place" that "switch-hits well for business or pleasure."

**Bombay Grille** [S] – | – | – | M

*6665 Dublin Ctr. Rd. (Snouffer Rd.), Dublin, 614-336-2610*

This Northwester is a contender in the local Indian sweepstakes, and while the setting is smoke-free, the menu offers all heat levels; big eaters will appreciate the upscale all-you-can-eat lunch buffet.

### Braddock's Grandview  – | – | – | M

*1470 Grandview Ave. (W. 5th Ave.), 614-487-0077*

Pungent Low Country cooking and other regional American styles get their tasty due the old-fashioned way at this bright, semi-formal Northwester that's convenient to Downtown: chef Michael Braddock whips up everything from scratch; what's more, it's moderately priced; N.B. dinner only.

### Cameron's [S]  25 | 21 | 23 | $24

*2894 E. Main St. (Enfield Rd.), Bexley, 614-235-3662*
*2185 W. Dublin-Granville Rd. (Linworth Rd.), Worthington, 614-885-3663*

◪ The Regional American fare is "creative", service is "friendly" and the surroundings are full of "good energy and vibes" at these Bexley and Linworth siblings; grumblers complain that they're "small, crowded" and "way too noisy", but for most it's "worth" the din and high-ish prices for "innovative" dining.

### Cap City Fine Diner & Bar [S]  22 | 21 | 21 | $18

*1299 Olentangy River Rd. (bet. 3rd & 5th Aves.), 614-291-3663*
*1301 Stoneridge Dr. (Hamilton Rd.), Gahanna, 614-478-9999*

◪ Even those who complain that these "trendy diners for the '90s" are "overpriced" and "overrated" "right down to the old Formica tables and the vinyl-covered bench seats" grudgingly admit that they're "glad they're here" because the "food is tasty" and the variety's "good, from the meat loaf to the salmon."

### Figlio Wood-Fired Pizza  25 | 20 | 22 | $17

*3712 Riverside Dr. (Fishinger Rd.), 614-459-6560*
*1369 Grandview Ave. (bet. 3rd & 5th Aves.), 614-481-8850*

■ It's "small", "noisy" and "always crowded", but the "great atmosphere" and "yuppie pizza at its finest" keep pulling 'em in to this Italian duo in Upper Arlington and on Grandview Avenue with a no-smoking policy; only the wines elicit pricing complaints.

### Fishermans Wharf  – | – | – | M

*2143 E. Main St. (College Ave.), Bexley, 614-236-0043*

The '70s are back in Bexley at this smaller-scale reincarnation of a onetime fish house landmark where nautical doodads decorate the marine-blue walls; nostalgically, shrimp cocktail still heads the list of appetizers, but the cooking has otherwise been updated, so diners won't have to endure the typical deep-fried and broiled seafood menus of yore; plus, Captain Niki is the consummate host.

### Giuseppe's Ritrovo Italian Café  – | – | – | M

*2268 E. Main St. (Drexel Ave.), Bexley, 614-235-4300*

A modest, family-run trattoria that's not generic Italian but a source for authentic Calabrian, Sicilian and other regional fare, where the tomato, garlic and olive reign; N.B. it's even better now that there's a wine license, and the wines are priced right.

### Handke's Cuisine  28 | 25 | 25 | $33

*520 S. Front St. (bet. Beck & Blenkner Sts.), 614-621-2500*

■ "Masterfully done" Eclectic–New American food by a "certified master chef" wins raves at this Brewery District wine cellar, even if the subterranean "vaulted-ceiling" setting draws mixed reactions: "wonderful", "unique" vs. "dark, dingy"; some also cite "slow service" and "nouvelle cuisine portions", but on the whole it's well "worth the effort" and cost to enjoy superlative "global cuisine."

## Harold's Cajun Glory Cafe    _ | _ | _ | M
*1355 Bethel Rd. (Godown Rd.), 614-538-1822*
Bringing a taste of the Big Easy to Columbus, this dinner-only cafe serves Cajun-Creole fare in the spiffed-up quarters of a former fast-food joint; what may be the lowest restaurant wine prices in Ohio are another plus.

## Hunan Lion S    24 | 22 | 23 | $17
*2038 Crown Plaza Dr. (Reed Rd.), 614-459-3933*
■ A "comfortable" setting for "high-class, first-rate Chinese" food in the Northwest with "white-linen" surroundings and "friendly, welcoming" service.

## Hyde Park Grille    26 | 21 | 24 | $29
*1615 Old Henderson Rd. (Larwell Dr.), 614-442-3310*
☑ You can start with the "best martini" during the "best happy hour in town", which makes it easier to endure "long waits" for this Upper Arlington's "excellent steaks" served in a "dark ambiance" that some find "elegant" but others call "tired."

## L'Antibes    28 | 23 | 25 | $33
*772 N. High St., Ste. 106 (Warren Ave.), 614-291-1666*
■ This Near North Side "classical and classy" French is "quiet and intimate" (some say it's "almost too small"), tucked into a setting as "cozy as someone's house"; the traditional and modern cuisine is so "superbly prepared", it was voted No. 1 for Food in Columbus.

## La Tavola    _ | _ | _ | I
*33 Beech Ridge Dr. (Powell Rd.), Powell, 614-848-4231*
Expect a traditional trattoria at this casual, family-run newcomer in Powell, replete with checkered tablecloths and authentic Central and Northern Italian food; the menu is abetted by an extensive wine list that represents even more regions, at reasonable prices to boot; the only downside is that they don't take reservations.

## Latin Rooster Rotisserie S    ▽ 21 | 12 | 19 | $12
*Stoneridge Plaza, 389 Stoneridge Ln. (bet. Morse & Hamilton Rds.), Gahanna, 614-471-4567*
■ "Finally, Latin American home cooking" wakes up taste buds in Gahanna at this "family-owned gem" that offers an "unusual menu" including Peruvian specialties; "interesting" dishes with "different" flavors make some wish the menu would be "expanded a bit."

## Lindey's Restaurant S    26 | 25 | 24 | $25
*169 E. Beck St. (Mohawk St.), German Village, 614-228-4343*
☑ Because it "has the best bistro atmosphere" in "trendy German Village" and "mouthwatering" New American fare, this "institution" is "always jammed"; some find it "too noisy" and "yup-oid" with "surly" service and "overrated" food, but they're outnumbered by those for whom Lindey's is "ever in and ever worthy of it."

## Morton's of Chicago S    26 | 24 | 25 | $38
*2 Nationwide Plaza, Ste. 100 (Chestnut St.), 614-464-4442*
☑ Even those who rave about "superb" beef, "some of the best service around" and the "pleasurable" ambiance at this "clubby" Downtown steakhouse find the portions "overwhelming"; there's unanimity about the cost ("huge" – "make sure you're on an expense account") and a grumble or two about cigar smoke.

## Refectory
27 │ 26 │ 26 │ $35

*1092 Bethel Rd. (near Rte. 315 at Kenny Rd.), 614-451-9774*
■ The "professional staff", "romantic" setting in an "old church",
"spectacular wine list" and "classic haute cuisine" leave surveyors
searching for superlatives to describe this Northwest French:
"world-class", "as close to perfection as we have", "nothing
else comes close"; it's Columbus' Most Popular restaurant and a
favorite "for that special evening."

## Restaurant Japan 🅢
26 │ 15 │ 21 │ $19

*Kenny Ctr., 1173 Old Henderson Rd. (Kenny Rd.), 614-451-5411*
■ Fortunately, it's no longer "always crowded" at this Northwest
ethnic that serves the "best Japanese" food in Columbus; if "no
one speaks English", that could be taken as further proof that
it's "really authentic."

## Rigsby's Cuisine Volatile
27 │ 24 │ 25 │ $29

*698 N. High St. (Lincoln Rd.), 614-461-7888*
■ The "bustling" atmosphere, live music and "stunning" setting
in Columbus' Short North "bohemian art district" don't distract
raters from servings of Eclectic-Mediterranean "bistro fare at
its best"; everything – starting with the bread and "even the
butter" – is judged "excellent" at this lively (and often "noisy")
"place to see and be seen."

## Rotolo's Pizza 🅢🚭
26 │ 9 │ 22 │ $9

*1749 W. Fifth Ave. (Glenn Ave.), 614-488-7934*
■ Whether you call it "the best", "great" or an all-time "favorite",
pizza's the thing at this Grandview-area carryout with "friendly"
service from a "hardworking family"; only the addition of "eat-in
facilities could improve" on this kind of pie "perfection."

## Sapporo Wind 🅢
25 │ 19 │ 19 │ $19

*6188 Cleveland Ave. (south of I-270), 614-895-7575*
■ A contender for "best Japanese", this "elegant" Northeaster
earns raves for its "artistic, exquisite" food ("didn't think fish
this fresh could get to Ohio"); despite a few reports of "slow
service", most find no faults with the "beautiful presentations"
or refined flavors.

## Shaw's Restaurant 🅢
24 │ 23 │ 23 │ $20

*123 N. Broad St. (Wheeling St.), Lancaster, 740-654-1842*
■ "Worth the drive" to Lancaster, this American country inn with
a monthly changing menu offers "all the food trends, plus steaks
and chops" and a "moderate wine list" in an "elegant, old-world"
setting; there's no grumbling about the "reasonable prices", but
"slow service" occasionally irritates.

## Taj Palace 🅢
– │ – │ – │ M

*3794 Fishinger Blvd. (Mill Run Shopping Ctr.), 614-771-3870*
This reasonably priced, professionally run and brightly decorated
Northwester is well on its way to being ranked one of the finest
Indian restaurants in Columbus; though it has the hottest tandoori
ovens around, there's no smoking allowed to compete with
its fragrant aromas.

## Trattoria Roma

25  15  21  $21

*Woodward Park, 1270 Morse Rd. (Maize Rd.), 614-888-6686*

■ "Don't be fooled" by the "cramped" setting in a Northeast strip mall – this trattoria is rated Columbus' "best Italian", offering "a wonderful dining experience" with "memorable polenta and porcini appetizers" enhanced by "a good wine list" and "knowledgeable" service; now that the dining room is smoke-free, "the food tastes even better."

## Worthington Inn S

26  25  24  $27

*649 N. High St. (Rte. 161), Worthington, 614-885-2600*

◪ Most find the atmosphere at this Worthington-area "historic" inn "quaint" and "charming", and the Traditional American menu "well-done and presented", if "pricey"; contrarians don't get the mix of "stars and moons with colonial decor" and call the food "uneven" and service "pompous", but they're outvoted.

# Dallas

## TOP 20 FOOD RANKING

| | | |
|---|---|---|
| **29** | French Room | Classic French |
| **28** | Riviera | French/Mediterranean |
| | Mansion on Turtle Creek | Southwestern |
| **27** | Pyramid Room | Continental/French |
| | Cafe Pacific | Seafood |
| | Laurels | Eclectic/International |
| | Bob's Steak & Chop Hse. | Steakhouse |
| | York St. | New American |
| **26** | Del Frisco's | Steakhouse |
| | Fogo de Chao | Brazilian/Steakhouse |
| | Nana Grill | New American |
| | Mediterraneo | Mediterranean |
| | Hôtel St. Germain | Continental/French |
| | Sea Grill | Seafood |
| | Grape | Eclectic |
| | Star Canyon | Southwestern |
| | Green Room | New American |
| | Chez Gerard | French Bistro |
| **25** | Morton's of Chicago | Steakhouse |
| | AquaKnox | Seafood |

## OTHER IMPORTANT PLACES

| | |
|---|---|
| Al Biernat's | Seafood/Steakhouse |
| Anzu | Pacific Rim |
| Arc-en-Ciel | Chinese/Vietnamese |
| Bistro A | Mediterranean |
| Capital Grille | Seafood/Steakhouse |
| Chamberlain's | Steakhouse |
| EatZi's | Eclectic |
| Javier's | Mexican |
| Lavendou | French Bistro |
| Liberty | Asian/Pacific Rim |
| Lombardi Mare | Italian/Seafood |
| Mainstream Fish House | Seafood |
| Matt's No Place | Regional American |
| Mi Piaci Ristorante | Northern Italian |
| Palomino Euro Bistro | Mediterranean |
| Sevy's Grill | New American |
| Sonny Bryan's | BBQ |
| Sullivan's | Steakhouse |

**Al Biernat's [S]** ▽ 26 26 26 $50

*4217 Oak Lawn Ave. (bet. Herschel & Wycliff Aves.), 214-219-2201*

■ Al Biernat, for many years the popular maitre d' of the Palm in Dallas, recently opened this eponymous Oak Lawn surf 'n' turfer; his lobster salad is already a hit, as are his "awesome" sea bass and hefty cuts of beef.

**Anzu ◐[S]** 24 24 21 $30

*4620 McKinney Ave. (Knox St.), 214-526-7398*

■ "Unique" describes both the food and decor at this McKinney Avenue fusion spot, where hundreds of colorful origami cranes dangling from the ceiling set the stage for "exquisite" Pacific Rim fare ranging from "wonderful sushi" to "excellent desserts" such as a chocolate mousse–filled giant fortune cookie; the only thing missing from the "great California feel" is "the Pacific outside."

**AquaKnox [S]** 25 26 23 $48

*3214 Knox St. (Cole Ave.), 214-219-2782*

◪ "A must for seafood lovers" is the word on this "sophisticated" Knox/Henderson standout; while the "gorgeous" decor is worth seeing, what really draws the "chic clientele" is "impeccable", imaginative fare from Stephan (Star Canyon) Pyles' "real jewel" of a menu; still, it's "expensive" and some cite "tons of attitude."

**Arc-en-Ciel [S]** 21 9 16 $14

*3555 W. Walnut St. (Jupiter Rd.), Garland, 972-272-2188*

■ This "huge" (1,600 seats), no-frills Garland Asian is "a true bargain", offering "possibly the best dim sum in town" ("get there early for the best variety") along with a "very wide menu" of other Chinese and Vietnamese fare; service is "average" and there's not much decor, but "even if you don't like Chinese food" it "makes you a believer"; call ahead to make sure it's not closed for a function.

**Bistro A [S]** 24 23 22 $32

*6815 Snider Plaza (Lovers Ln.), 214-373-9911*

◪ "Off to a great start", this "nice addition to Snider Plaza" earns solid ratings for its "wonderful" Mediterranean fare and "sleek" yet "informal" setting, though some wonder how long on-the-go chef Avner Samuel will stick around; despite grumbles about "small portions" and service slips, it's popular, so "make reservations."

**Bob's Steak & Chop House** 27 22 24 $38

*4300 Lemmon Ave. (Wycliff Ave.), 214-528-9446*

■ This Uptown "classic steakhouse" with the requisite "masculine, clubby" look serves some of "the best steak in town (best value too)" and is also lauded for its lamb chops and side dishes (it "wins the 'great carrot' prize" for its honey-glazed version); cynics cite "tight quarters" and warn "don't breathe in the lounge – full of cigars", but others find it the "most intimate" steakhouse around.

**Cafe Pacific** 27 26 25 $34

*24 Highland Park Village (Mockingbird Ln. & Preston Rd.), 214-526-1170*

■ "Best seafood in Dallas by far" rave fans of this "elegant" Highland Park bistro with "noteworthy" seviche and the "best damn New England clam chowder west of Boston"; "old money, old wine, new food" sums it up, and if a few complain of waiters "direct from France", more cite "polished service" and "people-watching" courtesy of the "Chanel/Escada/Hermès set."

## Capital Grille S
-  -  -  E

*500 Crescent Ct. (bet. Cedar Springs Rd. & McKinney Ave.), 214-303-0500*
The latest entrant in the high steaks restaurant war, this swank
East Coast chain's Uptown surf 'n' turfer dazzles diners with
massive portions of perfectly cooked prime beef and lobster; while
the elegant setting comes complete with the obligatory cigar
lounge as well as random celeb sightings, you might want to
double-check your corporate charge limit before entertaining;
N.B. there's jazz piano Tuesday–Saturday nights.

## Chamberlain's S
24  22  23  $39

*5330 Belt Line Rd. (bet. Montfort Dr. & Prestonwood Blvd.),
972-934-2467*
■ Besides offering "some of the best" beef in town, owner-chef
Richard Chamberlain is a "master of sauces and fish" and "makes
a lovely event of eating" at this Far North Dallas steakhouse; with a
"calm, cool" ambiance and "attentive" service, it's an "indulgent"
"guilty pleasure", but you may have to endure a long wait, "even
with reservations", to enjoy it.

## Chez Gerard
26  22  23  $34

*4444 McKinney Ave. (1 block south of Knox St.), 214-522-6865*
■ For "traditional Country French" dining, this "intimate, upscale"
bistro on McKinney Avenue "still works every time", offering
"outstanding" lamb, "terrific soufflés" and "great pommes frites"
along with "excellent" service; it's thoroughly Gallic, right "down to
the boutique wine list", and admirers rate it "one of the best French
for the price", but even they don't like waiting despite reservations.

## Del Frisco's
## Double Eagle Steakhouse
26  23  24  $47

*5251 Spring Valley Rd. (N. Dallas Pkwy.), 972-490-9000*
☑ Legions of loyalists consider this "the best" steakhouse not
just in North Dallas but "in the country" – "if my husband could
pick his last meal on earth, this would be the place"; nitpickers
fault "long" waits, sometimes "arrogant" service and "expense-
account" prices ("everything à la carte"), but most think it's "worth
the cost" to experience "steak heaven."

## EatZi's S
23  19  19  $14

*3403 Oak Lawn Ave. (Lemmon Ave.), 214-526-1515*
■ "A lifesaver", "incredible takeout" and "the best grocery store
ever" typify reaction to this Oak Lawn gourmet market/cafe, a
"novel concept" offering a "fantastic selection of fresh, hard-to-
get" provisions plus Eclectic prepared fare; it can be "chaotic"
and "crowded", but fans say it's the "best thing to happen to
Dallas since we found 'black gold'" – "wish there were more"
(there are, but in other cities).

## Fogo de Chao S
26  22  26  $37

*4300 Belt Line Rd. (Midway Rd.), Addison, 972-503-7300*
■ "Wow!" – this "new and different" Brazilian steakhouse in
Addison offers an unending parade of grilled meats and poultry
presented on swords by gaucho-esque waiters; it's mostly a "meat
lovers' haven", but there's also a "gorgeous" salad bar and it's hard
to beat for "great value and atmosphere"; "go hungry", and even
then you may feel "like a goose being force-fed for foie gras."

### French Room, The

29 | 29 | 28 | $61

*Adolphus Hotel, 1321 Commerce St. (bet. Akard & Field Sts.), 214-742-8200*

■ Rated No. 1 for Food, Decor and Service in Dallas, this "flawless" Downtown French combines "incredible" classic cuisine with a "beautiful, very formal" setting and "skilled service" to achieve the "ultimate dining experience" – this is "romance at its best" and, remarkably, most detect "no stuffy airs"; "*très cher*" it is, but such "very special" experiences rarely come cheap.

### Grape, The ●🖫

26 | 22 | 23 | $26

*2808 Greenville Ave. (bet. Monticello Ave. & Vickery Blvd.), 214-828-1981*

■ Aging "like fine wine", this Eclectic bistro on Greenville has been going strong for over 25 years and remains "one of the most romantic restaurants around"; with its dark, "comfy, laid-back room", "nifty wine" list and blackboard menu featuring the likes of "terrific mushroom soup" and pâté, it's an "all-time favorite."

### Green Room, The 🖫

26 | 20 | 21 | $32

*2715 Elm St. (Crowdus St.), 214-748-7666*

■ "Funky" and "eclectic" describe both the ambiance and the "creative food" at this "hip" Deep Ellum New American; Marc Cassel (ex Star Canyon) runs the kitchen, and his nightly four-course 'Feed Me' prix fixe ($36 without wine, $58 with) is a popular "good deal"; the "wonderful open patio" is a plus on fine evenings.

### Hôtel St. Germain

26 | 27 | 26 | VE

*Hôtel St. Germain, 2516 Maple Ave. (bet. Cedar Springs Rd. & McKinney Ave.), 214-871-2516*

■ The "exceptional European" ambiance of this Uptown Victorian home sets the stage for Continental-French fare that most find "exquisite" and "a bargain" even at the prix fixe tab of $85; considered the "epitome of elegance", it's a "classy" place that also holds "wine tastings."

### Javier's 🖫

25 | 24 | 23 | $26

*4912 Cole Ave. (Harvard Ave.), 214-521-4211*

■ "Excellent", "real Mexico City" eats, including the "best mole in Dallas" and "awesome black bean soup", are served in an "upscale" yet "low-key" ambiance at this North of Downtown "favorite"; it's "crowded and noisy", but "if you can get in, you can't go wrong"; N.B. the goat entree ranks as one of Dallas' best forkfuls.

### Laurels

27 | 27 | 23 | $49

*Westin Park Central Hotel, 12720 Merit Dr. (Coit Rd.), 972-851-2021*

■ Commanding an "excellent view" from atop the Westin Park Central, this 'global fusion' specialist offers what some call "the ultimate dining in Dallas"; chef Danielle Custer has foodies exulting over her "exciting", "innovative" Eclectic menu, which is served by a pro staff in an "elegant" ambiance – in sum, a "class operation."

### Lavendou

24 | 24 | 21 | $31

*19009 Preston Rd. (bet. Frankford Rd. & Plano Pkwy.), 972-248-1911*

◩ A "great addition to Far North Dallas" say admirers of this Provençal bistro that conjures up the real thing with its "quaint" interior and "well-prepared" fare along the lines of onion soup, soufflés and niçoise salads; despite critics who cite "slow service" and feel it sometimes "misses the mark", most call it a "keeper."

**Liberty [S]** 22 | 18 | 19 | $21

*5631 Alta Ave. (Greenville Ave.), 214-887-8795*

◪ "Flavors fire up in every bowl" at this "fashionable" Lower Greenville Asian offering "funky fusion" fare including a "wonderful assortment of noodle dishes"; some say the Pacific Rim menu could "be more risky", but the "happening atmosphere" and "reasonable prices" make it a most "welcome addition."

**Lombardi Mare [S]** 23 | 25 | 22 | $34

*Village on the Parkway, 5100 Belt Line Rd. (Montfort Dr.), Addison, 972-503-1233*

■ "The little black dress is alive and well" at this "very Uptown" Far North Italian seafooder, praised for its "excellent", "fresh" (albeit "a bit pricey") aquatic fare and "attentive service"; it's "worth a trip just to see" the place, especially the bar scene, which unfolds beneath goldfish swimming in bowls suspended overhead.

**Mainstream Fish House [S]** 22 | 15 | 19 | $19

*11661 Preston Rd. (Forest Ln.), 214-739-3474*

■ Landlocked locals say this "surprise" in a North Dallas strip mall can be relied on for "good, plain seafood" that's the "freshest around" and served at "reasonable prices"; standouts include New England chowder served in a 'bread pot', the "best gumbo" in town, legendary lobster enchiladas and a killer Key lime pie.

**Mansion on Turtle Creek [S]** 28 | 28 | 27 | $56

*Mansion on Turtle Creek, 2821 Turtle Creek Blvd. (Gillespie St.), 214-559-2100*

■ "Top class in every way", Dallas' Most Popular restaurant showcases the "awesome" Southwestern fare of Dean Fearing, who "sets the standard" with dishes like lobster tacos and tortilla soup; a "classy" Downtown setting and "knowledgeable" (a few say "stuffy") service are more reasons why it's "worth a splurge" – "when you hit the lottery, this is the place to celebrate!"

**Matt's No Place** ▽ 24 | 16 | 20 | $24

*Lakewood Theater Plaza, 6326 La Vista Dr. (Gaston Ave.), 214-823-9077*

■ "No other place like it" proclaim fans of this Lakewood Regional American with a "casual Texas theme" and a "club"-like feel (its phone number was unlisted until recently); followers appreciate its 'Texas prairie' fare with a "Mexican and chuck wagon" slant, including wild game, creek-bottom shrimp and smoked spuds.

**Mediterraneo [S]** 26 | 25 | 24 | $38

*18111 Preston Rd. (Frankford Rd.), 972-447-0066*

◪ "One of the first great ones in Far North Dallas" say fans of this Mediterranean with "imaginative food", "understated elegance" and "some of the best service in town"; on the downside, it can get "noisy", but it's a place "to be seen", not necessarily heard.

**Mi Piaci Ristorante [S]** 24 | 24 | 21 | $32

*14854 Montfort Rd. (Belt Line Rd.), Addison, 972-934-8424*

■ This "elegant, sophisticated" Addison Northern Italian is "a great package", with a "romantic" setting and "excellent" fare; chef Kevin Ascolese's monthly cooking demos are a hit, so perhaps it doesn't matter if a few grumble about service "attitude."

| F | D | S | C |
|---|---|---|---|

**Morton's of Chicago [S]** 25 | 23 | 24 | $43

*501 Elm St. (Houston St.), 214-741-2277*
*14831 Midway Rd. (Belt Line Rd.), Addison, 972-233-5858*

■ For the last word in "excellent prime beef from the Midwest", old-school meat eaters turn to this Downtown and Addison steakhouse duo; they're "expensive", but the combination of "large portions", "attentive service" and elegant atmosphere (with muted lighting, dark wood and etched glass) is sure to "impress clients"; cigars and a selection of port help make every meal an occasion.

**Nana Grill [S]** 26 | 27 | 25 | $44

*Wyndham Anatole Hotel, 2201 Stemmons Frwy. (I-35), 214-761-7470*

■ With its "breathtaking" view of the Downtown skyline, this New American in the Wyndham Anatole offers some of the "most romantic" dining around; it's also an ideal place to "entertain" or celebrate, thanks to "excellent food", "terrific service", a "superb wine list" and popular holiday buffets.

**Palomino Euro Bistro [S]** 23 | 26 | 23 | $32

*Crescent Court, 500 Crescent Ct. (bet. Cedar Springs Rd. & Pearl St.), 214-999-1222*

◪ "Beautiful" sums up the decor, the food and the clientele at this suave and "glitzy" Mediterranean yearling at the Crescent Court; it follows through with "very good service" and "reasonable prices", but predictably, skeptics find it too "trendy."

**Pyramid Room [S]** 27 | 27 | 27 | $51

*Fairmont Hotel, 1717 N. Akard St. (Ross Ave.), 214-720-5249*

■ This "well-kept secret" offers "everything you'd want" in Downtown Continental-French dining, i.e. "classy, quiet" ambiance and "outstanding" food and service; the prix fixe dinner ($46 for four courses) is a "wonderful value", and celebrants proclaim this "the place for anniversaries, proposals, birthdays and clinching" deals.

**Riviera, The [S]** 28 | 27 | 28 | $57

*7709 Inwood Rd. (Lovers Ln.), 214-351-0094*

◪ Some of "the best food in the city" (rated No. 2 in Dallas) gives this Inwood French-Med a strong start, and it goes the distance with a "suave" setting, "primo" wine list and a staff that treats each patron as a "pampered guest"; however, it stumbles a bit in the eyes of critics who find the prices and the noise level too high.

**Sea Grill [S]** 26 | 18 | 23 | $28

*2205 N. Central Expy. (Park Blvd.), Plano, 972-509-5542*

■ "Great chef, wish he weren't so far out" say Dallas-based fans of Andy Tun and his Plano fish house; it's called "one of the best" seafooders in the Metroplex, with "beautiful presentations" and "wonderful" fare with Asian touches; adding to the enjoyment: "good service", a quiet ambiance and reasonable prices.

**Sevy's Grill [S]** 22 | 22 | 20 | $27

*8201 Preston Rd. (Sherry Ln.), 214-265-7389*

◪ This New American on Preston Road is a "solid performer" that's considered "outstanding in its price range", with a "tasty" menu (including items like heavenly truffled mashed potatoes and a decadent butter pecan cheesecake) enhanced by "good wine selections"; "noise is a problem", but they're working on it, and the back room is ideal for groups in search of privacy.

| F | D | S | C |
|---|---|---|---|

## Sonny Bryan's [S] 21 | 11 | 15 | $11

*2202 Inwood Rd. (bet. Forest Park Rd. & Harry Hines Blvd.), 214-357-7120*
*Galleria Mall, 133-75 Dallas Pkwy. (bet. LBJ Frwy. & N. Dallas Tollway), 972-851-5131*
*4701 Frankford Rd. (bet. Dallas Pkwy. & Pear Ridge Rd.), 972-447-0102*
*302 N. Market St. (Pacific Ave.), 214-744-1610*
*Republic Towers, 325 N. St. Paul St. (bet. Bryan St. & Pacific Ave.), 214-979-0102*

■ Texas reveres its BBQ, and to loyalists this "legend" is simply "the best BBQ in Dallas since dirt", especially the Inwood original; "no out-of-town guest should depart the state before eating this good meat", nor before learning to "love those onion rings"; hard-core connoisseurs need no encouragement to "put on some old clothes and go wallow" in the 'cue – and they never fail to "take home some sauce."

## Star Canyon [S] 26 | 27 | 24 | $41

*3102 Oak Lawn Ave. (Cedar Springs Rd.), 214-520-7827*

■ Sure, it's "hard to get reservations" at this Oak Lawn Texan-Southwestern, but that's because so many people think "Stephan Pyles does it best" when it comes to "interesting combinations of tastes and flavors" and "impeccable presentation" of dishes like the "best bone-in rib eye ever"; "amazing", "Texan elegant" decor and sharp service help make it a "true Texas feast" that's worth the expense and effort to get in.

## Sullivan's – | – | – | E

*17795 N. Dallas Pkwy. (Briargrove Ln.), 972-267-9393*

The North Dallas offshoot of a chain steakhouse offers two cigar-friendly bars and a mammoth wine list, but deviates from the norm with a '40s theme, featuring a swing band Thursday–Saturday and impromptu dancing – even though there's no formal dance floor.

## York St. 27 | 22 | 26 | $39

*6047 Lewis St. (bet. Live Oak & Skillman Sts.), 214-826-0968*

■ This "cozy" "hidden gem" in Old East Dallas offers a "fabulous" New American menu enhanced by "personalized service" – there's "no friendlier staff in town than owner Felissa" Shaw and company; add a "romantic, intimate" setting and you have the ideal "date place" and "a real find."

# Denver Area &
# Mountain Resorts

## TOP 20 FOOD RANKING

| Restaurant | Cuisine Type |
| --- | --- |
| *28* Papillon Cafe | New French |
| Highlands Garden Cafe | New American |
| Sweet Basil | New American |
| *27* Renaissance | Med./New American |
| Keystone Ranch | New American |
| Palace Arms | Continental/Trad. Amer. |
| Splendido | New American |
| Sushi Den | Japanese |
| Wildflower | New American |
| Tante Louise | French |
| Grouse Mtn. Grill | Regional American |
| Charles Court | Continental/New Amer. |
| La Petite Maison | French |
| *26* Briarwood Inn | American/Continental |
| Alpenglow Stube | Regional American |
| Café Brazil | Brazilian |
| La Montaña | Mexican/Southwestern |
| Barolo Grill | Northern Italian |
| Piñons* | Regional American |
| Del Frisco's Double Eagle | Steakhouse |

## OTHER IMPORTANT PLACES

| | |
| --- | --- |
| Aubergine Cafe | French Bistro/Med. |
| Bang! | Traditional American |
| Beehive | Med./New American |
| Cafe Alpine | Regional American |
| Cafe Bohemia | French Bistro/New Amer. |
| Domo | Japanese |
| Flagstaff House | Continental/New Amer. |
| Full Moon Grill | Northern Italian |
| Gabriel's | Northern Italian |
| Kevin Taylor | New American |
| Left Bank | French |
| Little Nell | New American |
| New Saigon | Vietnamese |
| Picasso | French |
| Potager | New American |
| Radex | New American |
| Soupçon | French Bistro |
| Strings | American/Cal./Med. |
| Swan at Inverness | Continental |
| Syzygy | New American |
| 240 Union | New American |

* Tied with the restaurant listed directly above it.

## Alpenglow Stube 🅂    26   28   26   $56
*Keystone Resort, 154 Soda Ridge Rd. (top of Outpost), Keystone, 970-496-4386*
■ Diners yodel in favor of this Keystone Regional American, the country's highest restaurant at 12,000 feet, serving "terrific food in an unforgettable setting", backed up by "impeccable service"; it's "worth the money" for a "blow out celebration" – the gondola ride up and down "is the crème de la crème."

## Aubergine Cafe 🅂    26   22   24   $30
*225 E. Seventh Ave. (bet. Grant & Sherman Sts.), Denver, 303-832-4778*
■ For "true Mediterranean bistro food" in what some call the "most romantic setting in the city", fans head to this near-Downtown "friendly, comfortable and consistent" "little slice of heaven" with "innovative", "tasty" cooking, a "carefully selected wine list" and a "knowledgeable staff"; but this "like Provence" "gem" can be "a little crowded", so "make reservations early."

## Bang!    25   14   17   $14
*3609 W. 32nd Ave. (bet. Lowell Blvd. & Meade St.), Denver, 303-455-1117*
■ A "tiny", "bang-up", North Denver "hole-in-the-wall" serving "superb" "homestyle" American cooking ("wonderful soups", "great meat loaf") that's "exactly what mom should have cooked but couldn't"; despite "counter service", "fluorescent lighting" and the "competition to snag a table", addicts yearn for a "clone" in their nabe – though many also yearn for a liquor license.

## Barolo Grill    26   25   24   $37
*3030 E. Sixth Ave. (bet. Milwaukee & St. Paul Sts.), Denver, 303-393-1040*
■ "You can go to Italy or go here" rave fans of the "scrumptious" cooking at this "lovely" East Denver Northern Italian, where the "owner's attention to details shows", especially in the "best Italian wine list in the West"; although service, while "knowledgeable", strikes critics as "self-important", ratings support boosters who say this "class act" "just gets better every year."

## Beehive    –   –   –   M
*606 Corona St. (E. 6th Ave.), Denver, 303-832-5766*
A new addition to the Congress Park neighborhood, this hip Med–New American combines the winning duo of Janice Henning (chef) and hubby Tim Elenteny (sommelier) for terrific, hearty eats and super (mostly imported) wines.

## Briarwood Inn, The 🅂    26   27   26   $40
*1630 Eighth St. (near Hwy. 58 & US 6), Golden, 303-279-3121*
☑ "Don't eat the day before you dine here" advise patrons of this "lavish", "romantic" American-Continental in Golden known for "superb multicourse meals" in an atmosphere of "absolute elegance" that's "perfect for a special occasion"; though a few bicker it's "past its prime", it remains a "traditionalist's paradise" that's "expensive and worth it" for its loyal clientele.

## Cafe Alpine 🅂    26   21   22   $29
*106 East Adams Ave. (Main St.), Breckenridge, 970-453-8218*
■ In a "town not known for great restaurants", this "intimate", "clubby" Breckenridge Regional American with a "cozy mountain atmosphere" offers a "creative menu, outstanding presentation, attentive service and a fabulous tapas bar"; though "pricey", it's "excellent when you want something different."

### Cafe Bohemia 25 | 16 | 19 | $27

*1729 E. Evans Ave. (bet. Gilpin & Williams Sts.), Denver, 303-777-7222*

◪ "They have a vision" applaud devotees of this "creative, cheery" Central Denver French-American bistro, a "special secret" with a "perfectionist chef-owner" turning out "stylish" fare that's "not generic"; but what's a "cozy space" to some elicits groans over "hole-in-the-wall discomfort" from others, and service gets "totally overburdened" when it's hopping.

### Café Brazil 💳 26 | 17 | 23 | $25

*3611 Navajo St. (W. 36th Ave.), Denver, 303-480-1877*

■ The "smells will drive you crazy and make your tongue dance" gush admirers of the "fabulous food" you will "dream about and crave" at North Denver's "perennially hip" Brazilian "hideaway"; it may be just a "hole-in-the-wall with style", but it's "homey", service is "charming" and oh, the grub – an "indescribable, wonderful melding of flavors"; N.B. reservations are "a must" – and so is hard cash.

### Charles Court [S] 27 | 27 | 26 | $46

*Broadmoor Hotel, 1 Lake Ave., Colorado Springs, 719-634-7711*

◪ The Broadmoor's fine dining room in Colorado Springs, this "formal" Continental–New American offers "the perfect getaway for a romantic evening", with its "beautiful view of Broadmoor Lake", "elegant, comfortable setting" and "consistent, proven" food and service; although casual sorts find it too "costly" and "stuffy", ratings say it all for the majority: a "treat for special occasions."

### Del Frisco's Double Eagle Steak House 26 | 25 | 25 | $48

*Denver Tech Ctr., 8100 E. Orchard Rd. (I-25), Greenwood Village, 303-796-0100*

■ "Texas comes to Denver" at this "extremely expensive but excellent" Greenwood Villager, where a "top-notch" staff delivers "power dinners" of "great" martinis and mammoth hunks of seared steer in a "clubby setting" accented by a "fabulous cigar bar" (the largest in the state); though many find it "incredibly enjoyable", a few beef "big is not always beautiful" and warn you'll "spend a bundle."

### Domo 25 | 28 | 21 | $23

*1365 Osage St. (Colfax Ave.), Denver, 303-595-3666*

■ "A joy to the palate and a delight to the eyes" gush devotees of this "unique" Downtowner that's "like a Japanese country inn" with a "very traditional menu" ("no sushi, no sashimi") of "food you didn't even know existed"; but the "stunning" decor ("stone tables", "large Japanese garden") and unusual, "authentic" fare draw crowds, leading to "interminable waits" (no reserving), and "inept" service doesn't help matters.

### Flagstaff House [S] 26 | 27 | 25 | $48

*1138 Flagstaff Rd. (on Flagstaff Mtn.), Boulder, 303-442-4640*

■ Boulder's top "special-occasion" restaurant earns applause for its "elegant" and "imaginative" (albeit "pricey") Continental–New American dining, "amazing wine list" and, especially, for its "fantastic view" of the city below (it's the "best place to take out-of-state visitors" or "someone you love"); while most agree it has "few, if any, flaws", there are gripes about service that's "terribly impressed with itself."

**Full Moon Grill [S]** | 26 | 20 | 23 | $30 |

*Village Shopping Ctr., 2525 Arapahoe Ave. (bet. Folsom & 28th Sts.), Boulder, 303-938-8800*

■ Admirers wax heavenly about this Boulder "hidden gem" from executive chef Bradford Heap, touting the "creative", "superbly executed" Northern Italian menu, "well-organized" wine list and "great service", all of which have only "improved with age"; although the "cozy", "funky" space is simply "too crowded" to some and the "irresistible" dishes can be "slow" to arrive, "it's still the place to go casual and feel like a king."

**Gabriel's [S]** | 25 | 25 | 25 | $35 |

*5450 N. Hwy. 67 (Santa Fe Dr.), Sedalia, 303-688-2323*

■ A "charming Victorian setting" "in a house with many rooms" makes for "very special, romantic" dining at this Sedalia (south of Denver) Northern Italian where "lovely music on the porch", "decadent meat and cream dishes" and a "beautiful garden" clinch the deal; nitpickers whine "why couldn't they put it closer to the civilized world?", but devotees agree it's "worth" the "pretty drive."

**Grouse Mountain Grill [S]** | 27 | 26 | 25 | $47 |

*Beaver Creek Resort, 141 Scott Hill Rd. (Village Rd.), Avon, 970-949-0600*

■ "Gorgeous and delicious" sums up this "intimate, quiet" Beaver Creek Regional American with a "great view" of the Valley below, and "extraordinary food, decor and service", plus a "top-notch wine selection", inside; though the "delicious, large portions could serve two people", save room for the "excellent desserts."

**Highlands Garden Cafe** | 28 | 27 | 26 | $33 |

*3927 W. 32nd Ave. (bet. Osceola & Perry Sts.), Denver, 303-458-5920*

■ "Open your eyes, it's not a dream" counsel enthusiasts of this North Denver New American (No. 2 for Food in the *Colorado Survey*), where two "lovely older homes" renovated into softly lit dining rooms provide the setting for "one of Denver's very best" and well-priced menus; "if you eat inside, though, you've missed" the "fabulous gardens", so "dine by candlelight among the roses" at what may be the "most romantic restaurant in town."

**Kevin Taylor** | 25 | 26 | 25 | $54 |

*Hotel Teatro, 1106 14th St. (Arapahoe St.), Denver, 303-820-2600*

◪ Although star chef Kevin Taylor's Downtown New American scores highly, diners report mixed reactions: converts point to the "elegant, over-the-top" food, "ethereal" space, "amazing wine list" and "superb ingredients [that] justify the pricey menu", but detractors retort it's "too expensive for us to bear the growing pains" ("my wallet hurts just thinking about it") and claim its "reach exceeds its grasp"; ratings, however, side with the fans.

**Keystone Ranch Restaurant [S]** | 27 | 27 | 27 | $56 |

*Keystone Ranch Resort (2½ mi. west of Hwy. 6), Keystone, 970-496-4386*

■ "Elegant, excellent but expensive" are the three Es at this "must-go" Summit County New American in the "best setting imaginable" – a "historic ranch home" with "superb views" of Keystone Valley; although "pricey", consensus is it's "worth it" for the "gourmet" "prix fixe" meals ("excellent game"), "impeccable service" and "world-class setting."

## La Montaña ⑤    26 | 21 | 21 | $29

*Village Ctr., 2500 Village Dr. (Après Ski Way), Steamboat Springs,*
*970-879-5800*

■ "Excellent", "upscale" Mexican-SW food is the deal at this "sizeable but cozy, second-story" Steamboat Springs beanery; "unusual combinations" and "pretty presentations" add up to "outstanding" eats so be sure to "make reservations."

## La Petite Maison    27 | 25 | 27 | $34

*1015 W. Colorado Ave. (bet. 10th & 11th Sts.), Colorado Springs,*
*719-632-4887*

■ Colorado Springs' oldest French restaurant, set in a "darling house", offers "excellent" "classical" and "innovative" cooking "served with flair", plus a "nice wine list" and "very good individual service"; it's perfect "for a romantic dinner", although perhaps "a little too cutesy" for a few; P.S. insiders advise "try the pâté and try not to fill up on the bread."

## Left Bank ⑤    26 | 23 | 23 | $42

*Sitzmark Lodge, 183 Gore Creek Dr. (Main St.), Vail, 970-476-3696*

☑ It's "the only real French restaurant in the state" maintain advocates of this long-standing and pricey Vail gastrodome, a "romantic adult" place to enjoy "glorious", "consistently excellent" cooking and "great service" in a "beautiful setting"; critics moan that it's "staid" and "they are French and don't know the meaning of service", but they're outvoted; N.B. cash only.

## Little Nell Restaurant, The    26 | 26 | 26 | $49

*Little Nell Hotel, 675 E. Durant St. (Spring St.), Aspen,*
*970-920-6330*

■ It's "worth every dollar you will spend" purr enthusiasts of this "very cosmopolitan", "pricey" Aspen hotel dining room, where, despite chef turnover, pampered sybarites continue to enjoy "fantastic" New American fare and a "great wine list" in a "gorgeous, elegant" setting; don't miss the "great courtyard for an alfresco lunch" and remember that "Bobby Stuckey is one of America's best sommeliers."

## New Saigon ⑤    25 | 14 | 19 | $17

*630 S. Federal Blvd. (bet. Center & Gill Aves.), Denver, 303-936-4954*

■ "Best", "best", "best" beats the drum for this South Denver Vietnamese where the "outstanding" food from an "encyclopedia of a menu" (40 pages) and the "five-star service" seem even better at "one-[star] prices"; fans of the "complex, high quality" curries and "great noodle bowls" plead "it's full now – don't list it."

## Palace Arms ⑤    27 | 28 | 27 | $47

*Brown Palace Hotel, 321 17th St. (bet. Broadway & Tremont Pl.),*
*Denver, 303-297-3111*

■ The top-drawer dining room of the 104 year-old Brown Palace Hotel ("lots of history"), this Downtown Denver American-Continental is the "only superelegant, plush restaurant left", according to devotees who rave about its "old Denver" "class, class, class", "turn-of-the-century furnishings" and "impeccable" (if slightly "snooty") service; it may be "for the filthy rich", but it's "worth the price" to "feel like royalty"; N.B. jacket and tie required.

## Papillon Café S
28 | 25 | 25 | $38

*250 Josephine St. (bet. 2nd & 3rd Aves.), Denver, 303-333-7166*

■ No. 1 for Food and Popularity in our *Colorado Survey*, this Cherry Creek New French with Asian influences offers chef-owner Radek Cerny's "outstanding" cuisine that's "as beautifully presented as it is delicious" (though wags warn you "could get vertigo" from the vertical constructions); "well-coached servers" and an "intelligent" wine list leave little room for complaint, though one diner tries: "I hate restaurants where everything on the menu is great."

## Picasso
26 | 26 | 25 | $51

*The Lodge at Cordillera, 2205 Cordillera Way (7 mi. south of Hwy. 6), Edwards, 970-926-6988*

■ "It's all perfect, even after Paris" sigh fans who paint a "charming" picture of this "quiet and intimate", high-end Vail Valley French in a "gorgeous setting", with "splendid food and wines to match" and a "romantic" ambiance with fireplace; "it's worth the drive to get there" say those with "magical" memories, and if a few claim "it's inconsistent", they're soundly outvoted.

## Piñons Restaurant S
26 | 25 | 26 | $54

*105 S. Mill St. (Main St.), Aspen, 970-920-2021*

■ "Go for the venison" say boosters of this "pricey" Aspen Regional American attracting an "older crowd" with "excellent game" and other "delicious" fare enhanced by "wonderful service" and "gorgeous" Western decor; though a few gripe that the "menu hasn't changed in ten years", the majority applauds the fact that it "oozes consistency."

## Potager
25 | 22 | 22 | $31

*1109 Ogden St. (bet. 11th & 12th Aves.), Denver, 303-832-5788*

☑ Most agree that this "airy", "hip, urban" New American "addition to the Capitol Hill scene" does up a "clever menu" of "fab food in a funky" but "comfortable" setting (a former laundry in a war zone re-do) where the "outdoor seating in the back is a great touch"; "inconsistent" service is the main complaint, though even fans admit the "adventurous", "changing" bill of fare is "sometimes too avant-garde and confusing."

## Radex ◗S
25 | 23 | 23 | $29

*100 E. Ninth Ave. (Lincoln Ave.), Denver, 303-861-7999*

☑ "Wonderful martinis" and "interesting food" from "genius" chef-owner Radek Cerny conspire to make this less expensive Papillon sib "the best newcomer to Denver", according to its "beautiful people" clientele who rave this New American is "so, so cool, from the hip staff to the superchic interior" – though cynics claim the latter is "like unfinished South Beach"; N.B. live jazz is another draw, although it makes the "upbeat" setting even more "noisy."

## Renaissance S
27 | 25 | 26 | $57

*304 E. Hopkins Ave. (bet. S. Mill & S. Monarch Sts.), Aspen, 970-925-2402*

☑ "Well-heeled clients" shower encomiums on Aspen's toniest Med–New American, giving high marks to its "unbelievably professional staff" and "generally superb", "imaginative and creative" food in a "very elegant" setting that's good for "celebrity watching"; although a few cite occasional "misses" and find it a bit "pretentious", adherents who can handle the high tabs rate it one of the "best in the state" and a "favorite anywhere."

**Soupçon [S]** 26 | 24 | 25 | $36

*127-A Elk Ave. (bet. 1st & 2nd Alley), Crested Butte, 970-349-5448*

■ "Good things come in small packages" remind enthusiasts of this "delightful" Crested Butte French bistro; the "heavenly food" transports diners even if "from the outside it looks like an old garage with pink drapes" – "don't miss" this "real winner."

**Splendido [S]** 27 | 27 | 26 | $58

*The Chateau, 17 Chateau Ln. (Scott Hill Rd.), Beaver Creek, 970-845-8808*

■ This "elegant", "beautiful" New American in an "awesome" setting high above Beaver Creek Valley offers "sublime and creative" food and a "great wine list", delivered by a refreshingly "down-to-earth" staff that will nonetheless treat you "royally"; so while "expensive", the "fully satisfied" majority finds it "worth it" and advises: "save for a very special occasion."

**Strings [S]** 26 | 23 | 24 | $34

*1700 Humboldt St. (corner of 17th Ave.), Denver, 303-831-7310*

◪ "As close to casual but elegant dining as can be had in Denver" claim buffs of this "bright, appealing" and affordable Uptown Cal-Med-American "institution" that's *the* place for "power lunching"; however, there are grumbles about "uneven service" ("friendly", "attentive" vs. "snooty", "slow").

**Sushi Den** 27 | 24 | 20 | $30

*1487 S. Pearl St. (Florida Ave.), Denver, 303-777-0826*

◪ This Washington Park high-end Japanese "home to the beautiful people" may be "painfully hip" and as "chi chi as they come", but most concur it also "puts the fresh in sushi" and is "worth the wait you'll undoubtedly have"; wet blankets dis "arrogant" patrons and staff and insist "there's better sushi in Denver", but they're loudly overruled by a solid majority that swears "nothing ever compares."

**Swan at Inverness, The** 26 | 25 | 26 | $46

*Inverness Hotel & Golf Club, 200 Inverness Dr. West (bet. County Line Rd. & I-25), Englewood, 303-799-5800*

■ The "elegant", "soothing", "exquisite" setting at this "upscale" Englewood hotel Continental earns clucks and coos aplenty from those who appreciate a "place where you can dress up" and enjoy "outstanding food", "savvy service" and "excellent wines"; though a few quack "company expense accounts only", most trumpet this "very romantic" "place for a celebration."

**Sweet Basil [S]** 28 | 23 | 24 | $40

*193 E. Gore Creek Dr. (Bridge St.), Vail, 970-476-0125*

■ Whether it's the "ultra hip" cuisine, "well-done service", "great outdoor seating" or the "sound of the river below", the bottom line on this "best in Vail" New American is that it "reaches great heights without being unreasonably expensive"; not surprisingly, it's "always crowded" so "make reservations."

**Syzygy [S]** 25 | 24 | 23 | $49

*520 E. Hyman Ave. (bet. Galena & Hunter Sts.), Aspen, 970-925-3700*

■ "Wow" – the "beautiful waterfall" and "artfully prepared food in a setting to match" add up to a "romantic" experience that's "very pricey but actually worth it" at this "swanky" Aspen New American, a former haunt of Spider Sabich, among other notables; an "affordable wine list" and "great" live jazz are other pluses.

## Tante Louise                  27 | 26 | 26 | $42
*4900 E. Colfax Ave. (Eudora St.), Denver, 303-355-4488*

■ "A favorite after all these years", this East Denver French
veteran still delivers "intimate, romantic dining" and "unpretentious
elegance" in a "lovely old home"; "gracious host" Corky Douglass
"uncorks a great meal" and "oversees a great wine list", and if a
few callow souls consider this "classic" a "fossil", its adoring
clientele cherishes it as a "sanctuary for life before baseball
caps and jeans."

## 240 Union S                  26 | 22 | 24 | $31
*240 Union Blvd. (3 blocks south of 6th Ave. Frwy.), Lakewood,
303-989-3562*

■ It's unanimous: this "underappreciated" New American "jewel"
is "hands down the best restaurant on the West Side" of town,
serving a "creative", fabulous" menu (especially "super fish") in a
"congenial setting"; it's for "that special night" made better by
"superb service" – just beware "the noisy, yuppie lunch crowd."

## Wildflower Restaurant S       27 | 27 | 25 | $46
*Lodge at Vail, 174 E. Gore Creek Dr. (base of Vail Mtn.), Vail,
970-476-5011*

■ Superlatives abound for this "beautiful", "fabulous" and
"expensive" Vail New American, with diners throwing bouquets
for the "world-class", "impeccable", "superelegant" food,
"gorgeous" decor with "flowers everywhere" and "wonderful
service"; those in the know say it's "lovely to eat outside [on the
patio] in the summer"; in sum, it "sets a standard."

# Detroit

## TOP 10 FOOD RANKING

| Restaurant | Cuisine Type |
|---|---|
| **28** Lark, The | Eclectic/French |
| **27** Golden Mushroom | Continental |
|     Opus One | New American |
| **26** Zingerman's Deli | Deli/Sandwich Shop |
|     Cafe Bon Homme | New French |
|     Moro's Dining | N/S Italian |
| **25** Pike Street Restaurant | Traditional American |
|     Ritz-Carlton Grill | Traditional American |
|     Moveable Feast | American/Continental |
|     Morton's of Chicago | Steakhouse |

## OTHER IMPORTANT PLACES

| | |
|---|---|
| Cousins Heritage Inn | New American |
| Earle, The | French/Italian |
| Five Lakes Grill | New American |
| Forte | Californian/New French |
| Il Posto Ristorante | Northern Italian |
| Mon Jin Lau | Asian |
| Rattlesnake Club | New American |
| Ristorante di Modesta | Northern Italian |
| Steve's Backroom | Middle Eastern |
| Too Chez | New American |
| Tribute | New American |
| Whitney, The | New American |

| F | D | S | C |
|---|---|---|---|

### Cafe Bon Homme

| 26 | 23 | 24 | $29 |
|---|---|---|---|

*844 Penniman Ave. (bet. Harvey & Main Sts.), Plymouth, 734-453-6260*
◪ The "lovely" ambiance of this Plymouth "special-occasion" place is matched by Contemporary French cooking that most judge "outstanding"; a few critics claim that the "polished" service can be "slightly precious" and the "fancy" food isn't quite up to its rep, but as ratings attest, superlatives far outweigh grumbles.

### Cousins Heritage Inn

| 25 | 23 | 24 | $30 |
|---|---|---|---|

*7954 Ann Arbor St. (bet. Baker & Main Sts.), Dexter, 734-426-3020*
■ "Year after year", this "beautiful" old house "in a quiet town" just west of Ann Arbor is favored for celebrations thanks to softly lit, "dignified" rooms and a short New American menu featuring hard-to-find game; it's what "one hopes to find" in a country restaurant, except that it's perhaps "a bit cramped."

### Earle, The ⬛

| 25 | 22 | 22 | $24 |
|---|---|---|---|

*121 W. Washington St. (S. Ashley St.), Ann Arbor, 734-994-0211*
◪ Take "someone you love" to this "hideaway" in Ann Arbor that offers a candlelit setting for "first-rate" country French-Italian fare complemented by some of the region's best wines; on a simpler note, try its wine bar for a light dinner "without a large bill"; foes find the ambiance "gloomy" and food "heavy", but they're outvoted.

F | D | S | C

**Five Lakes Grill** — | – | – | M

*424 N. Main St. (Commerce Rd.), Milford, 248-684-7455*
Brian Polcyn (ex Pike Street and Acadia), arguably one of the most talented chefs hereabouts, is displaying his skills in this tiny village an hour northwest of Detroit; enjoy New American dishes such as his signature roast duck with apple-cider sauce, as well as rich specials like Maryland crab cakes with Boursin and chive sauce, and a series of light offerings for the diet-challenged.

**Forte** — | – | – | M

*201 S. Old Woodward Ave. (south of Maple Rd.), Birmingham, 248-594-7300*
Lighting up Birmingham's restaurant row is this hot eatery that features green velvet banquettes and a lively bar; it's a très chic hangout that offers innovative Californian fare inspired by the South of France, as well as prime people-watching.

**Golden Mushroom** — 27 | 23 | 25 | $32

*18100 W. Ten Mile Rd. (Southfield Rd.), Southfield, 248-559-4230*
■ Defining fine Continental dining in Detroit for two decades, this "classic" has been a training ground for many of the area's best chefs; the "professional" supervision by semi-retired "master chef" Milos Cihelka (Steven Allen now serves as executive chef) consistently produces "premier" meals, focusing on mushrooms and game, matched with "excellent" wines; even if some find the decor "dated", most advise "save up" to enjoy "one of the best."

**Il Posto Ristorante** — | – | – | E

*29110 Franklin Rd. (Northwestern Hwy.), Southfield, 248-827-8070*
When chef Giovanni Belsito moved his elegant Northern Italian restaurant from Naples, FL to the affluent Detroit suburb of Southfield, he established what many agree is the best thing to hit town in years; the excellent, traditional menu, accompanied by a reasonably broad wine list, is delivered by a refined staff.

**Lark, The** — 28 | 27 | 28 | $50

*6430 Farmington Rd. (north of Maple Rd.), West Bloomfield, 248-661-4466*
■ "World-class" cooking from an Eclectic-French kitchen (ranked No. 1 for Food in the Detroit area) combined with rustic Portuguese decor and the hands-on "hospitality" of Jim and Mary Lark earn this West Bloomfield boutique high ratings across the board; it's "hip to bash it" and it takes a "big wallet and a big stomach" to do justice to its prix fixe menu, but its status as Michigan's Most Popular Restaurant speaks for itself.

**Mon Jin Lau** ◐ [S] — 24 | 20 | 21 | $19

*1515 E. Maple Rd. (Stephenson Hwy.), Troy, 248-689-2332*
■ Not only does this "crowded", highly regarded suburban "nouveau" Asian boast "adventurous" cooking, but it also has "great wines", a "classy", "dine-out" setting and knows how to "mix a martini"; the menu blends Chinese, Thai and French influences, providing an "interesting twist on the old standbys."

**Moro's Dining** [S] — 26 | 16 | 22 | $19

*6535 Allen Rd. (Southfield Rd.), Allen Park, 313-382-7152*
◪ A long-standing Italian "secret" in the Southern suburbs for "outstanding scampi and veal", salad tossed tableside and flambéed desserts; some find the atmosphere "romantic", but as decor ratings indicate, not everyone agrees.

**Morton's of Chicago [S]** 25 | 23 | 24 | $34

*1 Towne Sq. (Northwestern Hwy., bet. Civic Center Dr. & Lahser Rd.), Southfield, 248-354-6006*

◪ "Double-meal" servings of top-quality "red meat" win praise from carnivores who like to "smoke cigars, listen to Frank Sinatra and enjoy their own wine" amidst the "men's-club ambiance" of this classy chain steakhouse; not everyone is into this kind of "beef feast" (e.g. "food on steroids", too many "pinky rings and 'nieces'"); those who are say "go starving" and "bring money."

**Moveable Feast, The** 25 | 24 | 22 | $31

*326 W. Liberty St. (2nd St.), Ann Arbor, 734-663-3278*

◪ It's "hard to go wrong" at what admirers call Ann Arbor's "best", a "high-toned", lace-edged Victorian with "beautifully presented" Continental-American fare; the ever-changing menu "can be very inventive", and if it "sometimes misses" (ditto the service), odds are you'll enjoy an "excellent" meal in a "quiet, refined" setting.

**Opus One** 27 | 26 | 26 | $36

*565 E. Larned St. (Beaubien St.), 313-961-7766*

■ "First-class in every way", from the "elegant" etched glass, marble and mahogany interior and personal "pampering" to the "top-notch" New American menu and "sensational" desserts; though "pricey", it's "reliably impressive" and a byword for business entertaining among Detroit's Downtown power brokers.

**Pike Street Restaurant** 25 | 22 | 23 | $29

*18 W. Pike St. (bet. Saginaw St. & Wide Track Dr.), Pontiac, 248-334-7878*

■ A "diamond in the rough" in Downtown Pontiac, this American standout remains "consistently good" and "cosmopolitan" despite the departure of chef Brian Polcyn; the "innovative" kitchen turns out "hearty, wholesome" fare that's beautifully presented in a turn-of-the-century wood-and-brick setting; most rate it "just plain excellent."

**Rattlesnake Club, The** 25 | 24 | 22 | $31

*Stroh's River Pl., 300 River Place Dr. (E. Jefferson Ave.), 313-567-4400*

■ New American star chef Jimmy Schmidt presides over this polished wood-and-marble, river-view dining room; its elegant "NYC"–style setting, culinary artistry and "outstanding quality" make "the Snake" a premier "client" and "special-events" spot; "excellent" wines are the icing on the cake.

**Ristorante di Modesta** 25 | 21 | 22 | $27

*29410 Northwestern Hwy. (12 Mile Rd.), Southfield, 248-358-0344*

◪ It's usually a "scene" at this Western suburban "media hangout" where "terrific" Northern Italian food is spiced by local celeb sightings; it's "trendy, tasty" and has "great atmo", but complaints of "arrogance" suggest they need to "turn down the attitude."

**Ritz-Carlton Grill [S]** 25 | 27 | 26 | $33

*Ritz-Carlton Hotel, Fairlane Plaza, 300 Town Ctr. Dr. (bet. Hubbard & Southfield Svc. Drs.), Dearborn, 313-441-2100*

■ An ambiance of sheer "luxury" and an "unobtrusive", "well-trained staff" enhance the American menu of grilled meats and seafood at this "impressive" hotel dining room opposite Ford World HQ; it gets high marks all around and it's "extra special for special occasions"; "it's the Ritz" says it all.

## Steve's Backroom

25 | 17 | 20 | $12

*19872 Kelly Rd. (bet. 7 & 8 Mile Rds.), Harper Woods, 313-527-7240*
■ In a tiny, "very clean" BYO cafe in the back of a well-run Middle Eastern market owned by a Lebanese couple, diners discover the "best grape leaves and kibbeh" they've "ever tasted" and have "never had anything I didn't like"; this Harper Woods hideout is "a real surprise for the unknowing."

## Too Chez

23 | 22 | 21 | $25

*27155 Sheraton Dr. (I-96), Novi, 248-348-5555*
☑ Snappy and "stylish", this "chic" New American (with Italian accents) is "a treat for the eyes" thanks to modern decor sparked by colorful art and a mosaic floor; most say it pleases the palate with "original" cooking (pizzas, pastas, house-smoked salmon), but critics judge the menu "hit or miss" and find the place "too trendy" and "loud"; in the NW suburbs next to a Sheraton and handy to I-96, it's popular for business lunches and lights up even more at dinnertime.

## Tribute

– | – | – | VE

*31425 W. 12 Mile Rd. (W. Orchard Lake Rd.), Farmington Hills, 248-848-1313*
Opulent white-linen, check-your-wallet-at-the door Western suburban Contemporary American with sophisticated International accents created by chef Takashi Yagihashi (from Chicago's vaunted Ambria); diners pay tribute to excellent (and sometimes flawless) meals and service, just as was intended; open Tuesday–Saturday.

## Whitney, The 🆂

25 | 28 | 24 | $36

*4421 Woodward Ave. (bet. Mack & Warren Aves.), 313-832-5700*
☑ If you "want to impress, take them here" say fans of this stunning 1890 mansion built by lumber baron David Whitney on Detroit's threadbare main drag; it boasts the most "majestic" decor around (cut glass, carved wood, a sweeping staircase), and though some say the changing New American menu "could be better", most are satisfied by the hefty offerings; the "awesome" Sunday brunch gets thumbs up from surveyors and there's a "terrific" bar with jazz on the third floor.

## Zingerman's Deli 🆂

26 | 18 | 20 | $12

*422 Detroit St. (Kingsley St.), Ann Arbor, 734-663-3354*
■ Mavens debate whether "Ann Arbor's pride" is the "best deli in the Western hemisphere" or merely in "the Midwest"; "huge, wonderful corned beef sandwiches" and a long menu of "fabulous" combos on "heavenly breads" mean it's always "crowded and noisy", despite having taken over the building next door for more tables; it's also a "serious" "gourmet grocery" with coffees, meats, cheeses, smoked fish and other exotica.

# Fort Lauderdale

## TOP 10 FOOD RANKING

| Restaurant | Cuisine Type |
|---|---|
| **28** Eduardo de San Angel | Mexican |
| Darrel & Oliver's Cafe Maxx | New World |
| **26** Armadillo Cafe | Southwestern |
| Mark's Las Olas | New American |
| Black Orchid Cafe | Continental |
| Primavera | N/S Italian |
| **25** Brooks | Continental |
| Sunfish Grill | Seafood |
| Hobo's Fish Joint | Seafood |
| By Word of Mouth | New American |

## OTHER IMPORTANT PLACES

| | |
|---|---|
| Bistro Mezzaluna | New American |
| Cafe Martorano | N/S Italian |
| Darrel & Oliver's/Grill | Eclectic/International |
| Himmarshee Bar & Grille | Regional American |
| Hot Chocolates | Eclectic |
| Left Bank | French Bistro |

| F | D | S | C |
|---|---|---|---|

### Armadillo Cafe 🗲

| 26 | 19 | 23 | $40 |
|---|---|---|---|

*4630 SW 64th Ave. (Griffin Rd.), Davie, 954-791-5104*

■ "Worth a trip" to "out-of-the-way" Davie, this culinary pioneer "brought Southwestern cooking to South Florida" and continues to produce "outstanding", "innovative" cuisine out of a recently expanded, but still "unlikely", strip mall storefront; expect a "quiet" atmosphere, "friendly" service and such signature dishes as porcini-dusted sea bass (a "must-try") and lobster quesadilla.

### Bistro Mezzaluna

| 23 | 20 | 21 | $37 |
|---|---|---|---|

*741 SE 17th St. (S. Federal Hwy.), 954-522-6620*

■ A Central Broward "place to be seen" for "trendy yuppies", especially at its "upbeat bar", this Italian-accented New American also delivers "wonderful" food ("the best veal chop around") in an "elegant setting"; while spoilers warn about a "loud" decibel level and an "aggravating" no-reservations policy (for less than six), a visit is usually "a treat"; P.S. try to make it for the "best happy-hour nibbles" in town.

## Black Orchid Cafe S · 26 | 23 | 22 | $43 |

*2985 N. Ocean Blvd. (south of E. Oakland Park Blvd.), 954-561-9398*

☒ This "very romantic" Central Broward Continental lives up to its film-noir name with live music, a "classy", orchid-filled setting and a "fantastic selection of exotic food", including African game pheasant, ostrich and buffalo steak, matched with "great wines"; it doesn't come cheap, but daring diners and flower fanatics confirm that "everything is wonderful."

## Brooks S · 25 | 23 | 24 | $38 |

*500 S. Federal Hwy. (south of Hillsboro Blvd.), Deerfield Beach, 954-427-9302*

■ An ideal "opportunity to dress up" in casual Deerfield Beach, this "classy", "upscale" Continental attracts "older" "groups" of diners who like to mark "special occasions" in its "intimate", formal rooms; whippersnappers find the atmosphere "stiff" and "not very exciting", but appreciate the "quality" food and deft service.

## By Word of Mouth · 25 | 15 | 22 | $38 |

*3200 NE 12th Ave. (E. Oakland Park Blvd.), 954-564-3663*

☒ Located in a Central Broward commercial district, this "unusual" Contemporary American (and well-known caterer) displays its entire menu in a refrigerated case for patrons to peruse before ordering; while the "small", lace-curtain setting is "not much to look at", "excellent" offerings such as the signature sun-dried tomato paté, plus an "attentive" staff that describes every dish in detail, make this a "delightfully different" experience.

## Cafe Martorano · 25 | 17 | 19 | $50 |

*3343 E. Oakland Park Blvd. (A1A), 954-561-2554*

☒ While it attracts a "superstar" clientele and serves undeniably "excellent" Philadelphia-accented Italian food ("world-class mussels") from a daily menu that's recited at tableside, this "very small", "trendy" Central Broward venue otherwise plays to mixed reviews, with dissenters reporting "very expensive" prices, service issues ("snooty") and a high decibel level fueled by loud music.

## Darrel & Oliver's Cafe Maxx S · 28 | 21 | 26 | $48 |

*2601 E. Atlantic Blvd. (east of A1A), Pompano Beach, 954-782-0606*

■ Chef Oliver Saucy ("a local treasure") continues to "set the standard" at this celebrated Pompano Beach foodie shrine, with a daily changing menu of "dependably excellent" New World cuisine ("superb sweet onion–crusted snapper"), an "excellent wine selection", "fine service" and a casual, upscale interior marked by an open kitchen; P.S. some feel the "Hawaiian chocolate soufflé cake is the best dessert in South Florida."

## Darrel & Oliver's East City Grill S · 25 | 23 | 24 | $47 |

*Riviera Hotel, 505 N. Ft. Lauderdale Beach Blvd. (bet. Las Olas & Sunrise Blvds.), 954-565-5569*

■ An awesome combination of "wonderful", "innovative" Eclectic/ International cuisine, "personable", "knowledgeable" service and a "tropical setting overlooking the ocean" ("sit on the covered patio" and "watch the bikinis go by") draws a "very sharp crowd" to this Central Broward offshoot of Cafe Maxx; signature dishes include wok-prepared snapper and nori-wrapped salmon.

## Eduardo de San Angel | 28 | 23 | 26 | $43 |

*2822 E. Commercial Blvd. (bet. Bayview Dr. & 28th Ave.), 954-772-4731*

■ Gifted chef Eduardo Pria has now rejoined his protégé and younger brother Luis at this "cozy", "romantic" source for "serious" "gourmet Mexican" (read: "no chips and salsa", but 50 wines by the glass); with the No. 1 Food rating in Broward, it will singlehandedly "change your idea" of this cuisine, and the service team, led by fellow sibling Jose, is "exquisite", making a visit "always a delight."

## Himmarshee Bar & Grille [S] | 25 | 19 | 21 | $37 |

*210 SW Second St. (NW 2nd Ave.), 954-524-1818*

■ "Conveniently" located two blocks from the Broward Center for the Performing Arts, this Central Broward Regional American is called a "great" pre- and post-performance choice because of its "innovative" nightly changing menu, "attentive" service, friendly mezzanine bar and outdoor tables that are ideal for "people-watching"; it can get "noisy", especially on weekends, but that's par for any "cool scene."

## Hobo's Fish Joint [S] | 25 | 19 | 20 | $39 |

*Palm Spring Plaza, 10317 Royal Palm Blvd. (Coral Springs Dr.), Coral Springs, 954-346-5484*

■ "Perhaps the best seafood restaurant in Broward County", this Coral Springs favorite offers "huge portions" of a dozen types of extremely fresh fish prepared any of 16 different ways; the masculine, steakhouse-style setting includes wood floors, dark ceilings and white tablecloths, which along with the menu's meat offerings make carnivores feel right at home.

## Hot Chocolates ◐[S] | 24 | 23 | 22 | $40 |

*3101 N. Federal Hwy. (Oakland Park Blvd.), 954-564-5552*

■ A marble-and-flower-filled, Erté-meets-the-Flintstones interior, Eclectic cuisine "on a par with the setting" and a "hot" after-dinner nightclub with live music and dancing ("couples all over each other") are why this late-night Central Broward newcomer "is fun from beginning to end."

## Left Bank Restaurant, The [S] | 24 | 21 | 23 | $44 |

*214 SE Sixth Ave. (north of Las Olas Blvd.), 954-462-5376*

■ Even though chef-owner Jean-Pierre Brehier has "delegated" his kitchen duties and is frequently "off doing his TV show", this "long-established" Central Broward French bistro continues to serve "excellent" Provençal cuisine complemented by a large, California-focused wine list; the "charming atmosphere" is evoked through lots of dark woods and a Renior-style centerpiece mural; N.B. reservations are recommended.

## Mark's Las Olas [S] | 26 | 24 | 24 | $49 |

*1032 E. Las Olas Blvd. (bet. 10th & 11th Sts.), 954-463-1000*

◪ An "attractive", "see-and-be-seen" crowd knows to "make reservations" before dining at chef-owner Mark Militello's globally accented Contemporary American in Central Broward, the Most Popular restaurant in the *Fort Lauderdale Survey*, which "does not disappoint" thanks to a "stylish" interior and "imaginative" dishes ("great duck and tuna") using "quality ingredients"; critics find it "noisy" and "overpriced", with a clientele that looks "too thin" to appreciate the "excellent food."

## Primavera S

26 | 22 | 23 | $43

*Primavera Plaza, 830 E. Oakland Park Blvd. (Dixie Hwy.), 954-564-6363*

■ "Our restaurant for celebrations", this long-standing Italian remains "a classic" with "consistently excellent" fare – including a tempting antipasti table, homemade pasta and "great" desserts – plus "very good", "formal" service and a "quiet", flower-filled setting; while the tab can be "expensive", the off-season prix fixe meal for two, which comes with a bottle of wine, is a bargain.

## Sunfish Grill

25 | 15 | 20 | $39

*2771 E. Atlantic Blvd. (east of N. Federal Hwy.), Pompano Beach, 954-788-2434*

■ Visitors to this "tiny", funky Pompano Beach grill say chef Tony Sindaco "really understands seafood", producing "excellent", "flavorful" dishes complemented by a moderately priced wine list; while fish is his forte, there's also steak, chicken and fine homemade breads and desserts, which help make this an overall "real find" ("would hate for it to be discovered").

## TOP 10 FOOD RANKING

| | Restaurant | Cuisine Type |
|---|---|---|
| **28** | Cacharel | New French |
| | Del Frisco's | Steakhouse |
| **27** | Saint-Emilion | French Bistro |
| **26** | Bistro Louise | Mediterranean |
| **25** | Railhead Smokehouse | BBQ |
| | Angeluna | New American |
| | Kincaid's | Hamburgers |
| | La Piazza | N/S Italian |
| **24** | Angelo's Barbecue | BBQ |
| **23** | Cafe Aspen | New American |

## OTHER IMPORTANT PLACES

| | |
|---|---|
| Buffet at the Kimbell | New American |
| Grape Escape | Eclectic |
| Joe T. Garcia's | Mexican/Tex-Mex |
| Paris Coffee Shop | Traditional American |
| Randall's Gourmet | Eclectic |
| Reata | Southwestern |
| Reflections | New American |

| | F | D | S | C |
|---|---|---|---|---|
| **Angelo's Barbecue ⊄** | 24 | 15 | 17 | $11 |
| **Angeluna [S]** | 25 | 23 | 22 | $29 |
| **Bistro Louise** | 26 | 25 | 22 | $27 |

### Angelo's Barbecue ⊄

*2533 White Settlement Rd. (University Dr.), 817-332-0357*

■ "Dark and smoky", "golden oldie" Fort Worth "museum of BBQ" that dishes up "the best damn 'cue in the state", or maybe "the universe", along with the "coldest beer"; if a few doubters say "good but no longer the best", more consider this "the real deal."

### Angeluna [S]

*215 E. Fourth St. (bet. Calhoun & Commerce Sts.), 817-334-0080*

◪ Some of "Fort Worth's most original food" can be found at this "trendy" Downtowner praised for its "nouveau" American fare and "light, airy" setting with a cloud-motif ceiling; though it also draws some complaints ("loud", "uneven", "all show"), it's a definite "hot spot" and a "great location for Bass Hall" concertgoers.

### Bistro Louise

*Stonegate Commons, 2900 S. Hulen St. (Oak Park Ln.), 817-922-9244*

■ With "lovely" decor that hints of Provence and the Riviera, Fort Worth's Most Popular restaurant is an "elegant, comfortable" retreat offering "fresh, innovative" Mediterranean fare that makes "excellent use of spices"; it's "perfect for a ladies' lunch" and enough of a "treat" to merit a "drive from Dallas."

**Buffet at the Kimbell, The** [S] | 19 | 23 | 16 | $12
*Kimbell Art Museum, 3333 Camp Bowie Blvd. (University Dr.), 817-332-8451*
■ This lunch favorite in the acclaimed Kimbell Art Museum boasts (no surprise) "beautiful surroundings" plus "interesting" New American food that's "outstanding for a museum" – in fact, some go for "lunch first, then art"; regulars are especially happy now that chef "Shelby's back"; N.B. dinner served Fridays only.

**Cacharel** | 28 | 25 | 26 | $40
*2221 E. Lamar Blvd. (bet. Ballpark Way & Hwy. 360), Arlington, 817-640-9981*
■ Rated No. 1 for Food in FW, this "exceptional" New French set atop an office building is "the place for any important occasion"; offering "very consistent" food (including "soufflés to die for"), a "quiet" setting and "attentive service" with an eye for "detail", it's "expensive" but could show other restaurants "how it's done."

**Cafe Aspen** | 23 | 20 | 22 | $26
*Frost Bank Shopping Plaza, 6103 Camp Bowie Blvd. (Bryant Irvin Rd.), 817-738-0838*
◪ A Fort Worth pioneer in New American cuisine that's still a "favorite" for "wonderful seasonal fare" served in a cozy, romantic setting by a "courteous" staff led by an owner "who's always there and concerned"; despite scattered reports of "disappointing" meals, the fact that it has a "steady loyal following" says a lot; P.S. "dinner in the bar is one of the best-kept secrets in town."

**Del Frisco's Double Eagle Steak House** | 28 | 26 | 26 | $47
*812 Main St. (8th St.), 817-877-3999*
◪ The "classiest joint to get a steak and still wear your boots" describes this dark, clubby "meat lover's paradise" with beef "to die for" (rated No. 2 for Food in Fort Worth); "superb service" is a plus, and though some find "cigar smoke a turnoff" and call it "too noisy" and "expensive", most consider it "well worth" the tab.

**Grape Escape** [S] | 21 | 21 | 22 | $22
*500 Commerce St. (4th St.), 817-336-9463*
◪ FW's first wine bar, in an ideal location facing Bass Performance Hall, is "a small, fun place" serving "surprisingly good" Eclectic nibbles in a stylish, "relaxed atmosphere"; though grumblers say it's hard to make "a full meal" out of the small plates and call it "pricey for what you get", most are happy to focus on the "great wine flights" served by an "extremely knowledgeable" staff.

**Joe T. Garcia's** [S]⇏ | 21 | 21 | 20 | $16
*2201 N. Commerce St. (bet. N. Main & 22nd Sts.), 817-626-4356*
◪ A Fort Worth "landmark" for over 60 years and "still going strong", thanks to some of "the best margaritas and Mexican food" around plus a "fantastic" patio ("sit by the pool") that makes "you feel you're really in Mexico"; not everyone agrees ("tourist-oriented", "bland food"), but to its "cult following" it's "unbeatable."

**Kincaid's Hamburgers** ⇏ | 25 | 14 | 18 | $8
*4901 Camp Bowie Blvd. (Eldridge St.), 817-732-2881*
■ "No decor, no service, who cares? – best burger ever" sums up this ancient grocery store beloved for its "good, old-fashioned, greasy burgers" made from "high-quality meat"; sit at a picnic table or follow the lead of regulars and eat standing at the counters.

## La Piazza S
25 ⎤ 25 ⎤ 22 ⎤ $33 ⎤

*University Park Village, 1600 S. University Dr. (I-30), 817-334-0000*

☑ Easily the most elegant Italian nook in town ("great for a date"), with a "loyal following" for its "consistently first-rate food"; but it doesn't come cheap and may be served with a side of "attitude."

## Paris Coffee Shop
22 ⎤ 14 ⎤ 23 ⎤ $9 ⎤

*704 W. Magnolia Ave. (Hemphill St.), 817-335-2041*

■ The "best home cooking" in the Hospital District entices folks into this longtime American "classic" (since 1930), and "marvelous Southern hospitality" courtesy of its "wonderful waitresses" keeps them here; fans say the "pies and plate lunches can't be beat" and there's "lots of food for the money"; breakfast and lunch only.

## Railhead Smokehouse
25 ⎤ 18 ⎤ 19 ⎤ $12 ⎤

*2900 Montgomery St. (I-30), 817-738-9808*
*5220 Hwy. 121 (Hall Johnson Rd.), Colleyville, 817-571-2525*

■ Rave reviews go to the "best all-around BBQ in FW", serving up "huge platters" of "superior" beef, ribs and chicken that are "worth the pounds" gained; a "clean, safe location" can mean long lines and noise, but it also means "lots of interesting customers" and a "great patio scene"; the Colleyville branch is new and unrated.

## Randall's Gourmet Cheesecake Co.
▽ 25 ⎤ 25 ⎤ 22 ⎤ $24 ⎤

*907 Houston St. (bet. 8th & 9th Sts.), 817-336-2253*

■ "Don't let the name fool you" – this "quiet, intimate" Downtown Eclectic hideout offers a "great overall dining experience"; the menu is "limited" but "delicious", enhanced by a "good wine list" and ambiance that makes you "feel you're in NYC"; in sum, a "little jewel" – and yes, "save room" for the cheesecake.

## Reata S
23 ⎤ 26 ⎤ 22 ⎤ $30 ⎤

*Bank One Bldg., 500 Throckmorton St., 35th fl. (bet. 4th & 5th Sts.), 817-336-1009*

☑ Perched high atop a bank building, this nouveau Southwestern named for the ranch in *Giant* offers "cowboy cuisine with an upscale twist that works" in a matching setting that's rated No. 1 for Decor in Fort Worth; though some call it "overpriced" and wish the "food matched" the "beautiful view", most like its "unique" style and call it the ideal place to impress "a Yankee."

## Reflections
▽ 26 ⎤ 25 ⎤ 26 ⎤ $43 ⎤

*Worthington Hotel, 200 Main St. (Houston St.), 817-882-1765*

☑ "Excellence in fine dining" is what admirers find at this stunning hotel dining room offering artistic presentations of New American fare in an elegant, "romantic" ambiance; the less impressed say it "can be wonderful – or not so", but solid ratings across the board side with those who call it "a treat", albeit a pricey one.

## Saint-Emilion
27 ⎤ 24 ⎤ 25 ⎤ $36 ⎤

*3617 W. Seventh St. (Montgomery St.), 817-737-2781*

■ A favorite for elegant Country French cuisine, this intimate winner is lovely for "an anniversary or special celebration" thanks to "superb duck" and other "authentic", "high-quality" bistro fare enhanced by a "very good wine list", attentive service and "romantic" ambiance; a caring owner is another reason why it's considered "one of the best."

# Honolulu

## TOP 20 FOOD RANKING

| Restaurant | Cuisine Type |
|---|---|
| **27** Alan Wong's | Hawaiian |
| La Mer | French |
| Roy's | Eurasian/Pacific Rim |
| **25** Hoku's | Eclectic/International |
| Hy's Steak House | Steakhouse |
| Orchids | Seafood |
| Yohei Sushi | Japanese |
| Azul | Mediterranean |
| 3660 on the Rise | Pacific Rim |
| Ruth's Chris | Steakhouse |
| Bali-By-The-Sea | Eurasian/Hawaiian |
| Kyo-Ya | Japanese |
| Cascada | Med./Pacific Rim |
| Golden Dragon | Chinese |
| **24** Ono Hawaiian Foods | Hawaiian |
| Prince Court | Pacific Rim |
| Kacho | Japanese |
| Legend Seafood | Chinese/Seafood |
| Sam Choy's | Hawaiian |
| Swiss Inn | Continental |

## OTHER IMPORTANT PLACES

| | |
|---|---|
| A Pacific Cafe | Pacific Rim |
| Chef Mavro's | Hawaiian |
| Ciao Mein | Chinese/Italian |
| Indigo | Eurasian |
| Mariposa | Regional American |
| Michel's | Classic French |
| Padovani's Bistro | French Bistro/Hawaiian |
| Palomino Euro Bistro | Mediterranean |

| F | D | S | C |
|---|---|---|---|
| 27 | 20 | 24 | $45 |

### Alan Wong's S
*McCully Ct., 1857 S. King St., 5th fl. (bet. Hauoli & Pumehana Sts.), 808-949-2526*

☑ Fans of "culinary genius" Alan Wong and his "brilliant" Hawaiian cuisine that "looks as good as it tastes" voted his namesake place Oahu's Most Popular restaurant; for most, the "imaginative" fare and "cutting-edge wine list" are worth the "long wait" and "pricey" tab, even if some bemoan "plain decor" that "doesn't equal the food."

## A Pacific Cafe S　　　　　　　23 21 21 $36
*Ward Ctr., 1200 Ala Moana Blvd. (bet. Piikoi St. & Ward Ave.), 808-593-0035*
☑ "Exquisite presentations" and a "lovely blend of flavors" have
harnessed a steady luncheon trade, although evening reviewers
find the "dinner menu a more worthy showcase" of Jean-Marie
Josselin's latest "imaginative" Pacific Rim entry in Ward Centre;
but the jury is out on the "Jules Verne meets Jacques Cousteau"
decor and reactions to service range from "excellent" to "slow."

## Azul　　　　　　　　　　　　25 24 25 $55
*Ihilani Resort & Spa, 92-1001 Olani St., Kapolei, 808-679-0079*
■ An "elegant, intimate" room with "classy decor", "impeccable
Mediterranean cuisine", the "best wine list in town" and some of
"the best service in Hawaii" mean this West Oahu resort's premier
restaurant is tailored for expense-account guests and "special-
occasion" local dining; count on the freshest fish and a "wow"
tab at this "fancy" "getaway."

## Bali-By-The-Sea　　　　　　　25 27 25 $46
*Hilton Hawaiian Village, 2005 Kalia Rd. (Ala Moana Blvd.), 808-941-2254*
■ "Elegant service" and "awesome" Eurasian fare with Hawaiian
accents (kiawe-grilled *opakapaka*) are just part of the charm of this
popular "class act" in Waikiki that also offers "romantic ambiance",
"outstanding ocean scenery", "splendid service" and a "good
wine cellar" complemented by a "knowledgeable wine staff."

## Cascada S　　　　　　　　　25 25 23 $36
*Royal Garden Hotel, 440 Olohana St. (bet. Alawai Blvd. & Kuhio Ave.),
808-945-0270*
■ This hotel hideaway has become a Med–Pacific Rim magnet that
draws local culinary sophisticates to Waikiki; while most reserve
this "romantic" "garden" "oasis", complete with a waterfall and a
"pool like a Roman castle's", for a "special-occasion" evening,
lunch is booming with the business crowd and vacationing foodies.

## Chef Mavro's S　　　　　　　– – – VE
*1969 S. King St. (McCully St.), 808-944-4714*
After creating a sensation as master chef at La Mer in the
Halekulani Hotel and again at Seasons in the Four Seasons on
Maui, chef George Mavrothalassitis is back in Honolulu with this
brilliant Hawaiian Regional, which also includes accents from his
native Provence; the setting is muted, the service impeccable,
and the cumulative experience exquisite.

## Ciao Mein S　　　　　　　　23 23 22 $32
*Hyatt Regency Waikiki, 2424 Kalakaua Ave., 808-923-2426*
■ A much-acclaimed Waikiki Chinese-Italian ("the best of both
worlds") producing "well-prepared", "clever" dishes with "an
interesting mix of flavors" served amidst "eclectic decor"; while
some find it "expensive", others counter that it's one of the "few
places that's worth what they charge."

## Golden Dragon S　　　　　　25 25 22 $34
*Hilton Hawaiian Village, 2005 Kalia Rd. (Ala Moana Blvd.), 808-946-5336*
■ There's "excellent food, decor and service" at this Waikiki
hotel Chinese with a "beautiful beachside locale"; it's "expensive
but tasty" and insiders insist "if you order just one dish, make it
lobster curry with fried *haupia* [coconut]" – "it's God's gift to food."

**Hoku's [S]** | 25 | 26 | 25 | $47

*Kahala Mandarin Oriental Hotel, 5000 Kahala Ave., 808-739-8779*

■ "Find any excuse to go" to this Eclectic-International "rising star" declare reviewers; diners appreciate the "exceptional" service and "classy yet unpretentious" ocean-view setting; many "would like to visit again" – "if [they] could afford it"; N.B. master chef Oliver Altherr recently departed, thus putting the above food rating in question.

**Hy's Steak House [S]** | 25 | 24 | 24 | $39

*Waikiki Park Heights Hotel, 2440 Kuhio Ave. (Uluniu Ave.), 808-922-5555*

◪ The "very caring" tableside service "spoils the customer" at this "elegant", "clubby" classic Traditional American steakhouse in Waikiki that's been lauded as the "absolute best in Honolulu" for 20 years ("so old, it's new again"); expect "top quality", from the "kiawe-grilled steaks that can't be beat" to the "don't-get-me-started" rack of lamb; all of it makes the "untouristy crowd" of locals "feel like a million dollars", which is why "expensive" but "worth it" is the consensus.

**Indigo** | 23 | 23 | 21 | $28

*1121 Nuuanu Ave. (Hotel St.), 808-521-2900*

◪ A highly rated but controversial Downtown "Bali-in-Chinatown" Eurasian; boosters applaud the "exciting", "exotic" "grazing" dishes using curries, peanut sauces, fish and lamb, as well as the "pleasant courtyard tables", weekend jazz and convenient location next to the Hawaii Theater; detractors complain about "teeny-weeny" portions and "flavors that don't always complement each other"; nightly valet parking weighs in on the plus side.

**Kacho [S]** | 24 | 22 | 22 | $37

*Waikiki Parc Hotel, 2233 Helumoa Rd. (Kalia Rd.), 808-921-7272*

◪ Reviewers are enraptured by this "classy" Waikiki "gem" offering "elegant" Kyoto-style dishes that for "flavor and beauty can't be beat"; but "authentic breakfasts" and "delicious lunches" at one of the "best Japanese restaurants on Oahu" don't come cheap – "I'm glad someone else paid."

**Kyo-Ya [S]** | 25 | 25 | 23 | $39

*2057 Kalakaua Ave., 808-947-3911*

■ Reserve a tatami room and be "treated like a shogun" at this "peaceful" and "modern" Waikiki Japanese where the artistic dishes are such "a feast for the eyes" ("great butterfish *misoyaki*") that "you don't want to ruin them" by taking a bite; most agree it's "pricey but worth the money spent" – "oh please, somebody take me again."

**La Mer [S]** | 27 | 28 | 27 | $65

*Halekulani Hotel, 2199 Kalia Rd. (beachfront at Lewers St.), 808-923-2311*

■ For the money-is-no-object crowd that wants to "pull out all the stops", this "romantic" open-air hotel dining room "right on the water" is "definitely worth the expense"; expect a "fabulous Diamond Head view", "the finest French cuisine" prepared by chef Yves Garnier, "impeccable service" and an atmosphere of "subdued elegance" – more than enough reason to "put on a jacket" (or a long-sleeved, collared shirt is required) and spend "three hours on dinner."

F | D | S | C

**Legend Seafood [S]** 24 | 14 | 15 | $20

*Chinese Cultural Plaza, 100 N. Beretania St. (River St.), 808-532-1868*

■ The specialty at this "busy-as-a-bee" Chinatown "favorite" "endorsed by lots of Asian patrons" is "the absolute best dim sum in Honolulu", although the seafood dishes are also "great"; surveyors say it's the "closest to real Hong Kong cuisine in Hawaii", so most don't mind that it's "without charm."

**Mariposa [S]** – | – | – | E

*Neiman Marcus, 1450 Ala Moana Blvd. 3rd fl. (opp. Ala Moana Park), 808-951-3420*

Honolulu branch of the tony Texas store whose restaurant boasts views of Ala Moana Park and the ocean; exec chef Douglas Lum offers three Regional American cuisines: Texan (Red River ribs), Northwestern (salmon) and Hawaiian–Pacific Rim; prices are about what you'd expect at Neiman Marcus.

**Michel's [S]** 22 | 26 | 23 | $53

*Colony Surf Hotel, 2895 Kalakaua Ave., 808-923-6552*

◪ Fans feel this "reborn" Classic French on the toe of Diamond Head "has it all" – a "breathtaking view of the surf", "decor that matches the setting" and "excellent food and service"; but equally vocal foes write it off as "ridiculously overpriced", with "supercilious service" and "overrated food"; still, it remains a favorite for "romantic dinners" and "special occasions."

**Ono Hawaiian Foods ⊄** 24 | 9 | 16 | $13

*726 Kapahulu Ave. (bet. Date & Winam Sts.), 808-737-2275*

■ "You'll never leave here hungry", but "be prepared to wait" at this "cramped" "hole-in-the-wall" "classic" on Waikiki's eastern boundary road that regulars cheer as "best in its class" for "cheap", "authentic Hawaiian" grub like the "biggest *laulaus* in town"; fans agree "the name [*Ono* means 'good'] says it all" at this "highly recommended local dive."

**Orchids [S]** 25 | 27 | 25 | $41

*Halekulani Hotel, 2199 Kalia Rd. (beachfront at Lewers St.), 808-923-2311*

◪ This oceanside seafooder blooms in the "most beautiful open-air setting on the beach" – a "romantic" "spot to watch the sun set and the moon rise"; its "exquisite cuisine" and "gracious" staff make it a "favorite" "for a special occasion"; the "amazing" Sunday brunch is a "must not miss", even though it's "very pricey."

**Padovani's Bistro & Wine Bar [S]** – | – | – | VE

*Doubletree Alana Hotel, 1956 Ala Moana Blvd. (Kalakaua Ave.), 808-946-3456*

After successful stints at the Hulopo'e Court and Ihilani at the Manele Bay Hotel on Lanai, acclaimed chef Philippe Padovani has hit Honolulu and struck out on his own, wowing fans with his French bistro–Hawaiian Regional cuisine served in an elaborate, spare-no-expenses interior.

**Palomino Euro Bistro [S]** 23 | 27 | 23 | $30

*Harbor Sq., 66 Queen St. (bet. Bethel & Nimitz Sts.), 808-528-2400*

◪ "Hot spot" and "promising" entry to the Downtown scene that earns a "gold medal" for its "gorgeous bar" and Mediterranean menu; "smart and trendy", it's already a "place to see and be seen", but surprisingly it's "very reasonably priced."

### Prince Court Restaurant S                24 | 22 | 22 | $36
*Hawaii Prince Hotel Waikiki, 100 Holomoana St. (Ala Moana Blvd.), 808-944-4494*

◪ "Innovative Pacific Rim" cooking makes "lunches and dinners terrific" and Sunday brunch is a serious contender for the "best in town"; "unbelievably courteous service" and "great views of the marina" add other dimensions to an "always pleasant experience."

### Roy's S                                    27 | 21 | 24 | $40
*6600 Kalanianaole Hwy. (Keahole St.), 808-396-7697*

■ This "expensive", "imaginative" Eurasian "crackles with the creativity" of Roy Yamaguchi, the "grandfather of Pacific Rim cuisine" and "still the master" of "beautifully presented", "gold-standard" "designer food"; it's "too noisy", "too crowded" and "too far from town" in Hawaii Kai, but "try the bar downstairs for a quieter dine."

### Ruth's Chris Steak House S              25 | 19 | 22 | $38
*Restaurant Row, 500 Ala Moana Blvd. (bet. Punchbowl & South Sts.), 808-599-3860*

■ Whether it's lauded for serving some of the "best steaks in town", "in the state" or "in the world", the same adjectives apply to this Restaurant Row establishment: "thick", "tasty", "juicy" and "succulent"; beef eaters boast you "can't beat the porterhouse for two" – it's "expensive" but "worth it."

### Sam Choy's Diamond Head S              24 | 20 | 22 | $35
*Hee Hing Plaza, 449 Kapahulu Ave., 2nd fl. (opp. Ala Wai Golf Course), 808-732-8645*

■ Sam's Hawaiian Regional "plate lunch has a college degree" cheer boosters of this "luxe" "local-style restaurant" on the fringe of Waikiki, with "wonderful decor", "no pretensions" and "hard-to-get reservations"; "humongous portions" lift "leftovers to a new height", but the "noise" and "erratic service" displease some.

### Swiss Inn S                             24 | 18 | 23 | $26
*Niu Valley Shopping Ctr., 5730 Kalanianaole Hwy. (E. Halemaumau St.), 808-377-5447*

■ It's hard to tell which is more popular, the "superb" Continental food that's like "eating in a chalet in the Alps" or the "friendly owners" ("Martin Wyss is a legend") at this "favorite old standby" in an East Honolulu shopping mall; dinner is a "good value" and many supporters swear that "Sunday brunch is the best in town."

### 3660 on the Rise S                      25 | 19 | 22 | $37
*Wilhelmina Rise, 3660 Waialae Ave., 808-737-1177*

■ Chef-owner Russell Siu "pairs the unusual with spectacular results" – "from appetizer to dessert it's perfection" – at this Kaimuki Pacific Rimmer; while some carp that the "tuna-can seating" is "like eating on a crowded bus", most feel the "quality of the food rises above the cramped and noisy atmosphere."

### Yohei Sushi                            25 | 17 | 20 | $28
*Kokea Business Complex, 1111 Dillingham Blvd., 808-841-3773*

◪ Located near West Honolulu's airport/industrial area, this is a "low-key" "power-lunch hangout" where the "most creative sushi chefs" produce "excellent" food that's the "epitome" of Japanese; fans don't even flinch at the "big prices" because of the "quality."

# Houston

## TOP 20 FOOD RANKING

| Restaurant | Cuisine Type |
|---|---|
| *28* DeVille | New French |
| *27* Rotisserie for Beef & Bird | Traditional American |
| Chez Nous | French Bistro |
| Cafe Annie | Southwestern |
| La Réserve | Continental |
| Mark's | New American |
| Brennan's | Creole |
| *26* Ruggles Grill | Southwestern |
| Riviera Grill | Mediterranean |
| Damian's | N/S Italian |
| Anthony's | Continental |
| Brenner's | Steakhouse |
| Patisserie Descours | Desserts/Sandwich Shop |
| Tony's | Continental/Italian |
| Lynn's Steakhouse | Steakhouse |
| *25* C & H Steak Company | Steakhouse |
| Pappas Bros. Steakhse. | Steakhouse |
| La Mora | Northern Italian |
| Churrascos | South Amer./Steakhouse |
| Nino's | N/S Italian |

## OTHER IMPORTANT PLACES

| Restaurant | Cuisine Type |
|---|---|
| Américas | South American |
| Golden Room | Chinese/Thai |
| Goode Co. Barbecue | BBQ |
| Hunan | Chinese |
| La Colombe d'Or | Classic French |
| La Griglia | N/S Italian |
| La Tour D'Argent | Classic French |
| McCormick & Schmick's | Seafood |
| Pappasito's Cantina | Tex-Mex |
| Rainbow Lodge | Regional American |
| Redwood Grill | New American |
| Scott Chen's | Asian |
| Sierra Grill | New Amer./Southwestern |
| Simposio | Northern Italian |
| Tasca | New Amer./Spanish |

### Américas
24 | 26 | 22 | $31

*Saks Pavilion, 1800 Post Oak Blvd. (bet. San Felipe & Westheimer),*
*713-961-1492*

■ "Holy Columbus! – what a discovery!"; gifted chef Michael Cordúa's "original", "exquisite" South American menu is "out of this world", spinning "imaginative" twists on New World ingredients; equal to the "exciting" cuisine is the "must-see" "knockout decor" that "looks like it was done by Picasso on drugs", a "superb" staff, and a "festive atmosphere"; the only drawback to this "winner" near The Galleria is its pandemonium decibel level.

### Anthony's
26 | 25 | 24 | $42

*Highland Village, 4007 Westheimer (Drexel), 713-961-0552*

■ "One of Houston's premier tables", this "sleek, sexy and tantalizing" Continental in Highland Village with "fabulous decor and service to match" is "much more relaxed" than Tony's, its older sibling; "the place to be seen", it offers "serious power meals" "prepared with care and flair", as well as a "top-notch wine list"; while a few deem it a bit pretentious", most revel in a "special dining experience" that "delivers luxurious excess with style."

### Brennan's of Houston 🖪
27 | 27 | 26 | $39

*3300 Smith (Stuart), 713-522-9711*

■ For decades, this "impressive" Downtown "Texanized" sibling of the renowned Commander's Palace in New Orleans has been ordained Houston's "Creole heaven", with a romantic courtyard and an "elegant" room; Carl Walker serves up "turtle soup that will cure whatever ails you", "creative fish dishes and divine bananas Foster", and dinner at his private table in the kitchen is "a classy treat"; all in all, this is "a superior restaurant in every respect."

### Brenner's Steak House 🖪
26 | 17 | 22 | $38

*10911 Katy Frwy./I-10 W. (near Wilcrest), 713-465-2901*

■ Cut into the best steak in Houston at this modest-looking Katy Freeway "old reliable", which has remained "virtually unchanged" for decades; most folks evidently like its retro ways, touting the "old-fashioned atmosphere" and "waitresses in white" who still recite the menu; you can't go wrong with the "mouthwatering steaks" and "excellent" German-style fried potatoes.

### Cafe Annie
27 | 26 | 26 | $48

*1728 Post Oak Blvd. (San Felipe), 713-840-1111*

■ "How many more awards can they win?" ask surveyors who have voted this Tanglewood American with a SW bent Houston's Most Popular restaurant; chef Robert Del Grande presents cuisine that's "world-class on all counts" in richly paneled rooms reminiscent of "dining on a fine luxury liner"; though "small portions at huge prices" give pause to a few, the overwhelming verdict is simply "drop-dead gorgeous in every respect."

### C & H Steak Company 🖪
25 | 25 | 23 | $33

*12000 Southwest Frwy. (bet. W. Airport & Wilcrest), Stafford, 281-277-9292*

■ Look forward to "excellent beef" that "meets all expectations" at this "fine" chophouse courtesy of über-restaurateurs Chris and Harris Pappas; though the "pricey" menu is strictly à la carte, the "beautiful interior" and "quiet atmosphere" pay off at this "good place to take clients when you're in the [Southwest] suburbs"; P.S. cognoscenti rate "the rib eyes better than the filets."

## Chez Nous 27 | 23 | 26 | $44

*217 S. Ave. G (Staitti), Humble, 281-446-6717*

■ Francophiles cheerfully trek the "zillion miles" to this "remote" French bistro in Humble (north of Bush Intercontinental Airport) to indulge in an "authentic European" experience; enthusiasts rate the food "close to perfection", singling out the "sublime" duck, fresh crab and "incredibly good" pâté; in addition, the staff is so "warm and friendly" that this spot is voted No. 1 for Service in the Houston area.

## Churrascos 25 | 21 | 22 | $28

*9705 Westheimer (Gessner), 713-952-1988*
*Shepherd Sq., 2055 Westheimer (S. Shepherd), 713-527-8300*
*1320 W. Bay Area Blvd. (bet. Baybrook Mall & Gulf Frwy.), Friendswood, 281-461-4100*

■ With its signature "melt-in-your-mouth" tenderloin, the Cordúa brothers' South American steakhouse trio is winning carnivorous converts far and wide; besides the "unbeatable beef", the menu includes "great vegetarian platters", plantain chips ("a hit") and a "*tres leches* dessert" to "dream about", presented by a "well-trained staff"; true believers tout it as "a must-visit."

## Damian's Cucina Italiana 26 | 23 | 23 | $34

*3011 Smith (Rosalie), 713-522-0439*

■ The "grande dame" of Downtown's southern edge, this Italian has earned "top-notch" status with its "superb food", "romantic" room and "professional service"; preserving a "Euro feel with a touch of class", it's "still firing on all cylinders" in spite of chef Luigi Ferre's departure, and partisans pardon its "stuffy" side because, after all, "they spoil me."

## DeVille 28 | 27 | 26 | $43

*Four Seasons Hotel, 1300 Lamar (Austin), 713-652-6250*

■ "The classiest place Downtown" is also the *Houston Survey*'s No. 1 for Food and Decor; chef Tim Keating has "restored this Cadillac to a shine" with his "creative, delicious" Contemporary French menu; neophytes may find the richly appointed hotel dining room "a little stiff", but the cuisine's "embarrassment of riches" and the staff's "attentive" treatment define "elegant" dining.

## Golden Room 21 | 18 | 19 | $19

*1209 Montrose (bet. W. Dallas & W. Gary), 713-524-9614*

■ With its rosy exterior and Siamese appointments, this "peaceful, pretty" Montrose Thai-Chinese offers an "intimate atmosphere" to enhance "fresh, authentic" dishes like "great curries and seafood" and heady soups; some compare the "close" seating to "eating in a living room", but followers find it "charming" and marvel that "even popularity hasn't caused it to suffer."

## Goode Co. Barbecue [S] 24 | 17 | 18 | $12

*5109 Kirby Dr. (bet. Bissonnet & Westpark), 713-522-2530*
*8911 Katy Frwy./I-10 W. (Campbell Rd.), 713-464-1901*

■ Perfuming the air of Kirby and the Katy Freeway, the "great and authentic Texas BBQ" at this duo has earned its share of "rabid loyalty"; 'cue connoisseurs rate it "best of breed", singling out the "great chopped-beef sandwich", "stellar" brisket and duck; and "don't skip the pecan pie."

## Hunan [S] 23 | 22 | 21 | $23

*Saks Pavilion, 1800 Post Oak Blvd. (bet. San Felipe & Westheimer), 713-965-0808*

■ Gigi Huang's old-guard Asian "feels like NY" (though it's actually in Tanglewood) and "sets the standard" for Chinese dining "elevated to an art form"; "personalized service" and "gorgeous decor" delight disciples, and even if the prices might be "hard to swallow", there's always the "chance of a George Bush sighting."

## La Colombe d'Or [S] 23 | 25 | 22 | $43

*La Colombe d'Or Hotel, 3410 Montrose (Harold), 713-524-7999*

◪ "Lots of great calories" lie in wait at this "elegant, incredibly romantic" Classic French housed in a Montrose luxury hotel that boasts the "best atmosphere" in Houston; mixed reactions – it "can be excellent or mediocre" – seem due to a "revolving-door chefs" problem, yet ratings suggest that this can be a "wonderful special occasion spot – if you get the right waiter."

## La Griglia [S] 24 | 23 | 22 | $29

*River Oaks Ctr., 2002 W. Gray (McDuffie), 713-526-4700*

■ "Always a place to be seen", this "happening" River Oaks Italian phenom lures a "beautiful crowd" who breezes in for "to-die-for seafood cheesecake" and, of course, the scene; as expected, this "festive" grill can be "too loud" and "too trendy" for some, but most call it "swinging" and advise "go early or wait at the bar."

## La Mora Cucina Toscana 25 | 22 | 23 | $28

*912 Lovett Blvd. (bet. Montrose & Westheimer), 713-522-7412*

■ Taking "Italian food to a higher level", this "hideaway" off Montrose seduces with "great Tuscan cuisine"; Florence-bred chef-owner Lynette Hawkins Mandola "learned well and is always there to keep things humming", though enough call this "lovely" spot a "well-kept secret" to suggest it might "need advertising."

## La Réserve 27 | 27 | 25 | $49

*Omni Hotel, 4 Riverway (S. Post Oak Ln. & Woodway), 713-871-8181*

■ Lauded by most as "perfect in every way", this Omni Hotel Continental has had a number of chefs in the past few years, leaving well-wishers with their "fingers crossed" for the latest arrival, toque Mercer Mohr; the many kudos for "fine civilized dining", however, are slightly offset by brickbats for "outdated", "overpriced" fare; stay tuned.

## La Tour D'Argent 22 | 25 | 22 | $40

*2011 Ella Blvd. (T.C. Jester), 713-864-9864*

◪ For "sophisticated dining" in a rustic ambiance, this Classic French just inside the North Loop "radiates class" and "drips with romance", though the stuffed animals adorning the "hunting-lodge" setting evoke some negative feedback ("see where the endangered species went"); still, most feel this is a "special place in time."

## Lynn's Steakhouse 26 | 21 | 24 | $40

*955 Dairy-Ashford (bet. Katy Frwy./I-10 W. & Memorial Dr.), 281-870-0807*

■ Lynn Foreman's "small" West Side steakhouse specializes in "melt-in-your-mouth" beef presented with extras like "superb gumbo and creamed spinach" and "endless freshly baked bread"; the "peaceful atmosphere" and "attentive" service also appeal, making this "best-kept secret in town" "perfect for a rendezvous."

## Mark's American Cuisine 🄂   27 | 24 | 23 | $37
*1658 Westheimer (bet. Dunlavy & Ralph), 713-523-3800*
■ Chef-owner Mark Cox brings a "serious pedigree" from his tenure at Tony's to his "great" New American venture in the Montrose area; in a "beautiful old church" with a "pretty ceiling", he creates dishes so "excellent" that his restaurant debuted with the sixth highest food rating in Houston; despite a few grumbles about "tables too close" together, the consensus is clear – "Cafe Annie better watch out."

## McCormick & Schmick's 🄂   – | – | – | M
*1151 Uptown Park (Post Oak Blvd.), 713-840-7900*
For some welcome relief from Houston's typical fried seafood, sail by this branch of the Portland-based chain that's making a splash in the Uptown Park mall with fin fare flown in daily from the Pacific Northwest – exotic choices like coldwater oysters, petrale sole, razor clams, monkfish, mako shark and Dungeness crab; all the details are well thought out here, from the sexy San Francisco–style bar to the air-conditioned patio.

## Nino's   25 | 21 | 22 | $26
*2817 W. Dallas (bet. Montrose & Waugh Dr.), 713-522-5120*
■ For 20 years, this "fun" Montrose Italian has been the Mandolas' most popular venue, a "spontaneous", "innovative", "authentic table" with "family recipes from Mamma M." and "excellent" pasta, veal and chicken dishes; the "gracious, professional" service ("they spoil me here"), "dark", "cozy" atmosphere and "reasonable" prices further explain why it remains an "enchanting treasure."

## Pappas Bros. Steakhouse   25 | 25 | 23 | $44
*5839 Westheimer (Bering), 713-780-7352*
🄵 It's those Pappas boys again, this time with a Morton's-style steakhouse in a "beautiful building" near The Galleria; supporters marvel over "fantastic, classic steaks", winning sides ("the [roasted] mushroom is unbelievable") and the "best cigar room in town"; dissenters say "hang onto your wallet" and prepare for an "unbearably noisy", "smoky" environment that exemplifies the "type of excess that leads to revolutions."

## Pappasito's Cantina 🄂   22 | 18 | 19 | $18
*2515 S. Loop W. 610 (bet. Buffalo Speedway & Kirby), 713-668-5756*
*11831 I-10 E. (Federal Rd.), 713-455-8379*
*20099 Gulf Frwy./I-45 S. (NASA Rd. 1), Webster, 281-338-2885*
*6445 Richmond Ave. (Hillcroft), 713-784-5253*
*15280 North Frwy./I-45 N. (Airtex), 281-821-4505*
*7050 FM 1960 W. (Cutten), 281-893-5037*
*13070 Northwest Frwy./290 (Hollister), 713-462-0245*
*13750 Southwest Frwy./59 S., Sugar Land, 281-565-9797*
*10005 FM 1960 Bypass (Hwy. 59 N.), Humble, 281-540-8664*
*10409 Katy Frwy./I-10 W. (Gessner), 713-468-1913*
■ These cheery "full-of-beans" Tex-Mex outlets, part of the Pappas dynasty, attract a young, exuberant crowd for "awesome" tortilla soup and the "best fajitas in town", in portions so large you can "expect to take some home"; a few complain they're "too crowded, too rushed" and "too noisy at peak times", but that's the price of success.

## Patisserie Descours
26 | 14 | 18 | $11
*1330-D Wirt Rd. (Westview), 713-681-8894*
■ Patrons swoon over the "tasty" soups, "fantastic sandwiches" and sweet "works of art" created at Marilyn Descours' Spring Branch pâtisserie and lunchroom, the No. 1 dessert stop in Houston and *the* source for the "best wedding cakes"; since it closes at 3 PM and tables are at a premium, it's best to "go early."

## Rainbow Lodge S
22 | 26 | 21 | $35
*1 Birdsall (Memorial Dr.), 713-861-8666*
■ "Who wouldn't want to eat" at this "romantic and rustic", antique-filled lodge with a "knock-your-socks-off" view of Buffalo Bayou and a Regional American menu featuring wild game and Gulf Coast seafood?; while "brunch is great too", and the service more than capable, voters can't help but focus on the "most interesting decor and grounds in Houston."

## Redwood Grill S
24 | 23 | 22 | $32
*Chelsea Mkt., 4611 Montrose (bet. Bissonnet St. & Richmond Ave.), 713-523-4611*
■ This Museum District New American sibling of the Post Oak Grill gets high marks from its suit-and-tie clientele who makes it "their number one business spot", thanks to an "elegant" setting where "one can talk without yelling"; "excellent", "imaginative" food, including the signature pistachio-crusted snapper, "fabulous blueberry-spinach salad" and top-notch breads also draw diehards.

## Riviera Grill S
26 | 15 | 21 | $32
*Radisson Suites, 10655 Katy Frwy./I-10 W. (Beltway 8), 713-974-4445*
■ "It's hard to imagine a better fish dish than the Chilean sea bass" prepared by chef-owner John Sheely at this "exquisite" Mediterranean in a "weird location" next to the Town & Country Mall; while the interior is "not much to look at", it hardly matters because the "innovative and flavorful" food "outshines" any drawbacks and "gives hotel dining a good name."

## Rotisserie for Beef & Bird
27 | 24 | 26 | $40
*2200 Wilcrest (north of Westheimer), 713-977-9524*
■ "Personable" chef-owner Joe Mannke and his staff always "make you feel welcome" at this Far West No. 1 Traditional American, beloved by Houstonians for "an anniversary dinner or a romantic night out"; expect "fantastic" game dishes ("wonderful, crispy duck"), an "extensive wine list" and historic American oil paintings that are an "education too"; the bottom line: "a class act that does everything well."

## Ruggles Grill S
26 | 18 | 18 | $29
*903 Westheimer (Montrose), 713-524-3839*
☑ There's no question that chef-owners Bruce and Susan Molzan "pile on" "always" "outstanding food" at this trendy Southwestern on Westheimer known for its "famous" grilled veggies and "out-of-this-world desserts"; however, hordes of surveyors take issue with the "frustrating environment", which includes a "deafening" noise level, "way-too-crowded seating" and most pointedly a much-despised "worthless" reservations policy which results in hour-long waits.

## Scott Chen's — | — | — | E

*6540 San Felipe (Voss), 713-789-4484*

Tuxedoed service, elegant surroundings and a superb wine list strike the appropriate notes at this new Tanglewood entry from chef-owner Scott Chen, the man behind Empress; anticipate a menu that's a sophisticated mix of Asian ingredients and styles refined with a prominent French accent, including such treats as shrimp in a puddle of caviar sauce and salmon steamed with balsamic vinegar.

## Sierra Grill [S] 23 | 19 | 20 | $29

*4704 Montrose (south of Southwest Frwy./59 S.), 713-942-7757*

■ Daring diners say "charming" chef-owner Charlie Watkins' Museum District Southwestern–New American showcases "the most creative menu in Houston", including "indescribably delicious" sesame-crusted tuna and "enchanting aged buffalo"; P.S. since it's now open only for dinner, "a lunch favorite is gone."

## Simposio [S] 22 | 17 | 19 | $29

*5591 Richmond Ave. (Chimney Rock), 713-532-0550*

■ "This one's a sophisticated keeper" declare fans of this Northern Italian that's ensconced on a corner of an otherwise featureless strip mall; expect a "*simpatico*" staff, an owner who "shows an interest in diners" and "excellent" food, especially the "heavenly" risotto; the only question – "why isn't this restaurant better known?"

## Tasca 23 | 24 | 22 | $28

*908 Congress (Travis), 713-225-9100*

■ Handsome New American–Spanish spot Downtown that wins raves for its "far-out tapas menu", "beautiful atmosphere" and weekend jazz; its roomy bar and wide selection of wines by the glass make it popular before or after a show, but some note that the "lines won't last if they don't start honoring reservations."

## Tony's 26 | 26 | 25 | $53

*1801 Post Oak Blvd. (south of San Felipe), 713-622-6778*

■ "Still the place to see and be seen", Tony Vallone's firstborn establishment, a safe refuge for Houston's uptrodden in The Galleria area, is "better than ever after a slump" say many advocates who caution that the Continental-Italian cuisine is "wonderful but priced like jewelry"; even the few critics who complain that eating here is "an over-produced epic" admit it's "fun to go and watch the ultrarich in action."

# Kansas City

## TOP 15 FOOD RANKING

| Restaurant | Cuisine Type |
|---|---|
| **28** Cafe Allegro | New American |
| **27** American Restaurant | New American |
| Tatsu's | Classic French |
| Ruth's Chris | Steakhouse |
| **26** Metropolis | New American |
| Lidia's | N/S Italian |
| Stolen Grill | New American |
| Cafe Sebastienne | New American |
| Stroud's | Traditional American |
| Starker's Reserve | New American |
| Plaza III | Steakhouse |
| Grille on Broadway | New American |
| Peppercorn Duck Club | New American |
| **25** Jun's Japanese | Japanese |
| JJ's | Seafood/Steakhouse |

## OTHER IMPORTANT PLACES

| | |
|---|---|
| Bluebird Cafe | Vegetarian |
| Bristol Bar & Grill | Seafood |
| Cafe Italia/Mission | Northern Italian |
| Fiorella's Jack Stack | BBQ |
| Garozzo's | N/S Italian |
| Grand St. Cafe | Eclectic |
| Hannah's Bistro | French Bistro |
| Japengo | Pacific Rim |
| Le Fou Frog | French Bistro |
| Savoy Grill | Seafood/Steakhouse |
| Stephenson's | Traditional American |
| Yia Yia's | International |

| F | D | S | C |
|---|---|---|---|

### American Restaurant
27 | 28 | 28 | $45

*Crown Ctr., 200 E. 25th St. (Grand Ave.), 816-426-1133*
■ "KC's showplace", this Downtown New American "continues to get better and better" thanks to "outstanding", "innovative" dishes from husband-and-wife chefs Michael Smith and Debbie Gold and a highly "knowledgeable" staff that's ranked No. 1 for Service in the *Kansas City Survey*; factor in a "breathtaking" setting with two-story-high windows offering "great night views" of the city, and it's clear why "everything is astounding – including the tab."

## Bluebird Cafe 🅂
22 | 19 | 19 | $11 |

*1700 Summit St. (17th St.), 816-221-7559*

■ "Healthy" Vegetarian Downtown that "dispels the myth" that the genre is just tofu and sprouts, with "tasty" choices often containing organic produce from the garden across the street; "for people-watching", it's an "essential" stop on the lunch circuit.

## Bristol Bar & Grill 🅂
25 | 24 | 23 | $25 |

*5400 W. 119th St. (Nall Ave.), Leawood, KS, 913-663-5777*

■ While many are "sorry it left" its Plaza digs for Johnson County, this finny "fave" still retains a staff that "makes you feel special", a "classy" if "noisy" setting and the "best seafood in KC"; the hooked insist that no visit is complete without a taste of the "to-die-for" sweet biscuits.

## Cafe Allegro
28 | 24 | 27 | $40 |

*1815 W. 39th St. (State Line Rd.), 816-561-3663*

■ Retaining its No. 1 ratings for Food and Popularity in KC, this "high-style" Westport New American proffers "beautifully presented" dishes prepared from seasonal ingredients; add an impressive wine list, "wonderful" service and an "elegant" setting for a "special-occasion place that makes the occasion."

## Cafe Italia/Mission
24 | 16 | 22 | $21 |

*Mission West, 6524 Martway St. (Lamar Ave.), Mission, KS, 913-262-9242*

■ "Seven years before Lidia's got all the credit" for introducing KC to "true" Northern Italian cuisine, this Johnson County "jewel" was serving similarly "exquisite" fare; while its low-ceilinged interior won't win it any design awards, the food is "fabulous."

## Cafe Sebastienne 🅂
26 | 26 | 22 | $17 |

*Kemper Museum, 4420 Warwick Blvd. (45th St.), 816-561-7740*

■ Reverent reviewers remark that chef Jennifer Maloney's "artistically presented" Contemporary American cooking is nicely complemented by a "colorful" setting in the Kemper Museum; although dinner is now served Fridays, many "wish it were open" the rest of the week, thanks to a "magnificent job" on everything.

## Fiorella's Jack Stack 🅂
25 | 21 | 21 | $16 |

*13441 Holmes Rd. (135th St.), 816-942-9141*
*9520 Metcalf Ave. (95th St.), Overland Park, KS, 913-385-7427*

■ This "upscale" BBQ landmark on the South Side now has a Johnson County sib, and both offer "big menus" that "go beyond" one's expectations to include "luscious lamb ribs"; "fabulous sides" ("excellent onion rings") further fuel their rep as "perfect" places to "take out-of-town guests."

## Garozzo's Ristorante
24 | 17 | 21 | $18 |

*526 Harrison St. (5th St.), 816-221-2455*

## Cafe Garozzo 🅂
*9950 College Blvd. (Mastin St.), Overland Park, KS, 913-491-8300*

## Garozzo's Ristorante Due 🅂
*12801 E. 40 Hwy. (east of Blue Ridge Mall), Independence, 816-737-2400*

■ Italian trio that supplies "food so good you will taste it in your dreams" in a "Sinatra's kind of hangout" setting; the draws include "frighteningly huge portions" and a signature chicken spiedini that's "among the best dishes in town"; converts cry "mama mia!", it's "well worth the wait – and there usually is one."

## Grand St. Cafe 🅂

25 24 24 $22

*Country Club Plaza, 4740 Grand St. (bet. 47th & Main Sts.), 816-561-8000*

■ "Grand in all ways", this "upscale" Plaza-area Eclectic is a bastion of "continued culinary innovation", home to the "best and biggest pork chop around" and specials that "make your mouth water", all delivered by "friendly" servers; "eating outside in the summer" is sublime, but indoorsy types can "sit at the counter and watch the cooking."

## Grille on Broadway, The 🅂

26 19 25 $28

*3605 Broadway (Valentine Rd.), 816-531-0700*

■ The "food, wine, owner and intimacy" are all pluses at this "tiny" Midtown New American, "a real gem" where the "superb" "fresh fish" stands out on the "imaginative menu"; owner "Sean Cummings is a wonderful, witty host" whose charming "blarney" suggests "being served in someone's dining room" – but "don't go if you're claustrophobic."

## Hannah's Bistro

– – – M

*3895 State Line Rd. (39th St.), 816-960-1300*

New French bistro fare makes this newcomer a perfect fit in Westport's 39th Street restaurant district; a judicious sprinkling of Asian and Arabic influences adds spice to the menu, the sampler trio of soups has proven popular, and simple, tasteful decor makes the most of a former Pizza Hut building.

## Japengo 🅂

23 25 22 $27

*600 Ward Pkwy. (Pennsylvania Ave.), 816-931-6600*

☑ KC goes Pacific Rim at this Plaza yearling with "stunning" decor and an "exciting" menu brimming with "exotic flavors"; the Japengo-style service – in which a table's entire order is served one dish at a time and diners are urged to share – earns mixed reviews ("pretentious" and "annoying" vs. ideal "for a group"), yet most concur this "trendy" place is "greatly needed."

## JJ's 🅂

25 23 24 $28

*910 W. 48th St. (Belleview St.), 816-561-7136*

■ "Always hopping with a trendy crowd", this "bright, airy" steakhouse-seafooder "tucked away on the edge of the Plaza" pairs a "stunning", award-winning wine list with a "superb" menu; fans add they "can't think of a better place for someone to buy me lunch."

## Jun's Japanese

25 18 20 $20

*7660 State Line Rd. (75th St.), Prairie Village, KS, 913-341-4924*

■ "Sit at the sushi bar and enjoy the show" at this Johnson County shrine to raw fish, "the one-and-only authentic Japanese" in the area, featuring "KC's best" toro and hamachi; when it comes to traditional cooked food, there's sukiyaki that's "an event" and terrific tempura and teriyaki too.

## Le Fou Frog 🅂

25 19 21 $29

*400 E. Fifth St. (Oak Tfwy.), 816-474-6060*

■ "Don't you have a rating above excellent?" ask surveyors smitten by this "chichi French bistro" Downtown, with "fish so fresh they're nearly swimming", "excellent sauces" and lots of nightly specials; a few quibblers say it can get "noisy" and "pricey at dinner", but overall, this is a "wonderful addition to the scene."

**Lidia's [S]** | 26 | 29 | 23 | $26 |

*101 W. 22nd St. (Baltimore Ave.), 816-221-3722*

■ Owned by Lidia Bastianich of NYC's Felidia, this Downtown Italian just might be KC's "best new restaurant in years"; it debuts with the No. 1 Decor score thanks to David Rockwell's "spectacular" design complete with a 30-foot fireplace; factor in a "very creative menu" and an "affordable wine list" and this is sure to be the "hottest ticket in town."

**Metropolis American Grill** | 26 | 22 | 24 | $29 |

*303 Westport Rd. (Central St.), 816-753-1550*

■ Some of the "most artistic", "beautifully presented" cooking in town can be found at this "innovative" Westport New American where "excellent" tandoori sea bass is the signature dish; a "cozy", "cosmopolitan" setting that oozes style combined with the "personal charm" of owners Steve Chick and David Rabinovitz make this "one of KC's finest"; P.S. "out-of-this-world catering" is available too.

**Peppercorn Duck Club, The [S]** | 26 | 26 | 26 | $34 |

*Hyatt Regency Crown Ctr., 2345 McGee St. (Pershing Rd.), 816-435-4199*

■ "If duck turns you on, they do it right" at this perennial New American in Downtown's Hyatt Regency, a "romantic" rendezvous for a "special evening"; everyone likes the "smiling", "gracious service", and chocoholics sigh the dessert buffet is a "work of art."

**Plaza III The Steakhouse [S]** | 26 | 24 | 24 | $32 |

*Country Club Plaza, 4749 Pennsylvania Ave. (Ward Pkwy.), 816-753-0000*

■ "One of America's top" beef palaces, this Plaza fave offers "excellent" steaks and an award-winning wine list; while some feel the "old-style" decor "could be updated" and find the "pricey" tabs too up-to-date, most say it's the "destination" for "power" dining.

**Ruth's Chris Steak House [S]** | 27 | 24 | 25 | $38 |

*700 W. 47th St. (Jefferson St.), 816-531-4800*

■ Native sons say it's "hard to admit a nonlocal can do the best" porterhouse or filet mignon, but this Plaza outpost of a high-end national chain "knows its business" well and wins many over with "luscious steaks" "drenched in butter", accompanied by "wonderful sides"; the "very elegant" dining room (reminiscent of a "men's club") is perfect for expense-accounters, but everyone else should "take out a loan."

**Savoy Grill [S]** | 24 | 24 | 23 | $31 |

*Hotel Savoy, 219 W. Ninth St. (Central St.), 816-842-3890*

◪ This nearly 100-year-old Downtown steakhouse-seafooder offers larger-than-life lobsters served in a "posh" atmosphere by a pampering staff; though modernists yawn it "needs a menu overhaul", traditionalists insist this treasured "time warp" (with its "Harry Truman booth") is "still the classiest place in town."

**Starker's Reserve** | 26 | 25 | 25 | $36 |

*Country Club Plaza, 201 W. 47th St. (Wyandotte St.), 816-753-3565*

■ While widely renowned as "the best spot for hosting a private party" in KC, this Country Club Plaza Contemporary American is also open to the public for dinner Tuesday–Saturday; "A+ food", a 1,600-label, award-winning wine list and one of "the most romantic views in town" most assuredly add up to "a perfect meal" for many.

**Stephenson's Old Apple Farm [S]** | 23 | 22 | 22 | $20

*16401 E. Hwy. 40 (Lee's Summit Rd.), Independence, 816-373-5400*

■ Set in a "quaint" East Side orchard, this "comfortable" American is "famous for its apple"-based specialties, ranging from dumplings to daiquiris, as well as "big portions" of "forget-the-diet" dishes; over a half-century old, it remains a "trusty favorite" when you're hankering for a meal just like "grandma's Sunday dinner."

**Stolen Grill, The** | 26 | 18 | 22 | $34

*904 Westport Rd. (Southwest Tfwy.), 816-960-1450*

■ Inspired surveyors "steal away" to this "wonderful addition to Kansas City's dining scene", a "hip" Westport Contemporary American that dazzles with "innovative" preparations courtesy of CIA-trained chef Patrick Weber; though a few quibblers call it "pricey", "crowded" and "too noisy even for an extrovert", many others wonder "why aren't there more like this in town?"

**Stroud's [S]** | 26 | 16 | 21 | $16

*1015 E. 85th Ave. (Troost Ave.), 816-333-2132*
*5410 NE Oak Ridge Dr. (bet. I-35 & Vivion Rd.), 816-454-9600*

■ "Drop your sophisticated veneer" and head for this South Side American or its Northland cousin, where "large portions" of the "best fried chicken on the planet" (and other "vehicles to get more gravy") are dished up; sure, this might be "the reason Kansas City is the fourth fattest city in the USA", but once you've "stuffed" yourself and found someone to "roll you out to the car", you'll agree it was "worth it" – even if the waits are "inhumane."

**Tatsu's** | 27 | 21 | 24 | $29

*4603 W. 90th St. (½ block east of Roe Ave.), Prairie Village, KS, 913-383-9801*

■ "Don't judge a restaurant by its exterior" say supporters of this "quietly charming" "jewel" in a Johnson County strip mall, where a Japanese-trained chef turns out Classic French cuisine "like Julia Child used to cook", including "outstanding carrot soup" and the "best salmon encroûte"; while critics note that the "limited", "old-fashioned" "menu doesn't change much, regulars never complain."

**Yia Yia's [S]** | 24 | 24 | 23 | $24

*4701 W. 119th St. (Roe Ave.), Overland Park, KS, 913-345-1111*

■ "PB&J's brightest jewel" is still "action central" when it comes to checking out "prairie yuppies" and the "beautiful people" of South Johnson County; they're drawn by a consistently "innovative International menu", very "friendly" service and smart-looking digs that combine to make for a "darn good all-around" experience.

## TOP 10 FOOD RANKING

| | Restaurant | Cuisine Type |
|---|---|---|
| 27 | Andre's | Classic French |
| | Michael's | Traditional American |
| | Portofino | N/S Italian |
| 26 | Steak House | Steakhouse |
| | Emeril's New Orleans | Cajun/Creole |
| | Palace Court | Classic French |
| | Drai's on the Strip | French |
| | Monte Carlo | New French |
| | Suzette's | Classic French |
| | Second Street Grill | Asian/Pacific Rim |

## OTHER IMPORTANT PLACES

| | |
|---|---|
| Aqua | Seafood |
| Aureole | New American |
| China Grill | Eclectic |
| Circo, Osteria del | Northern Italian |
| Eiffel Tower | Classic French |
| First Floor Grill | Traditional American |
| Le Cirque | Classic French |
| Lupo, Trattoria del | N/S Italian |
| Nobu | Japanese |
| Olives | Mediterranean |
| Onda | N/S Italian |
| Palm Restaurant | Steakhouse |
| P.F. Chang's | Chinese |
| Picasso | New French/Spanish |
| Pinot Brasserie | Californian/French Bistro |
| Prime | Steakhouse |
| Renoir | New French |
| Spago | New American |
| Star Canyon | Southwestern |
| Valentino | Northern Italian |

| | F | D | S | C |
|---|---|---|---|---|
| **Andre's** | 27 | 25 | 26 | $52 |

*Monte Carlo Resort, 3770 Las Vegas Blvd. S. (Tropicana Ave.), 702-798-7151* [S]
*401 S. Sixth St. (bet. Bridger Ave. & Las Vegas Blvd.), 702-385-5016*
■ "Drippingly romantic", this "exquisite" Downtown Classic French and its newer sibling in the Monte Carlo have been voted Most Popular and No. 1 for Food in Las Vegas, thanks to their "*magnifique*" fare, "top-of-the-line wine cellar" and "unmatched atmosphere"; granted, the original location might be "remote" and some say their "most outstanding feature is the price", but for "serious gourmets", they are "unquestionably the finest in LV."

## Aqua S  — — — E

*Bellagio Hotel, 3600 Las Vegas Blvd. S. (Flamingo Rd.), 702-693-7223*
Next to the Bellagio Gallery of Fine Art and the resort's Botanical Gardens, this transplanted SF seafooder, founded by Michael Mina and Charles Condy, now has Mark Lo Russo (former sous chef at the California locale) at its helm, who's turning out extravagant tasting menus and wine pairings in addition to à la carte offerings; the dynamite environment is all rare woods and sumptuous fabrics, and offers a fine view of the pool.

## Aureole S  — — — E

*Mandalay Bay Hotel, 3950 Las Vegas Blvd. S. (Hacienda Ave.), 702-632-7401*
Charlie Palmer's Mandalay Bay version of his celebrated NYC eatery boasts live swans, a view of a waterfall and a four-story wine tower accessed by sleek young women, hoisted in harnesses to retrieve bottles (there are some 9,000), yet the New American fare (courtesy of husband-and-wife chefs Megan and Joe Romano) is as memorable as the decor; à la carte and prix fixe menus in the main dining rooms, prix fixe only in the exceptional Swan Court.

## China Grill S  — — — M

*Mandalay Bay Hotel, 3950 Las Vegas Blvd. S. (Hacienda Ave.), 702-632-7404*
A very hip, high-energy eatery in Mandalay Bay, where the showstopping lighting and special features are a perfect foil for the excellent Eclectic fare; yes, it's noisy and frenetic, but one bite of the famous lamb ribs, along with a sip of one of the heady libations, and you won't even notice the din.

## Circo, Osteria del S  — — — E

*Bellagio Hotel, 3600 Las Vegas Blvd. S. (Flamingo Rd.), 702-693-8150*
Situated next to Le Cirque in the Bellagio, this Tuscan gem is a bit more casual than its tony cousin but still quite chic, with homestyle Italian fare courtesy of chef Enzo Secchi (working in conjunction with executive chef Marc Poidevin); a view of the fountain-filled lake and a premium wine cellar add to its allure.

## Drai's on the Strip S  26 27 24 $49

*Barbary Coast Hotel, 3595 Las Vegas Blvd. S. (Flamingo Rd.), 702-737-0555*
■ Despite a "strange location" in the Barbary Coast, this "very chichi" "hidden jewel" transcends its surroundings with a "sexy" setting that's No. 1 for Decor in LV; look for an "innovative" French Provençal menu that's "worthy of special note"; P.S. there's "exceptional jazz" on weekends in the smart library lounge.

## Eiffel Tower Restaurant S  — — — VE

*Paris Hotel, 3655 Las Vegas Blvd. S. (bet. Flamingo Ave. & Tropicana Rd.), 702-948-6937*
Chic and magnifique, this Classic French aerie in the Paris Hotel soars 11 stories above the Strip, offering a jawdropping view of the around-the-world-in-a-glance Vegas landscape; chef Jean Joho (of Chicago's equally stratospheric Everest) takes the kitchen to impressive heights, turning out sumptuous, innovative cuisine that might be très cher, but is worth every franc.

### Emeril's New Orleans Fish House 🅂 | 26 | 24 | 24 | $46 |
*MGM Grand Hotel, 3799 Las Vegas Blvd. S. (Tropicana Ave.),*
*702-891-7374*
■ It's "difficult to get reservations" at this "expensive" Cajun-Creole in the MGM Grand that's the brainchild of famed New Orleans chef Emeril Lagasse, and with good reason: enthusiasts exclaim the "extraordinary, beautifully presented food" is "perhaps the best in Vegas"; despite "parking that can be a chore" (think sensible shoes for the "long walk" to get there), dining at this delta transplant is "always a treat."

### First Floor Grill | − | − | − | E |
*Four Seasons Hotel, 3960 Las Vegas Blvd. S. (bet. Hacienda Ave. &*
*Russell Rd.), 702-632-5000*
Elegant and serene, this chic eatery in the posh new Four Seasons is a top choice for local movers and shakers who savor the mostly-American menu that highlights seafood and steaks; dieters suggest trying one of the low-cal, low-fat alternative selections as an entree before indulging in one of the wicked desserts (the pastry chef is a wonder).

### Le Cirque 🅂 | − | − | − | VE |
*Bellagio Hotel, 3600 Las Vegas Blvd. S. (Flamingo Rd.), 702-693-8100*
Manhattan's legendary restaurant, created by Sirio Maccioni, is a smashing success at this Classic French transplant in the Bellagio, where a festive, circus-inspired setting provides the backdrop for some culinary derring-do by toque Marc Poidevin (former chef de cuisine at NYC's Le Cirque); reserve well in advance unless you're staying in the hotel, and remember jackets and ties are required.

### Lupo, Trattoria del 🅂 | − | − | − | M |
*Mandalay Bay Hotel, 3950 Las Vegas Blvd. S. (Hacienda Ave.),*
*702-632-7410*
Wolfgang Puck's new family-style Italian at Mandalay Bay is a product of his travels abroad with Lupo chef Mark Ferguson (ex Spago), where the two gathered recipes and accessories for this inviting villa with a bay view; the menu is a mix of dishes from many regions of Italy.

### Michael's 🅂 | 27 | 23 | 27 | $63 |
*Barbary Coast Hotel, 3595 Las Vegas Blvd. S. (Flamingo Rd.),*
*702-737-7111*
■ "They make you feel like royalty" at this "fabulous" American veteran in the Barbary Coast that presents some of the "best Dover sole, stone crabs and coquille St. Jacques" around; reservations can be tough – or all but "unavailable to mere mortals" – but it does help if you're a hotel guest or a high roller; and yes, it's "ridiculously expensive", though devotees declare it's "worth every penny."

### Monte Carlo 🅂 | 26 | 24 | 26 | $56 |
*Desert Inn Resort, 3145 Las Vegas Blvd. S. (bet. E. Desert Inn Rd. &*
*Fashion Show Dr.), 702-733-4444*
■ "You'll think you're in heaven" at this venerable Contemporary French in the Desert Inn, thanks to a celestial assortment of some of "the best gourmet food" around; a "very quiet, very relaxing" ambiance and "excellent service" make it a favorite with showfolks who relish the "understated" feel of this "solid" spot.

**Nobu ◐** – | – | – | E

*Hard Rock Hotel, 4455 Paradise Rd. (Harmon Ave.), 702-693-5090*

Forget serene, forget tranquil: this Nouvelle Japanese in the Hard Rock Hotel is crackling with exotic Asian flavors jazzed up by a touch of Peru, thanks to the intuitive genius of executive chef/co-owner Nobu Matsuhisa, a famed name on both coasts (NY's Nobu, LA's Matsuhisa); hip picks include a silky signature black cod with miso and a splendid tasting menu, but desserts are the real surprise here – Japanese, no, delectable, yes.

**Olives ◐[S]** – | – | – | M

*Bellagio Hotel, 3600 Las Vegas Blvd. S. (Flamingo Rd.), 702-693-7223*

A spin-off of the celebrated Boston eatery created by Todd English, this Mediterranean delight in the Bellagio is always bustling, with a particularly high demand for seating on its glorious patio with a lakeside view; chef Victor LaPlaca (from the original Olives) replicates many of the Beantown favorites here and more, all utterly delicious.

**Onda [S]** – | – | – | E

*Mirage Hotel, 3400 Las Vegas Blvd. S. (Spring Mountain Rd.), 702-791-7111*

This charming contemporary Italian in the Mirage comes courtesy of Boston's renowned Todd English (Olives); look for an appealing, seasonally driven menu from the young Italian chef, Luke Palladino, who makes every meal a special occasion, thanks to exquisite creations like butternut squash ravioli with brown butter sauce.

**Palace Court [S]** 26 | 26 | 26 | $63

*Caesars Palace Hotel, 3570 Las Vegas Blvd. S. (Flamingo Rd.), 702-731-7731*

■ If "pomp and ceremony" turn you on, make an entrance at this "ultimate" Classic French in Caesars Palace that features "first-class everything": a "stunning setting", "food as good as the atmosphere" and "top service"; granted, it's "way expensive", but it's "absolutely worth it" for a "very special occasion"; P.S. "you just might see a movie star" here.

**Palm Restaurant [S]** 25 | 21 | 23 | $42

*Forum Shops at Caesars, 3500 Las Vegas Blvd. S. (Flamingo Rd.), 702-732-7256*

■ "Huge lobsters" and perhaps "the best porterhouse ever" keep this "always superb" steakhouse in the Forum Shops at Caesars packed with the "power elite"; true, it's "expensive" and can be "loud", but its uptrodden clientele can't get enough of its "tasty beef", crying "damn the cholesterol, full speed ahead."

**P.F. Chang's China Bistro [S]** 23 | 23 | 21 | $23

*4165 S. Paradise Rd. (Flamingo Rd.), 702-792-2207*

◪ "If you're looking for action", try this "trendy" "American idea of a Chinese restaurant" just East of the Strip, where the "upscale yuppie" crowd goes "to be seen", "but not heard" – it's "too noisy"; though diehards "can't get enough of those lettuce wraps" and are happily "willing to wait" for them ("no reservations accepted"), faultfinders dismiss the "franchise-style" fare and only show up "for the bar scene."

## Picasso 🅂　　　　　　　–　–　–　VE

*Bellagio Hotel, 3600 Las Vegas Blvd. S. (Flamingo Rd.), 702-693-7223*
An exquisite tribute to the artist in the Bellagio, where the master's
paintings and ceramics adorn the dining room and acclaimed SF
chef Julian Serrano (Masa's) creates another kind of art – a melding
of Contemporary French and Spanish dishes – in the kitchen; early
visitors say this flower-filled room with a lake view is as romantic
as it gets.

## Pinot Brasserie ●🅂　　　　　–　–　–　E

*Venetian Hotel, 3355 Las Vegas Blvd. S. (bet. Flamingo &
Spring Mtn. Rds.), 702-414-8888*
An authentic brasserie in the Venetian Hotel via überchef
Joachim Splichal (LA's Patina) that's casually elegant, with
Parisian flea market antiques artfully arranged throughout the
brass and burnished wood interior; its Cal-French bistro menu
draws from a large rotisserie and oyster bar for inspiration.

## Portofino　　　　　　　　27　24　25　$48

*Desert Inn Resort, 3145 Las Vegas Blvd. S. (bet. E. Desert Inn Rd. &
Fashion Show Dr.), 702-733-4495*
■ The "great remodeling job" and the arrival of a talented new chef
at this "elegant" Italian in the Desert Inn show in a remarkable
ratings jump since the last *Las Vegas Survey*; sure, it's "pricey",
but big spenders like the view "overlooking the casino" and
regulars rejoice in the braised oxtail on toasted brioche or the
lamb shank served with Israeli couscous.

## Prime 🅂　　　　　　　　–　–　–　E

*Bellagio Hotel, 3600 Las Vegas Blvd. S. (Flamingo Rd.), 702-693-7223*
Style comes to the steakhouse at this stunning new arrival in the
Bellagio conceived by award-winning chef and restaurateur
Jean-Georges Vongerichten (NYC's Jean Georges, Jo Jo, Vong);
the highest quality meats, seafood and chops, prepared by an
outstanding chef, Kerry Simon, are accompanied by a choice
wine list and served in an ethereal space done in shades of
chocolate brown and powder blue; pounce!

## Renoir 🅂　　　　　　　　–　–　–　VE

(fka Alex Stratta)
*Mirage Hotel, 3400 Las Vegas Blvd. S. (Spring Mountain Rd.),
702-791-7111*
Wooed from his post at a posh Phoenix hotel, award-winning chef
Alessandro Stratta has brought acclaim to this yearling at the
Mirage (formerly the pleasant, but not outstanding, Melange); it's
now an exciting, albeit expensive, dining experience featuring
creative Contemporary French cuisine that emphasizes seasonal
ingredients; N.B. jacket required.

## Second Street Grill ●🅂　　　26　23　24　$29

*Fremont Hotel, 200 Fremont St. (Casino Ctr. Blvd.), 702-385-6277*
■ It might be "the best reason to come Downtown" say fans of
this "innovative" Asian in the Fremont Hotel that specializes in
Pacific Rim dishes expertly prepared by one of the few female
chefs in LV; "reasonable prices" and "excellent specials" make it
sometimes "hard to get in."

## Spago S
| 26 | 24 | 24 | $37 |

*Forum Shops at Caesars, 3500 Las Vegas Blvd. S. (Flamingo Rd.),*
*702-369-6300*

■ "Beautiful people" populate this "loud, hip and trendy" New American in the Forum Shops at Caesars that's the brainchild of überchef Wolfgang Puck, the man who "generated the restaurant renaissance in LV"; whether you "eat in the little cafe in the front" that's "less expensive" or in the more formal, pricier dining room, expect some of "the best people-watching" around at this "phenomenal" experience that's a "must-do when in town."

## Star Canyon ◑S
| – | – | – | E |

*Venetian Hotel, 3355 Las Vegas Blvd. S. (bet. Flamingo &*
*Spring Mtn. Rds.), 702-414-3772*

Buckaroos and buckarettes are galloping over to the Venetian to dig into some mighty tasty Tex-Southwestern vittles courtesy of superchef Stephan Pyles at this clone of his famed Dallas eatery; droll, Lone Star State decor (a branded ceiling, plenty of cowboy boots, decorative barbed wire) sets the amiable tone for the dandy dishes that emerge from the kitchen's wood-burning oven.

## Steak House, The ◑S
| 26 | 23 | 24 | $34 |

*Circus Circus Hotel, 2880 Las Vegas Blvd. S. (Sahara Ave.),*
*702-794-3767*

■ "Too bad you have to walk through Circus Circus" to get to this "consistently good" chophouse, a "big surprise" that still draws diehards "despite its location"; carnivores say you'll find "Ruth's Chris–quality for much less" money here, which is why reservations are so tough to get, so plan ahead – way ahead.

## Suzette's S
| 26 | 25 | 26 | $46 |

*Santa Fe Hotel, 4949 N. Rancho Dr. (Hwy. 95 N.), 702-658-4900*

■ "A little-known hideaway" on the Northwest Side, this "tiny" Classic French "gem" has just 40 seats and they're usually filled with locals; sybarites say "you'll never feel so pampered", adding "they need to advertise" more.

## Valentino ◑S
| – | – | – | E |

*Venetian Hotel, 3355 Las Vegas Blvd. S. (bet. Flamingo &*
*Spring Mtn. Rds.), 702-414-3000*

Bask in the glory of Tuscany à la veteran restaurateur Piero Selvaggio at this Venetian Hotel Italian transplant from Santa Monica and helmed by chef Luciano Pellegrini (ex LA's Posto); with camera-ready fare backed by a legendary wine collection – over 24,000 bottles – that's displayed throughout the handsome space, this is just plain don't-miss dining; P.S. Italian Grill, nestled in the entryway, offers a lower priced, pared-down menu.

## TOP 25 FOOD RANKING

| Restaurant | Cuisine Type |
|---|---|
| **28** Matsuhisa | Japanese/Seafood |
| Sushi Nozawa | Japanese |
| Chinois on Main | Pacific New Wave |
| **27** Patina | Californian/New French |
| L'Orangerie | Classic French |
| Shiro | Asian/Cal./Seafood |
| Valentino | N/S Italian |
| Joe's | Californian |
| Bel-Air Hotel | Californian/New French |
| Belvedere, The | Asian/Cal./French |
| Spago Beverly Hills | Californian/New French |
| **26** Water Grill | Seafood |
| Jozu | Cal./Pacific New Wave |
| Diaghilev | French/Russian |
| Campanile | Cal./Mediterranean |
| Brent's Deli | Deli |
| Ruth's Chris | Steakhouse |
| Hirosuke | Japanese |
| R-23 | Japanese |
| Cafe Bizou | French Bistro |
| L'Ermitage | Continental |
| Citrus | Californian/French |
| Yujean Kang's | Chinese/Pan-Asian |
| Arnie Morton's | Steakhouse |
| Röckenwagner | Californian/Eclectic |

## OTHER IMPORTANT PLACES

| | |
|---|---|
| Bistro 45 | Cal./French Bistro |
| Cafe Blanc | Asian/New French |
| Chaya Brasserie | Asian/Cal./French |
| Devon | Californian |
| JiRaffe | Californian |
| Julienne | French Bistro |
| La Cachette | New French |
| Lawry's The Prime Rib | Steakhouse |
| Locanda Veneta | Northern Italian |
| Michael's | Californian/New French |
| Palm, The | Steakhouse |
| Parkway Grill | Californian |
| Pinot Bistro | Cal./French Bistro |
| Saddle Peak Lodge | New American |
| Spago Hollywood | Californian |

## Arnie Morton's of Chicago S

26 | 22 | 24 | $49

*435 S. La Cienega Blvd. (San Vicente Blvd.), LA, 310-246-1501*

■ One of the Big Boys in town when it comes to "superb", "huge" hunks of cow, this "ultimate, manly" "class of the field for steak and martinis" offers a "clubby, expense-account" setting where "everything is in excess, from the cholesterol to the check!"; not everyone likes the opening raw meat show, but the culinary finale earns raves: "orgasmic Godiva chocolate cake"; dinner only.

## Bel-Air Hotel S

27 | 29 | 27 | $54

*Bel-Air Hotel, 701 Stone Canyon Rd. (north of Sunset Blvd.), Bel-Air, 310-472-1211*

■ Perennially Number 1 for Decor in the *LA Survey* and the top-rated hotel restaurant for food, this "elegant", "civilized" dining room is universally considered "in a class of its own", a "fairy tale" experience in a "magical" setting with "impeccable service" and "imaginative" Nouvelle Cal-French cuisine; those in need of the "big occasion" should consider Table One, the private dining room in the kitchen, where up to eight can luxuriate in a glass bubble while the staff dazzles them with the best they can do.

## Belvedere, The S

27 | 28 | 27 | $55

*Peninsula Beverly Hills Hotel, 9882 Little Santa Monica Blvd. (Wilshire Blvd.), Beverly Hills, 310-788-2306*

■ After having muscled the Bel-Air out of the top slot for LA hotel dining last year, this "superb" Cal-French/Cal-Asian "celebration" spot slips back a hair into the No. 2 position, without losing any of its "pampering atmosphere"; a "good place to impress when wearing something new from Neiman", it offers a "gracious" experience along with much "power brokering" (CAA is next door), and earns raves for its "absolutely wonderful champagne brunch on Sunday."

## Bistro 45 S

26 | 23 | 24 | $43

*45 S. Mentor Ave. (bet. Colorado Blvd. & Green St.), Pasadena, 626-795-2478*

■ "As good a reason as any to visit Pasadena", this highly praised Cal-French bistro in an art deco building is an "all-time favorite" where owner "Robert Simon makes sure that all is perfect", from the "warm" ambiance and "excellent food" to the "great wine list"; admirers rate it "on par with any bistro on the Westside" and a "great spot for intimate gatherings and celebrations."

## Brent's Deli S

26 | 14 | 21 | $14

*19565 Parthenia Ave. (Tampa Ave.), Northridge, 818-886-5679*

■ Year in and year out, the highest-ranked deli in SoCal, beating out major names like Nate 'n Al's and Canter's with a pantheon of superlatives: "best hot pastrami", "best corned beef", "rye bread to die for", "terrific cabbage soup", "football-sized éclairs", all for the asking at this "authentic NY deli" in the 'burbs where "even the waitresses yell at you" – "Brooklyn, hang your head!"

## Cafe Bizou S

26 | 19 | 23 | $27

*14016 Ventura Blvd. (east of Hazeltine Ave.), Sherman Oaks, 818-788-3536*

■ "A star in every way" and easily one of the most popular restaurants in SoCal ("hurried" and "crowded" are its downsides), thanks to its "great French food" and to its being "absolutely the best buy in town" with an "amazing $2 corkage policy"; devotees rave "everything on the menu is great" at this "true oasis in the Valley" – though "you might be dead before you get a reservation."

**Cafe Blanc** | 25 | 16 | 22 | $40 |

*9777 Little Santa Monica Blvd. (Wilshire Blvd.), Beverly Hills, 310-888-0108*

■ This "very civilized" Asian–New French in a "storefront" offers "always exquisite" "creative delights" for the "adventurous" from chef Tomi Harase: appetizers that are "like Japanese kaiseki" and entrees that are "works of art"; it's a "treasure to discover" – a "minimalist setting but maximalist quality."

**Campanile [S]** | 26 | 24 | 23 | $42 |

*624 S. La Brea Ave. (bet. 6th St. & Wilshire Blvd.), LA, 323-938-1447*

■ One of the defining restaurants in the City of Angels (in a "unique" structure built by Charlie Chaplin), this "grand" and "gorgeous" Cal-Med is "always noisy and always crowded, always good" for "extraordinary", "rustic" grill fare from chef-owner Mark Peel and "astonishing breads" from co-owner Nancy Silverton's adjacent La Brea Bakery (No. 1 for bread in the *LA Marketplace Survey*); "try the Monday night family-style dinners", though do watch out for "attitude."

**Chaya Brasserie [S]** | 25 | 24 | 22 | $39 |

*8741 Alden Dr. (bet. Beverly Blvd. & 3rd St., east of Robertson Blvd.), LA, 310-859-8833*

■ "Still innovative" and "noisy as a brass monkey", this "scene" "loaded with agents" has been a "winner for years", packed nightly with "chic guys and gals" sampling "exotic", "over-the-top" Cal-French/Pan-Asian bistro creations; it manages to be both trendy and friendly: "go once and have a great meal . . . go twice and be treated like a regular."

**Chinois on Main [S]** | 28 | 22 | 23 | $48 |

*2709 Main St. (bet. Ocean Park Blvd. & Rose Ave.), Santa Monica, 310-392-9025*

■ Despite Spago's high profile, this "crowded, fun" and "pricey" Pacific New Waver is consistently the top-rated of Wolfgang Puck's many SoCal restaurants, a "cramped" yet stylish Santa Monican serving "creative" and "fantastically delicious dishes" ("especially the catfish"); even if some complain that "dinner is a shout-fest", most of the din comes from devotees shouting "Bravo Wolfie!"

**Citrus [S]** | 26 | 23 | 23 | $46 |

*6703 Melrose Ave. (1 block west of Highland Ave.), LA, 323-857-0034*

■ After all these years, the ratings are still impressive for this Cal-French "classic" that's "still terrific" with its quirky decor (sun umbrellas used indoors) and glass-fronted kitchen; an "awesome lunch" "oasis in Hollywood" that's "unusually welcoming for a trendy restaurant", it's an evergreen "culinary delight" where, as ever, you should "leave room for dessert."

**Devon [S]** | 25 | 21 | 24 | $40 |

*109 E. Lemon Ave. (Myrtle Ave.), Monrovia, 626-305-0013*

■ The least secret "secret gem" around, this "truly wonderful" Californian in the midst of Middle American Monrovia is a hit for its "imaginative cuisine" served in a storefront that keeps on expanding as word of its "exquisite food" spreads; fans who call it a "sensory treat" rate it "as good as the best on the Westside" and have only one complaint: "wish it were closer."

| | F | D | S | C |
|---|---|---|---|---|
| **Diaghilev** | 26 | 27 | 27 | $59 |

*Wyndham Bel Age Hotel, 1020 N. San Vicente Blvd. (Sunset Blvd.), W. Hollywood, 310-854-1111*

■ "A huge splurge", this highly rated, "most romantic" Franco-Russian "where Russians go to die from opulence" is the best place in town for "elegant" dining on caviar and "great vodkas" with the "best maitre d'" "out of central casting" to complete the mood; the smitten "could eat their pelmeni everyday" at this West Hollywood "favorite for a celebration" where there are "even balalaikas" along with a harpist from the Bolshoi; dinner only.

| | F | D | S | C |
|---|---|---|---|---|
| **Hirosuke** [S] | 26 | 16 | 22 | $27 |

*17237 Ventura Blvd. (Louise Ave.), Encino, 818-788-7548*

■ "Sushi doesn't get much better than this" attest admirers of this "friendly" Encino Japanese that's renowned for raw fish "as fresh as it gets"; many "almost hate to rave because it'll just get harder to get in", but they can't resist because it's staffed by "the nicest people"; P.S. "go before 6 PM or face a wait."

| | F | D | S | C |
|---|---|---|---|---|
| **JiRaffe** [S] | 25 | 21 | 22 | $39 |

*502 Santa Monica Blvd. (5th St.), Santa Monica, 310-917-6671*

■ Quondam co-owner Josiah Citrin (aka Ji) has split to open Melisse, and the jury is out as Raphael (Raffe) Lunetta carries on solo at this Santa Monica Californian; thus far the venture is hailed for its "fantastic menu" of "innovative dishes" matched with "terrific service" in a room that's "bright and airy" (if "a bit loud"); in sum, it's a "lovely experience" calculated to "impress your date."

| | F | D | S | C |
|---|---|---|---|---|
| **Joe's** [S] | 27 | 18 | 23 | $36 |

*1023 Abbot Kinney Blvd. (bet. Main St. & Westminster Ave.), Venice, 310-399-5811*

■ One of LA's top culinary destinations, this "out-of-this-world" Venice Californian consistently turns in an "absolutely awesome" performance; "the ultimate" in cooking is paired with "terrific" service, and "sweet" chef-owner Joe Miller offers his "fabulous menu" at a "gourmet value" – "when you can get in"; N.B. a post-*Survey* renovation is not reflected in the decor score.

| | F | D | S | C |
|---|---|---|---|---|
| **Jozu** [S] | 26 | 23 | 24 | $43 |

*8360 Melrose Ave. (4 blocks east of La Cienega Blvd.), W. Hollywood, 323-655-5600*

■ Call it "Pacific Rim Fusion", "Cal-Asian" or "French-Asian", the bottom line is this West Hollywood knockout delivers "fantastic", "beautifully presented food" in a "clubby" room "for the ultrahip"; some suggest it's "a little too Zen", though those in touch with their Inner Diner praise "very creative chef" Suzanne Tracht and owner Andy Nakano, whose "great attitude" is said to attract a celestial following ("God eats here – and always orders dessert").

| | F | D | S | C |
|---|---|---|---|---|
| **Julienne** | 25 | 21 | 20 | $20 |

*2649 Mission St. (bet. El Molino & Los Robles Aves.), San Marino, 626-441-2299*

■ Like a "little bit of France", this "extremely charming" "San Marino hangout" is a "hidden jewel" in the eyes of the "ladies who lunch and gentlemen golfers" who stop in for sandwiches on "wonderful rosemary bread", Provençal quiche and apricot chicken; it's also a hit with locals who "live for their sweets"; N.B. aside from the cafe, there's a gourmet market and caterer.

## La Cachette §　　　　　　26 | 25 | 24 | $46

*10506 Little Santa Monica Blvd. (bet. Beverly Glen Blvd. & Overland Ave.),*
*Century City, 310-470-4992*
■ Charismatic master chef Jean François Meteigner mixes "old-world charm" with "creative", "elegant" Modern French cooking at this "bit of la belle France plunked down in an alleyway"; a "hidden jewel box" with an ambiance that's "wonderful, but stuffy", it's a "pleasure" "from soup to soufflé" with the only quibbles over the room that's "lovely" but "loud when filled."

## Lawry's The Prime Rib §　　　25 | 23 | 24 | $36

*100 N. La Cienega Blvd. (½ block north of Wilshire Blvd.), Beverly Hills,*
*310-652-2827*
■ Not just "a classic" but "*the* classic", a "shrine to prime rib" where, in Zen terms, "they do what they do" – which is serve "succulent beef" carved tableside; it's a "tradition" to which generations of Angelenos have flocked to "feel like royalty", especially if you order the "Diamond Jim Brady cut"; "what can we say? Lawry's does it right"; dinner only.

## L'Ermitage §　　　　　　　26 | 26 | 25 | $51

*L'Ermitage Beverly Hills, 9291 Burton Way (bet. Foothill Rd. & Maple Dr.),*
*Beverly Hills, 310-278-3344*
■ You'll be "treated like royalty" at this "gorgeous", "intimate" hotel restaurant featuring a "magnificent" Continental menu with International accents and a setting of "old-world elegance"; it's "lovely" all around, especially "if someone else is paying."

## Locanda Veneta　　　　　　25 | 18 | 21 | $38

*8638 W. Third St. (bet. Robertson & San Vicente Blvds.), LA, 310-274-1893*
■ For many, this "perfect" Venetian is home to "hands down the best Italian food in LA", "heavenly preparations" served in a "sleek, high-class", albeit "cramped", setting ("try to get a booth to avoid banging elbows"); but most consider crowding a small price to pay for the "great risotto" and "incredible chocolate soufflé"; though the room is "boisterous and loud, the food is never tired."

## L'Orangerie §　　　　　　　27 | 28 | 27 | $63

*903 N. La Cienega Blvd. (bet. Melrose Ave. & Santa Monica Blvd.),*
*W. Hollywood, 310-652-9770*
■ Only Ginza Sushi-Ko is more costly than this "epitome of French style in LA", a Classic French dinner-only "favorite for special occasions" in a "grandiose room" ("Louis XIVth meets California") with a "delightful courtyard" and "flowers more expensive than my wedding"; those dazzled by the "impeccable" food say "all LA chefs should come here for lessons", and the "exceptional service" brings it "close to perfect" – "hope it stays forever."

## Matsuhisa §　　　　　　　28 | 18 | 23 | $54

*129 N. La Cienega Blvd. (north of Wilshire Blvd.), Beverly Hills, 310-659-9639*
■ This "awesome, creative" Japanese seafooder regains its top standing as the No. 1 restaurant for Food in LA, a "city of uncompromising Japanese food" where "Matsuhisa is a shrine" and the answer to the question "what else can you possibly do with sushi . . . wow!"; you may "need Krugerrands to pay" for this "orgasmic" experience, but few complain about the prices when what they're eating is "Asian food from God"; as they say on the street – "Nobu is the man!"

### Michael's
| 25 | 26 | 24 | $49 |

*1147 Third St. (north of Wilshire Blvd.), Santa Monica, 310-451-0843*
■ Consistently one of the top-ranked restaurants in LA, this "classic leader in California cuisine" remains a major influence on SoCal eating thanks to aging enfant terrible Michael McCarty, "still the genius" behind this "big shot" Cal-French; this "special-occasion place" "defines romance" with its "elegant haute cuisine", "attentive, professional service" and "beautiful garden."

### Palm, The S
| 25 | 19 | 21 | $48 |

*9001 Santa Monica Blvd. (bet. Doheny Dr. & Robertson Blvd.),*
*W. Hollywood, 310-550-8811*
■ A "boys' club" where "table-hopping" players learn whether they're in or out, this hub for "movers and shakers" is irreplaceable "for those who miss old NY"; the "classic" steakhouse treatment includes properly mixed cocktails, "great Gigi salad", "lobster with an attitude" and "mouthwatering" red meat; "loud", "casual" and "worth the big bucks", it's still "popular every night."

### Parkway Grill S
| 25 | 24 | 23 | $37 |

*510 S. Arroyo Pkwy. (bet. California & Del Mar Blvds.), Pasadena,*
*626-795-1001*
■ For a "Westside restaurant on the Eastside", try this "popular Pasadena spot", often dubbed the Spago of the San Gabriel Valley (Puck should charge royalties) for its "top-quality" California cuisine; citing the "flowers and skylights" and produce grown in an on-site garden, boosters gush it "never fails to delight."

### Patina S
| 27 | 24 | 26 | $57 |

*5955 Melrose Ave. (bet. Highland Ave. & Vine St.), LA, 323-467-1108*
■ "This is the big leagues, baby"; superlatives fly around LA's Most Popular restaurant, a "classic" "phenomenon" where every plate is an "exquisite" "work of art"; master chef Joachim Splichal's Contemporary Cal-French exhibits "flavors beyond belief" ("order everything"), and "first-class service" ensures everybody is "somebody"; the ultimate response is reverent: "on the eighth day, God created Patina."

### Pinot Bistro S
| 25 | 24 | 23 | $41 |

*12969 Ventura Blvd. (½ block west of Coldwater Canyon Ave.), Studio City,*
*818-990-0500*
■ The first (and for many the "best") of Joachim Splichal's more casual Patina spin-offs, this "designer French" "delight" "sets the standard" in the Valley with its "California takes on bistro food", matched with a "beautiful", "warm" room and "excellent service"; for bringing a taste of "France to the land of Valleyspeak", area admirers call it a culinary "raison d'être."

### Röckenwagner S
| 26 | 22 | 23 | $41 |

*2435 Main St. (bet. Ocean Park & Pico Blvds.), Santa Monica, 310-399-6504*
■ Named for chef-owner Hans Röckenwagner, this Cal-Eclectic showcases his German roots with "consistently first-rate", "creative cuisine" ("sublime crab soufflé", "excellent bread", memorable white asparagus) served in a "beautiful room" set in an ultramodern Main Street mini-mall; "everything works" here since "handsome, hands-on" Hans is "never content just to give you what you've always gotten before" – a philosophy that makes for a "stellar dining experience."

**R-23** 26 | 21 | 21 | $35

*923 E. Third St. (bet. Alameda St. & Santa Fe Ave.), Downtown LA, 213-687-7178*

■ "Simply remarkable" "urbane" decor (particularly the Frank Gehry–designed cardboard chairs) is but one of the highlights of this "minimalist" sushi bar, a Katsu spin-off located in a Downtown art district alleyway that leaves arrivistes "feeling smug about being in the know"; "melt-in-your-mouth-like-buttah sushi" and other "divine", "Zen-like" creations result in a "peaceful yet powerful dining experience", but "make sure you get directions" and "bring a compass" as it's "impossible to find."

**Ruth's Chris Steak House [S]** 26 | 21 | 23 | $43

*224 S. Beverly Dr. (bet. Olympic & Wilshire Blvds.), Beverly Hills, 310-859-8744*

■ "You'll never eat a better steak anywhere" than at this BH outpost of the national chain that's once again the top-rated chop shop in SoCal; expect "outstanding beef that comes sizzling in butter" (and so tender "you practically don't need a knife"), accompanied by "excellent" sides in a "clubby" environment; "meat-and-potatoes men" call it "an indulgence that neither you nor your Visa card will soon forget"; dinner only.

**Saddle Peak Lodge [S]** 25 | 28 | 25 | $46

*419 Cold Canyon Rd. (east of Malibu Canyon Rd.), Calabasas, 818-222-3888*

■ Take a journey that ends high in the Malibu "wilderness" at this "unique" "meat eaters'" mecca, an "LA getaway" that's a "cross between the Ritz and cowboy heaven", with "great wild game on the menu" to match the "animal heads on the walls"; though "not for the faint of heart", when it comes to a "safari on a plate", it's "the only game in town"; N.B. dinner and Sunday brunch only.

**Shiro [S]** 27 | 18 | 24 | $40

*1505 Mission St. (Fair Oaks Ave.), S. Pasadena, 626-799-4774*

■ "Catfish is king" at this "little jewel" of a South Pasadena Cal-Asian seafooder, where the house specialty is an "amazing" "whole fish" spiced with ponzu and cilantro that's "in a league of its own"; partialists "often dream of the catfish" (what would Freud say?), but anyone interested will also find seafood ravioli and even "well-prepared" chicken on the "less-is-more" menu; dinner only.

**Spago Beverly Hills [S]** 27 | 26 | 23 | $52

*176 N. Cañon Dr. (½ block north of Wilshire Blvd.), Beverly Hills, 310-385-0880*

■ Easily the most famous eatery in SoCal, Mr. Puck's flagship is a perpetual "hot spot" that "exceeds expectations", with "incredible" Cal-French cooking that's "as good as it gets", even if it's almost upstaged by "celebrities galore" and Barbara Lazaroff's "wild, eye-catching decor"; "beautiful food, room and people" says it all, and for the power brokers of Tinseltown, making this scene is simply "a must" – "if you can get in."

**Spago Hollywood [S]** 25 | 20 | 22 | $47

*1114 Horn Ave. (Sunset Blvd.), W. Hollywood, 310-652-3706*

■ Notwithstanding the buzz surrounding the BH branch, the West Hollywood original of this Californian powerhouse is "still fab", an "always crowded" "haven" for indulging in Wolfgang Puck's patented "creative pizzas" and "great salads" sans paparazzi madness; this is one Major Destination where "you can be seated even if you're not a star"; dinner only.

**Sushi Nozawa** 28 | 9 | 17 | $38 |

*11288 Ventura Blvd. (2 blocks west of Vineland Ave.), Studio City, 818-508-7017*

■ Where archrival Matsuhisa is a fusion seafooder, this Japanese storefront is all about "impeccably fresh", "melt-in-your-mouth" sushi, presented "hard-guy" chef Kazunori Nozawa's way or not at all; it's a minute space where "rules, rules, rules" abound – "and yes, you can be thrown out" – but the end result is "perfect artwork" on every plate; "sushi experts" attest it "lives up to the hype" – just don't forget "Nozawa is the man!"

**Valentino** 27 | 24 | 26 | $55 |

*3115 Pico Blvd. (west of #10 Frwy., bet. 31st & 32nd Sts.), Santa Monica, 310-829-4313*

■ "If you have time for only one meal when in LA", many voters nominate Piero Selvaggio's "haven away from the chaos", a "shrine" that's "as close to perfection as a restaurant can get" and perennially the top-rated Italian in SoCal; a "world-class" menu matched by a "wine cellar from heaven" and "impeccable service" make for one "extraordinary dining experience" that's only heightened if you let "Piero build you a meal" (but bring "lotsa lira"); N.B. lunch served Friday only.

**Water Grill [S]** 26 | 24 | 24 | $43 |

*544 S. Grand Ave. (bet. 5th & 6th Sts.), Downtown LA, 213-891-0900*

■ Almost from the day it opened, this "elegant" Downtowner has been ranked LA's best seafooder, a piscine pleasure palace that fin fans sum up in a word: "nirvana"; credit the "beautifully presented", "perfectly cooked" fish, one of the most opulent oyster bars on the West Coast and a "serene, regal" setting that's convenient if you're on the way to the Music Center; granted, it's "high-end" dining, but the overwhelming majority says it's "worth the price."

**Yujean Kang's [S]** 26 | 21 | 22 | $36 |

*67 N. Raymond Ave. (bet. Colorado Blvd. & Walnut St.), Pasadena, 626-585-0855*

*8826 Melrose Ave. (1 block west of Robertson Blvd.), W. Hollywood, 310-288-0806*

■ In the small world of "nouvelle Chinese" cuisine, Yujean Kang is king, a chef "in a class by himself" who "cooks with a lot of soul and passion" at this "pricey" Modern Asian duo that's a "great mix of East meets West"; his "adventurous" menu is abetted by an "inspired" wine list, "beautiful decor" and "lovely service", leading enthusiasts to sigh "we are blessed" that this "gourmet" "dining experience" is "still original after all these years."

# Miami/Miami Beach

## TOP 10 FOOD RANKING

| Restaurant | Cuisine Type |
|---|---|
| *27* Norman's | New World |
| Osteria del Teatro | Northern Italian |
| *26* Chef Allen's | New World |
| Tropical Chinese | Chinese/Dim Sum |
| Palm | Steakhouse |
| Pacific Time | Asian/Pacific Rim |
| Baleen | Seafood |
| Toni's Sushi Bar | Japanese |
| Joe's Stone Crab | Seafood |
| Caffe Abbracci | N/S Italian |

## OTHER IMPORTANT PLACES

| | |
|---|---|
| Astor Place | Floridian/International |
| Blue Door | New French |
| China Grill | Eclectic |
| Crystal Cafe | Continental |
| Escopazzo | N/S Italian |
| Forge, The | Continental |
| Il Tulipano Ristorante | Northern Italian |
| La Palme d'Or | French |
| Miss Saigon Bistro | Vietnamese |
| Morton's of Chicago | Steakhouse |
| Nemo | Eclectic |
| Ortanique on the Mile | Caribbean |
| Porcao | Brazilian/Steakhouse |
| Tuscan Steak | Northern Italian |
| Versailles | Cuban |
| Wolfie Cohen's Rascal House | Deli |
| Yuca | Nuevo Latino |

| F | D | S | C |
|---|---|---|---|
| 24 | 24 | 21 | $45 |

### Astor Place S

*Hotel Astor, 956 Washington Ave. (10th St.), Miami Beach, 305-672-7217*

■ "Wear black" and "pretend you're in Manhattan" at this "airy" "art deco" "hot spot" in an "elegant" Miami Beach hotel, which still boasts a "high-octane" bar and "people-watching" scene even if chef Johnny Vinczencz (creator of 'Caribbean Cowboy' cuisine) has surrendered the ovens; scenesters are confident that culinary wizard Norman Van Aken, now on board as a consultant, will keep the International-Floridian cuisine on the cutting edge.

**Baleen ◐[S]** | 26 | 27 | 20 | $53

*Grove Isle Hotel, 4 Grove Isle Dr., Coconut Grove, 305-858-8300*

■ Early response is in, and chef "Robbin Haas continues to be a marvel" with his "superb" seafood at this country-clubbish upstart at the Grove Isle Hotel; the "totally romantic" experience comes with "beautiful decor" and "one of the best views in town", though hedgers hint the "service could improve" given the "shockingly expensive" tabs.

**Blue Door ◐[S]** | 23 | 27 | 20 | $54

*Delano Hotel, 1685 Collins Ave. (17th St.), Miami Beach, 305-674-6400*

◪ "Wow!"; this "very chic" Nouveau French in the Delano Hotel presents chef Claude Troisgros' "amazing" cuisine against a candlelit backdrop of "floor-to-ceiling curtains that make you feel as if you're on stage"; it's "the perfect place for the glitterati to dine", and "the food is as beautiful as the people", though holdouts maintain the "service needs help."

**Caffe Abbracci ◐[S]** | 26 | 22 | 23 | $39

*318 Aragon Ave. (bet. Le Jeune Rd. & Miracle Mile), Coral Gables, 305-441-0700*

■ Thanks to "superb host" Nino Pernetti, local players "can always count on a wonderful meal" at this "elegant" Coral Gables Italian, a "power" scene that pulls in a "great-looking", celeb-studded clientele; for "consistently delicious food" and "professional service" it's "one of the best" in town, and its rep keeps it "crowded and noisy."

**Chef Allen's [S]** | 26 | 23 | 25 | $52

*19088 NE 29th Ave. (NE 191st St., 1 block east of Biscayne Blvd.), Aventura, 305-935-2900*

◪ "One of the greatest culinary experiences in South Florida – a must!" swear devotees of this "classy" star in an Aventura strip mall, created by "chef's chef" Allen Susser, one of the "mango mafia" that originated New World cuisine; the "pricey" "designer food" is cooked in an open kitchen, winning acclaim as "superb" and "imaginative", and though a few object that it "doesn't live up to its PR", most attest it's "always a pleasure."

**China Grill ◐[S]** | 23 | 23 | 19 | $47

*404 Washington Ave. (5th St.), Miami Beach, 305-534-2211*

◪ A celebrity "mob scene" attracts those who want to "see and be seen" – but not those "who want to hear and be heard" – at this "very loud" link in the growing national chain; it's still a popular night spot for the "glitzy" South Beach crowd, but even admirers of the "exceptional" Eclectic menu and "beautiful" setting snipe at service that's heavy on "attitude."

**Crystal Cafe [S]** | 25 | 20 | 25 | $34

*726 41st St. (bet. Chase & Prairie Aves.), Miami Beach, 305-673-8266*

■ Few establishments earn such consistently positive buzz as this "fabulous neighborhood" modern Continental run by "charming" chef-owner Klime Kovaceski and his wife; a Miami Beach standout, it racks up raves for osso buco "to die for", "wonderful" service and "outstanding value"; 'nuff said.

---

**Escopazzo ◐ [S]** 25 | 20 | 23 | $39

*1311 Washington Ave. (bet. 13th & 14th Sts.), Miami Beach, 305-674-9450*

■ A "perfect little gem", this recently expanded but still "tiny and terrific" South Beach Italian features owner Giuseppe 'Pino' Bodoni greeting patrons with "loving care" and feeding them "superb" hand-rolled pastas, authentic risottos and seafood; the "romantic" atmosphere is enhanced by "warm, friendly service", so while it's "expensive", most agree the "prices are fair" for the quality.

**Forge Restaurant, The [S]** 25 | 26 | 23 | $53

*432 Arthur Godfrey Rd. (Royal Palm Ave.), Miami Beach, 305-538-8533*

◪ Ever a "memorable experience", this "sentimental favorite" in Miami Beach continues to impress "the beautiful people" with "excellent" "old-fashioned" Continental fare and a "great wine list", presented in an "over-the-top" room; it's "still one of the best", though critics cry "overhyped" and no one disputes it's "pricey."

**Il Tulipano Ristorante [S]** 24 | 21 | 22 | $47

*11052 Biscayne Blvd. (110th St.), North Miami, 305-893-4811*

◪ This North Miami monument to "old-world elegance" is considered "one of the top Italians" in town for "luxury dining"; admirers pay "high prices" for its "intimate" charms, though modernists insist it's now "over the hill."

**Joe's Stone Crab [S]** 26 | 20 | 22 | $46

*11 Washington Ave. (S. Pointe Dr.), Miami Beach, 305-673-0365*

■ "The season is too short" lament fans of this Miami Beach seafood "landmark" (open mid-October through mid-May), where tourists, celebrities and natives all make the "pilgrimage" to feast on "the best stone crab ever", plus creamed spinach "you can easily OD on" and "awesome Key lime pie"; everyone crabs about the "looong waits" and suggests ways around them: "get there at 5 PM", "go for lunch" or "order takeout" from the adjacent store.

**La Palme d'Or [S]** – | – | – | VE

*Biltmore Hotel, 1200 Anastasia Ave. (Grand Blvd.), Coral Gables, 305-445-1926*

"Life never felt so good" as at this "most elegant" venue in the "historic" Biltmore Hotel, where visiting Michelin-starred chefs create "a splendid menu" that evolves monthly but always features "superb" French fare; "a table overlooking the magnificent pool" is perfect for basking in Gallic refinement against a backdrop that preserves a touch of the Jazz Age.

**Miss Saigon Bistro [S]** 24 | 13 | 23 | $25

*146 Giralda Ave. (Ponce de Leon Blvd.), Coral Gables, 305-446-8006*

■ For "fabulous" Vietnamese in a "friendly" setting, this Coral Gables entry is the new destination of choice; quarters may be "cramped", but the "knowledgeable" staff serves with "humor and pizazz", making every comer feel like a "guest in someone's home."

**Morton's of Chicago [S]** 25 | 23 | 22 | $50

*1200 Brickell Ave. (Coral Way), Miami, 305-400-9990*

*17399 Biscayne Blvd. (NE 173rd St.), North Miami Beach, 305-945-3131*

■ To every "carnivore's delight", these "classy" (and "pricey") outposts of the national chophouse chain offer a "private club" feel to enhance their "first-rate steak" and lobster, "exceptional wine list" and deadly Godiva chocolate cake; "smooth" and "comfortable" "standbys", they "never disappoint" the faithful.

**Nemo ◐[S]** 25 | 23 | 22 | $42

*100 Collins Ave. (1st St.), Miami Beach, 305-532-4550*

■ Sited in a "funky" art deco space in newly trendy SoFi, this "lively" Eclectic is the "epitome of South Beach cool"; attractions include "wonderful flavors" courtesy of chef-owner Michael Schwartz (ex LA's Chinois) and chef Frank Jeannetti, and, of course, "good scenery" featuring plenty of "models."

**Norman's** 27 | 25 | 26 | $55

*21 Almeria Ave. (Douglas Rd.), Coral Gables, 305-446-6767*

■ "Do believe the hype": rated No. 1 for Food and Popularity in the *Miami Survey*, this "striking" Gables "standard" setter is where "the chic meet" to indulge in "astonishingly good" "treats for the tongue" delivered by a "superb" staff; "chef Norman Van Aken is a master" of "exceptional", "inventive" New World cuisine, though the "super-premium prices" lead a fault-finding few to cite "mucho dinero" for such "small portions."

**Ortanique on the Mile** – | – | – | E

*278 Miracle Mile (Le Jeune Rd.), Coral Gables, 305-446-7710*

A spin-off of the defunct Norma's on the Beach, this colorful, upscale Caribbean next door to the Miracle Theatre lures in the smart set with its unique takes on specialties like smoked marlin, curried crab cakes and Blue Mountain coffee ice cream.

**Osteria del Teatro** 27 | 18 | 24 | $44

*1443 Washington Ave. (Española Way), Miami Beach, 305-538-7850*

■ "Consistently the best Italian" in town, this "little jewel" of a South Beach "storefront" is "famous" for its "excellent" Northern-style specialties, including seafood linguini in parchment; it's "charming", "hospitable" and "very Italian", and regulars ensure the "intimate" room stays "crowded."

**Pacific Time [S]** 26 | 21 | 22 | $47

*915 Lincoln Rd. (bet. Jefferson & Michigan Aves.), Miami Beach, 305-534-5979*

■ Lately a South Beach trendsetter, this "high-end, cosmopolitan" hot spot is home to chef-owner Jonathan Eismann's "fabulous" and "complex" Pan-Asian fusion creations, served in a "casual" space that's "busy" and "loud, loud, loud"; it's a showcase for "fresh, startling" fare, including some of the "best seafood anywhere" and a dynamite dessert list ("don't miss the chocolate bomb").

**Palm [S]** 26 | 20 | 24 | $52

*9650 E. Bay Harbor Dr. (Kane Concourse), Bay Harbor Islands, 305-868-7256*

■ It's "like going back to the '30s" at this "NY-type" Bay Harbor Islands chophouse where meat eaters can count on "big slabs" of "the best steak in Miami" as well as mammoth lobsters and all the classic sides, prepared "simply" and served by pros; it may be "plain" and "pricey", but hey, "everybody goes here."

**Porcao ◐[S]** 23 | 18 | 20 | $37

*801 Brickell Bay Dr. (SE 8th St.), Miami, 305-373-2777*

■ "Considering it's not Rio", the "outstanding Brazilian-cut meats" provide an "excellent" selection at this rodizio-style Downtown "beef lover's paradise"; insiders advise "come hungry" because between the "great salad bar" and the nonstop parade of grilled goodies served tableside, everyone's in for a "pig out."

### Toni's Sushi Bar ◑🅢
26 | 22 | 21 | $28

*1208 Washington Ave. (12th St.), Miami Beach, 305-673-9368*
■ SoBe's longest-standing sushi bar is also the "best on the beach" in the eyes of enthusiasts who extol the "wonderful presentations" of "A-1" fish, "beautiful" traditional Japanese decor and "pleasant" service; true sushi-heads just belly up to the bar, but couples note the booths are super "for a date."

### Tropical Chinese Restaurant 🅢
26 | 18 | 21 | $28

*Tropical Park Plaza, 7991 SW 40th St. (79th Ave.), Miami, 305-262-7576*
■ "Can't beat their dim sum" say supporters of this Cantonese-Mandarin powerhouse in Southwest Dade, where the steel carts roll daily; it's noted for its "superb" and "authentic" fare ("chicken feet shocked me"), and if the regular menu can be "pricey", it provides "Hong Kong quality" and the "long lines tell the story."

### Tuscan Steak ◑🅢
25 | 22 | 22 | $48

*433 Washington Ave. (5th St.), Miami Beach, 305-534-2233*
■ South Beach's "beautiful people" "arrive hungry" at this "very hip" Northern Italian meatery, favored for "plentiful" portions of "mouthwatering" Tuscan fare dished up "family style"; the "intense flavors" complement a "brilliantly renovated deco" space, and the "trendy" results are "expensive" and ever "so noisy!"

### Versailles ◑🅢
19 | 14 | 17 | $19

*3555 SW Eighth St. (SW 35th Ct.), Miami, 305-445-7614*
■ Even Anglos "appreciate the authenticity" at this "always buzzing" Cuban diner, a Little Havana "landmark" where the "courteous" staff makes everyone "feel at home"; the "affordable" "stick-to-your-ribs" fare is served in a spacious room that's "tacky in a charming way", evoking the French palace with glass, mirrors and chandeliers ("bring sunglasses!").

### Wolfie Cohen's Rascal House ◑🅢
22 | 11 | 18 | $18

*17190 Collins Ave. (172nd St.), Sunny Isles, 305-947-4581*
■ "Forever great", this 24-7 "gem" is "always packed" at peak hours, and the "wait is part of the scene" as "Miami Beach's Jewish population" sits down to "hearty servings" of "genuine NY deli" classics and "more desserts than you can shake a stick at"; it "lives up to its rep", though even advocates marvel that the "best deli in town" is "such a dump" – go figure.

### Yuca 🅢
21 | 20 | 19 | $43

*501 Lincoln Rd. (Drexel Ave.), Miami Beach, 305-532-9822*
◪ "Cuba meets Gucci" at this "excellent upscale" South Beach trendsetter, which offers "daring and original" Nuevo Latino cuisine in a "great location" that's ideal for scoping the passing crowd, though contras claim the package is "way overpriced"; music lovers converge on the upstairs nightclub, especially "when [popular Cuban singer] Albita is in town."

# Minneapolis/St. Paul

## TOP 10 FOOD RANKING

| Restaurant | Cuisine Type |
|---|---|
| **28** Goodfellow's | New American |
| **27** D'Amico Cucina | N/S Italian |
| Bayport Cookery | Eclectic |
| Manny's Steakhouse | Steakhouse |
| **26** Lucia's | New American |
| Ristorante Luci | N/S Italian |
| La Belle Vie | French/Mediterranean |
| Origami | Japanese |
| Kincaid's | Seafood/Steakhouse |
| 510 Restaurant | French/New American |

## OTHER IMPORTANT PLACES

| | |
|---|---|
| Aquavit | Scandinavian |
| Buca di Beppo | N/S Italian |
| Dakota Bar & Grill | Regional American |
| Local, the | Irish/American |
| Loring Cafe | New American |
| Oceanaire | Seafood |
| Palomino Euro Bistro | Mediterranean |
| St. Paul Grill | Traditional American |
| Table of Contents | Regional American |
| Zelo | Northen Italian |

| F | D | S | C |
|---|---|---|---|
| – | – | – | E |

### Aquavit
*IDS Ctr., 75 S. Seventh St. (Nicollet Mall), Minneapolis, 612-343-3333*
Twin Cities foodies are ecstatic about this smart Scandinavian in Downtown's IDS Center, transplanted from Manhattan under the aegis of NYC executive chef Marcus Samuelsson and under the supervision of chef Roger Johnsson, who oversees the daily operation; look forward to sleek, stylish and pricey Scando-Asian fusion in an airy Nordic atmosphere.

### Bayport Cookery S
*328 Fifth Ave. N. (Hwy. 95), Bayport, 651-430-1066*
■ Though its many fans "wish it were closer", that doesn't keep legions of serious foodies from this "unforgettable experience" in Bayport where "impressive" Eclectic fare is served in a "fastidiously prepared" five-course prix fixe extravaganza that changes weekly (don't miss the "annual morel mushroom dinners" in May and June); what's more, fans feel that a "leisurely" meal here "increases the chance that the evening will end romantically."

## Buca di Beppo 🖪    20 | 21 | 20 | $18

(fka Buca)

*1204 Harmon Pl. (Hennepin Ave.), Minneapolis, 651-638-2225*
*2728 Gannon Rd. (Shepard Rd.), St. Paul, 651-SPA-GETT*
*14300 Burnhaven Dr. (143th St.), Burnsville, 612-892-7272*
*7711 Mitchell Rd. (Hwy. 5), Eden Prairie, 612-724-7266*

☑ "Go with folks you like 'cause you're gonna share everything" at this "festive" Italian chain where the fare is served "family-style", and "loosen your belt" when the "ridiculously large portions" arrive; pros praise the "best garlic mashed potatoes ever" and "fair prices", but faultfinders fume that the "wait forever" for "bland" "factory food" is "not worth it."

## Dakota Bar & Grill 🖪    23 | 22 | 21 | $26

*Bandana Sq., 1021 E. Bandana Blvd. (Lexington Ave.), St. Paul, 651-642-1442*

■ "Hot food and hot jazz" are the hallmarks of this "class act" Midwesterner in St. Paul, overseen by Ken Goff, "one of the Twin Cities' best chefs"; foodies flock for his "amazing" seasonal recipes (like the signature Brie-and-apple soup), while hipsters pronounce it their "fave" for "sophisticated" jive; in sum, "eat and enjoy."

## D'Amico Cucina 🖪    27 | 26 | 25 | $43

*Butler Sq., 100 N. Sixth St. (bet. 1st & 2nd Aves.), Minneapolis, 612-338-2401*

■ Ranked No. 2 for Food and Popularity in Minneapolis/St. Paul, this Warehouse District contemporary Italian proffers a "gorgeous, glorious" menu that's "the standard" by which "all others are judged" (it "doesn't get much better than this" rave admirers); "phenomenal service", an "excellent wine list" and a "beautiful space" make this the quintessential "place to celebrate something special, or nothing at all" – but "save up" before you reserve.

## 510 Restaurant    26 | 23 | 25 | $38

*510 Groveland Ave. (Lyndale Ave.), Minneapolis, 612-874-6440*

■ "An old-time classic" near Loring Park, this French-American "institution for gourmets" is undergoing "an apparently successful transition" now that the next generation of owners has stepped in; while it still "reeks of old money", matching "first-class" dishes with a "very romantic" setting and "formal service" that "treats you like royalty", the younger crowd claims it's "a bit stuffy."

## Goodfellow's    28 | 26 | 27 | $43

*City Ctr., 40 S. Seventh St. (bet. Hennepin & Nicollet Aves.), Minneapolis, 612-332-4800*

■ "Delectable combinations" of "edible art" on every plate, plus a "gorgeous" deco room and an "awesome wine list" make chef Kevin Cullen's New American "hands down the best in town", ranking No. 1 for Popularity, Food, Service and (in a tie) Decor in the *Minneapolis/St. Paul Survey*; predictably, the "spectacular" package is priced up in "expense-account" territory.

## Kincaid's 🖪    26 | 24 | 25 | $32

*8400 Normandale Lake Blvd. (84th St.), Bloomington, 612-921-2255*

☑ The "suburban business" crowd favors this surf 'n' turfer in a Bloomington "office tower" for "excellent all around" meals, declaring that it defines yupscale dining and "oozes power at lunch"; skeptics say it's "cruising on reputation alone", citing "expensive cookie-cutter food" and a menu that "never changes except for the prices"; both camps concede that it's "hard to get in."

### La Belle Vie S   26 | 25 | 23 | $43
*312 S. Main St. (Nelson St.), Stillwater, 651-430-3545*
■ "Supercreative" French-Mediterranean cuisine courtesy of two former D'Amico Cucina chefs earns this "charming" Stillwater entry enthusiastic foodie support, and the "historic"setting is an eye-pleaser; while some speak only of "great promise" and opine it "could be outstanding", converts are convinced it's already a "very special" "escape" that's well "worth the drive."

### Local, the ●S   21 | 24 | 19 | $29
*931 Nicollet Mall (10th St.), Minneapolis, 612-904-1000*
☑ Pub partisans sense "a lot of potential" in this "nice addition" to the Downtown scene, an "upscale" Irish-American with a "warm" "Euro feel" installed in a "very hip" and "classy" storefront; an unconvinced minority finds it a "better place to drink than eat", citing "uneven food and service" and "pricey" tabs; all agree its "growing popularity" is likely to keep it "noisy" and "crowded."

### Loring Cafe S   22 | 25 | 17 | $28
*1624 Harmon Pl. (16th St.), Minneapolis, 612-332-1617*
☑ The "high funk factor" at this "very urban", "artsy" hangout tends to overshadow a "creative" New American menu that some find "surprisingly uneven"; nonetheless, with "bohemian" decor and a staff to match, it's "unlike anything in town."

### Lucia's S   26 | 22 | 24 | $27
*1432 W. 31st St. (Hennepin Ave.), Minneapolis, 612-825-1572*
■ Tucked into an Uptown storefront, this "beautiful spot" features a menu devoted to "imaginative" New American dishes created from the "best seasonal ingredients"; the "sensitive treatment of food and guests" and "excellent wine list" make it a "special-occasion place" – maybe even the "Minnesota Chez Panisse."

### Manny's Steakhouse S   27 | 23 | 26 | $43
*Hyatt Regency, 1300 Nicollet Mall (Grant St.), Minneapolis, 612-339-9900*
■ "Everything a beef lover wants" arrives in abundance at this "steakhouse *Satyricon*", a "macho" Downtown "powerhouse" where "fantastic" meat is delivered in "insanely huge portions", backed by "perfect service"; it's "expensive", but porterhouse partisans proclaim that "nobody does it better."

### Oceanaire S   – | – | – | E
*Hyatt Regency, 1300 Nicollet Mall (Grant St.), Minneapolis, 612-333-2277*
It's déjà vu all over again at this new Downtown supper club launched by the Parasole group in the former Pronto digs, which has been redone in a swanky '30s style; pro servers in white coats supply seafood as fresh and sassy (and costly) as the steaks served at nearby sibling Manny's, satisfying a sea of see-and-be-seeners at this latest spot to make a splash; N.B. dinner only.

### Origami S   26 | 21 | 21 | $26
*30 N. First St. (1st Ave.), Minneapolis, 612-333-8430*
■ It "feels like NY" at this "pristine" Warehouse District Japanese that proffers the "best sushi in town" (or at least the "best that can be expected in the middle of a continent"); though penny-pinchers say portions are "skimpy" for the price, sushiphiles feel that "every precious morsel" is "worth the splurge"; P.S. insiders suggest you "sit at the bar" – "the chefs are a blast."

| F | D | S | C |
|---|---|---|---|

### Palomino Euro Bistro ◐[S]

| F | D | S | C |
|---|---|---|---|
| 25 | 26 | 24 | $28 |

*825 Hennepin Ave. (9th St.), Minneapolis, 612-339-3800*

☑ "If you picked this horse, you've got a winner" say fans of this "upbeat" Downtown Mediterranean that's generating a "great buzz" thanks to an "artsy", "stylish" crowd who keeps coming back for some of the "best people-watching" around; wanna-bes sniff it's "full of itself", yet the beautiful ones rate it a "perfect night out."

### Ristorante Luci [S]

| F | D | S | C |
|---|---|---|---|
| 26 | 17 | 23 | $27 |

*470 S. Cleveland Ave. (Randolph Ave.), St. Paul, 651-699-8258*

☑ "Call way ahead" because it's "tough to get reservations" at this diminutive Highland Park "*trattorissimo*" that presents "outstanding" Italian fare complemented by a "brilliant" wine list; though the "cramped" "sardine-like" seating means your evening "won't be romantic", fans say "the lack of atmosphere *is* the atmosphere" and insist that this "fabulous" place should "never change a thing."

### St. Paul Grill [S]

| F | D | S | C |
|---|---|---|---|
| 25 | 26 | 24 | $33 |

*Saint Paul Hotel, 350 Market St. (5th St.), St. Paul, 651-224-7455*

☑ One of the most "popular" establishments in St. Paul, this "upscale" hotel grill has a "clubby feeling and historic setting" that alone "make it worthwhile" (ask for a "window seat for a wonderful view of Rice Park"); appointed with "beautiful wood paneling" and "cozy booths", it's "elegant in an F. Scott Fitzgeraldish way" and staffed by a "gracious" team; though "everything" on the Traditional American menu is "excellent", skeptics nitpick that the "old-school" cuisine "needs updating."

### Table of Contents [S]

| F | D | S | C |
|---|---|---|---|
| 24 | 21 | 22 | $29 |

*1310 Hennepin Ave. S. (13th St.), Minneapolis, 612-339-1133*
*1648 Grand Ave. (Snelling Ave. N.), St. Paul, 612-699-6595*

■ Each branch of these "hip" 'Midwest fusion' standouts "has its own personality": the Minneapolis venue is "romantic" and "upscale", with a marvelous martini bar, while the St. Paul site, attached to a campus bookstore, is "delightful" and "quaint"; both boast an "ever-changing" Regional American menu that celebrates "intelligent, creative cooking", but expect the dishes to arrive in "dieters' portions."

### Zelo ◐[S]

| F | D | S | C |
|---|---|---|---|
| – | – | – | E |

*Nicollet Mall, 831 Nicollet Mall (9th St.), Minneapolis, 612-333-7000*

From the owner of Bloomington's Ciao Bella comes this urbane Tuscan grotto whose contemporary Italian menu emphasizes things aquatic; generating almost as much buzz as the cooking is its breathtaking setting in the 1929 Medical Arts Building in Downtown's Nicollet Mall, which has been transformed into an avant-garde yet cozy hideaway, with abstract chandeliers, high ceilings and low lighting.

# New Jersey

## TOP 10 FOOD RANKING

| Restaurant | Cuisine Type |
|---|---|
| **28** Jeffrey's | New American |
| Saddle River Inn | French/New American |
| **27** Sagami | Japanese |
| Scalini Fedeli | Northern Italian |
| Ryland Inn | New French |
| Washington Inn | New American |
| Rosemary & Sage | New American |
| Chez Madeleine | Classic French |
| Cafe Panache | New French |
| 410 Bank Street | Cajun/Caribbean |

## OTHER IMPORTANT PLACES

| | |
|---|---|
| Bernards Inn | New American |
| Doris & Ed's | Seafood |
| Ebbitt Room | New American |
| Frog & the Peach | New American |
| Harvest Moon Inn | New American |
| Serenäde Restaurant | New French |
| Stage House Inn | New French |
| Waters Edge | New American |

| F | D | S | C |
|---|---|---|---|

### Bernards Inn, The      25 | 27 | 24 | $48
*The Bernards Inn, 27 Mine Brook Rd. (Quimbey St.), Bernardsville, 908-766-0002*
■ Plaudits pour in for this "perfect hideaway for a romantic interlude" in Bernardsville, an "elegant country inn" with a "hunt club" setting fit for "aristocracy"; the "excellent and original" New American menu developed by celebrated chef Edward Stone is "masterfully" prepared and presented by a "gracious staff"; in sum, it's "one of the best."

### Cafe Panache      27 | 20 | 23 | $43
*130 E. Main St. (Rte. 17), Ramsey, 201-934-0030*
☑ The "Aureole of NJ" gush admirers of chef-owner Kevin Kohler's New French Ramsey "gem", a BYO with a "beautifully presented" seasonal menu that "far exceeds" its "tight", "former Long John Silver's" setting; "discreet" service rounds out the picture of one of the Most Popular spots in the *New Jersey Survey*.

### Chez Madeleine      27 | 17 | 24 | $44
*4 Bedford Ave. (Washington Ave.), Bergenfield, 201-384-7637*
■ This Classic French "jewel" just might be "Bergen County's best gastronomic experience" due to its "top-notch" "seasonal" menu, ranging from "savory" cassoulet to "fabulous" soufflés; while the "cramped" setting suggests that it's time to "expand", all is forgiven when one comes under the spell of "charming" hostess-owner Madeleine and her "terrific" staff.

### Doris & Ed's 🔲
26 | 20 | 23 | $41

*348 Shore Dr. (Waterwich Ave.), Highlands, 732-872-1565*
■ Patrons of this "unequaled" James Beard Award–winner feel like they've "died and gone to seafood heaven", especially those who indulge in the "chef's elegant signature dishes" paired with a selection from the "excellent wine list"; the "well-heeled" types who frequent this "newly redecorated" Highlands destination don't mind the "eyebrow-raising prices", but could do without the "big waits."

### Ebbitt Room, The 🔲
26 | 25 | 24 | $42

*Virginia Hotel, 25 Jackson St. (bet. Beach Dr. & Carpenter's Ln.), Cape May, 609-884-5700*
■ "An absolute delight", this "civilized", "classy" Cape May New American "delivers on expectations" with "inspired" seasonal cuisine ("the best tuna this side of Maui") and "wonderful service" amidst "Victorian elegance"; factor in Steve LaManna on piano and a postdinner respite on the porch for a "very complete evening."

### 410 Bank Street 🔲
27 | 22 | 23 | $41

*410 Bank St. (bet. Broad & Lafayette Sts.), Cape May, 609-884-2127*
■ "Every trip" to Cape May should include dinner at this "amazing" Cajun-Caribbean "treasure" where chef Henry Sing Cheng is "a magician", mixing "exotic seasonings with quixotic presentations" that make "everything on the menu wonderful"; despite "long waits" and "cramped seating", this "gussied-up Victorian house" is always a "hopping scene" – so reserve well in advance; N.B. closed mid-October–April.

### Frog and the Peach, The 🔲
26 | 23 | 23 | $47

*29 Dennis St. (Hiram Sq.), New Brunswick, 732-846-3216*
■ "Don't miss the culinary adventure" at New Brunswick's "pricey" granddaddy of New American fine dining, still the premier restaurant in town after 16 years; it's stayed that way, despite chef changes, because owners Elizabeth Alger and James Black keep it "civilized and friendly", making it the "place for first dates, first anniversaries and first impressions", where diners happily "put as much work into eating the meal as the chef does in making it."

### Harvest Moon Inn 🔲
25 | 23 | 21 | $44

*1039 Old York Rd. (Rte. 202), Ringoes, 908-806-6020*
■ Set in an 1811 Historic Register building, this "out-of-the-way" Ringoes New American with "fabulous food" offers "a multi-sensory experience" and the kind of "quiet luxury" diners desire for "special occasions"; "one of the best all-around in NJ", it's actually two restaurants in one – a "formal dining room" plus a family-style tavern with a "great bar menu" and a "good piano player" on weekends.

### Jeffrey's
28 | 21 | 25 | $37

*73 Main St. (Washington St.), Toms River, 732-914-9544*
■ Garnering the No. 1 rating for Food in the *NJ Survey*, chef-owner Jeffrey Schneekloth's New American BYO in Toms River is an "impeccable" "oasis in Ocean County's restaurant desert", a place that exudes "pride in everything served"; fans of this "unforgettable dining experience" admit it's "pricey, but worth every penny", adding "don't wait till the last minute to reserve."

### Rosemary and Sage 🅂    27 ｜ 19 ｜ 25 ｜ $41

*26 Hamburg Tpke. (I-287, exit 53), Riverdale, 973-616-0606*

■ "Like wild herbs, it sprang up where least expected" and has grown into a "fabulous" New American serving "serious food in an unserious area" of Morris County; "knowledgeable servers" present a "creative", "changing menu" and "fine selection of wine" in "simple" but "soothing" surroundings, leading surveyors to sigh "you're in for a treat."

### Ryland Inn, The 🅂    27 ｜ 27 ｜ 26 ｜ $62

*Rte. 22W (8 mi. west of Bridgewater Commons), Whitehouse, 908-534-4011*

■ Some claim there are "not enough superlatives to describe how great this place is", but others go to town describing Craig Shelton's Contemporary French in Hunterdon County, voted the *NJ Survey*'s Most Popular restaurant; the "transcendent kitchen" is enhanced by "exquisite surroundings", an "extensive wine list" and a "knowledgeable staff", though a minority maintains that the experience is "not worth" the "week's salary" prices.

### Saddle River Inn    28 ｜ 26 ｜ 26 ｜ $49

*2 Barnstable Ct. (bet. E. Allendale Ave. & W. Saddle River Rd.), Saddle River, 201-825-4016*

■ A "world-class restaurant" that "puts special back in front of occasion", this New American–French in Saddle River "never fails to impress" thanks to its "country-elegant atmosphere" and chef-owner Hans Egg's "impressive" menu; "it all comes together" here at "the best BYO" around that's "worth the tremendous effort" to get a reservation; P.S. "try the balcony for privacy."

### Sagami 🅂    27 ｜ 17 ｜ 21 ｜ $29

*37 Crescent Blvd. (bet. Collingswood Circle & Haddon Ave.), Collingswood, 856-854-9773*

■ "Don't go anywhere else" if you want "the best sushi in Jersey": this top-rated Japanese BYO in Collingswood is the equivalent of "Disney World for adult dining", thanks to chef-owner Shigeru Fukuyoshi's "meticulously prepared" fare that's so fresh the "sashimi is practically wiggling"; despite "cramped" conditions (a "tight room", "low ceilings" and "small tables"), this "champion" is "worth a weekly trip" – if you can get in.

### Scalini Fedeli    27 ｜ 26 ｜ 25 ｜ $55

*63 Main St. (Parrot Mill Rd.), Chatham, 973-701-9200*

■ "Reservations are scarcer than hen's teeth" at this "romantic" Chatham Northern Italian BYO, a "gourmet's dream" where "everything's an A-plus" – from chef-owner Michael Cetrulo's "superb food" to the "beautiful country house setting" to the "attentive" servers who treat you like "kings and queens"; it's "expensive but worth every penny."

### Serenäde Restaurant    25 ｜ 26 ｜ 25 ｜ $52

*6 Roosevelt Ave. (Main St.), Chatham, 973-701-0303*

■ "A star is born" in the form of husband-and-wife team James and Nancy Laird, who operate this "outstanding" Chatham New French with "attention to detail and an obsession with freshness" that results in "truly luxurious eating"; it's a "place for elegant celebrations", complete with an award-winning wine list and "beautiful flowers surpassed only by the taste of the food."

| | F | D | S | C |
|---|---|---|---|---|
| **Stage House Inn** [S] | 26 | 24 | 23 | $46 |

*366 Park Ave. (Front St.), Scotch Plains, 908-322-4224*

■ "You'll forget you're in the suburbs" once seated in the "elegant rooms with fireplaces" of this "beautiful, romantic" 1737 structure in Scotch Plains, the home of a Contemporary French dining destination that can "hold its own against" NYC's finer restaurants; "hats off to chef-owner David Drake" for this "NJ gem."

| | F | D | S | C |
|---|---|---|---|---|
| **Washington Inn, The** [S] | 27 | 27 | 26 | $42 |

*801 Washington St. (Jefferson St.), Cape May, 609-884-5697*

■ "Frasier and Niles" would hang out at this "historic and classy" Cape May New American if they lived on the Right Coast, for its "as-good-as-it-gets" food and service arrive in a "top-notch Victorian" setting accompanied by an "extensive wine list"; P.S. "try to have dinner in the super-romantic cellar."

| | F | D | S | C |
|---|---|---|---|---|
| **Waters Edge** [S] | 26 | 23 | 24 | $43 |

*Beach Dr. (Pittsburgh Ave.), Cape May, 609-884-1717*

■ Chef-owner Neil Elsohn's "spectacular", "inventive" New American cuisine impresses voters at this "hippest dining spot in Cape May", a "sophisticated yet casual" restaurant with oceanfront dining, "contemporary" decor and a black marble bar that's a "great meeting" place; even better, the location is "mercifully removed from the tourist crush."

# New Orleans

## TOP 20 FOOD RANKING

| Restaurant | Cuisine Type |
|---|---|
| **28** Grill Room | Eclectic |
| Peristyle | Contemporary Louisiana |
| **27** Gabrielle | Contemporary Louisiana |
| Brigtsen's | Cajun |
| Ruth's Chris | Steakhouse |
| Emeril's | Contemporary Louisiana |
| Bayona | International/New Amer. |
| Commander's Palace | Creole |
| Lafitte's Landing | Cajun/Creole |
| La Provence | French |
| Le Parvenu | Creole/New American |
| **26** Galatoire's | Classic French/Creole |
| NINJA | Japanese |
| Crozier's | Classic French |
| Young's | Steakhouse |
| Gautreau's | American/New French |
| Bistro at Maison de Ville | French Bistro |
| Kim Son | Vietnamese |
| Dakota, The | American |
| Louis XVI | French |

## OTHER IMPORTANT PLACES

| | |
|---|---|
| Antoine's | Creole/French |
| Arnaud's | Creole/French |
| Brennan's | Creole |
| Christian's | Classic French/Creole |
| Clancy's | Creole/Eclectic |
| Delmonico | Creole |
| Gerard's Downtown | French |
| Irene's Cuisine | N/S Italian |
| La Riviera | N/S Italian |
| Lemon Grass Cafe | Vietnamese |
| Metro Bistro | French Bistro |
| Mr. B's Bistro | Creole |
| Nine Roses | Vietnamese |
| Nola | Contemporary Louisiana |
| Pelican Club | Contemporary Louisiana |
| Rib Room | American/Continental |
| Upperline | Eclectic |

## Antoine's ⎣ 24 ⎦⎣ 25 ⎦⎣ 25 ⎦⎣ $44 ⎦
*713 St. Louis St. (bet. Bourbon & Royal Sts.), 504-581-4422*
☑ This "special occasion" French-Creole "grande dame" may be "past its prime" and a bit "faded", but it still has a devoted following that believes "some things never go out of style", namely "classic elegance" and "charm"; insiders say the "appetizers are fantastic" and note that having "a great waiter really helps" to enjoy this "quintessential New Orleans restaurant."

## Arnaud's 🖫 ⎣ 23 ⎦⎣ 25 ⎦⎣ 24 ⎦⎣ $41 ⎦
*813 Bienville St. (bet. Bourbon & Dauphine Sts.), 504-523-5433*
☑ "Lovely atmosphere" makes this elegant, 19th-century French Quarter classic one of "the great old New Orleans restaurants", even if opinions on the French-Creole fare range from "excellent" ("shrimp remoulade alone is worth the trip") to "average food in a beautiful restaurant"; but all agree Sunday brunch is a standout.

## Bayona ⎣ 27 ⎦⎣ 26 ⎦⎣ 25 ⎦⎣ $39 ⎦
*430 Dauphine St. (bet. Conti & St. Louis Sts.), 504-525-4455*
■ "Consistently great year after year" is the verdict on this "beautiful" French Quarter New American–International spot; chef Susan Spicer "works magic" for most diners, turning out "very creative" food that's usually "right on target", and though a few wish she would offer "more new dishes more often", most never tire of this "gem" that "continues to dazzle."

## Bistro at Maison de Ville 🖫 ⎣ 26 ⎦⎣ 24 ⎦⎣ 24 ⎦⎣ $38 ⎦
*Maison de Ville, 727 Toulouse St. (bet. Bourbon & Royal Sts.), 504-528-9206*
■ Chef Greg Picolo is following in some big footsteps at this "tiny", "charming" (a few say "cramped") French bistro, which has produced some superb New Orleans chefs, including Susan Spicer and the late John Neal; admirers say he's doing a "great" job turning out "sophisticated fare" that's served in one of the French Quarter's coziest "hidden treasures"; it's always crowded, so reservations are strongly recommended.

## Brennan's 🖫 ⎣ 25 ⎦⎣ 27 ⎦⎣ 25 ⎦⎣ $44 ⎦
*417 Royal St. (bet. Conti & St. Louis Sts.), 504-525-9711*
☑ "Still good after all these years" say admirers of this "romantic" Haute Creole French Quarter "landmark" with "the most lavish courtyard in the city"; all agree that "breakfast is spectacular" (but "expensive"), and even foes feel it has "great ambiance."

## Brigtsen's ⎣ 27 ⎦⎣ 21 ⎦⎣ 25 ⎦⎣ $35 ⎦
*723 Dante St. (bet. Maple St. & River Rd.), 504-861-7610*
■ "Wonderful food" that's "truly memorable" is what most diners find at this family-run Cajun that's ranked in New Orleans' Top Five for food and set in a "quaint house" in the Riverbend area; it can be "too crowded", but for "an exquisite meal" in an "intimate" room with "personal service", this gem is "a winner all-around" – "make reservations early."

## Christian's ⎣ 25 ⎦⎣ 24 ⎦⎣ 23 ⎦⎣ $33 ⎦
*3835 Iberville St. (S. Scott St.), 504-482-4924*
■ "Amen" exclaim converts to this Mid-City stalwart serving superb Classic French–Creole food in the "elegant ambiance" of an old converted church; "don't tell the tourists about this one" plead pros whose main complaint about this favorite is "cramped tables."

### Clancy's　　　　　　　　26 | 21 | 23 | $33
*6100 Annunciation St. (Webster St.), 504-895-1111*
■ "Clubby Uptown hangout" "away from tourists" that enjoys a "strong local following" for its "first-rate" Creole-Eclectic fare and "see and be seen" ambiance; this "diamond in the rough" may be "noisy", but it's a "classic" New Orleans neighborhood place.

### Commander's Palace ▣　　27 | 28 | 27 | $43
*1403 Washington Ave. (Coliseum St.), 504-899-8221*
■ "The pinnacle of Creole food" say the myriad fans of the Brennan family's "New Orleans classic", which perennially ranks as the city's Most Popular restaurant; set in the heart of the Garden District, it's "pricey" but provides a "rarely matched experience", complete with "beautiful rooms" and "incredible service"; don't forget the "best jazz brunch" in town on weekends.

### Crozier's　　　　　　　　26 | 21 | 23 | $34
*Petite Esplanade, 3216 W. Esplanade Ave. N. (bet. Causeway Blvd. & Severn Ave.), Metairie, 504-833-8108*
■ "Classic French cuisine" that may be the "best food in Metairie", especially the "divine steak au poivre", can be had at this "often-overlooked jewel"; nothing avant-garde here, just "authentic", well-presented fare, "unhurried" service and pleasant decor, making for dining "so wonderful you forget you're in a shopping center."

### Dakota, The　　　　　　　26 | 23 | 23 | $32
*629 N. Hwy. 190 (¼ mi. off I-12), Covington, 504-892-3712*
■ "Duck spring rolls, a great wine list and cool art" are just a few of the reasons why fans say this North Shore "class act" serving Louisiana-accented American cuisine is "well worth the 40-minute drive"; "excellent", "innovative food" (especially the "superb crab and Brie soup") and nicely appointed surroundings cause many to declare it "best of the North Shore places."

### Delmonico ▣　　　　　　　– | – | – | VE
*1300 St. Charles Ave. (Erato St.), 504-525-4937*
An instant success, Emeril Lagasse's latest venture, set in a historic building in the Lower Garden District with elegant, muted decor, is drawing crowds with 'grand Creole cuisine' featuring classic New Orleans dishes; it's very 'in', upscale and pricey, with welcome valet parking; N.B. if unable to climb stairs, request first-floor seating.

### Emeril's　　　　　　　　　27 | 22 | 25 | $43
*800 Tchoupitoulas St. (Julia St.), 504-528-9393*
■ A "must-go experience" say fans of Emeril Lagasse's "vibrant" culinary flagship in the Warehouse District; while his Contemporary Louisiana cuisine is "pricey", it's "consistently excellent" and service is "fantastic", but just as many say it may be the "noisiest place in town"; even so, it's a "special-occasion treat."

### Gabrielle　　　　　　　　27 | 21 | 25 | $36
*3201 Esplanade Ave. (bet. Broad St. & Carrollton Ave.), 504-948-6233*
■ "It may be small, but it's superb" is the consensus on this "intimate", "friendly" Contemporary Lousiana cafe with Creole accents that's ranked in the top five for food and is near the New Orleans Museum of Art; "great adaptations of local ingredients" result in "ab fab" cooking, but while many enjoy the "cozy" room, others find it "cramped" (enclosing the patio has added 20 seats).

**Galatoire's [S]** 26 24 26 $37

*209 Bourbon St. (Iberville St.), 504-525-2021*

■ "Don't ever change" plead locals who love this French Quarter "tradition"; New Orleans' No. 2 favorite restaurant, it's a "classic" French–Haute Creole serving the likes of "the best trout meunière" in "elegant", turn-of-the-century surroundings; those "in the know" say "it's the place to be" for Friday lunch; N.B. the no-reserving policy has been eased for parties of eight Tuesdays–Thursdays.

**Gautreau's** 26 23 24 $36

*1728 Soniat St. (Danneel St.), 504-899-7397*

◪ A "hidden" Uptown "neighborhood gem" serving "fine" New French–American fare in a "cozy" converted old drugstore complete with original tin ceiling; the food is "innovative" (a few say "uneven") and the atmosphere is "low-key elegant", but most agree the "acoustics are horrible."

**Gerard's Downtown** – – – E

*500 St. Charles Ave. (bet. Lafayette Park & Poydras St.), 504-592-0200*

Once the guiding light of Mr. B's Bistro, talented Gerard Maras has returned to NO to anchor the inviting dining room at the CBD's recently opened Parc St. Charles Hotel; the French-influenced menu includes the likes of lobster ravioli.

**Grill Room, The [S]** 28 29 27 $50

*Windsor Court Hotel, 300 Gravier St. (bet. S. Peters & Tchoupitoulas Sts.), 504-522-1992*

■ "Tops in all categories" rave surveyors who rate this "superior" Eclectic in the posh Windsor Court Hotel No. 1 for Food, Decor and Service in New Orleans; it offers the city's "swankiest gourmet experience", complete with "superb"cuisine, "excellent" staff and "impeccable surroundings."

**Irene's Cuisine [S]** 25 21 22 $29

*539 St. Philip St. (Chartres St.), 504-529-8811*

■ "Long waits" and no reserving are "a turnoff" for some, but a "cozy" interior welcomes those who finally get inside this "find" serving "true Italian" food (plus some Gallic dishes) in a "romantic" Quarter setting; "Irene's rosemary chicken is the best" and prices are "affordable" – no wonder "word has spread."

**Kim Son** 26 15 20 $17

*349 Whitney Ave. (W. Bank Expy.), Gretna, 504-366-2489*

■ The somewhat spartan decor is nothing to brag about at this West Bank Vietnamese, but who cares given moderate prices for such "fantastic", "imaginative" food as "subtle" clay pot meals and "great" salt-baked seafood to "make your taste buds dance"; no question, it's so "delicious and cheap that it's habit-forming."

**Lafitte's Landing [S]** 27 24 23 $33

*Bittersweet Plantation, 404 Claiborne Ave. (Railroad Ave.), Donaldsonville, 225-473-1232*

■ "Wonderful local cuisine" based on classic Cajun-Creole recipes with French flair describes the food at this elegant plantation house, called "a must" by admirers of chef John Folse and his "beautiful presentations"; all agree "it's well worth the [one-hour] drive" from the French Quarter, and if you're looking for the perfect end to a day of plantation touring, "this is it"; N.B. it's brunch only on Sundays.

---

**La Provence [S]** 27 | 26 | 24 | $40

*25020 Hwy. 190 E. (bet. Lacombe & Mandeville), Big Branch, 504-626-7662*

■ For "luxurious food in a cozy provincial setting" nothing beats this North Shore country French inn, which is a 40-minute drive across Lake Pontchartrain; "chef Chris [Kerageorgiou] keeps going and going and his food is fabulous", making for a "superb" experience, especially in winter by the fireplace.

**La Riviera** 24 | 20 | 22 | $30

*4506 Shores Dr. (bet. N. Clearview Pkwy. & W. Esplanade Ave.), Metairie, 504-888-6238*

■ Fans extol "the best" fried calamari and osso buco in town plus "excellent veal and fish dishes" at this Metairie Italian "that's still good after many years"; it may be "loud", but "the crabmeat ravioli is worth the trip alone."

**Lemon Grass Cafe [S]** 23 | 16 | 20 | $23

*Int'l House Hotel, 217 Camp St. (bet. Common & Gravier Sts.), 504-523-1200*

*216 N. Carrollton Ave. (bet. Bienville & Canal Sts.), 504-488-8335*

◪ A new location in a very smart CBD "boutique" hotel has upscale minimalist decor quite different from that of the simpler Mid-City venue; both offer "superb, nouvelle Vietnamese" that's a "little expensive" but "always wonderful."

**Le Parvenu [S]** 27 | 23 | 24 | $29

*509 Williams Blvd. (bet. Airline Hwy. & Jefferson Ave.), Kenner, 504-471-0534*

◪ Upscale decor in a "charming" house along with American-Creole fare that's "delicious" and "different" explain why fans applaud this "outstanding" yearling in Kenner; while the folks in the 'burbs are lavish in their praise of this "delightful" addition, some are not so kind about the staff, citing service that's "too laid-back" or just plain "slow."

**Louis XVI [S]** 26 | 26 | 25 | $49

*St. Louis Hotel, 730 Bienville St. (bet. Bourbon & Royal Sts.), 504-581-7000*

◪ This "impressive" Quarter "classic" serves "real" French cuisine that's "elegant and refined" amidst "gorgeous surroundings"; though faulted by some for being "very expensive" with "waiters who hover too much", it remains a "special-occasion" rendezvous.

**Metro Bistro [S]** – | – | – | VE

*200 Magazine St. (Common St.), 504-529-1900*

The latest venture from the folks at Charley G's, this good-looking urban chic CBD French bistro is turning out highly touted fare from steamed mussels to duck cassoulet; a totally redesigned interior (it was formerly Graham's) has made it more comfortable and quieter, so it's already a big hit with the Downtown crowd.

**Mr. B's Bistro [S]** 25 | 24 | 24 | $31

*201 Royal St. (bet. Bienville & Iberville Sts.), 504-523-2078*

■ "Superb food in the Brennan family tradition" is what you can expect at this "popular" Haute Creole run by Ralph Brennan and sister Cindy of the Commander's Palace Brennans; "one of the best" rendezvous in the Quarter, it's always "crowded", with good reason – i.e. "top-quality", "creative" food ("gumbo ya-ya is a must"), "service supreme" and a "vibrant, casual" ambiance.

## Nine Roses ☒                    25 | 17 | 20 | $15

*1100 Stephen St. (Stumpf Blvd.), Gretna, 504-366-7665*

■ "Memorable" and "terrific" typify the glowing comments about this West Bank Vietnamese; it's an affordable, neat, white-tablecloth place that's "wonderful for families" and a "great discovery" for fans of Asian cooking who say it transports them "back to old Saigon."

## NINJA                           26 | 14 | 19 | $19

*8115 Jeanette St. (S. Carrollton Ave.), 504-866-1119*

☒ Even those who say this Carrollton Japanese has "the best sushi in town" admit that it's a "bit slow"; it's also low on decor, but this tiny, converted house is staffed by "friendly people" and offers a wide variety of affordable dishes and "very good" box sushi.

## NOLA ☒                          25 | 23 | 23 | $34

*534 Rue St. Louis St. (bet. Chartres & Decatur Sts.), 504-522-6652*

■ Trendy celeb chef Emeril Lagasse's "casual" Quarter "in-spot" earns high marks for its "innovative, excellent" Contemporary Louisiana cuisine, good service and "with-it atmosphere"; "noisy" and "crowded", it may not be relaxing, but it's a "feel-good place" and "more user-friendly" than Emeril's pricier flagship.

## Pelican Club ☒                  25 | 24 | 23 | $37

*312 Exchange Alley (Bienville St.), 504-523-1504*

☒ A "best-kept secret" hidden in a tiny French Quarter alley presenting "excellent" Contemporary Louisiana dishes with "Asian touches"; the "comfortable" setting may be plagued by "bad acoustics", but most find it a "happy" experience even if it's a bit "overpriced."

## Peristyle                       28 | 23 | 25 | $36

*1041 Dumaine St. (bet. Burgundy & N. Rampart Sts.), 504-593-9535*

■ Raves abound for this French Quarter "jewel", a "tiny but exquisite" Contemporary Louisiana spot rated No. 2 for Food in New Orleans; "wonderful, innovative" and "fit for the gods" typify praise for chef-owner Anne Kearney's "exciting" fare; N.B. a fire has temporarily closed the restaurant, which is scheduled to reopen in spring 2000.

## Rib Room ☒                      25 | 25 | 23 | $37

*Omni Royal Orleans Hotel, 621 St. Louis St. (bet. Chartres & Royal Sts.), 504-529-7046*

■ An "elegant" Quarter American-Continental that's been "a winner for years", serving the likes of "excellent prime rib" and the "best crab bisque on earth"; "clubby" and "consistent", it's a "power lunch place" providing some of the "best people-watching."

## Ruth's Chris Steak House ☒      27 | 21 | 25 | $39

*711 N. Broad St. (Orleans Ave.), 504-486-0810*
*3633 Veterans Memorial Blvd. (Causeway Blvd.), Metairie, 504-888-3600*

■ "Incomparable", "consistently great", "fantastic" – and so the praise goes for the "institution" that launched the nationwide steakhouse chain and is rated in the top five for Food in New Orleans; its trademark is mouthwatering meat "sizzling" in butter plus divine sides such as creamed spinach; the Broad Street original is a real power scene, especially at Friday lunch when it's a "politico heaven."

**Upperline** [S] 24 | 22 | 23 | $32

*1413 Upperline St. (bet. Prytania St. & St. Charles Ave.), 504-891-9822*

■ At this "consistently good" Uptown "neighborhood" Eclectic, "a bohemian interpretation of Cajun-Creole food served with wit and style" awaits diners; "great food, great artwork, great service" and "moderately elegant" decor add up to a "very comfortable", "always enjoyable" experience; all agree that owner JoAnn Clevenger is the "best hostess in town."

**Young's** 26 | 16 | 19 | $24

*850 Robert Blvd. (Gause Blvd.), Slidell, 504-643-9331*

◪ "Spectacular steaks with all the trimmings" can be yours at this simple North Shore steakhouse, *if* you can find it – there's still no sign outside; the fish is terrific too, and while there's not much charm in the setting, it's neat, clean and inexpensive, a winning combination that brings in crowds; be prepared for a "long wait."

# New York City

## TOP 20 FOOD RANKING

| | Restaurant | Cuisine Type |
|---|---|---|
| **28** | Le Bernardin | New French/Seafood |
| | Daniel | Classic French |
| | Peter Luger | Steakhouse |
| | Nobu | Japanese |
| | Chanterelle | New French |
| | Jean Georges | New French |
| | Aureole | New American |
| **27** | Lespinasse | New French |
| | La Grenouille | Classic French |
| | Nobu, Next Door | Japanese |
| | Il Mulino | Northern Italian |
| | Union Square Cafe | New American |
| | Gotham Bar & Grill | New American |
| | Gramercy Tavern | New American |
| | Café Boulud | Classic French/Eclectic |
| | La Côte Basque | Classic French |
| | Tomoe Sushi | Japanese |
| | Montrachet | French Bistro |
| | Oceana | Seafood |
| **26** | Four Seasons | Continental |

## OTHER IMPORTANT PLACES

| | |
|---|---|
| Aquavit | Scandinavian |
| Babbo | N/S Italian |
| Bouley Bakery | New French |
| Café des Artistes | Classic French |
| Carnegie Deli | Deli |
| Cello | New French/Seafood |
| Eleven Madison Park | New American |
| La Caravelle | Classic French |
| Le Cirque 2000 | Classic French |
| Lutèce | New French |
| Manhattan Ocean Club | Seafood |
| March | New American |
| Mercer Kitchen | New Amer./New French |
| Milos, Estiatorio | Greek/Seafood |
| Oyster Bar | Seafood |
| Palm | Steakhouse |
| Park Avenue Cafe | New American |
| Periyali | Greek |
| Picholine | Mediterranean |
| Rao's | Southern Italian |
| River Cafe | New American |
| Russian Tea Room | Russian |
| Shun Lee Palace | Chinese |
| Smith & Wollensky | Steakhouse |
| Sushisay | Japanese |
| Sylvia's | Soul Food/Southern |
| Tabla | New American |
| Tavern on the Green | New American |
| '21' Club | Traditional American |
| Union Pacific | New American |
| Veritas | New American |
| Windows on the World | New American |

**Aquavit [S]** 25 25 24 $55

*13 W. 54th St. (bet. 5th & 6th Aves.), 212-307-7311*

■ Chef Marcus Samuelsson "makes magic" at this Midtown "Scandinavian paradise" where the "exquisite" fare is as "pure" as the "dramatic" atrium space with a "mesmerizing waterfall"; it's not cheap ($64 prix fixe dinner), but the upstairs cafe is a "great deal."

**Aureole** 28 26 26 $68

*34 E. 61st St. (bet. Madison & Park Aves.), 212-319-1660*

■ "Deserves its halo" say devotees of Charles Palmer's East Side paragon that's "still one of the tops", offering "wondrous", albeit pricey, New American food (rated No. 1 for that cuisine in NYC), architectural desserts worthy of "MoMA" and a duplex townhouse that's even lovelier after a post-*NYC Survey* redo by Adam Tihany; if some find it "a bit crowded" and "stuffy", far more call it a "dining dream", especially the prix fixe lunch; dinner is $69 prix fixe only.

**Babbo ◐[S]** 26 23 24 $56

*110 Waverly Pl. (bet. MacDougal St. & 6th Ave.), 212-777-0303*

■ "An instant hit for good reason", this Village Italian owned by Joe Bastianich (Becco, Frico Bar) and chef Mario Batali (Pó) was voted the most popular newcomer in this year's *NYC Survey*; "absolutely delicious, inventive cuisine", "perfectly choreographed service" and a "beautiful" bi-level setting give rise to only one complaint – "too bad it's hard to get a table."

**Bouley Bakery ◐[S]** 26 21 23 $55

*120 W. Broadway (Duane St.), 212-964-2525*

■ "It's not the original, but what is?" note fans of David Bouley's nonetheless "extraordinary", elegantly "casual" (and recently expanded) TriBeCa bakery/restaurant with "wonderful breads baked on premises", "delightful" New French fare and what most call "impeccable" service; of course it's "pricey", but fans call Bouley "the Houdini of food since everything he cooks is magical."

**Café Boulud [S]** 27 22 25 $63

*Surrey Hotel, 20 E. 76th St. (bet. 5th & Madison Aves.), 212-772-2600*

■ "Any place associated with chef Daniel Boulud has to be great, and it is" say devotees of this "low-key", modern Upper East Side cafe, whose "minimalist" French-Eclectic fare inspires "bravos" from "food groupies"; it's pricey, with "cheek-by-jowl" seating, but most would "love to eat like this all the time."

**Café des Artistes ◐[S]** 24 27 23 $55

*1 W. 67th St. (bet. Columbus Ave. & CPW), 212-877-3500*

■ Like dining "in a Valentine's card", George and Jenifer Lang's "romantic" "classic" near Lincoln Center makes diners "feel like they're in an opera before going to one" with its "lush", "nymph-filled" setting; even if the French food "weren't so good, you'd still have to love" this "top choice" for celebrations and proposals.

**Carnegie Deli ◐[S]⊘** 20 9 12 $22

*854 Seventh Ave. (55th St.), 212-757-2245*

◪ At this renowned Midtown deli "institution", it's part of the shtick to "jostle tourists, fight with waiters" and enjoy super "sandwiches so big, you need Mick Jagger's mouth to eat them"; plan on primo pastrami, cheesecake and other "cholesterol" classics at this Woody Allen–style "only in NY" experience.

## Cello ▤

_53 E. 77th St. (bet. Madison & Park Aves.), 212-517-1200_

| – | – | – | VE |

Had this handsome East Side French seafooder-cum-garden been open at the time of our _NYC Survey_, it might well have rated as the city's best newcomer of 1999; as it is, well-heeled locals have kept it packed since opening day, so despite top-of-the-line prices, it's already one of the toughest tickets in town.

## Chanterelle

_2 Harrison St. (Hudson St.), 212-966-6960_

| 28 | 26 | 27 | VE |

■ "Sheer perfection", "angels feast on lesser food" is how the accolades flow for Karen and David Waltuck's "serene", now 20-year-old TriBeCa New French, where "every dish shows the creative mind behind it", the decor exudes "understated elegance" and service is "seamless" and welcoming "whether you come" for the "top value" prix fixe lunch ($35) or a blowout dinner ($75 prix fixe only); in sum, "one of NYC's very best."

## Daniel ◑

_60 E. 65th St. (bet. Madison & Park Aves.), 212-288-0033_

| 28 | 26 | 26 | $75 |

■ "Heavenly as is Daniel [Boulud] does" sigh the many bec fins who find his "formal" Classic French "as great as ever" in its "spacious" new East Side home; acclaimed for his "creative perfection", this master chef's "superb" food (ranked No. 2 in NYC) gets "better all the time" and is backed up by "service with finesse" and newly softened decor, making this a place to celebrate "life's special moments"; just be sure to book "months ahead" and save up in the interim, or try the bar, with a less pricey à la carte menu and same-day reserving.

## Eleven Madison Park ▤

_11 Madison Ave. (24th St.), 212-889-0905_

| 25 | 25 | 25 | $58 |

■ "Danny Meyer strikes again" with this Madison Square Park "evocation of a bygone" era set in a "gorgeous" art deco space with "soaring ceilings"; most find chef Kerry Heffernan's New American fare equally "memorable", ditto Meyer's signature "superb" service, and if a few critics feel its early performance "falls a bit short", that's probably due to the "high expectations" his name inspires.

## Four Seasons

_99 E. 52nd St. (bet. Lexington & Park Aves.), 212-754-9494_

| 26 | 27 | 26 | $67 |

■ "For all seasons" and all reasons, from the definitive "power lunch" in the Grill Room to celebrations in the "glorious" Pool Room, this "peerless" NY "classic" has "set the standard" for over 40 years with its "exceptional" Continental cuisine, "superb" service and Philip Johnson's "landmark" design; if you hesitate to blow your "child's college tuition" here, try the Grill Room's $59 prix fixe dinner.

## Gotham Bar & Grill ▤

_12 E. 12th St. (bet. 5th Ave. & University Pl.), 212-620-4020_

| 27 | 25 | 25 | $57 |

■ Still "at the top of its game", this Village New American retains all the pluses that have made it a perennial Most Popular contender (No. 3 in NYC this year): Alfred Portale's "towering", "pure genius" cuisine, "tack-sharp service", a "beautiful" room and "glamorous crowd"; what's more, the $20 prix fixe lunch and special wine deal put this "rarefied" Gotham glory within everyone's reach.

**Gramercy Tavern** [S] 27 | 26 | 26 | $60

*42 E. 20th St. (bet. B'way & Park Ave. S.), 212-477-0777*

■ "All the senses come alive" at Danny Meyer's masterpiece of "friendly elegance" (NYC's No. 2 for Popularity), which "opened big and has lasted" as a "star" of Flatiron/Gramercy; Tom Colicchio's food is "the essence of first-rate American" cuisine and finds a "perfect" home in the smartly "rustic" setting staffed by "gracious" pros; not surprisingly, all this care is costly ($62 prix fixe dinner), but "each meal is a new high" and the casual front tavern is "a steal" that doesn't require reserving.

**Il Mulino** ◐ 27 | 19 | 23 | $60

*86 W. Third St. (bet. Sullivan & Thompson Sts.), 212-673-3783*

■ Perennially NYC's No. 1 Italian, this "lively garlic madhouse" in the Village piles on a lot of "delicious", "filling" food and almost too-"friendly" service; it's a "formidable" feast that "overshadows the noise, crowds and waits" ("even with a reservation") and is "worth every penny"; for a more leisurely meal, try lunch.

**Jean Georges** [S] 28 | 26 | 27 | $78

*Trump Int'l Hotel, 1 Central Park West (bet. 60th & 61st Sts.), 212-299-3900*

■ This "world-class" "dazzler" off Columbus Circle proffers chef Jean-Georges Vongerichten's "brilliantly" executed New French cuisine in an "elegant, contemporary setting" made all the more "comfortable" by an "impeccable" staff that pays "attention to all details"; you may need to "arrange financing" (dinner is $85 prix fixe), but most feel it's still a "small price to pay to know that for a few hours, life will be perfect"; the less formal front room, Nougatine, is more affordable and there's an outdoor terrace in summer.

**La Caravelle** 26 | 25 | 25 | $66

*Shoreham Hotel, 33 W. 55th St. (bet. 5th & 6th Aves.), 212-586-4252*

■ NYers have had "over 30 years of wonderful meals" at André and Rita Jammet's Midtown French grande dame; offering Cyril Renaud's "superb" food in an "elegant" room, it's that rare "formal" restaurant that extends "warm" "VIP" service to all, making it one of the city's "most civilized places to eat"; prix fixe only: dinner $68, lunch $38.

**La Côte Basque** [S] 27 | 26 | 26 | $67

*60 W. 55th St. (bet. 5th & 6th Aves.), 212-688-6525*

■ "Traditional French at its best" sums up this renowned Midtown "beauty" whose murals "transport you" to the Basque coast while Jean-Jacques Rachou's "superior" cuisine and accompanying "silken" service recall haute dining as it "used to be"; if "a bit stuffy", most say "don't change a thing", surely not the "bargain" $35 lunch; dinner is $63 prix fixe.

**La Grenouille** ◐ 27 | 27 | 26 | VE

*3 E. 52nd St. (bet. 5th & Madison Aves.), 212-752-1495*

■ For elegant "big-deal" dining, few places match the Masson family's Midtown Classic French "showstopper", where one "sits among kings" and other VIPs enjoying "top-of-the-line" food and service in a flower-filled setting that's "what Paris wishes it looked like in the spring"; it's prix fixe and pricey ($45 lunch, $90 dinner), but it "doesn't get much better" and the upstairs private room is one of NY's secret treasures.

**Le Bernardin ◐** 28 | 27 | 28 | $75

*155 W. 51st St. (bet. 6th & 7th Aves.), 212-489-1515*

■ The pinnacle of "piscatory perfection", Maguy LeCoze's French seafood stunner nets NYC's Top Food and Top Service honors this year, making it the city's overall "king of the sea"; it's "expensive" (prix fixe only: $43 lunch, $75 dinner), but with chef Eric Ripert's works of "genius", a "soothingly elegant" Midtown setting and "polished" service, it's leagues above most and a sure bet when you "need to impress", business-wise or otherwise.

**Le Cirque 2000 [S]** 26 | 26 | 25 | $74

*NY Palace Hotel, 455 Madison Ave. (bet. 50th & 51st Sts.), 212-303-7788*

◪ It's not like "the old days", but this "Y2K-ready" version of Sirio Maccioni's NY legend, now in Midtown's Villard Houses, is still a "spectacle", with Sottha Khunn's "terrific" French food, Jacques Torres' superb desserts, Adam Tihany's must-see, if not must-like, "elegantly trippy" decor and, as always, electric people-watching; even given "attitude", "uneven" meals, high costs and "tourists", this "big top" is the town's best "show."

**Lespinasse** 27 | 28 | 27 | $81

*St. Regis Hotel, 2 E. 55th St. (bet. 5th & Madison Aves.), 212-339-6719*

■ Though Gray Kunz is "missed", his talented successor, Christian Delouvrier, is "hardly a letdown" and this "gorgeous" Midtown French (No. 1 for Decor in NY) remains a "sumptuous", "spacious" setting for "phenomenal meals" with "service fit for royalty" – "they do everything for you" in what can only be described as an "awesome" "indulgence", and $10,000 later you go home.

**Lutèce** 26 | 25 | 26 | $70

*249 E. 50th St. (bet. 2nd & 3rd Aves.), 212-752-2225*

■ While memories of the André Soltner glory years at this "elegant" East Midtown haute French duplex townhouse will never fade, this "old champ" "still shines" under another outstanding chef, Eberhard Mueller, who is leading it into the new millennium in "his own style", producing "sublime" food (largely grown at his wife's farm) served by an "outstanding" staff; it's "dining at its luxurious, unpretentious best", and well worth the prix fixe tabs (lunch $38, dinner $65).

**Manhattan Ocean Club ◐[S]** 25 | 22 | 23 | $56

*57 W. 58th St. (bet. 5th & 6th Aves.), 212-371-7777*

■ "Fish doesn't come any better" than at this Midtown seafooder that's "tops in its class" with "not a bad dish in the place" and a "quiet, understated beauty" in the "great NY tradition of power dining"; it's like flying first class – "you get what you pay for."

**March [S]** 26 | 25 | 26 | $73

*405 E. 58th St. (bet. 1st Ave. & Sutton Pl.), 212-754-6272*

■ "Go in like a lion and come out like a lamb" at this "memorable" Sutton Place New American, an "ultraromantic" "charmer" in an "intimate townhouse" complete with a "lovely garden"; "ace" chef Wayne Nish creates a "phenomenal" small-dish, prix fixe menu ($68 dinner) with "a revelation in every mouthful", abetted by a "brilliant sommelier" and "flawless service"; "if you can afford it – go!"

## Mercer Kitchen, The ●ⓈＳ

23 | 23 | 19 | $50

*Mercer Hotel, 99 Prince St. (Mercer St.), 212-966-5454*

☑ "Everything you've heard is true" about this "nearly perfect" American-Provençal in the Mercer Hotel basement that "outshines everything else in SoHo"; "Jean-Georges Vongerichten doesn't let up" with an "unbelievable, innovative" menu that's presented to a "very hot crowd" either at "communal tables" or in the "architecturally pleasing" main room; the only drawbacks: "no windows", "wild food-swings", "sticker shock."

## Milos, Estiatorio ●ⓈＳ

26 | 24 | 22 | $61

*125 W. 55th St. (bet. 6th & 7th Aves.), 212-245-7400*

■ "Sleek" surroundings set the "chic" tone at this high-ceilinged Midtowner, the *NYC Survey*'s top-rated Greek and a "beautiful temple" to all things piscatory, with "fish so fresh they almost bite back at you"; but the "staggering" per-pound pricing leads some to suggest you "stick to the wonderful appetizers to stay solvent."

## Montrachet

27 | 21 | 24 | $61

*239 W. Broadway (bet. Walker & White Sts.), 212-219-2777*

■ "Glorious eating", a "wine list to make your head spin" and "attentive service" make some ask "does it get any better?" than Drew Nieporent's "essential" TriBeCa French bistro; while a few feel the "decor needs an overhaul", most tout this "masterpiece" as simply "the top" (especially Friday's "great buy" prix fixe lunch).

## Nobu Ｓ

28 | 24 | 24 | $63

*105 Hudson St. (Franklin St.), 212-219-0500*

■ Nobu Matsuhisa's TriBeCa Japanese, "like a shiatsu massage of the tongue", inspires "sheer bliss" among its bicoastal, "star-studded" clientele, offering "sushi at its finest" and other unique Japanese-Peruvian fare presented amid delightful David Rockwell–designed decor; however, this brand of "culinary perfection" "ain't cheap" and "you can make a career of getting a dinner reservation" – fortunately, it's easier to get a table for lunch.

## Nobu, Next Door ●

27 | 23 | 23 | $54

*105 Hudson St. (Franklin St.), 212-334-4445*

■ Rated as this year's No. 1 NYC newcomer and more than just a replica of its renowned next-door neighbor, this TriBeCa standout delivers some of the "best Japanese in town", perfecting the "art of sushi" and soba in a bamboo-bedecked room; it's "less of a scene" and the "no-reservations policy" for parties under five promises access to "ordinary people" – "finally, a table!"

## Oceana

27 | 24 | 25 | $61

*55 E. 54th St. (bet. Madison & Park Aves.), 212-759-5941*

■ "Exceptional" seafood is "done to perfection" at this marvelous Midtowner with "glitzy" "luxury-liner" decor and silky-smooth service; fish fanciers consider it "transcendent" eating that's "worth every penny" (prix fixe only, $42 lunch, $65 dinner).

## Oyster Bar

22 | 17 | 16 | $40

*Grand Central, lower level (42nd St. & Vanderbilt Ave.), 212-490-6650*

■ An undisputed "NY classic", this "cavernous", "noisy" Grand Central seafooder serves "fine fish with flourish" from a menu with "more choices than at a Greek diner", but the serious shucking at the "top raw bar" is where the real action is.

F | D | S | C

**Palm** ◐[S] — 25 | 16 | 19 | $54

*837 Second Ave. (bet. 44th & 45th Sts.), 212-687-2953*

**Palm Too** [S]

*840 Second Ave. (bet. 44th & 45th Sts.), 212-697-5198*

**Palm West** [S]

*250 W. 50th St. (bet. B'way & 8th Ave.), 212-333-7256*

◪ Now a trio, these Midtown cow palaces are "nothing fancy", but their fab "football-sized filets" and marvelous "monster" lobsters keep the he-men coming; caricature-covered walls, "curmudgeonly waiters" and "NY attitude" please the regulars, but a few outsiders find the "sawdust-caked" look and "macho" mentality "very dated."

**Park Avenue Cafe** [S] — 24 | 23 | 22 | $55

*100 E. 63rd St. (bet. Lexington & Park Aves.), 212-644-1900*

■ "David Burke is a magician" who conjures up an "incredible" "blend of tradition and modernism" at this East Side New American whose "delicious" cooking is matched by "first-rate" service and an attractive "Americana"-oriented setting; from the "yummy bread basket" to the "stunning desserts", the "svelte patrons dive in" "with zest"; P.S. a "special table in the kitchen" offers a unique perspective.

**Periyali** — 25 | 21 | 23 | $49

*35 W. 20th St. (bet. 5th & 6th Aves.), 212-463-7890*

■ "What Odysseus was surely looking for", this "chic Greek" "pacesetter" offers an "elegant and delicious" "taste of Athens" in the Flatiron area; it wins a chorus of kudos for its "spectacular seafood", "attentive service" and "understated" room, but be advised this is not the place to start breaking plates.

**Peter Luger Steak House** [S]⊄ — 28 | 15 | 19 | $55

*178 Broadway (Driggs Ave.), Brooklyn, 718-387-7400*

■ For the 16th year running, surveyors have voted this Williamsburg heavyweight NY's No. 1 steakhouse – we may have to retire the title – praising its "porterhouse perfection"; beef-eaters brave the "not-so-great" macho service, German "beer-hall atmosphere" and "cash-only" policy in exchange for "amazing meat" "sizzling in butter" and the full pantheon of sides and rich desserts, fully expecting "paramedics to bring the check."

**Picholine** ◐[S] — 26 | 23 | 24 | $61

*35 W. 64th St. (bet. B'way & CPW), 212-724-8585*

■ Proving that "there is life on the West Side", this "inspired" "showstopper" courtesy of chef-owner Terrance Brennan is the city's top-rated Mediterranean and "far and away the best near Lincoln Center"; besides Brennan's sensational cooking, which inches up in our ratings each year, highlights include NYC's best cheese cart, "unobtrusive" service and a "bargain" prix fixe lunch.

**Rao's** ⊄ — 24 | 17 | 22 | $53

*455 E. 114th St. (Pleasant Ave.), 212-722-6709*

■ "A unique ambiance" (think "*Goodfellas* video"), "guaranteed" celebrity sightings and "lots" of very good Southern Italian food await at this amazing "East Harlem landmark" – that is, "if you can get a reservation" before the year 3000 (if you know owner Frank Pellegrino, maybe he can do something for you); parking is no problem, the bodyguards out front will watch your car.

## River Cafe ●🄂
24 | 27 | 23 | VE

*1 Water St. (Brooklyn Bridge), Brooklyn, 718-522-5200*
■ The "breathtaking" Downtown NYC skyline view from this "romantic" East River barge restaurant lures the most jaded Manhattanites to Brooklyn, where a "star-studded" ambiance, "excellent" American food and a "soft", gilt-edged "formality" enhance the "magical" setting; "I fell in love that night – with NY"; dinner is $70 prix fixe only.

## Russian Tea Room ●🄂
– | – | – | E

*150 W. 57th St. (bet. 6th & 7th Aves.), 212-974-2111*
With Tavern on the Green's showman owner Warner LeRoy at the helm, it's no surprise that the newly rebuilt four-level Russian Tea Room – opened in 1927 by Russian émigré ballet stars and for decades a glittering nexus for NY's theatrical and literary sets – is an eye-popping extravaganza, with such touches as the old Maxwell's Plum ceiling and a 16-foot-high crystal bear filled with live fish; RTR has just about everyone in NY, not just foodies, waiting to partake of its vodka, caviar and blini.

## Shun Lee Palace ●🄍🄂
24 | 22 | 22 | $46

*155 E. 55th St. (bet. Lexington & 3rd Aves.), 212-371-8844*
■ "Chinese reaches a new level" at Michael Tong's "classy" East Midtown flagship; it costs more than the norm, but is "fit for an emperor" with "superb" food, "elegant" Adam Tihany decor and "formal" service from waiters who "know what you like" better than you do – so take their advice and enjoy NY's "best luxe Chinese."

## Smith & Wollensky ●🄂
23 | 17 | 20 | $53

*797 Third Ave. (49th St.), 212-753-1530*
■ In just over 20 years, this East Midtown duplex has become entrenched as a "classic NY steakhouse" with all the genre's best attributes – "melt-in-your-mouth" steaks, "sublime" wines, a "manly" ambiance and "Armani suit" crowd, plus "deafening" noise and studiously "tough waiters"; now it's branched out to other cities with equal success.

## Sushisay
26 | 18 | 21 | $48

*38 E. 51st St. (bet. Madison & Park Aves.), 212-755-1780*
■ "Clean, spare, traditional" in appearance and "incredibly well-run", this "very authentic" Nipponese's "fresh, perfectly seasoned and prepared" sushi and sashimi bring "Ginza taste, and also prices", to Midtown's "best" Japanese business lunch; "you're in capable hands", so go ahead and "indulge."

## Sylvia's 🄂
19 | 13 | 17 | $28

*328 Lenox Ave. (bet. 126th & 127th Sts.), 212-996-0660*
■ A justly celebrated Harlem institution whose "sink to the bottom of your belly Soul Food", rich desserts, "warm energy" and live music, all at low tabs, keep it "mobbed with tourists", "famous people" and jazz buffs; the "gospel choir" brunch is a real experience.

## Tabla 🅂                                26 | 26 | 25 | $58
*11 Madison Ave. (25th St.), 212-889-0667*
■ Another Danny Meyer "grand slam", this new Indian-spiced American on Madison Square Park became an instant hit thanks to chef Floyd Cardoz's "exciting" food, an "exotic", stylish duplex setting and "super" service; if a few cite "weird" combos, the vast majority says "everything works" and "the hype", and cost ($52 prix fixe dinner, except at the Bread Bar downstairs), are "justified."

## Tavern on the Green 🅂                 17 | 25 | 18 | $51
*Central Park West (bet. 66th & 67th Sts.), 212-873-3200*
🅉 A "must-see" "NYC extravaganza", Warner LeRoy's world-famous Central Park "fairyland" with its "glitz and glitter" decor is "magical" at any time, but even more so "when snow falls" or outdoors in summer; its American food can be quite good if kept simple and has never stopped it from drawing tourists and not a few Gothamites who admit it's "a hell of a show" and one of NYC's best party sites; P.S. check out the early-bird prix fixe.

## Tomoe Sushi                           27 | 9 | 15 | $32
*172 Thompson St. (bet. Bleecker & Houston Sts.), 212-777-9346*
🅉 "Heaven on rice", "an orgasm in your mouth" are how surveyors describe the sensational sushi that draws "masses" to this "zero" ambiance Village Japanese; it would be "a bargain at twice the price."

## '21' Club                             22 | 23 | 22 | $57
*21 W. 52nd St. (bet. 5th & 6th Aves.), 212-582-7200*
■ "As old school as you can get" and proud of it, this Midtown "icon" remains a "total power place", offering "class, style and history" plus American fare that's "excellent" and still "getting better" under chef Erik Blauberg; even the likes of burgers and chicken hash come at "high-end prices" here, but that also buys you some of the world's most expert "coddling" and most intriguing surroundings, including the extraordinary wine cellar and handsome rooms for private parties.

## Union Pacific                         25 | 25 | 24 | $65
*111 E. 22nd St. (bet. Lexington Ave. & Park Ave. S.), 212-995-8500*
■ In a "gorgeous", "serene" Gramercy setting with a "mesmerizing waterfall", Rocco DiSpirito's "supremely creative" and "beautifully presented" New American cuisine "takes risks and delivers", backed up by "excellent service" and "extraordinary wines"; if a few find the food and prices "a little far out", far more say "all aboard" for "truly exciting" dining; dinner is $65 prix fixe only.

## Union Square Cafe 🅂                   27 | 24 | 26 | $55
*21 E. 16th St. (bet. 5th Ave. & Union Sq. W.), 212-243-4020*
■ "Danny Meyer's masterpiece" and New York's Most Popular restaurant for four years running, this New American remains "unsurpassed" as a "fully satisfying dining experience" because its "formula works": offer "fabulous food" (from Michael Romano) in a "relaxed" yet "classy" space with "gold standard" service for less than your competition; "if you can get in", odds are it will "steal your heart."

F | D | S | C

## Veritas S
25 | 23 | 25 | $67

*43 E. 20th St. (bet. B'way & Park Ave. S.), 212-353-3700*
■ "In truth, a stunner": Scott Bryan and Gino Diaferia's Flatiron New American is certainly a contender for NYC rookie of the year; it's not only an oenophile's "paradise" with a "phenomenal" cellar ("not a list, it's a novel"), but the food also "dazzles" and is "graciously served" in an "intimate", "elegant" room; however, with dinner at a prix fixe $62 sans wine, this "wow" can easily turn into an "ouch!"

## Windows on the World S
21 | 27 | 22 | $57

*1 World Trade Ctr., 107th fl. (West St., bet. Liberty & Vesey Sts.), 212-524-7000*
◪ "Just looking out the window" makes this huge, 107th-floor New American a "wow"; maybe it won't "take your breath away" like the view, but Michael Lomonaco's cooking has "really made a difference" with "much-improved" food that "rounds out a great evening" including fine wines and "gracious" service; N.B. the pre-theater prix fixe helps keep costs earthbound at this must for out-of-town visitors.

# Orange County

## TOP 10 FOOD RANKING

| Restaurant | Cuisine Type |
|---|---|
| **28** Pascal | French |
| **27** Troquet | New French |
| Ramos House Cafe | New American |
| Gustaf Anders | Continental/Swedish |
| Ritz, The | Continental |
| **26** Ritz-Carlton Laguna Niguel | French/Mediterranean |
| Five Feet | Asian/French |
| Pavilion | Cal./Mediterranean |
| Pinot Provence | French Bistro |
| **25** Zov's Bistro/Bakery | Mediterranean |

## OTHER IMPORTANT PLACES

| | |
|---|---|
| Antonello | Northern Italian |
| Aubergine | Californian/French |
| Bistango | New American |
| Five Crowns | Continental |
| Splashes | Mediterranean |

| F | D | S | C |
|---|---|---|---|

### Antonello

| 25 | 25 | 25 | $42 |
|---|---|---|---|

*S. Coast Plaza Village, 1611 Sunflower Ave. (Plaza Dr.), Santa Ana, 714-751-7153*

■ For "consistently flawless", "perfectly executed" Northern Italian cuisine, this "eternal verity" has few peers, particularly given its "elegant" surroundings and "gracious" service befitting its quintessential power crowd; devotees declare "it's worth the drive from LA" (or as a stop on the way to the nearby OC Performing Arts Center) and though it's "expensive", many advise "reward yourself!"

### Aubergine

| – | – | – | E |
|---|---|---|---|

*508 29th St. (Newport Blvd.), Newport Beach, 949-723-4150*

The venue that put Tim and Lisa Goodell on SoCal's culinary map, this Cal-French predecessor to Costa Mesa's trendy Troquet is now reopened after many months of renovation; a small beachside cottage expanded to accommodate more diners, it's said to be sweeter than ever and the perfect frame for chef Tim's elegant prix fixe choices.

### Bistango **S**

| 24 | 24 | 23 | $35 |
|---|---|---|---|

*19100 Von Karman Ave. (north of Campus Dr.), Irvine, 949-752-5222*

■ At this "dramatic" atrium restaurant–cum–art gallery, "creative, delectable presentations" of New American standouts ("excellent steaks", "wonderful lamb") vie with an "artsy" ambiance and live contemporary jazz for the attention of OC movers and shakers; no wonder locals "take out-of-towners here."

**Five Crowns** [S] 24 | 25 | 24 | $38

*3801 E. PCH (Poppy St.), Corona del Mar, 949-760-0331*

■ "Tradition rules" at this "venerable" Continental that's famed as a "prime rib paradise", a "genteel" "haven" for Anglophiles (credit its "warm English decor") and "a must" destination at Christmastime when "live carolers" make things merry; though trendy types dismiss its "time warp" menu and shrug the whole enterprise is "resting on its laurels", loyalists insist "this historic charmer hasn't lost a beat"; dinner and Sunday brunch only.

**Five Feet** [S] 26 | 19 | 21 | $40

*328 Glenneyre St. (bet. Forest Ave. & Mermaid St.), Laguna Beach, 949-497-4955*

■ "Everything is succulent" at this "inventive" Asian-French with Pacific Rim flourishes, a "classy" dinner-only hot spot that draws acclaim for its "incredible presentations of fabulous food" (notably "the outstanding catfish special"); though there's "sardine-style seating", "enthusiastic service" helps ease the crush.

**Gustaf Anders** [S] 27 | 23 | 25 | $44

*S. Coast Plaza Village, 3851 Bear St. (Sunfower Ave.), Santa Ana, 714-668-1737*

■ One of the only Scandinavians in SoCal and certainly the most renowned, this taste of "Sweden in OC" is a "piece of heaven", made all the more celestial by its "great aquavit collection" and "outstanding holiday smorgasbord"; "tranquil and laid-back", it's "worth a detour" for "expensively excellent" dining.

**Pascal** 28 | 23 | 25 | $47

*1000 N. Bristol St. (Jamboree Rd.), Newport Beach, 949-752-0107*

■ "It doesn't get any better" than this "bit of French countryside" in OC that regains its No. 1 rating for Food this year; Francophiles laud chef Pascal Olhats' "lovely" Provençal menu, the "romantic" setting "filled with fresh roses", the "superb service" and overall "high quality" (despite its strip mall setting); P.S. "get a friend who doesn't like fish to try it here – you'll hook them."

**Pavilion** [S] 26 | 27 | 26 | $49

*Four Seasons Hotel, 690 Newport Center Dr. (Santa Cruz Dr.), Newport Beach, 949-760-4920*

■ "Casual elegance is the rule" at this "always satisfying" Cal-Med in the Four Seasons that earns raves as "one of the top hotel restaurants in the country" and a "favorite for special occasions"; enthusiasts say this "all-around superb dining experience" is "fantastic" on every level ("delicious food", "beautiful setting", "excellent service"), and though the price for all this perfection can be steep, some find it "quite reasonable" for the bliss it evokes.

**Pinot Provence** [S] 26 | 26 | 24 | $43

*Westin S. Coast Plaza, 686 Anton Blvd. (bet. Bristol St. & Town Center Dr.), Costa Mesa, 714-444-5900*

■ Mr. Splichal goes to OC with this "junior Patina", a Gallic "slice of authentic Provence in palm tree land" that just might be the "prettiest of all the Pinots"; natives rave this "dream come true" is a "wonderful alternative when going to the Performing Arts Center" (or for a "fabulous Sunday brunch" or "delightful" $19.99 prix fixe lunch); in sum, this "welcome addition" near the Westin South Coast Plaza has "instantly" made itself "one of the best" in the area.

### Ramos House Cafe 🅂  27 | 19 | 21 | $19

*31752 Los Rios St. (2 blocks east of Del Obispo St.), San Juan Capistrano, 949-443-1342*

■ An "adventure to find", this highly rated "rustic cottage" set in a "historic part" of San Juan Capistrano provides a "lovely outdoor setting" that sets the mood for "perfecto" dining; expect a "great overall" New American menu with Cajun and Southern flourishes at this "step back in time" that only does breakfast and lunch.

### Ritz, The 🅂  27 | 27 | 27 | $47

*Newport Fashion Island, 880 Newport Center Dr. (Santa Barbara Ave.), Newport Beach, 949-720-1800*

■ Once again, this ritzy Continental ranks as OC's Most Popular (as well as No. 1 for Service), amassing plaudits for its "classically served" "perfect food" and the "old-world opulence" of its "magnificent room"; "extremely popular with the power elite", this is dining "as plush as it gets" that "feels like NYC, but with better prices" – in short, an "awesome experience."

### Ritz-Carlton Laguna Niguel  26 | 28 | 26 | $50

*Ritz-Carlton Laguna Niguel, 1 Ritz-Carlton Dr. (PCH), Dana Point, 949-240-5008*

■ "Heaven on earth" can be attained at this "elegant", "top-shelf" French-Med, a "first-class restaurant in a first-class hotel" perched atop a bluff overlooking the Pacific; "adventurous cuisine with prices to match" arrives in a room decked out with "artwork that rivals the Getty" (earning it the No. 1 Decor score in OC), and though it can be "easy to feel underdressed" at this "splurge location", for "formal, serious dining" regulars say a "Ritz is a Ritz is a Ritz"; dinner only.

### Splashes 🅂  22 | 26 | 21 | $36

*Surf & Sand Hotel, 1555 S. PCH (Bluebird Canyon Dr.), Laguna Beach, 949-497-4477*

■ "It's so close to the Pacific, you actually feel the splashes" at this appropriately named Mediterranean with a "perfect setting" "right on the sand"; the food is "better than expected", the patio "relaxing" and the indoor fireplace "romantic", so "bring the out-of-towners" for a taste of the "best seaside dining" around.

### Troquet  27 | 23 | 23 | $45

*S. Coast Plaza, 3333 Bristol St. (Town Center Dr.), Costa Mesa, 714-708-6865*

■ After displacing Pascal last year as OC's No. 1 spot for Food, this Contemporary French "masterpiece" slips to No. 2 with its rival's resurgence but remains a "sophisticated bistro" where the "gorgeous interior" and "fantastic cuisine" are "just like in Paris"; in spite of an incongruous "mall setting" and "pricey" tabs, it offers "exceptionally fine dining" that leaves true believers tongue-tied: "I can't say enough."

### Zov's Bistro & Bakery Cafe  25 | 18 | 21 | $28

*Enderle Ctr., 17440 E. 17th St. (Yorba St.), Tustin, 714-838-8855*

■ The "smell of freshly baked breads" and other "peerless Levantine" treats entice the faithful into this "tiny" Tustin standout where the "diverse menu" of "delicious and imaginative" fare ranges from rack of lamb, salads, pastas and couscous to pastries prized as "well worth the calories"; "brilliant" chef-owner Zov Karamardian can claim a "very loyal following", built the old-fashioned way: "she can cook."

# Orlando

## TOP 10 FOOD RANKING

| Restaurant | Cuisine Type |
|---|---|
| **28** Victoria & Albert's | Traditional American |
| La Coquina | New World |
| Del Frisco's | Steakhouse |
| Le Coq au Vin | French Bistro |
| **27** California Grill | Californian |
| Flying Fish Cafe | Seafood |
| **26** Chatham's Place | Continental |
| Manuel's on the 28th | Eclectic/New American |
| Morton's of Chicago | Steakhouse |
| Artist Point | Northwestern |

## OTHER IMPORTANT PLACES

| | |
|---|---|
| Antonio's La Fiamma | N/S Italian |
| Bahama Breeze | Caribbean |
| Chez Vincent | Classic French |
| Citricos | Mediterranean |
| Emeril's Restaurant Orlando | Cajun/Creole |
| Enzo's on the Lake | Northern Italian |
| Fulton's Crab House | Seafood |
| Harvey's Bistro | French Bistro/New Amer. |
| Johnny Rivers' | BBQ |
| Le Provence | New French |
| Maison et Jardin | Continental |
| Park Plaza Gardens | Continental/Eclectic |
| Pebbles | Californian/New Amer. |
| Peter Scott's | Continental |
| Rolando's | Cuban |
| Sergio's | N/S Italian |
| Winnie's Oriental Garden | Chinese |

| F | D | S | C |
|---|---|---|---|

**Antonio's La Fiamma**    | 25 | 22 | 22 | $26 |
*611 S. Orlando Ave. (Maitland Ave.), Maitland, 407-645-1035*
■ Expect "an evening of pampering" from this immensely popular Maitland Italian with "an excellent deli downstairs and fine dining upstairs"; the "authentic" cuisine is served "with an emphasis on keeping the customers happy" by a "knowledgeable staff" in a "lovely", albeit "painfully noisy", setting; some say the wine list is reason enough to go.

F | D | S | C

## Artist Point [S]

26 | 26 | 24 | $30

*Disney's Wilderness Lodge, 901 Timberline Dr. (World Dr.), Lake Buena Vista, 407-824-1081*

■ "Deliciously unique Pacific Northwest food" is the specialty of this rustic yet "breathtaking" room at Disney's Wilderness Lodge that's "like eating at Frank Lloyd Wright's house"; "still undiscovered by the crowds", it draws kudos for its "great salmon, wild game" and extensive regional wine list; for those seeking a "dining adventure, not a quick meal", this is a "hands-down favorite."

## Bahama Breeze ◐[S]

22 | 24 | 20 | $17

*8849 International Dr. (1 mi. south of Sand Lake Rd.), 407-248-2499*
*499 E. Altamonte Dr. (Palm Springs Blvd. & State Rd. 436), Altamonte Springs, 407-831-2929*

■ From the folks who brought you Red Lobster and The Olive Garden comes this "peppy" Caribbean-flavored chain with "inexpensive" food and "islandish", "party atmosphere"; though a few say it "reeks of franchise", nonetheless it's "always crowded", so "go early or wait forever" to get in.

## California Grill [S]

27 | 27 | 25 | $36

*Disney's Contemporary Resort, 4600 N. World Dr., Lake Buena Vista, 407-824-1576*

■ One of Disney's "finest", this "superb" Californian atop the Contemporary Resort has it all: an "adventuresome" menu by chef Clifford Pleau, an "exciting wine program" with many by-the-glass choices and an "awesome" view, all of which come together so well that it's voted Orlando's Most Popular restaurant; no surprise, it "can be difficult to get into", so reserve far in advance and "time your dinner for the Magic Kingdom fireworks."

## Chatham's Place [S]

26 | 22 | 25 | $33

*Phillips Pl., 7575 Dr. Phillips Blvd. (Sand Lake Rd.), 407-345-2992*

■ Although the Chatham family no longer owns it, this Continental remains a local fave (despite its proximity to touristy International Drive) for a "really delightful evening"; admirers like the fact that you can "dress up or down" and that everyone "is treated with the same attention as frequent guests"; regulars recommend the signature pecan-crusted grouper, calling it simply "world-class."

## Chez Vincent

24 | 21 | 21 | $28

*533 W. New England Ave. (Park Ave.), Winter Park, 407-599-2929*

◪ "Sharp, sophisticated and intimate", chef Vincent Gagliano's Classic French in Winter Park's redeveloped West End might be on the "wrong side of the tracks", but many call this "perfect little bistro" a "great addition to the scene" (though a few hedge that the "food is *almost* there"); though some dub the service "slaphappy", most maintain it's "trying hard and should get even better."

## Citricos [S]

25 | 26 | 26 | $40

*Disney's Grand Floridian Resort & Spa, 4401 Grand Floridian Way, Lake Buena Vista, 407-939-3463*

■ "Chef Roland Muller's innovative food" draws applause at this Disney Mediterranean at the Grand Floridian Resort, where the "stunning" decor and "very attentive service" also impress; though it might be a bit "noisy" and "a little pricey", the word on the boardwalk is that it's a "great new restaurant to try"; N.B. the wine pairings – for an additional $20 – come highly recommended.

**Del Frisco's Steakhouse** 28 | 22 | 24 | $37

*729 Lee Rd. (1½ blocks west of I-4), 407-645-4443*

■ "Steaks are the signature", but "everything from appetizers to desserts is exquisite" say the many supporters of this "very special" Lee Road "guy place" with "dark wood" decor and a "clubby atmosphere" (the guys think it's "a great place to close a deal"); the few who "wish there were more nonbeef items" seem to miss the point: it's aimed at carnivores who "don't care about prices" given "humongous portions" of "excellent food."

**Emeril's Restaurant Orlando [S]** – | – | – | E

*Universal Studios Escape, Universal CityWalk, 407-224-2424*

Superchef Emeril Lagasse's latest venture is the hands-down culinary star of Universal's CityWalk, thanks to resourceful Cajun-Creole cooking that showcases basic ingredients in unusual combinations; its techno-industrial setting, reflecting its New Orleans' warehouse roots and featuring an open kitchen, is jammed with locals who have displaced tourists who didn't think of making reservations.

**Enzo's on the Lake** 26 | 24 | 23 | $33

*1130 S. Hwy. 17-92 (State Rd. 434), Longwood, 407-834-9872*

■ "Enzo Perlini is hands-on" at his eponymous, "high-end" Longwood restaurant that some say is the "closest thing to an Italian trattoria in North America"; young lovers sigh it's a "first-rate first date place" as "there's passion in the food and staff", even if others claim nonregulars are "treated like you crashed a party"; most concur, however, "you'd swear you're in Italy having a meal in the country" thanks to its "beautiful location" on Lake Fairy.

**Flying Fish Cafe [S]** 27 | 26 | 25 | $34

*Walt Disney World Boardwalk Resort, 2101 N. Epcot Resorts Blvd. (Buena Vista Dr.), Lake Buena Vista, 407-939-2359*

■ "Disney outdid itself" at this Boardwalk seafooder where "cutting-edge cuisine" served amid "fantastic decor" makes it "too good to pass up"; especially notable is the open kitchen view ("get a seat at the bar and watch them in action") and a "not-to-be-missed" chocolate volcano cake that will "knock your socks off."

**Fulton's Crab House [S]** 21 | 21 | 20 | $27

*Downtown Disney, 1670 Buena Vista Dr., Lake Buena Vista, 407-934-2628*

◪ "Terrific oysters without the fear" can be found at this Downtown Disney seafooder that prides itself on freshness and "good variety"; a few nonbelievers say "leave it to the tourists" and everyone warns "hold onto your wallet" as the tab can be "ridiculous", yet the "stunning" location (it's housed on an old paddle wheeler) and knowledgeable staff sway many.

**Harvey's Bistro** 24 | 23 | 22 | $23

*NationsBank Bldg., 390 N. Orange Ave. (Livingston St.), 407-246-6560*

■ It might be the Downtown "office building location", but this New American–French bistro has a "big city feel" that's "unlike Orlando" and helps make it popular "after work" or "before a basketball game" or the theater; the "inventive menu" utilizing fresh seasonal ingredients also earns respect, as does the "great ambiance and service."

**Johnny Rivers' Shanks Smokehouse [S]** – – – M

*5370 W. Colonial Dr. (Kirkman Rd.), 407-293-5803*

Owner Johnny Rivers has converted an abandoned Red Lobster into an upscale barbecuerie in West Orlando and is packing in locals who come to sample a creative menu that includes turkey shank, BBQ ribs and pulled pork; make sure to save room for the Hershey bar bread pudding.

**La Coquina [S]** 28 27 27 $41

*Hyatt Regency Grand Cypress, 1 Grand Cypress Blvd. (State Rd. 535), 407-239-1234*

■ "A class act that's hard to follow", this "very elegant" New World restaurant in the Grand Cypress Resort delivers a "romantic, special experience" in a "fairy-tale setting for grown-ups"; its "artistically presented" food, "top-shelf" service and "pretty surroundings" make it arguably "the most wonderful" dining adventure in Orlando; P.S. don't miss the "best Sunday brunch on Planet Earth."

**Le Coq au Vin [S]** 28 22 25 $29

*4800 S. Orange Ave. (Holden Ave.), 407-851-6980*

■ Chef-owner Louis Perrotte's "tried-and-true" South Orlando bistro is "where Orlando's chefs dine" on their nights off, and with good reason: its Country French cuisine is so "affordable and unpretentious" and the setting so "warm" that you'll "hate to leave"; some fanatics go "just for the crème brûlée" or the "must-have soufflés", but everyone concurs "do not miss this" – "it's very popular, so make reservations."

**Le Provence** 26 23 23 $33

*50 E. Pine St. (bet. Magnolia & Orange Aves.), 407-843-1320*

■ "The food gets better every year" claim devotees of this Downtown Contemporary French that's called "consistently delightful", with "attentive service" and "stylishly updated" cuisine presented with "real flair" in an "intimate and serene" atmosphere; for a "romantic evening", *"c'est si bon."*

**Maison et Jardin [S]** 26 27 26 $37

*430 S. Wymore Rd. (½ mi. south of 1-4 & State Rd. 436), Altamonte Springs, 407-862-4410*

■ This "romantic", "special-occasion" Altamonte Springs Continental in an "older house" with a "lovely garden setting" is "of another time and place", serving flaming desserts and "beef Wellington that dreams are made of"; "impeccable service" and an "exciting wine list" complement the "wonderful" though "pricey" menu, and while a tad "stuffy" for some (jackets requested), most say dining at the 'Mason Jar' (as it's known locally) is a "don't miss" experience.

**Manuel's on the 28th** 26 28 27 $49

*NationsBank Bldg., 390 N. Orange Ave. (Livingston St.), 407-246-6580*

■ Considered by some "the top restaurant in Florida" (and not just because of its 28th-floor location in Downtown Orlando), this "sophisticated" Eclectic–New American serves "world-quality" cuisine and "creative specials" in a "stunning" yet "intimate" room with a "view so good you'll forget the prices"; "attentive" "service teams" are the final touch that make it "spectacular all the way around" – this is "Orlando at its best."

| | F | D | S | C |
|---|---|---|---|---|
| **Morton's of Chicago [S]** | 26 | 23 | 24 | $45 |

*Goodings Marketplace, 7600 Dr. Phillips Blvd. (Sand Lake Rd.), 407-248-3485*

◪ This "top-notch" chain steakhouse near Universal Studios serves beef that's "as close to perfect as you can get", topped off by the likes of a "Godiva hot chocolate cake to die for"; a "classy place for local execs", it exudes "a big city feeling" (i.e. it's "noisy" and filled with "cigar smoke") and can be "very expensive"; some say "go if you're not paying."

| | F | D | S | C |
|---|---|---|---|---|
| **Park Plaza Gardens [S]** | 22 | 25 | 21 | $33 |

*319 Park Ave. S. (New England Ave.), Winter Park, 407-645-2475*

◪ Bringing the outdoors indoors, the "beautiful" covered-courtyard setting of this Winter Park Eclectic-Continental makes it "absolutely the prettiest dining room in Central Florida"; though some say the "overpriced" food "is only half as good as the decor", a redesigned menu and a new sidewalk cafe have fans cheering.

| | F | D | S | C |
|---|---|---|---|---|
| **Pebbles** | 24 | 22 | 22 | $20 |

*17 W. Church St. (Orange Ave.), 407-839-0892* [S]
*Saks Fifth Ave., Florida Mall, 8001 S. Orange Blossom Trail (Sand Lake Rd.), 407-816-5354*
*Crossroads Plaza, 12551 State Rd. 535 (I-4), Lake Buena Vista, 407-827-1111* [S]
*2110 W. State Rd. 434 (Douglas Ave.), Longwood, 407-774-7111* [S]
*2516 Aloma Ave. (State Rd. 436), Winter Park, 407-678-7001* [S]

■ "A touch of California cuisine in a town of Disney dining", this New American chain offers what some call the "best total package for the money" thanks to its "gourmet-on-the-cheap" philosophy; fans rave about its "unusual", "always changing" menu, "great wine list" and "creative" salads (ask for the zucchini dressing); throw "reasonable prices" and good service into the mix and you have the "best 'every night' restaurant" in town.

| | F | D | S | C |
|---|---|---|---|---|
| **Peter Scott's** | 25 | 25 | 24 | $41 |

*Longwood Village, 1811 W. State Rd. 434 (I-4), Longwood, 407-834-4477*

■ An "elegant dinner club with entertainment, dancing" and "a '40s flair", this Longwood "lovers' retreat" is the "perfect place to propose" almost anything; Dover sole is among the favorites on a Continental menu that pleases an "older crowd" at this "very expensive" (some say "overpriced") "special-occasion spot."

| | F | D | S | C |
|---|---|---|---|---|
| **Rolando's [S]** | 24 | 11 | 20 | $13 |

*870 E. State Rd. 436 (Red Bug Lake Rd.), Casselberry, 407-767-9677*

■ Some of the "best Cuban food north of Havana" is served at this Casselberry "fave", a "wonderful, family-operated restaurant" with "homestyle" cooking in a "neighborhood cafe atmosphere"; though the room could use a little brightening ("decor, what decor?"), you'll feel like "part of the family" as it's so "very friendly."

| | F | D | S | C |
|---|---|---|---|---|
| **Sergio's [S]** | 25 | 24 | 23 | $31 |

*355 N. Orange Ave. (Robinson St.), 407-428-6162*

■ "When you first walk into" this Downtown Italian, "you get the feeling this is a class act" thanks to its "charming" ambiance and sophisticated touches like "roses for the ladies"; though some say "service could be more attentive", the "delicious food" and "great wine" maintain the "upscale everything" tone of this "special-occasion", "NY-style" place.

## Victoria & Albert's 🅂     28 | 29 | 29 | VE |

*Disney's Grand Floridian Resort & Spa, 4401 Grand Floridian Way, Lake Buena Vista, 407-824-2591*

■ This American "crown jewel of fine dining" in Disney's Grand Floridian takes Metro Orlando's triple crown, placing No. 1 for Food, Decor and Service; the "best dress-up place in town", it offers "pure luxury" in the form of chef Scott Hunnel's "flawless" seven-course feast that includes "your own personalized menu" and "a rose for milady"; you must "book way in advance" (especially for the coveted chef's table in the kitchen) and though "you'll be treated like royalty, it costs a king's ransom."

## Winnie's Oriental Garden     23 | 22 | 21 | $19 |

*1346 Orange Ave. (Hwy. 17-92), Winter Park, 407-629-2111*

■ The "most upscale, fine dining" Chinese around is how fans describe this Winter Park yearling serving "exquisite, jewel-like food" that's evidence of a "delicate touch in the kitchen"; add "gracious hosting" and "stark, clean decor" to the mix and you have one of the "classiest" dining experiences in town; P.S. "check out the sinks in the bathrooms."

# Palm Beach

## TOP 10 FOOD RANKING

| | Restaurant | Cuisine Type |
|---|---|---|
| *28* | Four Seasons Restaurant | Regional American |
| *27* | Maison Janeiro | New French |
| | La Vieille Maison | New French |
| | Kathy's Gazebo Cafe | Classic French/Continental |
| *26* | Morton's of Chicago | Steakhouse |
| | Cafe L'Europe | International |
| | Chez Jean-Pierre | New French |
| | Cafe Chardonnay | New American |
| *25* | Chef Reto's Restaurant | International |
| | La Petite Maison | French Bistro/Med. |

## OTHER IMPORTANT PLACES

| | |
|---|---|
| Acquario | Mediterranean |
| La Finestra | Northern Italian |
| La Tre Vietnamese | Vietnamese |
| Max's Grille | New American |
| 100 South Ocean | Continental |
| 32 East | New American |

F | D | S | C

**Acquario** 23 | 23 | 21 | $47

*Esplanade, 150 Worth Ave. (bet. S. County Rd. & S. Ocean Blvd.), Palm Beach, 561-655-9999*

■ Hard to find due to an ongoing construction project, this Palm Beach Mediterranean is worth the search for Theo Schoenegger's top-notch cuisine, complemented by an "efficient", "nonsnooty" staff and a "visually exquisite" setting, including a stunning saltwater aquarium behind the bar; N.B. insiders recommend ordering the lobster and asparagus risotto, pineapple carpaccio and, if money is not an issue, the tasting menu.

**Cafe Chardonnay** [S] 26 | 22 | 25 | $44

*Garden Square Shoppes, 4533 PGA Blvd. (Military Trail), Palm Beach Gardens, 561-627-2662*

■ Atmosphere buffs say sit upstairs when dining at this art-filled Palm Beach Gardens New American, which features "professional service", cuisine that's "a joy for the palate" ("try the crab cakes and chocolate pecan pie") and an "enormous", 500-label wine selection (25 by the glass); while it's a "great dining experience" any time, a visit is especially appealing off-season (May–October) when flights, vin-focused dinners and a prix fixe menu are available.

## Cafe L'Europe
26 | 26 | 25 | $53

*331 S. County Rd. (Brazilian Ave.), Palm Beach, 561-655-4020*

■ "Dress up" to mingle with "Palm Beach jet-setters" ("society with a capital S") at this "classy" International with a wide variety of "wonderful food", "outstanding service" and "plush" surroundings, which include stunning flower arrangements, lots of dark wood and mirrors and a "great" caviar bar with a baby grand piano (music nightly); overall, it's a delightful "piece of old Europe" "and one of Florida's best."

## Chef Reto's Restaurant S
25 | 20 | 24 | $46

*41 E. Palmetto Park Rd. (N. Federal Hwy.), Boca Raton, 561-395-0633*

■ Bring your map to this Boca Raton International where every month the eponymous chef, working out of a glass-enclosed open kitchen, creates a new menu reflecting a different geographic region (like Tuscany or the Pacific Northwest); even though the "excellent" victuals span the planet, the decor and "outstanding" service remain constant; nonetheless, despite all the kudos, this "gem" continues to be a local "secret."

## Chez Jean-Pierre
26 | 23 | 24 | $52

*132 N. County Rd. (bet. Sunrise & Sunset Aves.), Palm Beach, 561-833-1171*

■ This always busy Palm Beach Contemporary French bistro has a "cozy" first floor highlighted by "a lovely" long bar (smoking permitted), mirrors, trompe l'oeil paintings and an eat-in wine cellar; upstairs is distinguished by a pecky-cedar ceiling and collages on the walls, but no matter where you sit there's "great food" ("excellent Dover sole") "served well."

## Four Seasons Restaurant ●S
28 | 28 | 26 | $57

*Four Seasons, 2800 S. Ocean Blvd. (Southern Blvd. Bridge),
Palm Beach, 561-582-2800*

■ Everything is "taken to another level" at this PB "special-occasion" venue where chef Hubert Des Marais' "magnificent" Regional American (aka 'Floribbean') cuisine earns the No. 1 ranking in the *Palm Beach Survey;* pastry chef Tom Worhach's desserts are off the chart ("fabulous"), the staff "pampers" and the "glamorous" formal dining room, with white tablecloths, velvet upholstered chairs and a "beautiful view", is pure "elegance"; bottom line: you can bank on an overall "great experience."

## Kathy's Gazebo Cafe S
27 | 23 | 22 | $48

*4199 N. Federal Hwy. (Spanish River Rd.), Boca Raton, 561-395-6032*

☑ Despite the unfortunate passing of its founder and namesake, this "formal", chandelier-filled Boca Raton destination continues to serve "consistently excellent" Classic French–Continental cuisine from an open kitchen fronting the bar; even though most feel this is one of "the best restaurants in Florida", impatient types warn that "reservations mean nothing."

## La Finestra
22 | 21 | 21 | $42

*171 E. Palmetto Park Rd. (Mizner Blvd.), Boca Raton, 561-392-1838*

■ "It's dress-up time" for diners heading to this regally appointed Boca Raton Northern Italian sporting Belle Époque lithographs, starched linen tablecloths, fresh red roses on every table and nightly piano music, to complement its "serious food and service"; signature items include chicken and pork with wild mushrooms and a seafood crêpe stuffed with eggplant.

## La Petite Maison    | 25 | 22 | 24 | $45 |

*366 E. Palmetto Park Rd. (bet. SE 3rd & 4th Aves.), Boca Raton, 561-750-7483*
■ Reviewers gush that chef Guy Augier and his wife Sylvia "make you feel like part of their family" at this "small", "charming" Boca Raton French-Med set in a lovely old house with an enclosed patio; look for such "serious" signatures dishes as escargot with spinach au gratin, broiled lobster with aioli and duck with red wine sauce, as well as the summertime prix fixe ("reasonably priced").

## La Tre Vietnamese Restaurant S    | 24 | 15 | 22 | $29 |

*249 E. Palmetto Park Rd. (east of US 1), Boca Raton, 561-392-4568*
■ "Glad they're back" declare fans of this relocated and renamed (fka Le Truc) family-run Vietnamese operating out of an unassuming Boca Raton storefront, where an "eager-to-please" staff serves "medium-priced" French-inspired presentations of "excellent" dishes such as tamarind squid; locals add "we need more ethnic restaurants" like this one.

## La Vieille Maison S    | 27 | 28 | 27 | $56 |

*770 E. Palmetto Park Rd. (2½ mi. east of I-95), Boca Raton, 561-737-5677*
■ "Romantics" say "try for a private room" when dining at this 30-year-old Contemporary French "standby" in a "charming", Mizner-era "old mansion" in Boca Raton; with "beautiful", "grand-style" surroundings (flowers, Impressionist-inspired art, antiques, reproduction furniture), "excellent" cuisine, "superb service" and "a fine wine list", it's not surprising that this is once again the Most Popular restaurant in the *Palm Beach Survey*; P.S. it's "pricey", but there's a "great prix fixe deal" during the summer.

## Maison Janeiro    | 27 | 26 | 25 | $57 |

*191 Bradley Pl. (bet. Oleander & Seminole Aves.), Palm Beach, 561-659-5223*
■ Tuxedo-clad waiters serve renowned chef Gerard Reuther's "excellent" Contemporary French fare (including a choice of 25 soufflés) "on Versace-designed plates" at this Palm Beach young-and-old, high-society "place to be seen", which is "beautifully" decorated with tomato soup–colored walls, zebra-patterned banquettes and vintage Gallic posters; N.B. an 850-label wine list means oenophiles should plan ahead.

## Max's Grille S    | 23 | 20 | 21 | $34 |

*Mizner Park, 404 Plaza Real (N. Federal Hwy.), Boca Raton, 561-368-0080*
■ "Try the meat loaf" and pork chops declare surveyors about the "wide range" of "solid", "hearty" "upscale" New American "comfort food" that emerges from the open kitchen of this stylishly "casual" Boca Raton "old favorite", with a cozy, brown-wood dining room and an attractive outdoor patio that's ideal for "people-watching"; P.S. with no reservations (except for six or more), expect "big crowds" and "long waits" ("busy, busy, busy").

## Morton's of Chicago S    | 26 | 24 | 24 | $50 |

*777 S. Flagler St. (bet. Chase St. & Lakeview Ave.), West Palm Beach, 561-835-9664*
*5050 Town Center Circle (Military Trail), Boca Raton, 561-392-7724*
■ "Plentiful portions" of "terrific" prime, aged beef ("wonderful NY strip") and lip-smacking, succulent chops are the hallmarks of this high-end steakhouse chain's outlets in West Palm Beach and now Boca; expense-accounters can expect "fine service" and an attractive "club-like" ambiance that will impress even the picky.

## 100 South Ocean [S] — | — | — | E

*Ritz-Carlton Palm Beach, 100 S. Ocean Blvd. (E. Ocean Ave.), Manalapan, 561-533-6000*

"Elegant dining" defines this Manalapan Ritz-Carlton destination where chef Stefan Kauth's frequently changing menu of Continental cuisine takes advantage of local seasonal products, the impeccable staff works gracefully and the intimate, European-style dining room comes with an ocean view, harpist, white linen tablecloths and huge fresh flower arrangements.

## 32 East [S] 24 | 21 | 21 | $42

*32 E. Atlantic Ave. (bet. 1st & Swinton Aves.), Delray Beach, 561-276-7868*

■ "There's a new menu every day" based upon what's good at the market at this two-story Delray Beach New American where chef Nick Morfogen takes "food to another level" (and makes his own breads and desserts); the mahogany dining room has a cosmopolitan, San Francisco–like feel and the crowd oozes "sophistication"; N.B. look for an adjacent nightclub, 32 Degrees, to open imminently.

# Philadelphia

## TOP 20 FOOD RANKING

| Restaurant | Cuisine Type |
|---|---|
| **29** Le Bec-Fin | Classic French |
| Fountain Restaurant | Continental/New French |
| Le Bar Lyonnais | French Bistro |
| **27** Brasserie Perrier | New French |
| Susanna Foo | Asian/French |
| Deux Cheminées | Classic French |
| Mainland Inn | New American |
| Swann Lounge & Cafe | American/Continental |
| Jake's | New American |
| Dmitri's | Mediterranean/Seafood |
| Dilworthtown Inn | American/Classic French |
| **26** Ciboulette | New French |
| Striped Bass | Seafood |
| Coventry Forge Inn | Classic French |
| Morton's of Chicago | Steakhouse |
| Tacconelli's Pizza | Pizza |
| Overtures | Mediterranean |
| Monte Carlo Living Room | N/S Italian |
| Evermay on the Delaware | New American |
| La Famiglia | Italian |

## OTHER IMPORTANT PLACES

| | |
|---|---|
| Arroyo Grille | Southwestern |
| Audrey Claire | Mediterranean |
| Bistro St. Tropez | French Bistro |
| Buddakan | Asian/Eclectic |
| DiPalma | Northern Italian |
| Fork | New American |
| La Veranda | Italian/Seafood |
| Moshulu | International |
| Nan | French/Thai |
| Opus 251 | New American |
| Pasion! | South American |
| Prime Rib | Steakhouse |
| Rococo | New American |
| Rouge 99 | American/Continental |
| Vetri | N/S Italian |
| White Dog Cafe | New American |

### Arroyo Grille 🖻

15 | 20 | 16 | $25

*Leverington & Main Sts., 215-487-1400*

☑ This "super trendy" Southwestern yuppeteria on its own little island in Manayunk is prized for its "attractive" clientele, "funky" interior and "great deck"; noise, "mediocre" food and "slow service" from the "young and the careless" only slightly diminish its appeal, especially for "good margaritas" "on a sultry summer night."

### Audrey Claire 🖻⌿

22 | 17 | 20 | $26

*276 S. 20th St. (Spruce St.), 215-731-1222*

■ The "light and breezy" atmosphere, "innovative" Med cooking and "young, hip" Center City crowd ("it feels like the TV show *Friends*") make this BYO the "new in spot"; a no-reservations policy and "long waits" mean "get there early."

### Bistro St. Tropez

24 | 20 | 20 | $31

*2400 Market St., 4th fl. (23rd St.), 215-569-9269*

■ An "artsy", "offbeat" location in the Marketplace Design Center sets the stage for this "authentic" French bistro, a "hip"place for "excellent food" at "reasonable prices for the quality"; toss in "great views" overlooking the Schuylkill, "cute waiters whose suggestions you should always take", jazz on Thursday nights and it all adds up to a "hidden jewel."

### Brasserie Perrier 🖻

27 | 27 | 25 | $50

*1619 Walnut St. (bet. 16th & 17th Sts.), 215-568-3000*

■ "Another Georges Perrier masterpiece" rave legions of admirers blown away by this "suave", "art deco" New French, a "great addition" to Restaurant Row at "more reasonable prices" than its older sibling, Le Bec-Fin; expect "wonderful presentations" and "complex tastes" from chef Francesco Martorella and a "superbly trained" staff; a few grumblers scoff at the 'brasserie' tag and "pricey wine", but overall – "believe the hype."

### Buddakan 🖻

– | – | – | E

*325 Chestnut St. (bet. 3rd & 4th Sts.), 215-574-9440*

A chic, sleek setting that's as stylish as a movie set – complete with a glass-enclosed waterfall – dominates this Old City Asian-Eclectic, which opened with one of the biggest splashes in years; owner Stephen Starr (The Continental) has installed chef Scott Swiderski (ex Miami's China Grill) in the kitchen; the staff is arguably the best-looking and tallest in the city, with a level of competence that's equally high.

### Ciboulette 🖻

26 | 24 | 24 | $52

*Bellevue Bldg., 200 S. Broad St. (Walnut St.), 215-790-1210*

■ Acolytes gush that Bruce Lim's "heavenly" New French in a "lovely" room in the Bellevue "lives up to its reputation"; and while his "appetizer portion" concept "adds up quickly", it also "allows for a taste of many wonderful selections" including "foie gras to quack about"; save room for the "fabulous dessert cart."

### Coventry Forge Inn

26 | 25 | 24 | $45

*3360 Coventryville Rd. (1½ mi. west of Rte. 100), Pottstown, 610-469-6222*

■ Even after 45 years, the Callahans' "long-standing favorite" in Pottstown "hasn't lost its touch" for "traditional" French fare (the Saturday night prix fixe is an "excellent value") in a "serene" country setting that even city folk don't mind driving to.

## Deux Cheminées | 27 | 28 | 26 | $65

*1221 Locust St. (bet. 12th & 13th Sts.), 215-790-0200*

■ If you "forgot what it was like to have your senses exhilarated", Fritz Blank's "romantic" Classic French in an "elegant" Center City townhouse will remind you; "rich" dishes are "so amazing you'd swear they came from heaven" and service is "unobtrusive", though a few contend that at these prices "I want to eat on Limoges, not buy it."

## Dilworthtown Inn, The [S] | 27 | 27 | 26 | $44

*1390 Old Wilmington Pike (Brinton Bridge Rd.), West Chester, 610-399-1390*

■ "What a romantic treat" sigh reviewers lovestruck by this West Chester country inn ("the prettiest of them all") that has "come back strong" after a fire; as the "Le Bec-Fin of the 'burbs", expect "wonderful " Classic French–American cooking, an "outstanding" wine list, "impeccable" service and an "incredible attention to detail" overall – the "goblets and silver glisten."

## DiPalma | – | – | – | VE

*114 Market St. (bet. Front & 2nd Sts.), 215-733-0545*

This handsome Old City Northern Italian is named for chef-owner Salvatore DiPalma, an alum of both the Ritz-Carlton and Roscoe's Kodiak Cafe, who's known for his skill with grilled meats and fish; power types and celebrating couples alike are deftly dealt with by a polished yet unassuming staff, and the slick downstairs bar and winning wine cellar are already hits.

## Dmitri's [S]💳̸ | 27 | 13 | 19 | $23

*795 S. Third St. (Catharine St.), 215-625-0556*

■ It may be a "claustrophobic's nightmare", but this "fabulous" Mediterranean BYO in Queen Village is an "all-time favorite" for "consistently fresh" seafood ("the best octopus on the planet"); regulars recommend you "arrive at 5 PM" (with cash) or be prepared to "camp out for the evening"; P.S. "sit at the counter" to watch how "two cooks feed 40 people."

## Evermay on the Delaware [S] | 26 | 26 | 26 | $54

*River Rd. (Headquarters Rd.), Erwinna, 610-294-9100*

■ A "best bet for romance", this "most impressive" New American "hidden charmer" north of New Hope is prized for "well-prepared" "three-hour dinners" with "impeccable" service in a "classic setting"; though a few workaholics growl about the "limited" menu and hours ("any chef who serves three meals a week is on vacation"), the sybaritic majority dubs it "definitely a go"; the attached B&B gets high marks as well.

## Fork [S] | 24 | 25 | 22 | $31

*306 Market St. (bet. 3rd & 4th Sts.), 215-625-9425*

■ "My new favorite restaurant" sums up reactions to this "casual", "low pressure" New American in Old City that oozes style, from its "cool chandeliers", "way hip" plates and "imaginative cutlery" to a clientele that's "as well-dressed as the decor"; toss in "fabulous food" and "so far, so good."

## Fountain Restaurant 🖪    29 | 29 | 28 | $60
*Four Seasons Hotel, 1 Logan Sq. (Benjamin Franklin Pkwy. & 18th St.), 215-963-1500*

■ For "the most sophisticated dining in Philadelphia", it would be hard to top Jean-Marie Lacroix and company (and their ratings) at this "consistently fabulous" Continental-French in the Four Seasons; business people tout it as a "super meeting place" for a power lunch, and the brunch-and-dinner crowd says it's a "wow" for "imaginative", "sublime" food and "flawless" service in a room that's "elegance personified"; it "keeps Le Bec-Fin on its toes."

## Jake's 🖪    27 | 22 | 24 | $42
*4365 Main St. (bet. Grape & Levering Sts.), 215-483-0444*

■ Bruce Cooper's "first-class" New American is "Manayunk's bright star", an "understated" "wonder" with "knowledgeable" servers, an "outstanding" wine list and the "best nouvelle cuisine around", though when it's crowded you can "feel like a sardine"; don't leave without trying the crab cakes or salmon.

## La Famiglia 🖪    26 | 23 | 23 | $51
*8 S. Front St. (bet. Chestnut & Market Sts.), 215-922-2803*

■ An "amazing wine list", "fabulous" food, "wonderful old-world charm" and "professional service" make this "authentic" Old City Italian one of the best "special-occasion" spots in town; while a few find the atmosphere "stuffy" and "pretentious", the majority maintains it's "still great after all these years."

## La Veranda 🖪    23 | 21 | 19 | $41
*Penn's Landing, Pier 3, Columbus Blvd. (bet. Arch & Market Sts.), 215-351-1898*

■ A "hangout" for "politicos" and other "well-connected" types, this Penn's Landing Italian seafooder serves "superb" food in "generous portions" and offers "great waterfront views"; however, even admirers admit "unless you're somebody, service is slow" and "snooty", and the "wait is bad even with reservations."

## Le Bar Lyonnais    29 | 24 | 25 | $42
*1523 Walnut St. (bet. 15th & 16th Sts.), 215-567-1000*

■ "Why pay Le Bec-Fin prices when you have Le Bar downstairs?"; this "cozy" "gathering place" beneath Georges Perrier's older, "pomp and circumstance" shrine features a "sophisticated" French bistro menu and is a "romantic spot" for drinks and dessert"; it may be "cramped" and "smoky", but "it's where those who really know great food at great prices go."

## Le Bec-Fin    29 | 29 | 29 | VE
*1523 Walnut St. (bet. 15th & 16th Sts.), 215-567-1000*

■ It's No. 1 across the board for Food, Decor, Service and Popularity in Philadelphia and "everything they say about" Georges Perrier's "world-class" Classic French on Restaurant Row "is true": "exquisite" cuisine, "gorgeous" decor and "impeccable" yet "unintimidating" service; while it's "expensive" (the prix fixe dinner is $118), devotees dub the $36 lunch a "bargain" because "if you die and go to 'food heaven', Le Bec-Fin will be the name over the door."

**Mainland Inn** [S] 27 25 26 $42

*17 Main St. (Sumneytown Pike), Mainland, 215-256-8500*

■ This "hard to beat" New American in an "idyllic pastoral setting" near Lansdale might be the "best-kept secret" in rural Montco; the "sophisticated menu", "excellent food" and "lap of luxury" atmosphere are lovingly maintained by "owners and a staff with a passion that makes for a great restaurant"; acolytes urge "if you haven't been there yet, go."

**Monte Carlo Living Room** [S] 26 24 24 $51

*150 South St. (2nd St.), 215-925-2220*

■ An "elegant" Italian with "warm, attentive" service that's a "romantic" retreat from the hustle of South Street; chef Nunzio Patruno "has hands of gold", and the "decadent" disco upstairs is the place to work off the calories; it's "expensive", but a "wonderful special event experience."

**Morton's of Chicago** [S] 26 21 23 $49

*1411 Walnut St. (Broad St.), 215-557-0724*

■ The new Walnut Street location of this "decadent" chain continues to be "always reliable" for "huge portions" of "top-quality" steaks, with a side of cigars; it's "especially good for expense accounts", pulling in "power people" who are there to "chew the fat."

**Moshulu** [S] 17 25 18 $38

*735 S. Columbus Blvd. (South St.), 215-923-2500*

◪ "Sailors never had it like this" on a "beautifully appointed" ship berthed on the southern edge of Penn's Landing; while some call it a "pleasant" place to "entertain out-of-towners" because it "harbors tasty" International fare, others pan "ho-hum food" and "steerage-class" "attitude."

**Nan** – – – M

*4000 Chestnut St. (40th St.), 215-382-0818*

A French-Thai BYO in University City with sublime food from the chef of the late, great Alouette, and a restful, inviting atmosphere; it's certainly one of the better newcomers.

**Opus 251** [S] 23 23 22 $41

*Philadelphia Art Alliance, 251 S. 18th St. (Rittenhouse Sq.), 215-735-6787*

■ "An outstanding newcomer", this "innovative" American with Asian accents in the Art Alliance off Rittenhouse Square serves "exquisitely prepared food" in an "elegant" atmosphere with a "European feel" and "attentive service"; "lunch on the patio is wonderful."

**Overtures** [S] 26 24 23 $36

*609-611 Passyunk Ave. (bet. Bainbridge & South Sts.), 215-627-3455*

■ Insiders insist this Mediterranean BYO "hideaway" off South Street is the "city's best value"; "astonishingly" "sophisticated" cuisine, "European service at its most professional" and a "romantic atmosphere" add up to a "great date" place for making amorous overtures.

F | D | S | C

### Pasion! ◑🅂
_____ | _____ | _____ | E

_211 S. 15th St. (bet. Locust & Walnut Sts.), 215-875-9895_

Chef Guillermo Pernot, who set palates ablazin' at Vega Grill, partners with Michael Dombkoski (ex Susanna Foo) at this lush Center City South American that's one of the city's hottest newcomers in every sense of the word; foodies are packing the seviche bar and the richly appointed dining room where they're rewarded with bold tastes and superior presentations (not to mention dazzling Latin desserts); the bilingual staff excels at explaining the unfamiliar and is especially helpful with wine pairings.

### Prime Rib 🅂
_____ | _____ | _____ | E

_Warwick Hotel, 1701 Locust St. (17th St.), 215-772-1701_

The showy D.C. and Baltimore steakhouse chain has swanked up a smashing space in the Warwick, with plush, leopard-print carpet, onyx walls and a baby grand, all to attract an older crowd hungering for the old days; huge portions of excellent, traditional food (the signature prime rib can feed an army) are served impeccably.

### Rococo 🅂
22 | 26 | 19 | $38

_123 Chestnut St. (2nd St.), 215-629-1100_

■ This "hip", "New York–like" Contemporary American is "the place to see and be seen" in Old City; expect everything to be "beautiful", from the food ("fantastic" "nouvelle" treats) to the people ("wear black, be thin") to the decor ("breathtaking room", "sexy cigar" lounge and "happening bar"); the only drawback is that it can get "so loud that it's difficult to hold a conversation."

### Rouge 99 ◑🅂
_____ | _____ | _____ | M

_Rittenhouse Claridge Apt. Bldg., 205 S. 18th St. (bet. Locust & Walnut Sts.), 215-732-6622_

Neil Stein, of Striped Bass fame, has turned the wine shop in the Rittenhouse Claridge into a sexy, '20s Paris salon with a comfy bar; delicious Euro-American food from chef Michael Yeamans keeps the crowd around into the wee hours.

### Striped Bass 🅂
26 | 28 | 24 | $56

_1500 Walnut St. (15th St.), 215-732-4444_

■ Neil Stein's "power heavy", "destination" seafooder in the heart of Center City's Restaurant Row has a new chef, Terence Feury (ex NYC's Le Bernardin), whose culinary derring-do is only matched by the "knockout" old bank vault decor; though the usually "stellar" service can occasionally be "snotty" and you might holler "holy mackerel!" when the check arrives, this place is "never dull", and remains one of Philly's favorites.

### Susanna Foo 🅂
27 | 26 | 25 | $49

_1512 Walnut St. (bet. 15th & 16th Sts.), 215-545-2666_

■ "The blending of Asian and French cuisines is a marriage made in heaven" at this Restaurant Row "favorite", where the "smashing", "understated" "new decor" (up four notches from the last _Philadelphia Survey_) now lives up to the "sublime", "sparkling" creations and "fine", "attentive" service; there's still some quibbling over the "skimpy portions" but overall, it's easily No. 1 in its genre.

| F | D | S | C |
|---|---|---|---|

## Swann Lounge & Cafe ◐[S]

| F | D | S | C |
|---|---|---|---|
| 27 | 27 | 26 | $38 |

*Four Seasons Hotel, 1 Logan Sq. (bet. Benjamin Franklin Pkwy. & 18th St.), 215-963-1500*

■ "Civilized", "relaxing" American-Continental in the Four Seasons singled out for the "lovely floral arrangements", lunch buffet, "best afternoon tea", Saturday night dessert bar and Sunday brunch; since it's "almost as good as the Fountain", it's (even at these prices) "a best value."

## Tacconelli's Pizza [S]🚫

| F | D | S | C |
|---|---|---|---|
| 26 | 8 | 15 | $15 |

*2604 E. Somerset St. (bet. Almond & Thompson Sts.), 215-425-4983*

■ Where else but this incredibly popular, 50-year-old, cash-only Port Richmond parlor would patrons be required to reserve their dough in advance to get a piece of the "best pizza in the world" ("especially the white" version); but remember, since it's just pizza, period, you may want to "bring your own salad" and wine; P.S. it's dethroned DeLorenzo's as No. 1 pizzeria in the *Philadelphia Survey*.

## Vetri

| F | D | S | C |
|---|---|---|---|
| – | – | – | VE |

*1312 Spruce St. (bet. Broad & 13th Sts.), 215-732-3478*

Seldom has a newcomer hit its stride (and become booked solid) as quickly as this romantic Italian in the Center City space that once housed early incarnations of Chanterelles, Ciboulette and Le Bec-Fin; it's clear that chef Marc Vetri and his dedicated staff are up to the challenge, and although portions aren't huge, each course incorporates rare ingredients and shows serious thought; bonus points go to the winsome wine list.

## White Dog Cafe [S]

| F | D | S | C |
|---|---|---|---|
| 24 | 21 | 20 | $32 |

*3420 Sansom St. (34th St.), 215-386-9224*

■ Even if you "don't like her politics" (what some call a "politically correct atmosphere"), "your tail won't stop wagging" after sampling Judy Wicks' "consistently creative" and "delish" New American food; the dog-themed, "eclectic" Penn campus setting has "cozy little rooms" that get "noisy" and "crowded", but everyone agrees this is a "unique Philadelphia restaurant."

# Phoenix/Scottsdale

## TOP 10 FOOD RANKING

| Restaurant | Cuisine Type |
|---|---|
| **29** Pizzeria Bianco | Pizza |
| **28** Vincent Guerithault | Southwestern |
| **27** Mary Elaine's | Eclectic/New American |
| Los Dos Molinos | Mexican |
| Ruth's Chris | Steakhouse |
| Marquesa | Spanish |
| Morton's of Chicago | Steakhouse |
| **26** Chaparral | Eclectic/New Amer. |
| Golden Swan | Southwestern |
| RoxSand | International |

## OTHER IMPORTANT PLACES

| | |
|---|---|
| Arizona Kitchen | Southwestern |
| Christopher's Fermier | French Bistro |
| Christo's | Continental/N. Italian |
| Convivo | N/S Italian |
| Latilla Room | Regional American |
| Lon's at the Hermosa Inn | New American |
| Michael's at the Citadel | Eclectic |
| Palm Court | Continental |
| Restaurant Hapa | Asian/New American |
| Restaurant Oceana | Seafood |
| Roaring Fork | Regional American |
| Roy's | Pacific Rim |
| Tarbell's | New American |
| T. Cook's | Italian/Med./Spanish |

| F | D | S | C |
|---|---|---|---|

**Arizona Kitchen**  ▽ | 24 | 23 | 25 | $30 |

*Wigwam Resort, 300 E. Wigwam Blvd. (bet. Dysart & Litchfield Rds.), Litchfield Park, 623-935-3811*
■ "Excellent", "imaginative Southwestern dishes" using regional ingredients combined with a "charming" ambiance of whitewashed stucco, beamed ceilings and brick floors make the trip "off the beaten path" to the "grand old" Wigwam Resort on the far Westside well worthwhile.

**Chaparral [S]** 26 | 26 | 26 | $37

*Marriott's Camelback Inn, 5402 E. Lincoln Dr. (Tatum Blvd.), Scottsdale, 480-948-1700*

■ Long regarded as an "upscale time warp", this "top-notch" Paradise Valley restaurant has always been a grand destination for "traditional" Continental food served by a staff adept at giving the "royal treatment"; however, both the menu and decor have been stylishly updated (thus putting the above ratings in question) to showcase New American-Eclectic cuisine in a frontier moderne room.

**Christopher's Fermier Brasserie [S]** – | – | – | E

*Biltmore Fashion Park, 2584 E. Camelback Rd. (24th St.), Phoenix, 602-522-2344*

What happens when one of the Valley's best chefs 86's the white tablecloths and la-ti-da service he was famous for to open a comfortable brasserie in the Camelback Corridor?; people come in droves to dine on burgers and brewed-on-the-premises beer as well as foie gras and Sauternes; the bistro-style menu still has a discernible French accent, and many of Chris Gross' specialties have been retained (to prevent rioting, no doubt), but this high-end hangout is fresh and fun.

**Christo's** 26 | 21 | 25 | $24

*6327 N. Seventh St. (bet. Maryland Ave. & Rose Ln.), Phoenix, 602-264-1784*

■ "First-class" Continental–Northern Italian food set down by some of the "top waiters in the Valley" in an "elegant", "intimate" and "welcoming" setting spell "a cosmopolitan delight" for just about everyone; what's more, "fair prices" and "consistently good" cooking "every day" make it among the "best values in Phoenix" at lunch or dinner; "outstanding" on all counts sums it up.

**Convivo** – | – | – | M

*7000 N. 16th St. (Glendale Ave.), Phoenix, 602-997-7676*

Mark Bloom, who headed up the kitchen at Tarbell's for so long, has opened his own place with wife Pat, a wine wonk who acquired much of her savvy working next door at Sportsman's Liquor; the result is a small, ultra-personal operation in North Phoenix that's dedicated to simple, sophisticated, quasi-Italian food and affordable wines.

**Golden Swan [S]** 26 | 27 | 26 | $34

*Hyatt Regency Scottsdale, 7500 E. Doubletree Ranch Rd. (Scottsdale Rd.), Scottsdale, 602-991-3388*

■ A "breathtaking" setting and "amazing" food are the hallmarks of this two-tiered Southwestern with an "exquisite" patio and "romantic" dining gazebos set in a "lovely" koi-filled lagoon; diners enjoy "first-class service and food" including the "best BBQ salmon" and "most interesting Sunday brunch around"; "if you can afford it, go."

**Latilla Room [S]** ▽ 26 | 28 | 25 | $44

*Boulders Resort, 34631 N. Tom Darlington Dr. (Carefree Hwy.), Carefree, 480-488-9009*

■ "One of the best resort dining rooms", this "elegant" American Regional "is as good as it gets" according to delighted surveyors (and although voting was light, sky-high ratings back up the claim); a very few balk at "stuffy" service, but others find it "sophisticated."

## Lon's at the Hermosa Inn §
| 23 | 26 | 19 | $30 |

*Hermosa Inn, 5532 N. Palo Cristi Rd. (Stanford Dr.), Paradise Valley, 602-955-7878*

◪ This "rustic" redo of a "delightful" historic ranch house makes for what admirers call a "feel-good" "getaway place", with a "fabulous" new Contemporary American menu accented with Southwestern flavors (that may put the above food rating in question), including a "great" Sunday breakfast; but reports of "spotty" service and "inconsistent", "overpriced" food have "faded" the charm for a few.

## Los Dos Molinos
| 27 | 18 | 20 | $13 |

*8646 S. Central Ave. (south of Baseline Rd.), Phoenix, 602-243-9113*
*260 S. Alma School Rd. (bet. Broadway Rd. & Main St.), Mesa, 480-835-5356 ⌂*

■ "Not for the fainthearted", these "funky", friendly, no-frills siblings are "a fire-eater's paradise" for "truly great", "Santa Fe–style" Mexican food that "doesn't get any better"; there's no reserving, but the blue corn tortillas, near-flammable salsas (featuring Hatch, New Mexico chiles) and "exceptional carne adovada" make the "too-long waits" well "worth it."

## Marquesa §
| 27 | 28 | 26 | $38 |

*Scottsdale Princess Resort, 7575 E. Princess Dr. (Scottsdale Rd., north of Bell Rd.), Scottsdale, 480-585-4848*

■ Surveyors applaud this "regional treasure" with "bright, authentic" Spanish colonial decor, "superb service", "excellent paella" and other "outstanding" dishes that pay homage to Cataluña and the Basque region; it's "elegant and relaxing", with a "noteworthy" Spanish market–style Sunday brunch on the garden patio and a tasty tapas menu.

## Mary Elaine's
| 27 | 28 | 26 | $45 |

*Phoenician Resort, 6000 E. Camelback Rd. (60th St.), Scottsdale, 602-423-2530*

■ Despite a recent ownership change at the Phoenician, this "magnificent", "elegant" rooftop restaurant remains a "posh" spot for making "monumental memories", especially at "a window table" looking out over a "beautiful sunset"; with esteemed George Mahaffey (ex Little Nell Restaurant in Aspen) at the helm, the Eclectic menu will focus more on New American fare, but pampered diners can still expect a premier wine list and "sparkling service"; in sum, it's "perfect but a little pricey."

## Michael's at the Citadel §
| – | – | – | E |

*8700 E. Pinnacle Peak Rd. (Pima Rd.), Scottsdale, 480-515-2575*

Before opening this stylish Eclectic venue (formerly 8700) in North Scottsdale, Michael DeMaria made a name for himself at Lon's at the Hermosa Inn and T. Cook's; but since the food here ranges from wonderful to what's-the-big-deal?, best bets are drinks and appetizers by the fire in the bar or a private party at the chef's table overlooking the kitchen.

## Morton's of Chicago §
| 27 | 26 | 26 | $47 |

*Esplanade Complex, 2501 E. Camelback Rd. (24th St.), Phoenix, 602-955-9577*

◪ "Big beef" and "upscale" mahogany surroundings at the Valley's "new player" make what admirers call the "best steak in town" a "sybaritic experience"; but it's "pricey", as you'd expect, and the "cigar smoke" is "too much" for some.

**Palm Court** [S] 24 | 25 | 24 | $35

*Scottsdale Conference Resort, 7700 E. McCormick Pkwy. (bet. Hayden & Scottsdale Rds.), Scottsdale, 602-991-9000*

■ "Quiet elegance", "fine" Continental cuisine and "outstanding tableside" preparation make this "wonderful hotel restaurant" a "favorite celebration" destination as well as a place for "serious dinners" anytime; but what's a "delightful experience" to most is too "expensive" and "stuffy" to a few casual types, who object to "the dress code in the summer heat"; N.B. be sure to check out the "excellent" Sunday brunch.

**Pizzeria Bianco** [S] 29 | 17 | 21 | $17

*Heritage Sq., 623 E. Adams St. (7th St.), Phoenix, 602-258-8300*

■ This recently relocated but still "too small" pizzeria specializes in "outstanding" "Neapolitan-style" pizza made from scratch by an Italian master, baked in a brick oven and topped with homemade mozzarella and other "top-quality ingredients" that also go into the "terrific salads" and sandwiches; the No. 1 food rating in Arizona – and "long waits" – speak volumes; N.B. the decor score doesn't reflect the spiffy new digs.

**Restaurant Hapa** – | – | – | E

*6204 N. Scottsdale Rd. (Lincoln Dr.), Scottsdale, 602-998-8220*

Half-Japanese, half-American, James McDevitt is *hapa* ("half-and-half") in Hawaiian slang – a word that also helps account for his exceptional ability to blend New American and Asian cuisines at this intimate spot in Central Scottsdale; since McDevitt and his wife Stacey (dessert-maker extraordinaire) do nothing by halves, it's a cinch you'll leave Hapa happy.

**Restaurant Oceana** – | – | – | E

*8900 E. Pinnacle Peak Rd. (Pima Rd.), Scottsdale, 480-515-2277*

San Francisco emigrants Ercolino and Laura Crugnale know all the angles when it comes to fish, and they've opened this small seafooder in North Scottsdale to prove that there's more to life, piscatorially speaking, than Friday night fish fries and omnipresent ahi; smelts, skate, sardines, sea urchins and farm-raised scallops are a few sibilant examples of the top-quality products FedExed in daily.

**Roaring Fork** – | – | – | E

*7243 E. Camelback Rd. (east of Scottsdale Rd.), Scottsdale, 602-947-0795*

Chef-owner Robert McGrath is part-cowboy and all-man, the kind of guy you wouldn't expect to be so danged handy in the kitchen; the bold Western American cuisine he creates (broader in perspective than Southwestern) is the real draw, but it doesn't hurt that his welcoming Scottsdale spot echoes the elegant rusticity of his food – where else could you have homemade beef jerky with your martini?

**RoxSand** [S] 26 | 24 | 23 | $31

*Biltmore Fashion Park, 2594 E. Camelback Rd. (24th St.), Phoenix, 602-381-0444*

■ "Electric" describes this "place to be seen" with "stunning" decor and "new taste sensations" switched on by a "master" of transcontinental "fusion cooking" ("save room" for the "fabulous desserts"); it's also "excellent" for "quiet" meals on the balcony.

## Roy's S

− | − | − | E

*Scottsdale Seville, 7001 N. Scottsdale Rd. (Indian Bend Rd.),*
*Scottsdale, 480-905-1155*

Some people hate the noise and crowds at this corporate restaurant, named for chef-and-empire-builder Roy Yamaguchi, but whatever you think of the see-and-be-seen scene, there's no denying that the trendy (but not tortured) Pacific Rim cuisine is well prepared and nicely presented; those who go for the bright-lights, big-city feel of the place should position themselves at the bar for optimal meeting and greeting (as well as for furtive ogling).

## Ruth's Chris Steak House S

27 | 23 | 24 | $36

*2201 E. Camelback Rd. (22nd St.), Phoenix, 602-957-9600*
*7001 N. Scottsdale Rd. (Indian Bend Rd.), Scottsdale, 602-991-5988*

☑ Many beef lovers hope there's "a Ruth's Chris in heaven" – here on earth, they go to these "friendly", "dark", "opulent rooms" for "large" hunks of the "best steak imaginable", though at these prices they should "throw in a potato"; they also love the "excellent fish" and "best cheesecake", yet some could do without the sizzling "mess" of butter on which the steaks are served ("ruined too many ties").

## Tarbell's S

24 | 24 | 23 | $31

*Camelback East Shops, 3213 E. Camelback Rd. (32nd St.), Phoenix,*
*602-955-8100*

☑ Clean, contemporary decor and an open kitchen turning out "exciting" New American cuisine cause diners to proclaim this an "excellent" addition that "fits like a glove"; not everyone agrees ("pretentious", "inconsistent") and even admirers find it "pricey", but "good wines by the glass" and "solid service" help win over the majority.

## T. Cook's S

− | − | − | M

*Royal Palms Inn, 5200 E. Camelback Rd. (56th St.), Phoenix,*
*602-808-0766*

Featuring Tuscan, Spanish and Mediterranean fare cooked on an open-hearth grill, this expanded restaurant in the beautifully renovated Royal Palms Inn offers delectables that both comfort and pique the palate; you can look forward to being served such dishes as loin of lamb with wild mushrooms and couscous or rotisserie-roasted chicken by a casual yet precise staff; N.B. don't miss the 250-year-old Mexican fountain.

## Vincent Guerithault on Camelback S

28 | 25 | 26 | $42

*3930 E. Camelback Rd. (40th St.), Phoenix, 602-224-0225*

☑ At this "national treasure", country French ambiance and classic cooking techniques are combined with SW ingredients by chef Guerithault, yielding "superb" food many rate "best in the area", enhanced by exceptional wines and "irresistible desserts"; though a small faction claims that the menu, while "still very good", "needs re-energizing", for most this "romantic", *"très élégante"* "event" is "worth every penny" – explaining why its voted Most Popular in Arizona.

# Portland

## TOP 10 FOOD RANKING

| | | |
|---|---|---|
| **29** | Genoa | Northern Italian |
| **28** | Paley's Place | Northwestern |
| **27** | Couvron | New French |
| | Heathman | French/Northwestern |
| | Tina's | Northwestern |
| **26** | Caprial's Bistro & Wine | Northwestern |
| | Restaurant Murata | Japanese |
| | 3 Doors Down Cafe | N/S Italian |
| | Cafe des Amis | French Bistro |
| | Wildwood | Northwestern |

## OTHER IMPORTANT PLACES

| | |
|---|---|
| Atwater's Restaurant & Bar | New American |
| Cafe Azul | Mexican |
| Caffe Mingo | N/S Italian |
| Castagna | French/Italian |
| Higgins Restaurant & Bar | Eclectic |
| Lucy's Table | Med./Northwestern |
| Saucebox Cafe & Bar | Asian |
| Tapeo | Spanish/Tapas |
| Typhoon! | Thai |

| F | D | S | C |
|---|---|---|---|

### Atwater's Restaurant & Bar S    24 | 26 | 25 | $40
*US Bancorp Tower, 111 SW Fifth Ave., 30th fl. (W. Burnside St.),
503-275-3600*
☑ "Every plate is a party" at this New American "dress-up treat"
on the 30th floor of the Downtown US Bancorp Tower, offering
"the best view in town"; though a few hedge that "altitude isn't
everything" and say the "food doesn't live up to the setting", the
majority finds the "monthly-changing menu" to be "terrific", and
the "great jazz in the lounge" (Tuesday–Saturday) pleases imbibers.

### Cafe Azul    25 | 23 | 23 | $30
*112 NW Ninth Ave. (bet. Couch & Davis Sts.), 503-525-4422*
☑ There's "no compromising" at this "sophisticated" Pearl District
Mexican where the kitchen turns out "creative cuisine and sauces"
("the best mole on earth") and "lots of organics"; critics' main carp
is that it's "extraordinarily overpriced" "for what you get", but
otherwise many call it close to "perfect."

### Cafe des Amis    26 | 24 | 27 | $35
*1987 NW Kearney St. (20th Ave.), 503-295-6487*
■ "From pâté to dessert", everything's "fabulous, darling" at this
"classy" NW District French bistro that's particularly distinguished
for its extraordinary service (voted No. 2 in Portland); loyalists love
the intimate setting at this "great romantic spot" and are amazed
by its "consistency" – "this good for this long is astonishing!"

174

## Caffe Mingo [S] 25 | 20 | 22 | $24

*807 NW 21st Ave. (bet. Kearney & Johnson Sts.), 503-226-4646*

■ "Delicious, simple fare" is the forte of this "excellent" NW District Italian trattoria that also offers a "relaxed atmosphere", "knowledgeable waiters" and "reasonable prices"; it's no surprise that this "small, intimate space" can get "too crowded" and it's "irritating" there are "no rezzies" for parties less than six, but even though fans "wish it weren't so tough to get a table", they "keep coming back."

## Caprial's Bistro & Wine 26 | 19 | 22 | $27

*7015 SE Milwaukie Ave. (Bybee Blvd.), 503-236-6457*

■ "Local celebrity" Caprial Pence – author and cooking show host – might "greet you at the door" of her Pacific Northwest bistro in Westmoreland; "inspired meals" that are a "feast for the eyes" thrill enthusiasts, while "low wine prices" win the hearts of penny-pinching oenophiles; N.B. a recent expansion has doubled the dining area and added an open kitchen.

## Castagna – | – | – | E

*1752 SE Hawthorne Blvd. (bet. 17th & 18th Aves.), 503-231-7373*

Expect incredibly fresh, seasonal ingredients prepared French-Italian style at this Hawthorne newcomer, where minimalism informs both the food presentation and the decor; husband and wife owners Kevin Gibson and Monique Siu (ex Genoa and Zefiro, respectively) show great attention to detail in everything from the cork and limestone floors to the roasted quail stuffed with fresh figs soaked in cognac.

## Couvron 27 | 23 | 25 | $53

*1126 SW 18th Ave. (Madison St.), 503-225-1844*

■ "World-class ambitions" inform everything about this "upscale" West Side New French that offers "unusual presentations" of "outstanding" cuisine along with "very attentive" service that's "perfect for a special occasion"; though the "too-small space" and "spendy" tabs leave some gasping for air, most take a deep breath and declare "it's worth saving up for."

## Genoa 29 | 24 | 28 | $55

*2832 SE Belmont St. (29th Ave.), 503-238-1464*

■ Rated No. 1 for Food and Service, this Italian "treasure" in Southeast has also garnered the title of Portland's Most Popular restaurant, and stalwarts say "everything is impeccable", from the "inspired", seven-course prix fixe menu to the "intimate atmosphere" and "unsurpassed" staff; though a minority moans it's "too dark" and "very spendy", the majority agrees that "quality has never faltered" at this "still special experience."

## Heathman [S] 27 | 24 | 26 | $36

*Heathman Hotel, 1001 SW Broadway (Salmon St.), 503-241-4100*

■ Chef Philippe Boulot unveils "superb" French-NW cuisine at this "sublime" Downtown hotel dining room that's "class all the way"; a "top-notch wine list", "casual but sharp" service and a "sophisticated" setting gladden its "gourmet guests", and despite a few who mumble "overrated", the majority considers this a "truly adult experience"; N.B. a gradual remodeling should be completed in 2000.

**Higgins Restaurant & Bar [S]** 25 | 23 | 24 | $34
*1239 SW Broadway (Jefferson St.), 503-222-9070*
■ "Greg Higgins is the man", for his Eclectic with a pronounced French accent elates acolytes with "fresh, smart" dishes that make for a "premier food experience"; though faultfinders fuss there's "sometimes too much happening on one plate", most call it "absolute perfection", especially "Portland's art elite", who make the bar their own after the theater lets out.

**Lucy's Table** 24 | 22 | 23 | $31
*706 NW 21st Ave. (Irving St.), 503-226-6126*
◪ This dimly lit, "delightful" "new kid" (on a Northwest block that could be renamed 'Restaurant Row') features a "creative" Med–NW menu loaded with "interesting flavors", and service that's "almost too good"; only the cautious say "too soon to tell."

**Paley's Place [S]** 28 | 25 | 26 | $36
*1204 NW 21st Ave. (Northrup St.), 503-243-2403*
◪ "Outstanding", "refined" Northwest Regional cuisine using local and organic ingredients awaits diners at Vitaly and Kimberly Paley's "intimate" bistro in a turn-of-the-century NW home; expect some of the "most personal service in town" and more stylish digs, thanks to a nifty redo that added "cozy banquettes", a "charming" bar, "great vintage posters" and five points to the decor rating; N.B. the sweetbreads and crème brûlée are a must.

**Restaurant Murata** 26 | 18 | 21 | $27
*200 SW Market St. (bet. 2nd & 3rd Aves.), 503-227-0080*
■ Surveyors report "excellent sushi" from master chef Ryoshiro Murata at this Downtown Japanese in a "traditional" setting (i.e. a "bit formal"); to get a sense of how "unusual and authentic" his offerings are, call 48 hours in advance for the *kaiseki ryori,* a multicourse dinner whose price you set ($45 minimum).

**Saucebox Cafe & Bar** 22 | 21 | 19 | $22
*214 SW Broadway (Burnside St.), 503-241-3393*
■ "Very chic", "dark" and "narrow", this Downtown Pan-Asian appeals to both the "beautiful people" who "drip coolness" while sipping cocktails and "hip" foodies who appreciate the "assortment of fresh fish and noodle dishes", especially the "fantastic Javanese salmon"; those who don't fit in find it "too trendy."

**Tapeo** 25 | 23 | 22 | $24
*2764 NW Thurman St. (28th Ave.), 503-226-0409*
◪ The closest thing to an "authentic" tapas bar in the metro area, this Northwest Iberian gets heaps of praise from those who "love" to fashion a "fantastic" meal out of "a little bit of everything" and sip on one of the innumerable sherries from the "great Spanish wine list"; a "wonderful" chef-owner who "makes you feel at home" and a "lovely", "intimate" dining room further its appeal.

**3 Doors Down Cafe** 26 | 22 | 24 | $25
*1429 SE 37th Ave. (Hawthorne Blvd.), 503-236-6886*
■ Acolytes gush "three thumbs up" for the "perfectly cooked pasta", "intimate" setting ("very flattering" lighting) and "informed" "servers who are glad to see you" at this Hawthorne Italian; sure, there's "always a line to get in" and "no reservations", but the price is a "value" and to some it's "consistently the best meal in town."

## Tina's S     27   21   25   $30
*760 Hwy. 99 W. (opp. fire station), Dundee, 503-538-8880*
■ The big news at this French-accented Northwestern in the Wine Country is the renovation that has doubled the size of the dining area and added a fireplace and "cute little bar"; while the atmosphere's "clearly better", the kitchen has always turned out "superb", "creative" dishes and the "outstanding staff" deftly knows its way around the vino list, which is heavily weighted toward local pinot noir treasures.

## Typhoon! S     25   19   20   $21
*2310 NW Everett St. (23rd Ave.), 503-243-7557*
## Typhoon! on Broadway S
*Imperial Hotel, 400 SW Broadway (Stark St.), 503-224-8285*
■ "The most creative", "gorgeous" Thai food in Portland, served on "cool plates", can be found at this top-rated "yuppie haven" that's opened a new branch in the Imperial Hotel; while portions can be "small" and prices "high", this "amazing experience" is "breaking new ground", and the Broadway location reputedly has the largest tea selection (150 choices) of any restaurant in the country.

## Wildwood S     26   23   23   $34
*1221 NW 21st Ave. (Overton St.), 503-248-9663*
◩ "Like a San Francisco restaurant" is the big city compliment respondents pay to this "trendy" "exponent of Northwest" cuisine, known for chef-owner Cory Shreiber's "bold" seasonal food, "snappy service" and "avant-garde" decor; the "cramped seating" and "noisy" room annoy a few of the "pretty people", but overall it's still a top-five "favorite."

# Salt Lake City & Mountain Resorts

## TOP 10 FOOD RANKING

| | Restaurant | Cuisine Type |
|---|---|---|
| 27 | Fresco Italian Cafe | Northern Italian |
| | Grapevine | Continental |
| | Mariposa | New American |
| 26 | New Yorker Club | American/Continental |
| | Glitretind Restaurant | New American |
| | Martine | Med./New American |
| | Spencer's | Steakhouse/Trad. Amer. |
| | Chez Betty | American/Continental |
| | Ichiban Sushi | Japanese |
| | Metropolitan | New American |

## OTHER IMPORTANT PLACES

| | |
|---|---|
| Cafe Diablo | Southwestern |
| Cafe Trang | Vietnamese |
| Goldener Hirsch | American/Continental |
| Grappa Italian | N/S Italian |
| La Caille | French |
| Log Haven Restaurant | Eclectic/New American |
| Mandarin | Chinese |
| Market Street Grill | Seafood |
| Red Butte Cafe | Southwestern |
| Red Iguana, The | Mexican |
| Sundance Tree Room | New American |
| Tuscany | Northern Italian |

F D S C

**Cafe Diablo** [S] ▽ 25 19 21 $27

*599 W. Main St. (N. Center St.), Torrey, 435-425-3070*

■ The "best place to get a real meal after a week of camping" out is at this "oasis in the desert" in remote Torrey, near Capitol Reef National Park; the few who know about this straightforward Southwesterner run by a husband-and-wife team feel that its "hot and spicy" food is "surprisingly good for a small town"; N.B. open May–mid-October.

**Cafe Trang** [S] 24 13 19 $15

*818 S. Main St. (bet. 800 & 900 South), Salt Lake City, 801-539-1638*
*Cottonwood Mall, 4835 S. Highland Dr., Holladay, 801-278-8889*

◪ Long-standing SLC Vietnamese featuring "outstanding noodles, soups" and a "large vegetarian menu"; aesthetes assert that the decor is "dingy", but "consistently" "cheap eats" keep the crowds coming; N.B. there's a new, unrated suburban branch in Holladay.

### Chez Betty S          26 | 20 | 23 | $41

*Copperbottom Inn, 1637 Short Line Rd. (Deer Valley Dr.), Park City, 435-649-8181*

■ It may take a map to locate this Continental-American in a nondescript Park City hotel lobby, but its "consistently excellent" food and "polished service" help offset the "somewhat gloomy decor"; fans who find it the "most pleasing and least pretentious" eating experience in Utah ask "why dine anywhere else?"

### Fresco Italian Cafe S          27 | 24 | 25 | $34

*1513 S. 1500 E. (bet. Emerson & Kensington Aves.), Salt Lake City, 801-486-1300*

■ Rated No.1 for Food in the *Utah Survey*, this SLC "perennial favorite" serves "excellent" and "delicious" Northern Italian food in a "lovely setting" (an adjoining bookstore adds ambiance); "dining on the patio [and garden] in summer is preferred", but in any season since it's "an intimate pleasure that never disappoints", "reservations are a must."

### Glitretind Restaurant S          26 | 26 | 25 | $45

*Stein Eriksen Lodge, 7700 Stein Way (Royal St.), Deer Valley, 435-645-6455*

■ At this "sophisticated but not stuffy" New American in Deer Valley, the "outstanding" "food is as gorgeous as the mountain setting" ("what a view"!); sure, it's "pricey" and the "place to see and be seen" ("look for Stein [Eriksen] wanna-bes"), but "it's great for a special occasion."

### Goldener Hirsch S          24 | 25 | 24 | $42

*Goldener Hirsch Inn, 7570 Royal St. E., Deer Valley, 435-649-7770*

■ A "ritzy atmosphere" with "fine European decor" and ravishing mountain views, plus "consistent" cuisine and an "excellent wine list" help this Deer Valley Continental-American claim what some call "the best clientele in Utah."

### Grapevine, The          27 | 25 | 26 | $33

*129 N. 100 East (bet. 100 & 200 North), Logan, 435-752-1977*

■ "An unbelievable find" tucked away in a historic Victorian home surrounded by lavender-and-grapevine-filled gardens, this chef-owned-and-operated Logan "gem" steals the crowds from Cache Valley and beyond "given there's no competition" when it comes to the "always excellent" Continental cuisine; limited hours (dinner only, Wednesday–Saturday) mean it's "almost always full."

### Grappa Italian Restaurant S          24 | 27 | 22 | $46

*151 Main St. (Swede Alley), Park City, 435-645-0636*

☑ The "place to be in Park City", particularly for a "romantic supper date", is this "atmospheric" Italian filled with "beautiful people"; while opponents opine it's "overpriced" and "overrated", most maintain "freshness reigns" here, making for an "unforgettable meal" that's "worth every penny."

**Ichiban Sushi & Japanese Cuisine [S]** 26 | 25 | 20 | $29

*336 S. 400 East (bet. 300 & 400 South), Salt Lake City, 801-532-7522*

■ Even if "you think you don't like sushi, the Japanese-trained female chef will teach you" to ("try the Funky Charlie"– just one of the "very creative" "killer" offerings here); while regulars "thank God" this longtime Park City spot moved to a spiffed up Downtown SLC location in an old church, several respondents specify that you take a "seat at the sushi bar" because service can be "slow" elsewhere in the room.

**La Caille [S]** 20 | 29 | 23 | $53

*Little Cottonwood Canyon, 9565 S. Wasatch Blvd., Sandy, 801-942-1751*

◪ "One of the most beautiful restaurants in the country" and voted No.1 for Decor in the *Utah Survey* is this "idyllic" Sandy French "château retreat"; while critics carp about the sky-high tab ("you pay for the ambiance and bosoms" – i.e. the waitresses' "period uniforms are revealing"), atmosphere addicts insist this "exceptional special-occasion place" deserves attention, while business types tout it as "great for the expense-account crowd."

**Log Haven Restaurant [S]** 25 | 27 | 23 | $37

*6451 E. 3800 South (Wasatch Blvd., 4 mi. up Millcreek Canyon), Salt Lake City, 801-272-8255*

■ Its "unsurpassed", "spectacular" "mountain setting" – a "revived" lodge nestled in thick pines and wildflowers accented by a lily-pad pond – is "worth the trip" up Millcreek Canyon; almost as highly rated is the "consistently innovative" and "delicious" American-Eclectic cuisine; all in all, for "celebrations and romance", it's one of the "best dining experiences" in the area.

**Mandarin** 25 | 19 | 20 | $18

*348 E. 900 North, Bountiful, 801-298-2406*

■ A trip to Bountiful could bring you to the "best Chinese ever", an "always crowded" stalwart with a "vast" menu, "consistently fresh, flavorful, quality ingredients" and "fab-o food"; some insiders advise "ordering the Peking duck 48 hours ahead – it's the only way to get a reservation" and avoid the "much too long wait."

**Mariposa, The [S]** 27 | 26 | 25 | $47

*Silver Lake Lodge, Deer Valley Resort, 7600 Royal St., Deer Valley, 435-645-6715*

■ This "great retreat" at Deer Valley Resort's Silver Lake Lodge is a "class act" offering "imaginative" New American dishes that are "as good as it gets", a "quietly elegant" atmosphere and "amazing service"; it may "flatten your credit card", but that doesn't stop a "clientele of beautiful people" from packing the place; N.B. open December–mid-April.

**Market Street Grill [S]** 25 | 22 | 22 | $25

*54 Market St. (Main St., bet. 300 & 400 South), Salt Lake City, 801-322-4668*

■ Seafooder and "Salt Lake mainstay" – anchor of the successful Gastronomy Inc. group – that some label "a neighborhood wonder" for "fresh fish", the "best blackened chicken plate (and it's not even on the menu") and "good breakfasts"; yes, it's "noisy", "but that's the fun" and locals rely on it for "regular dinners out."

## Martine
26　23　24　$30

*22 E. 100 South (bet. Main & State), Salt Lake City, 801-363-9328*

■ "Off to a strong start and getting better", this Med–New American yearling is "just what SLC needs – a hip, delicious place Downtown"; "imaginative", "unusual dishes" include "fun to graze on tapas", which underscore the evening offerings, while the "pub menu at lunch is a proven winner"; devotees declare that they do "things right" and are "consistent enough to recommend" anytime.

## Metropolitan
26　26　23　$51

*173 W. Broadway (bet. 200 West & West Temple), Salt Lake City, 801-364-3472*

◪ "Someone brought an urbane New York bistro and dropped it in Salt Lake" is what surveyors say about this Contemporary American with "exquisite food" (albeit presented in "dime-sized portions") and an "unforgettable tasting menu" served in a "beautiful" room; the less sophisticated snipe that the "pretentious" atmosphere means you "must wear black – or sit behind the fern", and wallet-watchers warn that the tab may be "reason to take out a second mortgage", but sybarites simply shrug that the "big splurge is worth it."

## New Yorker Club
26　26　25　$45

*60 Market St. (Main St., bet. 300 & 400 South), Salt Lake City, 801-363-0166*

■ Longtime "chef Will Pliler is a master" at this Downtown American-Continental that, despite a basement setting, remains Gastronomy Inc.'s "ritzy" "crown jewel"; the "consistently excellent food", "gracious service" and "great wine list" set a "benchmark for excellence" and draw the "pretty people", making it a place "to go to close a deal" or when "you're feeling romantic."

## Red Butte Cafe S
21　19　18　$18

*Foothill Village Shopping Ctr., 1414 Foothill Dr. (S. 2300 East), Salt Lake City, 801-581-9498*

■ Suburban SLC Southwestern in a hectic mini-mall that earns a "local treasure" tag from fans who feel that the "lively", "interesting" fare like "well-prepared" pastas and "good cakes and pies" from the in-house bakery can "always be counted on"; it's "loud", but since it's convenient to the University, "casual" and reasonably priced, it qualifies as a "great date spot."

## Red Iguana, The S
25　13　18　$14

*736 W. North Temple (bet. 700 & 800 West), Salt Lake City, 801-322-1489*

■ This "gastronomic gem" may be a "hole-in-the-wall", but many surveyors say it's the "best Mexican" in SLC, serving "great moles" and other "authentic" entrees that always draw a crowd; despite the "kitchy", "very east LA decor" and "lack of seating", devotees decree that it's the place for "killer food" – "I crave it in my sleep."

## Spencer's For Steaks & Chops S
26　24　23　$39

*Doubletree Hotel, 255 S. West Temple (bet. 200 & 300 South), Salt Lake City, 801-238-4748*

■ "Classic", "very upscale" Downtown American whose "good, high-end steaks" are the "best Chicago beef in the region"; a "cigar-friendly bar" and a "great selection of martinis" make this "unique for Utah" addition a "place where you can remember what being on expense account was like."

**Sundance Tree Room [S]** 25 | 26 | 22 | $40

*Six mi. up Provo Canyon (North Fork Canyon Rd.), Sundance, 801-223-4200*

■ There's a "gorgeous mountain ski resort setting" for this American with a western accent that's co-owned by Robert Redford; with "very creative food" and a "comfortable", "inviting" ambiance, it's the "the best of the best" ("only the tree is dead – the rest is a true treasure").

**Tuscany [S]** 23 | 27 | 22 | $33

*2832 E. 6200 South (Holladay Blvd.), Salt Lake City, 801-277-9919*

■ "Impress out-of-towners with SLC chic" at this "favorite" destination, which showcases "romantic Northern Italian dining" with a "luxurious setting" and "great atmosphere" in which to savor "innovative cuisine", accompanied by a "wonderful wine list" and served by an "impeccable" staff; "though it's quite big", it's a "gorgeous" "place to be seen", so prepare for a "mob scene."

# San Diego

## TOP 10 FOOD RANKING

| | Restaurant | Cuisine Type |
|---|---|---|
| 28 | El Bizcocho | Classic/New French |
| 27 | WineSellar & Brasserie | New French |
| | Mille Fleurs | New French |
| | Sushi Ota* | Japanese |
| | Azzura Point | Californian/Med. |
| | Pamplemousse Grille | Californian/New French |
| 26 | Rancho Valencia | Californian/Continental |
| | George's at the Cove | New American |
| | Belgian Lion | Belgian/French |
| | Laurel | New French |

## OTHER IMPORTANT PLACES

| | |
|---|---|
| Cafe Japengo | Asian/Eclectic |
| Cafe Pacifica | Seafood |
| Delicias | Californian |
| Greystone | Steakhouse |
| Mixx | Eclectic |
| Morton's of Chicago | Steakhouse |
| Rainwater's | Steakhouse |
| Salvatore's | Northern Italian |
| Star of the Sea | Seafood |
| Taka | Asian/Eclectic |
| Tapenade | French Bistro |
| Thee Bungalow | Classic French |
| Twins | Classic/New French |
| Vignola | New French |
| Vivace | Northern Italian |

| | F | D | S | C |
|---|---|---|---|---|
| **Azzura Point [S]** | 27 | 26 | 25 | $45 |

*Loews Coronado Bay Resort, 4000 Coronado Bay Rd. (Silver Strand Blvd.), Coronado, 619-424-4477*

■ This airy room with "smashing" decor on the second floor of the view-endowed Loews Coronado Bay Resort is where "serious" foodies join hotel guests for chef Michael Stebner's "innovative" Cal-Med fare, as well as for some "great sunsets"; it's a "special-occasion vacation in our hometown."

* Tied with the restaurant listed directly above.

### Belgian Lion, The
| 26 | 21 | 23 | $36 |

*2265 Bacon St. (W. Point Loma Blvd.), 619-223-2700*

◤ "Expensive but very good" Belgian-French in Ocean Beach that reminds some of "grandma's parlor" with its lace doily–strewn setting, "wonderful cassoulet" and other "hearty" fare; though some claim service isn't always doting, regulars revel in "personal attention" and find this Coulon family veteran "still great"; open Thursday–Saturday, dinner only.

### Cafe Japengo S
| 25 | 24 | 20 | $29 |

*The Aventine, 8960 University Ctr. Ln. (bet. La Jolla Village & Lebon Drs.), 858-450-3355*

◤ Emphatically "too noisy", this "yuppie heaven" at the epicenter of the Golden Triangle offers "excellent", "artistic sushi" and other Asian-inspired food in an "elegant Japanese setting" that's such a "place to be seen" for singles that those over 30 head to quieter tables in the back; while staffers are "great for viewing", they can be "slow", which fuels critics who say "overrated."

### Cafe Pacifica S
| 25 | 22 | 22 | $31 |

*2414 San Diego Ave. (Old Town Ave.), 619-291-6666*

■ "Tremendous seafood" with an "innovative" edge is the specialty of this "consistently strong" performer on the border of historic Old Town, which "never disappoints" the knowledgeable locals and tourists who come here for "great sunsets" and a well-priced menu that draws on solid Californian cuisine traditions; while undeniably "charming", it "could use more space around the tables."

### Delicias S
| 25 | 26 | 24 | $36 |

*6106 Paseo Delicias (La Granada), Rancho Sante Fe, 858-756-8000*

■ "Fresh flowers" and "beautiful" country French decor serve as the backdrop for an equally good-looking crowd at this "cozy", "comfortable" Californian in the heart of wealthy Rancho Santa Fe; while the "warm, intimate" ambiance attracts the most comments, high ratings also go to the "excellent" food and "careful" service; in sum, it's "worth a visit", especially for lunch.

### El Bizcocho S
| 28 | 26 | 26 | $44 |

*Rancho Bernardo Inn, 17550 Bernardo Oaks Dr. (Rancho Bernardo Rd.), Rancho Bernardo, 858-675-8550*

■ The last bastion of black-tie service in town, this grand hotel dining room in Rancho Bernardo may be "far" from Downtown, but it takes top honors for its "world-class" Classic and New French cuisine – in fact, it was voted No. 1 for Food in SD; the "sublime" service – also voted No. 1 in SD – and "elegant decor" add to the appeal, and while it's "pricey", most agree the raves are "well-deserved"; P.S. don't overlook the "best brunch" in town.

### George's at the Cove S
| 26 | 26 | 25 | $37 |

*1250 Prospect St. (bet. Cave & Ivanhoe Sts.), La Jolla, 858-454-4244*

■ This "real La Jolla tradition" is consistently voted SD's Most Popular restaurant, but now the culinary accolades go to the New American cuisine and sterling seafood specialties of new chef Trey Foshee; the triple-tiered setting still offers "romantic", "less-expensive" dining "on the roof terrace under a full moon", a pricier ground-floor main room that "can't miss for business" meals and a bar in between where singles mingle and nibble on light bites.

**Greystone, The Steakhouse ◐[S]** – | – | – | E

*658 Fifth Ave. (G St.), 619-232-0225*

Former San Diego Padre Kevin Ward is the host (and a partner) at this beefy new venture in the Gaslamp Quarter where the dressiest sidewalk tables in town fill up early and stay jammed late; inside, the upscale decor pleases the mixed crowd of conventioneers and locals as much as the snappy service and top-notch steaks, seafood and pastas; needless to say, such a premium meal comes with a premium price tag.

**Laurel Restaurant & Bar [S]** 26 | 26 | 22 | $38

*505 Laurel St. (5th Ave.), 619-239-2222*

◪ "The place to take guests who think SD is a hick town" is this "sleek, sexy", dinner-only New French near Balboa Park with a "big-city feel" that gives an extra edge to Douglas Organ's "superb" cuisine; as you'd expect from the younger sister of WineSellar & Brasserie, there's an "excellent wine list", so even if some find it noisy, with uneven service, more "wish they were open for lunch."

**Mille Fleurs [S]** 27 | 27 | 26 | $54

*Country Squire Courtyard, 6009 Paseo Delicias (Avenida de Acacias), Rancho Santa Fe, 858-756-3085*

◪ Set in a blissfully beautiful Mediterranean-style villa in rural Rancho Santa Fe, this "big-bucks" Contemporary French "for the horsey set" features "wonderful" food served in a "romantic" (a few say "stuffy") setting that "looks like France"; if some find the service "pompous" and the "small portions" "grossly overpriced", the majority considers owner Bertrand Hug's discreet retreat "the ideal special-occasion restaurant."

**Mixx [S]** 23 | 20 | 21 | $28

*3671 Fifth Ave. (Pennsylvania Ave.), 619-299-6499*

◪ "Innovative food" 'without boundaries' wins 'em over at this "reasonably priced" Eclectic in "trendy" Hillcrest that's quietly decorated to show off the youngish "see-and-be-seen" crowd; the only points of contention are service that "could be better" and the weekend blues and jazz, which some would nix but others savor.

**Morton's of Chicago [S]** 26 | 24 | 25 | $48

*285 J St. (bet. 2nd & 3rd Aves.), 619-696-3369*

■ Meat lovers would gladly "take out a second mortgage" to finance a trip to this "dark", "woody", casually elegant Downtown steak palace serving notoriously "huge portions" of the "best beef this side of Chicago"; of course, cost isn't an issue for the expense-account crowd that heads here for "first-class" food and service, and though a few find the raw-meat menu cart shtick too much, most admirers aren't cowed by it.

**Pamplemousse Grille [S]** 27 | 24 | 25 | $43

*514 Via de la Valle (Jimmy Durante Blvd.), Solana Beach, 858-792-9090*

■ "Beautiful people" and horse-racing types (in season) jockey for a table at this "noisy", art-filled, understatedly elegant Cal-French near the sea, where former NYer Jeffrey Strauss' "imagination and talent" fuel an "exceptional, exciting" menu that's "always a treat", right down to "the best tarte Tatin in SD"; still, some label it "overpriced."

**Rainwater's on Kettner ◐ [S]** 25 | 22 | 24 | $38

*1202 Kettner Blvd. (B St.), 619-233-5757*

◪ "Our version of Morton's of Chicago, but better" say some San Diegans of this homegrown steakhouse, a spacious, clubby "power location" "for a business lunch" on the second floor of a restored building near the Downtown waterfront; it pleases expense-account "big shots" with "delicious beef" and a "wine room for parties", but foes find it "stuffy" and "overrated."

**Rancho Valencia [S]** 26 | 29 | 25 | $44

*Rancho Valencia Resort, 5921 Valencia Circle (Rancho Diegueno Rd.), Rancho Sante Fe, 858-759-6216*

■ Surveyors say "you can't beat the ambiance" at this smashingly "beautiful" dining room (voted No. 1 for Decor in SD), part of the "exclusive" Rancho Valencia Resort near Rancho Santa Fe; besides "superb" Cal-Continental fare with Pacific Rim accents, it boasts a "great view", "leisurely service" and the "prettiest patio" on which to "lose the day"; in sum, it's well "worth the drive."

**Salvatore's [S]** 25 | 23 | 23 | $34

*750 Front St. (G St.), 619-544-1865*

■ This long-running, "classy" favorite in Downtown's most exclusive condominium tower produces "good old-fashioned Northern Italian" fare in a "sophisticated", handsomely "rococo" setting; the "high-quality" kitchen is overseen by Raffaella Gangale while "charming" husband Salvatore plays host – so successfully that some think he "makes the experience."

**Star of the Sea [S]** 23 | 22 | 23 | $39

(fka Anthony's Star of the Sea)

*1360 N. Harbor Dr. (Ash St.), 619-232-7408*

◪ An extravagant renovation of this "classic" place to "impress out-of-towners" on the Downtown waterfront has resulted in a much less "formal" mood at this "pricey" 31-year-old seafood house; the new love seat–like chairs at tables for two set against glass walls overlooking the bay delights those who dismissed the former "'60s" decor and creates a romantic backdrop in which to enjoy the imaginative, seasonal dishes of recently arrived chef Brian Johnston; the staff (now sans tuxedos) remains as professional as ever, but has adopted a less stiff tone.

**Sushi Ota [S]** 27 | 13 | 17 | $26

*4529 Mission Bay Dr. (Balboa Ave.), 858-270-5670*

■ Despite an "odd location" near the freeway at the back side of Pacific Beach, this Japanese shrine is "always crowded" because the chef is an "artist with a knife", turning out "creative" sushi that's "the best in SD"; the food is so good that "visitors from Tokyo specifically request" a visit here, and it more than makes up for "lunch-counter decor" and "inconsistent service."

**Taka [S]** 26 | 19 | 21 | $29

*555 Fifth Ave. (Market St.), 619-338-0555*

■ The "trendy" young things who populate the Gaslamp Quarter agree that this is the "best" and "hippest" Downtown sushi bar, and its Asian fusion menu offers a "superb" alternative to the Italian fare that predominates in the neighborhood; while the claim that "beautiful folks" get top treatment is open to debate, there's no denying the "long lines", so hunker down.

### Tapenade 🖲
| – | – | – | E |

*7612 Fay Ave. (bet. Kline & Pearl Sts.), La Jolla, 619-551-7500*
Jean-Michel and Sylvie Diot left behind successful restaurants in
NY for sunny SD, and their French venture in La Jolla has drawn
raves from day one, offering a seafood-heavy bistro menu in a
breezy, South of France–like setting; it's fairly "pricey", but the
well-heeled clientele doesn't seem to mind.

### Thee Bungalow 🖲
| 25 | 19 | 23 | $34 |

*4996 W. Point Loma Blvd. (Bacon St.), 619-224-2884*
🔲 For more than a decade, chef Edmund Moore has followed a
successful recipe blending generous portions, hearty French
cuisine and reasonable prices at this "excellent standby" in an
"old Ocean Beach house"; the older "regular crowd" sings the
praises of the "best roast duck", "bargain" early-bird menu and
"fantastic"-value wine list, drowning out the few who think the
food's too "heavy" and the decor "needs updating."

### Twins ◐🖲
| – | – | – | E |

*Encinitas Lumberyard Shopping Ctr., 937 S. Coast Hwy. (Leucadia Blvd.),
Encinitas, 760-635-1962*
Named to honor the proprietors' twin daughters, this stylish
Encinitas newcomer fills a crying need for formal, fine French
dining along the North County coast; in a spacious room, affluent
yuppies and their elders smack their lips knowingly over the Classic
and Contemporary cuisine of chef Renè Herbeck, while the quiet
ambiance allows them to listen to their own sparkling conversation,
as well as the trilling of water flowing down the marble wall.

### Vignola
| ▽ | 26 | 20 | 24 | $34 |

*Ramada Inn, 828 Sixth Ave. (bet. E & F Sts.), 619-231-1111*
■ Simply but pleasantly decorated, this Gaslamp Quarter French
earns praise for its "awesome foie gras" and "innovative fare"
from "hot" chef Fabrice Poigin, who is warmly remembered from
previous stints around town; "reasonable prices" and a smoothly
trained young staff are pluses.

### Vivace 🖲
| 22 | 25 | 21 | $41 |

*Four Seasons Resort Aviara, 7100 Four Seasons Point (bet. Aviara Pkwy.
& Poinsettia Ln.), Carlsbad, 760-603-6999*
🔲 This "beautiful" Northern Italian in Carlsbad's Four Seasons
Resort Aviara is a "welcome addition" to the North County scene;
though the well-heeled suburbanites who flock to this "elegant"
enclave express some reservations (at these prices, they "need to
work harder on the food"), the more lenient note that it's improving.

### WineSellar & Brasserie
| 27 | 20 | 25 | $42 |

*9550 Waples St. (bet. Mira Mesa Blvd. & Steadman St.), 858-450-9557*
■ Douglas Organ is too old now to be the *enfant terrible* of SD
chefs, but his casually chic New French "hidden gem" in Sorrento
Mesa remains an "original" that's "worth a trip to the warehouse
district", offering "the best marriage of food and wine", as well
as "attentive service"; some find it "too expensive for the decor",
but with 3,000 wines to choose from and a six-variety tasting
every Saturday (lunch optional), it's "heaven" for oenophiles.

# San Francisco Bay Area*

## TOP 20 FOOD RANKING

| Restaurant | Cuisine Type |
|---|---|
| 29 French Laundry/N | New American/French |
| 28 Sent Sovi/S | New French |
| Masa's | New French |
| Ritz-Carlton Dining Room | New French |
| 27 La Folie | New French |
| Fleur de Lys | New French |
| Chez Panisse/E | Californian/Med. |
| Terra/N | Californian/French |
| Aqua | New American/Seafood |
| Boulevard | New American |
| Chez Panisse Cafe/E | Californian/Med. |
| 26 Campton Place | French |
| Charles Nob Hill | Californian/New French |
| Erna's Elderberry House/S | Californian/French |
| Domaine Chandon/N | Californian/New French |
| Pacific's Edge/S | Californian |
| Postrio | Californian |
| Emile's/S | Classic French |
| Woodward's Garden | New American |
| Fringale | French Bistro |

## OTHER IMPORTANT PLACES

| | |
|---|---|
| Bistro Jeanty/N | French Bistro |
| Bouchon/N | French Bistro |
| Eos Restaurant & Wine Bar | Asian/Eclectic |
| Farallon | Seafood |
| Gary Danko | New American |
| Globe | New American |
| Grand Cafe | Californian/New French |
| Hawthorne Lane | Californian |
| Jardinière | New French |
| Lark Creek Inn/N | Traditional American |
| Meetinghouse, The | New American |
| Moose's | Californian/Med. |
| Oliveto Cafe & Restaurant/E | Northern Italian |
| PlumpJack Cafe | Mediterranean |
| Rose Pistola | Italian/Seafood |
| Rubicon | Californian/New French |
| Shanghai 1930 | Chinese |
| Slanted Door | Vietnamese |
| Spago Palo Alto/S | Californian |
| Tra Vigne/N | N/S Italian |
| 231 Ellsworth/S | French |
| Vivande Porta Via | N/S Italian |
| Zuni Cafe | Mediterranean |

* E=East of San Francisco, N=North of San Francisco and
  S=South of San Francisco.

### Aqua
27  26  24  $57

*252 California St. (bet. Battery & Front Sts.), 415-956-9662*

■ Aqua-lytes gush that "everything is special" at this top-dollar Downtown New American, from the "very glam" crowd to chef Michael Mina's "stunningly presented", "awesome" seafood ("I didn't know they could do that to a lobster!") to the "gorgeous" flowers; noise levels are high and there's minor carping about "cold-as-fish" service, but as the *SF Survey*'s second Most Popular restaurant, this is definitely a "jewel in our culinary crown."

### Bistro Jeanty S
25  21  22  $39

*6510 Washington St. (east of Hwy. 29), Yountville, 707-944-0103*

■ "Forget Berkeley" – there's "absolutely authentic bistro food" at Philippe Jeanty's jaunty French spot in Yountville, which "hits on all cylinders" and "wow, wow, wows" our wide-eyed critics with "outstanding food" at "fair prices" and "convivial" ambiance; if the "Paris *ouest*" menu makes it "hard to decide what to eat", then just "order everything."

### Bouchon ●S
23  25  22  $42

*6534 Washington St. (east of Hwy. 29), Yountville, 707-944-8037*

■ Highly touted chef Thomas Keller (of SF's No. 1 rated French Laundry) and his brother Joseph are behind this "beautiful" Yountville yearling with a "NY-Parisian" feel and "excellent" French bistro food; a few feel the menu "doesn't reach far enough" and dub the service "disjointed", but the majority maintains "what's there is stellar" and it's a "wonderful addition to the Napa Valley scene."

### Boulevard S
27  26  24  $48

*1 Mission St. (Steuart St.), 415-543-6084*

■ "The girl can cook" declare reviewers blown away by chef Nancy Oakes' "always amazing" New American food at this Pat Kuleto–designed SoMa "art nouveau carnival", with "three distinctive rooms" and a "professional" staff that's "genuinely pleased to serve you"; so "get the company credit card and go" to what is once again the Most Popular restaurant in the *SF Survey*.

### Campton Place S
26  25  26  $54

*Campton Pl. Hotel, 340 Stockton St. (bet. Post & Sutter Sts.), 415-955-5555*

■ This hotel-based Downtown "oasis of refinement" is a "quiet", "spacious" "grown-up place" with a polished staff and "excellent" food; while chef Todd Humphries has departed, Laurent Manrique (ex NYC's Gertrude's) and his new Southern French menu are expected to maintain the same high culinary standards.

### Charles Nob Hill S
26  25  26  $61

*1250 Jones St. (Clay St.), 415-771-5400*

■ "Solid gold" chef Ron Siegel – victorious on the Japanese cult TV cooking show *Iron Chef* – "deserves awards" for "extraordinary" Cal–New French cuisine according to the "older crowd" that patronizes this "romantic" "hideaway" in a Nob Hill residential building; there's also a "professional" staff that makes diners feel "taken care of", but "wow, I'm glad it was on expense account."

### Chez Panisse
27 23 25 $64

*1517 Shattuck Ave. (bet. Cedar & Vine Sts.), Berkeley, 510-548-5525*

■ Culinary "goddess" Alice Waters' Berkeley "mother church" still draw raves ("a national treasure") for its "harmonious" use of the "freshest" ingredients in "barely embellished" Cal-Med dishes; since everyone goes in "expecting perfection", naturally a few "fail to understand" the "unadulterated" "magic" of the cuisine, but the overwhelming majority says it's definitely worth the "difficult reservations."

### Chez Panisse Cafe
27 22 24 $39

*1517 Shattuck Ave. (bet. Cedar & Vine Sts.), Berkeley, 510-548-5049*

■ This Berkeley Cal-Med cafe upstairs from Chez Panisse is called a "better value" than its parent, with a "more flexible" menu and equally "wonderful" food; an "unexpectedly informal" setting adds to its appeal as a "gem" that's "guaranteed to impress" – "if ya can get in" (same-day reservations only).

### Domaine Chandon [S]
26 25 25 $53

*1 California Dr. (Hwy. 29), Yountville, 707-944-2892*

■ "We oohed over every course" at this Yountville Californian–New French with a "spectacular setting" in the vineyards ("sit outside"); a "fine wine list" complements the "fantastic food", and an "attentive staff pampers" diners; in sum, it's still a "quintessential wine country destination" – just "rob a bank" beforehand.

### Emile's
26 21 23 $51

*545 S. Second St. (bet. Reed & William Sts.), San Jose, 408-289-1960*

■ "High-powered brokers and celebrities" dine at this pricey San Jose pioneer featuring "great" "Classic French with modern edges"; "caring service", an "elegant" ambiance and "fine wines" are other reasons why it's "always a treat."

### Eos Restaurant & Wine Bar [S]
25 19 20 $40

*901 Cole St. (Carl St.), 415-566-3063*

◪ Boosters rave they're "always amazed" at Arnold Wong's "daring" Asian fusion bistro in Cole Valley, where "gorgeously creative" cuisine comes with "provocative" selections from the "exceptional" wine bar next door; it may be "a little precious" for some, but it's "a must for foodies and wine geeks."

### Erna's Elderberry House [S]
26 27 27 $66

*48688 Victoria Ln. (Hwy. 41), Oakhurst, 559-683-6800*

■ Our furthest-flung restaurant is this "first-class" Cal-French in Oakhurst (right outside Yosemite National Park), a "special getaway that creates memories" with an "elegant, comfortable" ambiance and a "dining experience that's four-star from beginning to end"; you can overnight at the adjoining Château du Sureau, but some frustrated foodies still whine: "why is it so good yet so far?"

### Farallon [S]
24 28 23 $51

*450 Post St. (bet. Mason & Powell Sts.), 415-956-6969*

◪ Chef Mark Franz works "sheer magic with seafood" while Pat Kuleto's "drop-dead gorgeous" "underwater fantasy" decor is like "Captain Nemo on acid" at this "expense-account" Downtowner; while a disenchanted few say "attitude is an ingredient" here and claim they "need a microscope to find the appetizers", most advise "take the dive" for simply "sublime" coastal cuisine.

## Fleur de Lys
27 | 27 | 26 | $68

*777 Sutter St. (bet. Jones & Taylor Sts.), 415-673-7779*
■ Hubert Keller's "flawless creations" ("if it weren't so classy, you'd lick the plate") still stun reviewers at this "always superb" Downtown New French, which also offers an excellent vegetarian tasting menu; the "opulent" decor is "tops for elegance" and the service is "attentive", making it a "best splurge" for a "gala, romantic evening."

## French Laundry S
29 | 26 | 27 | $78

*6640 Washington St. (Creek St.), Yountville, 707-944-2380*
■ "Two whole days on redial" might score you a reservation at Thomas Keller's "dazzling" and deliriously expensive Yountville Contemporary American with French influences that's voted No. 1 for Food in the *SF Survey*; the "whimsical, playfully serious" cuisine is backed by the "finest service ever", and "monastic" decor adds to the "religious experience"; the spiritual predict it's "how we'll eat in heaven" and caution it's "just about as easy to get in to."

## Fringale
26 | 19 | 22 | $39

*570 Fourth St. (bet. Brannan & Bryant Sts.), 415-543-0573*
■ "Like a sunny Cézanne still life" come alive, Gerald Hirigoyen's highly rated and "charmingly petite" SoMa French is "buoyant" and "so bistro-y" ("about as authentic as you'll get"), with some "unparalleled" dishes and an "interesting wine list that consistently delivers"; the place is always "crowded", but "use your high school French and get a bump up in service" from the "flirtatious waiters."

## Gary Danko S
– | – | – | VE

*800 North Point St. (Hyde St.), 415-749-2060*
Bay Area super-chef Gary Danko left Viognier in San Mateo to open this eponymous French-influenced New American on the former Chez Michel site near Fisherman's Wharf, along with partner and maitre d' Nick Peyton (ex Ritz-Carlton Dining Room); with a large, seasonal menu available in a user-friendly, three-to-six-course format, a 600-bottle wine list and a sophisticated, contemporary art–filled setting, this is sure to be one of the hottest tickets for some time.

## Globe ●S
21 | 17 | 18 | $36

*290 Pacific Ave. (bet. Battery & Front Sts.), 415-391-4132*
☑ With a "post-industrial buzz" and "hip NYC feel", this "casually upscale" Downtown late night "scene" is where "chefs from around the city" and "foodies come to eat" Joseph Manzare's "innovative" New American cuisine in "a dark setting that feels so cool"; though some "don't get the attraction" and suggest the "uppity" staff "needs to smile", many feel it's "the only place to be at midnight."

## Grand Cafe S
21 | 26 | 20 | $37

*Hotel Monaco, 501 Geary St. (Taylor St.), 415-292-0101*
■ "Grand it is" – this "sophisticate's dream" Downtown is set in a "magnificently decadent" space with "fabulous high ceilings" and "beautiful art"; "the room is sheer heaven" and seems to "improve" the Cal–New French cuisine, which while "not up to the surroundings", is "commendable"; the staff is "knowledgeable", and the tabs "reasonable."

## Hawthorne Lane 🅂　　26 25 24 $50
*22 Hawthorne St. (bet. 2nd & 3rd Sts.), 415-777-9779*
■ Anne and David Gingrass' "fancy" SoMa Californian virtually "defines sophistication" and is "designed to impress"; "swoon" over the "gorgeous", "artful decor" while reveling in "superlative" cuisine turned out by a kitchen that "knows how to respect good ingredients"; the staff is "attentive" to "every detail" and most rejoice in an "incredible dining experience."

## Jardinière 🅂　　26 26 23 $54
*300 Grove St. (Franklin St.), 415-861-5555*
■ "Incredible talent" Traci Des Jardins (ex Rubicon) is "in full bloom" in the kitchen of this "cosmopolitan" Civic Center New French, turning out "peerless" cuisine with "memorable flavors"; equally "dazzling" is the "opulent" room designed by Pat Kuleto, with a "way cool round bar" that affords "great people-watching"; despite "too-small portions", most feel this "magical place" is "as close to perfection as it gets" and applaud "bravo!", "certain it'll become a SF classic"; P.S. "a balcony table over the bar is the best seat in town."

## La Folie　　27 23 25 $65
*2316 Polk St. (bet. Green & Union Sts.), 415-776-5577*
■ Chef Roland Passot's "divine" culinary "artistry" at this Van Ness/Polk New French reminds reviewers "why we loved nouvelle in the first place"; there's "romantic" decor and "informal" service that "looks after every detail", but with "half the pretension of comparable restaurants"; the tab will be a "savings drainer", but this "favorite" "deserves its spot as one of SF's best."

## Lark Creek Inn 🅂　　24 24 23 $45
*234 Magnolia Ave. (Madrone Ave.), Larkspur, 415-924-7766*
■ "Tried and true" with "top-notch" food is what surveyors say about Brad Ogden's "charming" Larkspur American in a "delightful old house"; considered a "classic", "Bradley's benchmark" is a "sentimental favorite" and "what a country restaurant should be."

## Masa's　　28 25 26 $75
*Hotel Vintage Court, 648 Bush St. (bet. Powell & Stockton Sts.), 415-989-7154*
☑ "All superlatives seem inadequate" when it comes to describing this "quiet", "very formal" Downtown Contemporary French shrine that "hasn't skipped a beat" since former chef Julian Serrano left, and continues to produce "unbelievable magic" courtesy of Chad Callahan's "imaginative" "works of art"; "flawless service" also makes it easier to swallow the prix fixe menu's "stratospheric" prices.

## Meetinghouse, The 🅂　　25 21 24 $37
*1701 Octavia St. (Bush St.), 415-922-6733*
■ "A perfect match of food and decor" characterizes this Pacific Heights New American with "upscale", but "straightforward" cooking and a "homey", yet "elegant", "Shaker-inspired" interior; factor in "personal attention" from an "excellent" staff and you have a place that's "just like going home . . . only much better."

F | D | S | C

## Moose's [S] — 22 | 21 | 21 | $38

*1652 Stockton St. (bet. Filbert & Union Sts.), 415-989-7800*

◩ Host extraordinaire Ed Moose's eponymous North Beach Cal-Med bistro is a "hub" for a "social-column" crowd attracted to the "lively bar" and nightly jazz; rounding out "the warm SF environment" is a "strong new chef's" "terrific" food ("better than it needs to be"), which is complemented by an "awesome wine list."

## Oliveto Cafe & Restaurant [S] — 24 | 21 | 21 | $42

*5655 College Ave. (Shafter Ave.), Oakland, 510-547-5356*

◩ "Shades of Tuscany" await visitors to Paul Bertolli's Oakland Northern Italian where diners "love the purity" of the flavors in the "simple", "unadorned" dishes; there's an open kitchen and decor that epitomizes "rustic elegance" too, but that doesn't stop a chorus of dissenters from declaring that the place is "overpriced" and "not as good as its rep"; N.B. to hedge your bets, consider the less expensive cafe downstairs.

## Pacific's Edge [S] — 26 | 28 | 24 | $57

*Highlands Inn, Hwy. 1 (Highland Dr.), Carmel, 831-622-5445*

■ "Nature provides the ambiance" at this top-dollar Californian in the Highlands Inn, which is voted No. 1 for Decor in the *SF Survey* and situated on a "spectacular stretch" of the Carmel coast; however, the vista "doesn't overshadow the truly fine food", which is likely to remain highly rated despite the departure of chef Cal Stamenov (now at Marinus); since it "excels in every way", the only question is whether the "world-class views" are "best at lunch at a window table" or "right before sunset."

## PlumpJack Cafe — 24 | 22 | 23 | $44

*3127 Fillmore St. (bet. Filbert & Greenwich Sts.), 415-563-4755*
*PlumpJack Squaw Valley Inn, 1920 Squaw Valley Rd., Olympic Valley, 530-583-1576* [S]

■ Oozing "star quality", this "stylish", "clubby" Union Street Med entices with an "always changing, always great" menu, paired with a "tantalizing" retail-priced wine list (thanks to the owners' nearby spirits shop); a few sniff "how good can hype really taste?", but most praise the "upscale dining" experience; N.B. there's also a branch in Olympic Valley.

## Postrio [S] — 26 | 26 | 24 | $52

*Prescott Hotel, 545 Post St. (bet. Mason & Taylor Sts.), 415-776-7825*

■ Prepare to be thoroughly "dazzled" by this "striking" Wolfgang Puck creation Downtown – sip a cocktail at the "energized" bar, "make your grand entrance" down the "fabulous" stairway, ease into the "plush" dining room, bask in the "star-studded scene", and revel in chefs Steven and Mitchell Rosenthal's "sensational" Cal cuisine; "they hit all the marks" and "get everything right from A-Z."

## Ritz-Carlton Dining Room — 28 | 28 | 28 | $68

*Ritz-Carlton Hotel, 600 Stockton St. (bet. California & Pine Sts.), 415-773-6198*

■ "Treat yourself to the good life" at this Nob Hill New French wallet-wrencher where "talented" Sylvain Portay always produces something "incredible" and "elegance takes on new meaning" after spending an evening in the "rarefied" room; a harpist and a "pampering" staff (No. 1 in the *SF Survey* for service) complete the "seldom-less-than-extraordinary" experience.

**Rose Pistola ◐[S]** 21 | 20 | 18 | $38
*532 Columbus Ave. (bet. Green & Union Sts.), 415-399-0499*
◪ Reed Hearon's "trendy" North Beach Italian-seafooder attracts a "diverse crowd" ("big blondes, yuppies, gay couples") and generates an equally wide range of responses: boosters love the "hip" atmosphere and "family-style" portions of "excellent" Ligurian dishes; naysayers find it "overhyped" with a "brutal noise level" and a staff that's generous with the "attitude."

**Rubicon** 24 | 21 | 22 | $49
*558 Sacramento St. (bet. Montgomery & Sansome Sts.), 415-434-4100*
◪ An "attractive crowd" of "business diners" packs this celebrity-backed Downtown Californian–New French for the dynamic combination of chef Scott Newman's "exceptional" food and super sommelier Larry Stone's "spectacular wine list"; quibblers find the "understated" setting "slightly stuffy" and "corporate", but concede the place "still has the buzz."

**Sent Sovi [S]** 28 | 22 | 25 | $56
*14583 Big Basin Way (5th St.), Saratoga, 408-867-3110*
■ The "treasure of Saratoga" is David Kinch's "perfect small restaurant", an "exquisite find" with "imaginative" New French food, which is backed up by highly rated service; it's "pricey", but the experience is "always extremely enjoyable."

**Shanghai 1930 [S]** 20 | 23 | 18 | $40
*133 Steuart St. (bet. Howard & Mission Sts.), 415-896-5600*
◪ "Exotic elegance" best describes the decor of George Chen's "sophisticated" SoMa Chinese supper club, a "classy" celebrity hangout with a "super bar", "great jazz" and "some novel, excellent dishes" ("go with a mouth ready to experiment"); foes bemoan sometimes "spotty service", "small portions" and "expensive" tabs.

**Slanted Door [S]** 25 | 17 | 19 | $31
*584 Valencia St. (17th St.), 415-861-8032*
■ This "outstanding", "unique twist on" Vietnamese in the Mission District has "cool", "spartan" decor, "waiters who stay on their toes" and some of the "most exciting", "creative" cuisine in town ("I'll never forget the clay-pot chicken") that's "pure flavors and textures"; "unreal" wines only add to the misery of those who find it "impossible to get in"; N.B. there's now valet parking.

**Spago Palo Alto [S]** 24 | 23 | 22 | $51
*265 Lytton Ave. (Bryant St.), Palo Alto, 650-833-1000*
■ "Wolfgang works his magic" at this "chi-chi" ("just smell all that new money") Palo Alto hot spot and "sequel" to the original in LA, with the trademark "hip decor" and "fabulous people-watching" ("get off the cell phone already"); while some sniff it's "noisy" and "overrated", the majority maintains that the Californian food is "excellent" – as usual, "Puck knows what he's doing."

**Terra [S]** 27 | 25 | 25 | $52
*1345 Railroad Ave. (bet. Adams & Hunt Sts.), St. Helena, 707-963-8931*
■ Husband-and-wife team Hiro Sone and Lissa Doumani's highly-rated St. Helena Franco-Californian with Asian accents "has it all" – "gorgeous" cuisine served by an "amazing staff" in a "romantic", "quietly elegant" room; a few are Terra-fied by the prices, but all agree it's "definitely a destination place that always delivers."

**Tra Vigne [S]** | 24 | 26 | 22 | $42 |
*1050 Charter Oak Ave. (Hwy. 29), St. Helena, 707-963-4444*
◪ "Hang out with the who's who of Napa Valley" at this "brassy, classy, sassy" St. Helena Italian; they come for chef Michael Chiarello's "marvelous food that's made with love", a "lovely", "spacious" setting with a "fabulous interior design" that evokes Tuscany and an outdoor terrace that's "truly sublime" in summer.

**231 Ellsworth** | 25 | 22 | 24 | $47 |
*231 S. Ellsworth Ave. (bet. 2nd & 3rd Aves.), San Mateo, 650-347-7231*
■ High-end French "gem" in San Mateo with "elegant, refined food" that's "never a disappointment", making it the "nearby choice for special occasions"; while the "dull interior" doesn't excite those with design on their minds, the prix fixe lunch offers a "great deal on gourmet dining."

**Vivande Porta Via [S]** | 22 | 16 | 18 | $31 |
*2125 Fillmore St. (bet. California & Sacramento Sts.), 415-346-4430*
■ Find "stellar preparations" of Italian dishes (particularly Sicilian specialties) at Carlo Middione's Pacific Heights trattoria, "a restaurant disguised as a deli" where you can dine in or get the "appealing" fixings to go; while it may be "a bit pricey" considering "the deli atmosphere", most maintain "I've loved this place for years."

**Woodward's Garden [S]** | 26 | 15 | 21 | $37 |
*1700 Mission St. (Duboce St.), 415-621-7122*
■ A "real miracle" in a "lousy", "under-the-freeway" Mission District location, this "extremely cozy" (only 31 seats) New American "treasure" somehow "feels like a secret though everyone knows it's so good"; the "gem of a menu" is "unique" yet accessible, offering "some of the best food in SF", and it's served by an "endearing" staff that ensures it's "always a treat" – "even with a view of the exit ramp."

**Zuni Cafe ◐[S]** | 23 | 20 | 19 | $37 |
*1658 Market St. (bet. Franklin & Gough Sts.), 415-552-2522*
◪ "Joy radiates from the kitchen", an "artistic clientele" swarms the "hippest zinc bar in the city" and there's a "never-ending celebration" in the "cool" dining room of this Civic Center Med "scene"; from the "steadily brilliant menu", the famous and the famished feast on the "best roasted chicken on the planet"; even if it's "a little too-too", baby, "you're nobody in this town if you haven't been seen here."

# Santa Fe

## TOP 5 FOOD RANKING

| Restaurant | Cuisine Type |
|---|---|
| **25** Santacafe | Eclectic |
| Cafe Pasqual's | Southwestern |
| **24** Coyote Cafe | Southwestern |
| Carlos' Gospel Cafe | Sandwich Shop |
| India Palace | Indian |

## OTHER IMPORTANT PLACES

| | |
|---|---|
| El Farol | Mexican/Spanish |
| Geronimo | Southwestern |
| Inn of the Anasazi | Southwestern |
| La Casa Sena | New Mexican/SW |
| La Choza | New Mexican |
| Old House | Continental/SW |
| Old Mexico Grill | Mexican |
| Pink Adobe | Continental/SW |
| Pranzo Italian Grill | N/S Italian |
| Rancho de Chimayo | New Mexican |
| Shed, The | New Mexican |

| F | D | S | C |
|---|---|---|---|

### Cafe Pasqual's S

| 25 | 19 | 21 | $21 |
|---|---|---|---|

*121 Don Gaspar Ave. (Water St.), 505-983-9340*
☑ There's "always a line" at this "funky and fun" midpriced Southwestern cafe a block south of the Plaza in Santa Fe, but it's "worth the wait" for "the best people-watching in town" and creative cuisine like salmon burritos and "simply the best Sunday breakfast anywhere"; but dissenters liken it to a "cattle call."

### Carlos' Gospel Cafe ⇴

| 24 | 16 | 21 | $9 |
|---|---|---|---|

*125 Lincoln Ave. (bet. Marcy St. & Palace Ave.), 505-983-1841*
■ A local Santa Fe favorite, this lunch-only soup-and-sandwich cafe with a "nice little patio" is renowned for dishes like 'hangover stew', the Alice B. Toklas sandwich and "the best lemon meringue pie anywhere"; it's "not fancy, just good."

### Coyote Cafe S

| 24 | 24 | 23 | $38 |
|---|---|---|---|

*132 W. Water St. (bet. Don Gaspar Ave. & Galisteo St.), 505-983-1615*
☑ While some Santa Fe natives consider chef Mark Miller's place an "overrated" "tourist trap", plenty of "locals do dine here and love it", praising "the most creative menu in town" and voting it Santa Fe's Most Popular restaurant; his "innovative" Southwestern cuisine, marked by "big flavors" and an original "use of chiles", is "always a surprise" and, for most, "well worth the cost."

### El Farol S
20 | 21 | 18 | $24

*808 Canyon Rd. (Camino del Monte Sol), 505-983-9912*

■ A "heavy local scene" in Santa Fe for "drinking and dancing", this "classic", cozy adobe Mexican-Spanish is fun for solo travelers; the tapas are "interesting", "especially the calamari with romesco sauce", but "can easily become a very expensive meal."

### Geronimo S
24 | 26 | 22 | $35

*724 Canyon Rd. (Camino del Monte Sol), 505-982-1500*

■ Housed in a "beautiful" 150-year-old adobe, this pricey "hidden gem" on Santa Fe's old artist road is "classy without being snobby" and offers what admirers call "the most creative Southwestern contemporary cooking"; apart from a few complaints about service, most say it provides a "lovely experience anytime."

### India Palace S
24 | 21 | 23 | $21

*227 Don Gaspar Ave. (Water St.), 505-986-5859*

■ "One of Santa Fe's best, most consistent and friendliest", this "absolutely great all-around" Indian serves what devotees call the "best curry this side of Bombay"; white tablecloths and candles give it a "special occasion" feel, although some note the "staff always seems to be better attired than the guests."

### Inn of the Anasazi S
24 | 25 | 23 | $38

*Inn of the Anasazi, 113 Washington Ave. (bet. Marcy St. & Palace Ave.), 505-988-3236*

☑ "Pricey" Santa Fe Southwestern offering "nouvelle and natural" cuisine with an emphasis on vegetarian and seafood specials; handcrafted elegance gives this SW-style inn the look of a "European hotel", and the food presentation is as "gorgeous" as the decor; while dissenters find both food and service "uneven", ratings attest they're outvoted.

### La Casa Sena S
22 | 24 | 22 | $30

*125 E. Palace Ave. (Washington Ave.), 505-988-9232*

☑ Yes, there was a fire, but the "charming, cozy decor" at this historic Sena Plaza casa in Santa Fe has been preserved and the New Mexican–Southwestern cooking still has flair, with praise going to the trout cooked in clay and "heavenly" chicken enchiladas; it "may be touristy, but it exudes charm" and singing waiters belt out some "great tunes" in the adjoining cantina.

### La Choza
23 | 19 | 20 | $14

*905 Alarid St. (bet. Cerrillos Rd. & St. Francis Dr.), 505-982-0909*

■ A "nice alternative to touristy New Mexican"; Santa Fe locals don't like to tell folks about this place (it has the same owner as The Shed) and its "fabulous green chile" and red enchiladas – not to mention the mocha cake and homemade hot fudge on vanilla ice cream – all of which makes for a "good, inexpensive family dinner"; lunch lines are shorter than The Shed's.

### Old House, The S
– | – | – | E

*Eldorado Hotel, 309 W. San Francisco St. (Guadalupe St.), 505-988-4455*

Still something of a secret, this dinner-only Continental-SW in Santa Fe's Eldorado Hotel gets high marks from regulars for its elegant ambiance, knowledgeable staff, extensive wine list and imaginative, seasonal cuisine; just one taste of chef Martin Rios' achiote-rubbed halibut will make you want to move in.

### Old Mexico Grill S

23 | 18 | 19 | $20

*2434 Cerrillos Rd. (St. Michaels Dr.), 505-473-0338*

■ "Fine dining in a strip mall" is what you get at this Santa Fe eatery with "no atmosphere, but who cares?" – its "open grill" turns out "true Mexican food" including "the best fajitas"; according to surveyors, it's "like a visit to Mexico without worrying about any gastrointestinal consequences."

### Pink Adobe S

21 | 24 | 21 | $27

*406 Old Santa Fe Trail (Alameda St.), 505-983-7712*

◨ Housed in a "cozy" old pink adobe, this "piece of history" in Santa Fe with a Continental-Southwestern menu still offers what some call the "best steak around", especially steak dunnigan, "the standard setter" (served with mushrooms and green chile); "gypsy stew on a snowy day" can't be beat, but modernists say "they need to add to the menu" and some find the setting "too crowded."

### Pranzo Italian Grill S

22 | 22 | 21 | $23

*540 Montezuma Ave. (Guadalupe St.), 505-984-2645*

◨ "Best Italian for the price" say fans of this "consistent old standby" in Santa Fe offering "excellent value in a town where that's never the case"; "good pizzas" and salads and service "without attitude" make it a "great local" resource, but it sometimes feels "too crowded and rushed."

### Rancho de Chimayo S

20 | 24 | 19 | $20

*Santa Fe County Rd. 98 (¼ mi. off Hwy. 76), Chimayo, 505-351-4444*

◨ "Not a restaurant – an experience"; drive to this New Mexican in Chimayo at sunset, sit on the patio, have a blue margarita and the *carne adovada* burrito and you'll see why it's "an institution" and "worth the trip"; but critics cite "average" food and say "beware of tour buses."

### Santacafe S

25 | 25 | 23 | $37

*231 Washington Ave. (bet. Marcy St. & Paseo de Peralta), 505-984-1788*

◨ With its Southwestern and "Asian slant" on Eclectic cuisine and "elegant", "minimalist decor", this favorite (voted No. 1 for Food in Santa Fe) is "still king of the hill"; fans love its "creative" appetizers, "superb wine list" and historic adobe setting with courtyard dining a block north of Santa Fe's Plaza, but a handful find it "overpriced" and "too snooty."

### Shed, The

21 | 20 | 19 | $17

*113½ E. Palace Ave. (bet. Cathedral Pl. & Washington Ave.), 505-982-9030*

■ In a "great old building" (circa 1692) with "low doors and bright paint", this "adorable" New Mexican is a "local institution" in Santa Fe and "perennial Downtown lunch favorite"; prices are low and its "red chile is the benchmark", so expect "long lines" – "if you can get in, it's worth it."

## TOP 15 FOOD RANKING

| | | |
|---|---|---|
| **28** | Rover's | New French |
| | Campagne | French |
| **27** | Tosoni's | Continental |
| | Fullers | Northwestern |
| | Shiro's Sushi | Japanese |
| | Wild Ginger | Asian |
| **26** | Cafe Campagne | French Bistro |
| | Nishino | Japanese |
| | Dahlia Lounge | Northwestern |
| | Kingfish Café | Southern/Soul |
| | Inn at Langley | Northwestern |
| | Il Terrazzo Carmine | Northern Italian |
| | Szmania's | Northwestern |
| | Le Gourmand | Classic French |
| | Cafe Juanita | Northern Italian |

## Other Important Places

| | |
|---|---|
| Brasa | Mediterranean |
| Cafe Lago | N/S Italian |
| Canlis | Northwestern |
| Cascadia | Northwestern |
| Etta's Seafood | Seafood |
| Flying Fish | Seafood |
| Georgian Room | Northwestern |
| Harvest Vine | Spanish/Tapas |
| Herbfarm | New American |
| Lampreia | Northwestern |
| Painted Table | Asian/Northwestern |
| Salumi | N/S Italian |

| F | D | S | C |
|---|---|---|---|
| _ | _ | _ | M |

**Brasa** ◑
*2107 Third Ave. (Lenora St.), 206-728-4220*
This bold Belltown beauty marks the long-awaited return of ex
Campagne chef Tamara Murphy and her contemporary rendition
of Mediterranean cuisine, much of it cooked over open fire; the
sensuous dining room is designed for lingering, and the bar is a
prime site for a pre- or post-event bite.

## Cafe Campagne S
26 | 23 | 23 | $25
*Pike Place Mkt., 1600 Post Alley (Pine St.), 206-728-2233*
■ "Ooh la la!", this "first-class bistro" is Post Alley's own "slice of Paris", serving French comfort fare that "rivals its big sister [Campagne] upstairs" for "consistency and quality", amounting to "champagne food at beer prices"; the Gallic setting is ideal for a "rainy-day breakfast", "terrific Sunday brunch" or romantic dinner – this is a "treat" at a cost that "can't be beat."

## Cafe Juanita S
26 | 20 | 23 | $34
*9702 NE 120th Pl. (97th Ave.), Kirkland, 425-823-1505*
■ "Sometimes forgotten", this "creekside" Kirkland Northern Italian is a "warm and inviting" "class act" that's "worth the money" and "the drive" to experience chef John Neumark's evolving menu; standouts include "fantastic lamb shanks", rabbit, housemade bread and "wonderful desserts", matched with "personal service" and "perhaps the best vino list for the money in town" (the Cavatappi winery is annexed to the cafe).

## Cafe Lago S
25 | 18 | 21 | $25
*2305 24th Ave. E. (bet. Lynn & McGraw Sts.), 206-329-8005*
■ There are "long lines" and "great smells" at this "intimate and 'in'" Montlake Italian; regulars arrive early to get the most from the "limited" menu, which includes "wonderful antipasti", "excellent lasagna" and pizza raised "to an art"; a "friendly" staff adds to the charm, and if faultfinders grumble "pricey and crowded", for most "this is the real thing."

## Campagne ●S
28 | 25 | 25 | $44
*Inn at the Market, 86 Pine St. (bet. 1st Ave. & Post Alley), 206-728-2800*
■ "Elegant" country French cooking (voted Seattle's No. 2 for Food) coupled with "impeccable service" make for a "superb dining experience" at this Pike Place Market "treasure", and "only the clank of *boules* could make it more Provençal"; chef James Drohmen "works miracles", and the "intimate setting" enhances both business and pleasure (even if you have to "mortgage your house for wine" from the "outstanding" list); bottom line: it still "sets the standard" for "class."

## Canlis
25 | 27 | 27 | $48
*2576 Aurora Ave. N. (Halladay St.), 206-283-3313*
■ The panoramic view of Lake Union remains "unmatched" and the "food has really improved" at this "old favorite", a "grand old lady" with a "marvelous" makeover; chef Greg Atkinson gives the Pacific NW "steak-and-seafood" menu "a '90s twist", and the "superb service" is rated No. 1 in the *Seattle Survey*; "luxury" is "expensive", though, and this is still "blue-blood" home turf.

## Cascadia
– | – | – | VE
*2328 First Ave. (bet. Battery & Bell Sts.), 206-448-8884*
Belltown's newest showplace features luxe trappings (an etched-glass water wall, plush banquettes, a baby grand and acres of cherry wood paneling) that set the appropriate tone for chef/owner Kerry Sear's sumptuous Northwestern menu; delicacies like partridge in wild grasses and wild king salmon on cedar fronds satisfy the adventurous, while those seeking more casual nibbles stake out its low-key bar.

### Dahlia Lounge Ⓢ　　　　26　24　23　$34

*1904 Fourth Ave. (Stewart St.), 206-682-4142*

■ Chef-restaurateur Tom Douglas' firstborn is in full bloom, with a menu of "flavorful, Asian-influenced" Northwestern cuisine that extends the "food as art" philosophy from "innovative entrees" to "incredible daily specials"; the "eccentric, stylish" Downtown room exudes "comfort and elegance", and the "top-notch" staff pays "amazing attention to detail"; overall it's "one classy joint" that can deliver "a sublime experience."

### Etta's Seafood Ⓢ　　　　25　21　22　$30

*2020 Western Ave. (bet. Lenora & Virginia Sts.), 206-443-6000*

■ "Tom Douglas does seafood" at this "upbeat" eatery "on the water" that's noted for its "daring", "innovative approach" and "first-class ingredients" – the "exquisite salmon" is pit-roasted and spice-rubbed, and the sashimi and crab cakes are "unsurpassed"; too "trendy" for some, its proximity to Pike Place Market makes it "hard to get in" and, inevitably, "touristy."

### Flying Fish ●Ⓢ　　　　25　22　21　$33

*2234 First Ave. (Bell St.), 206-728-8595*

☑ "Fish from all over the world" surface at this "super-trendy", "high-energy" Belltown seafooder where chef-owner Christine Keff works "Asian-inspired culinary magic" to create "crowd-pleasers" like whole fried snapper, wok-seared "crab by the pound" and other "magnificent" presentations of "superbly prepared" aquatics; it's a "fun and sophisticated" scene, but phobes frown on "uneven quality", "slow service" and "the din" – "what's the big deal?"

### Fullers　　　　27　25　25　$46

*Sheraton Hotel & Towers, 1400 Sixth Ave. (bet. Pike & Union Sts.), 206-447-5544*

■ It's an "art gallery" exhibiting "top-flight" food say admirers of this Downtowner's "exquisite" style; celeb chef Monique Barbeau has passed the toque to her sous, Tom Black, but surveyors remain enthusiastic about the "dramatic" Northwestern meat-and-seafood menu and "gracious service"; a minority gripes it's too "expensive" and "stuffy", but it remains "a must for the self-respecting gourmet."

### Georgian Room Ⓢ　　　　25　28　26　$51

*Four Seasons Olympic Hotel, 411 University St. (bet. 4th & 5th Aves.), 206-621-7889*

■ "Guys, dust off your jackets", 'cause Downtown's "grande dame" is still unmatched for "elegant hotel dining"; it boasts "beautiful", ornate decor that scores No. 1 in the *Seattle Survey,* and new exec chef Gavin Stephenson oversees an "outstanding" Pacific NW seasonal menu complemented by a vast wine list; whether for a "power breakfast" or to "celebrate an occasion", it's "pricey but worth it" for a "fabulous" experience in an oh-so-"civilized" milieu.

### Harvest Vine　　　　–　–　–　M

*2701 E. Madison (27th St.), 206-320-9771*

Order a bottle of Pesquera to pass the time while you wait for a table at this minuscule Madison Valley tapas bar where regulars hold out for a seat at the copper-topped counter since the show is too good to miss; anticipate authentic little dishes from Spain (fresh grilled sardines, lamb, octopus, blood sausages, even baby eels) and impressive paellas, along with some mighty fine desserts.

## Herbfarm, The 🖻    – – – VE
*195 NE Gilman Blvd. (Front St.), Issaquah, 206-784-2222*
"Legendary and awesome but not yet rebuilt" after a fire destroyed
it in 1997, this fabled outpost is now occupying a 40-seat wine-aging
room at the Hedges Cellars Winery in Issaquah (15 miles from the
farm site in Fall City); here, chef Jerry Traunfeld is creating his
"exquisite" "once-in-a-lifetime experience for the palate" for the
few lucky gourmands who "can get a reservation" to indulge in a
"superb" NW-accented New American prix fixe feast.

## Il Terrazzo Carmine    26  24  24  $38
*411 First Ave. S. (bet. Jackson & King Sts.), 206-467-7797*
■ Owner Carmine Smeraldo, "the godfather of Seattle's Italian food
scene", is "always there to greet" the "sophisticated clientele"
that frequents this "stylish", "festive" "standout" near Pioneer
Square; expect "white-glove treatment all the way" and "few
compromises on the authentic" menu, composed of "first-class"
Northern specialties like "great venison farfalle"; "important
dinner coming up and want to impress? – go here."

## Inn at Langley    26  25  25  $48
*Inn at Langley, 400 First St. (Park Ave.), Langley, Whidbey Island, 360-221-3033*
■ Open for dinner on weekends only, this relaxed Whidbey Island
inn provides an "incredible" "adventure for palate and soul";
reserve at least two months in advance and hope for a seat at "the
communal table", though all diners in the small room "get a cooking
lesson" while watching talented chef Stephen Nogal prepare a
"fabulous" five-course Pacific NW feast in the open kitchen; "plan
for a long, leisurely meal and an educational experience."

## Kingfish Café 🖻⇴    26  23  21  $22
*602 19th Ave. E. (Mercer St.), 206-320-8757*
■ The "beautiful" "Coaston sisters have taken Soul Food to another
level" at their Capitol Hill hitter where chef Kenyatta Carter's "big
portions" and "lovely interpretation of Southern standards" help
make this "unique" spot with the "artsy-funky" atmo every bit "as
good as the buzz"; "get there a half-hour before the place opens"
say regulars who "hate the wait."

## Lampreia    25  21  22  $48
*2400 First Ave. (Battery St.), 206-443-3301*
☑ Much applause for owner Scott Carsberg, a "near perfectionist"
whose seasonal Pacific NW menu features "absolutely simple,
perfect food" that's "exquisite"; "tiny, delectable portions" wow
loyalists, as do the "elegant, romantic atmosphere", "beautiful
tableware", "refined service" and a "great cheese course"; a
minority calls the setting "sparse", claiming this Belltowner is
"the most overrated, pretentious restaurant in Seattle."

## Le Gourmand    26  20  24  $46
*425 NW Market St. (6th Ave. NW), 206-784-3463*
■ "Caring, intelligent" chef-owner Bruce Naftaly is a "treasure"
who "prepares everything with love" at this "classic" "fine French
restaurant in an unlikely Ballard location"; there's "nothing trendy"
about this unassuming house where "the freshest ingredients"
often come from the chef's own trees, vines and garden; "great
sauces" are essential to his seasonal, prix fixe menu, which is
"unbeatable for the money – hell, almost unbeatable, period."

**Nishino** [S] 26 | 22 | 22 | $33

*3130 E. Madison St. (Lake Washington Blvd.), 206-322-5800*

■ Tatsu Nishino (ex LA's Matsuhisa) serves "creative", "cutting-edge" cuisine at this "graceful" Madison Park Japanese; his "beyond description chef's-choice dinner" and "great sushi bar", where everything is "beautifully presented", are "impressive"; though some complain about "tiny", "overpriced" portions, most feel the food is "wonderful" and "can't wait to return."

**Painted Table, The** [S] 24 | 24 | 22 | $37

*Alexis Hotel, 92 Madison St. (1st Ave.), 206-624-3646*

■ "Artsy and elegant", the Alexis Hotel's "romantic", newly renovated dining room is "great for a business meeting or an intimate dinner"; "talented chef" Tim Kelley's "innovative" and "imaginative menu" relies on "NW and Asian influences"; a few doubters cry "overrated", complaining of "tiny portions", but most maintain it's "well worth the price for that special occasion."

**Rover's** 28 | 24 | 27 | $65

*2808 E. Madison St. (28th Ave.), 206-325-7442*

■ "Gifted chef" Thierry Rautureau presides over "the best special occasion place in the Northwest", where you can "indulge all your senses" with "impeccable everything"; "is there an award he hasn't won?" ask surveyors who have voted this "charming" Frenchman's "romantic" Madison Park hideaway No. 1 for Food in Seattle; "always superb", the "world-class" prix fixe menu is "spendy", but well worth the "splurge" for "ambrosia on a plate."

**Salumi** – | – | – | I

*309 Third Ave. S. (Main St.), 206-621-8772*

Chef Armandino Batali preserves ancient Italian food traditions at this diminutive Pioneer Square cafe–cum–cured meat factory where delicious, sausage-laden sandwiches delight devotees; it only serves lunch and take-out suppers, except on Saturdays when a group can book the communal table for a multicourse feast – and can assist in preparing the mozzarella and rolling the pasta dough.

**Shiro's Sushi** [S] 27 | 17 | 21 | $31

*2401 Second Ave. (Battery St.), 206-443-9844*

■ Celebrated sushi chef Shiro Kashiba made his name at Nikko, but his followers now flock to his eponymous Belltowner for "sushi from heaven" that makes it Seattle's No. 1 for Japanese; "sit at the counter and watch an artist in action", but "get there when they unlock the door or you'll have to give people the evil eye" as you wait; the decor is "simple and classy", though "elbow-to-elbow" tables and "paper napkins disappoint."

**Szmania's** [S] 26 | 23 | 25 | $36

*3321 W. McGraw St. (34th Ave.), 206-284-7305*

■ "Out-of-the-way" Magnolia affords a chance to get "away from the trendy scene" and into chef Ludger Szmania's "fabulous food" at this "Northwest treasure" with a German accent; with its "delectable entrees" (the "half-portion concept is brilliant"), "romantic atmosphere" enhanced by a "subtle and warm remodel" and "highly professional" service, this "neighborhood" "gem" "has it all."

## Tosoni's
| 27 | 15 | 25 | $34 |

*14320 NE 20th St. (bet. 140th & 148th Aves.), Bellevue, 425-644-1668*

■ "A slice of Europe in Bellevue?" – chef-owner Walter Walcher and his wife Wendy prove it can be done ("in a strip mall, no less"), wowing crowds at this "Eastside sleeper" with an "ambitious menu" that leans on Italy for inspiration; the fare is weighted toward "great meats", the service toward personal attention.

## Wild Ginger 🖫
| 27 | 23 | 22 | $30 |

*1400 Western Ave. (Union St.), 206-623-4450*

■ "Oh the flavors, the smells, the crowds!"; the "definitive Seattle Pan-Asian" with the "chic, sparse decor" and booming satay bar remains the city's Most Popular restaurant – and possibly the noisiest; James Beard Award winner Jeem Han Lock has a "wicked way with spice" and continues to conduct "a concert of flavors without a clash of cultures"; N.B. an expansion/move (to Third and Union) is scheduled for Spring 2000.

## TOP 15 FOOD RANKING

| | Restaurant | Cuisine Type |
|---|---|---|
| **28** | Fio's La Fourchette | French/Swiss |
| | Tony's | N/S Italian |
| **27** | Trattoria Marcella | N/S Italian |
| | Dominic's | N/S Italian |
| | Café de France | French |
| | Giovanni's | N/S Italian |
| | Sidney Street Cafe | New American |
| **26** | Faust's | New American |
| | Malmaison | Classic French |
| | Zinnia | New American |
| | Ritz-Carlton Grill | New American |
| | Harvest | New American |
| | Al's Restaurant | Steakhouse |
| **25** | Crossing, The | New American |
| | Citizen Kane's | Steakhouse |

## OTHER IMPORTANT PLACES

| | |
|---|---|
| Bar Italia Ristorante | Northern Italian |
| Cafe Balaban | New American |
| Cafe Mira | New American |
| Cafe Provençal | French Bistro |
| Cardwell's at the Plaza | New American |
| Eddie's Steak & Chop | Steakhouse |
| Frazer's Traveling Brown Bag | Regional American |
| Pueblo Solis | Mexican |
| Remy's Kitchen & Wine Bar | Mediterranean |
| Shiitake | Pacific Rim |

| F | D | S | C |
|---|---|---|---|
| 26 | 20 | 25 | $45 |

### Al's Restaurant
*1200 N. First St. (Biddle St.), 314-421-6399*
■ "A place to impress people", this edge-of-Downtown steakhouse has been a "wonderful" "special-occasion" site exuding "old-world" charm since 1925 (it's "almost as old as the waiters"); granted, its industrial neighborhood is kind of a "shock" and the "no-menu, no-prices" policy can be an "annoyance", but when it comes to "awesome steaks", look no further.

F | D | S | C

**Bar Italia Ristorante** [S] 24 | 15 | 20 | $23
*13 Maryland Plaza (Euclid Ave.), 314-361-7010*
■ "Simple, stylish and fresh", this Central West End trattoria is "as good as a trip to Northern Italy without the jet lag", and its recent "move to larger quarters is a blessing" (though not yet reflected in the decor score); "slow service" is a drag for a few, but most say this "underrated" spot is the "only St. Louis restaurant that could make it in NY."

**Cafe Balaban** [S] 24 | 21 | 21 | $30
*405 N. Euclid Ave. (McPherson Ave.), 314-361-8085*
◪ "Consistently high standards" keep this "Central West End anchor" an "old reliable" "year in and year out"; though there are complaints that the "tables are too close together" and suggestions that the New American "menu needs updating", the majority deems this "soigné" spot a "rock-solid adult dining experience."

**Café de France** 27 | 24 | 25 | $42
*410 Olive St. (4th St.), 314-231-2204*
■ "Uncompromising excellence" is yours at this "classy" Downtown French "gem" that "runs like a well-oiled machine" thanks to owner-chef Marcel Keraval's "beautifully presented" menu that's "full of surprises" and a "helpful" staff that "isn't all over you"; "plan on haute prices" ("whew!"), but it's "worth every penny (and calorie)" when you want "a fancy night out."

**Cafe Mira** 25 | 23 | 22 | $36
*12 N. Meramec Ave. (Forsyth Blvd.), Clayton, 314-721-7801*
◪ "Every dish is a work of art" at this "avant-garde" Clayton New American courtesy of Mike Johnson, "one of the best new chefs in town"; his "very trendy tall food" ("nothing you could ever make at home") arrives in a "chic" but "noisy" space populated by a "stylish" crowd who keeps busy "air-kissing" one another; overall, it's "superb – if money is no object."

**Cafe Provençal** 24 | 20 | 22 | $27
*34 N. Central Ave. (bet. Forsyth Blvd. & Maryland Ave.), Clayton, 314-725-2755* [S]
*427 S. Kirkwood Rd. (Clinton Ave.), Kirkwood, 314-822-5440*
■ These "delightful" French bistros win uniform raves for their "Parisian feel", "wonderful prix fixe" menu, "solid wine list" and "passionate service", though the newer Kirkwood branch seems to have the edge: it's "easier on the ears" and not "overcrowded" like its Clayton sibling (where you just might need to "bring a shoehorn" to squeeze in); either way, fans call them the "best fine dining value in St. Louis."

**Cardwell's at the Plaza** [S] 25 | 23 | 22 | $27
*94 Plaza Frontenac (Clayton Rd. & Lindbergh Blvd.), 314-997-8885*
■ "After a tough morning at the spa", the ladies who lunch head for this "trendy" New American that's "the best thing to happen to Plaza Frontenac"; it's also just the ticket "after shopping" (Neiman Marcus is next door) or for "business dinners" thanks to its "innovative" menu served in a "relaxing atmosphere"; however, snobs sniff it's "too good for its [mall] location."

**Citizen Kane's [S]** | 25 | 19 | 22 | $30

*133 W. Clinton Pl. (Lindbergh), 314-965-9005*

◪ Kirkwood chophouse that might not be "as good as the movie" it's named after, but still has great word of mouth for its "heavenly steaks" and "attentive service" at a price that's many "dollars less than Morton's"; but don't expect any kind of "aesthetic experience" in these "humble surroundings" until they "turn down the lights" and "get rid of the plastic tablecloths."

**Crossing, The** | 25 | 22 | 23 | $39

*7823 Forsyth Blvd. (Central Ave.), Clayton, 314-721-7375*

■ There's "star quality" at work at this Clayton New American "up-and-comer" where chefs Jim Fiala and Cary McDowell bring "big city–type food" (notably an "unbelievable beet salad") to St. Louis; despite objections that "prices are rising faster than Internet stocks", most agree this "strong new performer" "exceeds expectations" and is "great for a splurge."

**Dominic's** | 27 | 25 | 26 | $43

*5101 Wilson Ave. (Hereford Ave.), 314-771-1632*

■ "In a league of its own", this "quintessential" "old-world Italian" where "limos double-park nightly" just might be the "classiest restaurant on the Hill"; "dazzling" cooking and "truly lovely decor" "make you feel special", though a few say that the otherwise impeccable service verges on being "almost too much"; sure, it's costly, yet most "don't mind paying the price" for this exercise in "pure class."

**Eddie's Steak & Chop** | – | – | – | E

*40 N. Central Ave. (Maryland Ave.), Clayton, 314-725-1661*

Restaurateur Eddie Neill unveils a new Clayton steakhouse on the former site of Cafe Provençal; anticipate remarkable steaks, chops and roasts at prices lower than Morton's, a high-style wine list with a modest markup and an overall mellow mood complemented by relaxingly calm service.

**Faust's [S]** | 26 | 26 | 24 | $41

*Adam's Mark Hotel, 315 Chestnut St. (Memorial Dr.), 314-342-4690*

■ Named for 19th-century St. Louis restaurateur Tony Faust, this "cosmopolitan" New American in the Adam's Mark Hotel maintains his high standards with "superb dining and attention to detail", one of the "best wine stewards" in town and a "beautiful view of the Arch"; "underappreciated by locals" but "adored by travelers", it's just the place for "a long, sensuous meal" and "elegance without ostentation."

**Fio's La Fourchette** | 28 | 26 | 28 | $49

*7515 Forsyth Ave. (Jackson Ave.), Clayton, 314-863-6866*

■ This "consistently superb" French-Swiss "pearl in Clayton" has garnered "très formidable" ratings in the *St. Louis Survey* (voted Most Popular, No. 1 for Food and No. 2 for Service), causing many to sigh it's the closest they'll come to Paris "without TWA's help"; special kudos go to the "heart-safe menu items", the "free seconds" on "any part of the meal" and the "pure romance" of the setting; as for the pricing, it's "well worth the arm and the leg."

## Frazer's Traveling Brown Bag    24 | 17 | 20 | $21
*1811 Pestalozzi St. (Lemp St.), 314-773-8646*

■ "If there ever was a born cook, it's Frazer Cameron", whose eponymous American with Cajun accents lures crowds to the "out-of-the-way" South Side, near the Anheuser-Busch brewery; ok, there's "no atmosphere", but the "darn good chow" "just keeps improving" at this "offbeat" spot, and there's a groundswell among voters that "it should be open for lunch."

## Giovanni's    27 | 24 | 25 | $41
*5201 Shaw Ave. (Edwards Ave.), 314-772-5958*

■ "Great for a special event", this "outstanding" Italian vet in the heart of the Hill offers a "beautiful dining room" and equally "beautiful food"; it might be "high-priced" (so "eat *all* your pasta"), but the enraptured sigh it's worth it for an "always perfect evening" at what some deem the "best all-around restaurant in St. Louis."

## Harvest S    26 | 24 | 23 | $36
*1059 S. Big Bend Blvd. (Clayton Rd.), 314-645-3522*

☑ "The menu changes with the season" at this "hip, happening" New American in Richmond Heights where diners reap the benefits of an "incredible, varied menu" of "vertical food", topped off by some "heavenly bread pudding"; hairsplitters hedge it "can be too loud" and "a little pretentious", but the majority finds it simply "amazing" or, at least, "never boring"; P.S. "reserve well in advance."

## Malmaison S    26 | 27 | 25 | $42
*St. Albans Rd. (off Hwy. T), St. Albans, 636-458-0131*

■ "It's a long drive" to this "destination" Classic French in St. Albans, but fans say it's "worth the effort" for an "outstanding dining experience" in the "most romantic place" around (the "best fireplace in St. Louis" helps); Marseilles-born chef Simone Andujar uses herbs grown by the front door in her "superb" wild game dishes, causing devotees to sigh "it doesn't get any better than this."

## Pueblo Solis S    24 | 17 | 21 | $17
*5127 Hampton Ave. (Delor St.), 314-351-9000*

■ St. Louis' top-rated Mexican, this "authentic" South Sider has "mama in the kitchen" (Oralia Solis, mother of owner Alfredo) and she's turning out "different", "not typical" south of the border dishes as well as standards like "excellent guacamole" and "chicken enchiladas to kill for"; better yet, this "outstanding" spot is a "bargain too" – so don't be surprised to find it "packed."

## Remy's Kitchen & Wine Bar    25 | 22 | 22 | $26
*222 S. Bemiston Ave. (Bonhomme Ave.), Clayton, 314-726-5757*

■ Lisa Slay is cooking in the kitchen of this "chic" yet laid-back Mediterranean cafe in Clayton, turning out a "creative" "mix-and-match" menu of "small and large plates" backed up by "always interesting wine flights"; it's "understandably packed" and "noisy" because it's "more fun than [owner] Tim Mallett's other places" (Big Sky Cafe, Blue Water Grill) – and the fact that it's "open fairly late" keeps night owls alert.

### Ritz-Carlton Grill S
26 | 27 | 26 | $40

*Ritz-Carlton Hotel, 100 Carondelet Ave. (Hanley Rd.), Clayton, 314-719-1484*

■ Taking top honors once again for Decor in St. Louis, this "elegant" hotel New American in Clayton is "a great place to make an impression" or "for that special dinner"; one of the "most opulent brunches in town" and "impeccable service" also make this "very pleasant return to civilization" "worth the splurge."

### Shiitake
– | – | – | E

*7927 Forsyth Blvd. (Central Ave.), Clayton, 314-725-4334*

Part of the Del Pietro group of high-style restaurants (which includes another mushroom-named spot, Portabella), this splendid, dinner-only newcomer is the latest pricey entry in the burgeoning Clayton restaurant scene; chef Thom Zoog produces an ingenious Pacific Rim menu from which gingery, lemon-grass dining dreams come true.

### Sidney Street Cafe
27 | 24 | 25 | $32

*2000 Sidney St. (Salena St.), 314-771-5777*

■ When you feel like going "gourmet all the way", savor this "unique" South Side New American where "wonderful meals" arrive in "charming" surroundings with "zero attitude" ("if you can get in", that is); the only debate involves its "chalkboard menus" – some "love" them, while others say they should "spring for" printed versions.

### Tony's
28 | 26 | 28 | $52

*410 Market St. (Broadway), 314-231-7007*

☑ "Still the standard for the others to shoot for", this longtime Downtown Italian "landmark" has been voted No. 1 for Service (as well as No. 2 for Food and Popularity) in the *St. Louis Survey*, and you can plan on being "pampered" with "food so luscious you can't describe it"; while a few nitpickers shrug it's "the most overrated", many more feel that "no one else even comes close."

### Trattoria Marcella
27 | 18 | 24 | $29

*3600 Watson Rd. (Pernod Ave.), 314-352-7706*

■ "St. Louis Italian has never been better" than at this South Sider with a "stellar reputation" for food that "looks and tastes different" from the competition (especially the "riveting" lobster risotto); despite "plain" decor and a sometimes "noisy" room, "decent prices" keep it very "popular", and although it has "recently expanded", it's "still hard to get in" – so "reserve ahead."

### Zinnia S
26 | 21 | 24 | $30

*7491 Big Bend Blvd. (Shrewsbury Ave.), Webster Groves, 314-962-0572*

■ "Cozy" Webster Groves New American that "continues to outperform itself" with "fresh ideas" on the menu matched by "fresh flowers on every table"; "don't let the purple building throw you off" (or "the fact that it used to be a gas station") – this is "unpretentious elegance", where everything's "well executed" and "very imaginative."

# Tampa Bay/Sarasota

## TOP 10 FOOD RANKING

| Restaurant | Cuisine Type |
|---|---|
| **28** Mise en Place | New American |
| Beach Bistro | Med./New American |
| **27** Bern's Steak House | Steakhouse |
| Blue Heron | Eclectic |
| Euphemia Haye | Eclectic |
| Bijou Café | Continental/New Amer. |
| Michael's on East | New American |
| **26** Ophelia's | Eclectic |
| Morel | Eclectic/New American |
| Armani's | Northern Italian |

## OTHER IMPORTANT PLACES

| | |
|---|---|
| Café L'Europe | Continental |
| Ceviche Rest. & Tapas Bar | Spanish/Tapas |
| Maritana Grille | Floridian/New Amer. |
| Mise en Place Market Bistro | French Bistro |
| Oystercatchers | Seafood |
| Salt Rock Grill | Seafood/Steakhouse |
| Shula's Steak House | Steakhouse |
| SideBern's | Asian/Eclectic |
| Trattoria Primadonna | N/S Italian |

| F | D | S | C |
|---|---|---|---|

**Armani's**     | 26 | 28 | 27 | $46 |

*Hyatt Regency Westshore, 6200 Courtney Campbell Causeway (Hwy. 60), Tampa, 813-874-1234*
■ "Just the place to wear a little black dress", this "elegant" Northern Italian in Tampa's Hyatt Regency Westshore has it all: "terrific food", "classy atmosphere", "wonderful service" and "views to the nth degree"; but "don't forget your wallet", as this "premier dining experience" comes at a steep price – though the consensus is it's "worth it" for a "top-of-the-line" evening at one of the Gulf Coast's finest.

**Beach Bistro** Ⓢ     | 28 | 23 | 26 | $41 |

*6600 Gulf Dr. (66th St.), Holmes Beach, 941-778-6444*
■ Foodies from Anna Maria and beyond can't resist this "intimate" Mediterranean–New American, a "restaurant with charisma" that offers "outstanding service", "fabulous" sunset views and "always remarkable" fare; true, it's "pricey" and "limited seating" might make it "too crowded", but the majority feels it's "worth it" to enjoy one of the area's "best overall", a place that "would make it in Paris or NY."

## Bern's Steak House 🄢          27 | 22 | 27 | $42

*1208 S. Howard Ave. (bet. Marjorie & Watrous Sts.), Tampa,*
*813-251-2421*
■ Since 1956, this "national treasure for beef" in Tampa's Hyde
Park has been gathering accolades for its "famous, fabulous"
steaks and the "best wine list in the world"; while not everyone
likes its "bordello-like", "red flocked wallpaper" decor, most give
all-around high marks to this "dining event" and recommend you
"tour the kitchen and wine cellar, then feast in the dessert room."

## Bijou Café          27 | 23 | 24 | $34

*1287 First St. (Pineapple St.), Sarasota, 941-366-8111*
■ This "elegant little" Theater Districter is Downtown Sarasota's
"most sophisticated" cafe despite its unlikely location in a former
"1930s service station"; "they work hard at" their "inventive"
Continental–New American menu, serving "perfect food" that's
enhanced by "excellent" wines and "gentle service"; though
"jammed on opera nights", it exudes a "laid-back" atmosphere.

## Blue Heron, The 🄢          27 | 22 | 24 | $33

*Shoppes at Clover Pl., 3285 Tampa Rd. (bet. Lake St. George & US 19),*
*Palm Harbor, 727-789-5176*
■ "A rare combination of food and sauces" distinguishes the
Eclectic mix served by this posh Palm Harbor veteran, whose
recent renovation is yet to be reflected in its already respectable
decor score; devotees adore the "high-quality" cuisine so fervently
that they beg "please open for lunch", but for now it's dinner only.

## Café L'Europe 🄢          26 | 25 | 24 | $37

*431 St. Armands Circle (Hwy. 41), Sarasota, 941-388-4415*
■ The "grande dame of Sarasota" recently celebrated its 26th
anniversary, and this Continental "fixture on St. Armands Circle"
is "still tops", a "model dining spot for food, wines, decor and
service"; this "haven" can seem "a bit fussy" and "expensive"
(some call lunch "a better value"), but most think it's "worth it"
for one of the "most romantic" experiences in town.

## Ceviche Restaurant &          ▽ 21 | 18 | 18 | $27
## Tapas Bar ◑🄢

*2109 Bayshore Blvd. (Howard Ave.), Tampa, 813-250-0203*
■ A newcomer to Tampa's stylish SoHo neighborhood, this tapas
bar draws crowds with its "interesting menu" of Spanish finger
foods, despite its unconventional location in a Bay Shore residential
high-rise; up-all-night types applaud the late-late weekend
hours ('til 2:30 AM) and everyone finds the weekend flamenco
dancers quite snappy.

## Euphemia Haye 🄢          27 | 23 | 23 | $41

*5540 Gulf of Mexico Dr. (Gulf-to-Bay Rd.), Longboat Key, 941-383-3633*
■ It's "hard to beat" this "classy" Longboat Key Eclectic for
"world-class dining" in a "romantic" setting; it can be "cramped
downstairs" ("hope you like your neighbors"), but claustrophobes
can opt for the upstairs Haye Loft piano bar, where a "light menu"
or a "wonderful choice of desserts" await; up or down, there's a
"wine list that touches all bases" as well as "attentive service."

**Maritana Grille** [S] ▽ | 27 | 28 | 25 | $47 |

*Don CeSar Beach Resort, 3400 Gulf Blvd. (Pinellas Bayway), St. Petersburg Beach, 727-360-1882*

■ Experience "nirvana" at this Floribbean gem, the signature dining room of St. Pete's historic Don CeSar Resort, where beachside panoramas from the terrace and indoor saltwater aquariums make it one of the most striking rooms on the Gulf Coast; the "fabulous, creative" fare, prepared over a pecan and cherry wood grill, gives the view a run for its money.

**Michael's on East** | 27 | 26 | 25 | $40 |

*Midtown Plaza, 1212 East Ave. S. (bet. Bahia Vista & Prospect Sts.), Sarasota, 941-366-0007*

■ Again voted Sarasota's Most Popular restaurant, this "posh" New American has "just been redesigned" and its "striking", "drop-dead gorgeous" new look has also "greatly improved the noise level"; the "superb", "up-to-date" menu attracts a "very glitzy crowd" in search of "a special night on the town" and though it can be "a little pricey", most say it's "well worth it" to savor Sarasota's "brightest star."

**Mise en Place** | 28 | 24 | 24 | $35 |

*442 W. Kennedy Blvd. (Grand Central St.), Tampa, 813-254-5373*

■ "Incredibly inventive cuisine" at "fair prices" attracts gourmands to this Downtown New American, rated No. 1 for Food on the Gulf Coast; its "state-of-the-art combinations", "creative presentation" and "great wine selection" make this "as good as it gets in Tampa", and those who say the "only flaw is the wait" will be happy to know that it has just begun accepting reservations.

**Mise en Place Market Bistro** [S] | – | – | – | M |

*2616 S. MacDill Ave. (W. Palmira Ave.), Tampa, 813-839-3939*

Casual offshoot of the ever-popular Mise en Place, this South Tampa French bistro rarely misses a trick with notable salmon and chicken dishes, what just might be Tampa's best pâté and nearly three dozen wines by the glass; everything arrives in a comfortable bi-level setting that also offers outdoor dining as well as gourmet takeout.

**Morel** | 26 | 20 | 24 | $33 |

*3809 S. Tuttle Ave. (north of Bee Ridge Rd.), Sarasota, 941-927-8716*

■ This "tiny" Sarasota Eclectic–New American thrills fans with its "memorable" cuisine and "superb preparation and presentation" ("smooth service" doesn't hurt either); though in an "unlikely location for such a fine restaurant" – a "tacky storefront" "in a strip mall" – stalwarts say "this lovely little bistro" is always "pleasant" and "friendly"; dinner only.

**Ophelia's** [S] | 26 | 25 | 24 | $35 |

*9105 Midnight Pass Rd. (south of Turtle Beach), Sarasota, 941-349-2212*

■ "Sit outside if you can" at this "pretty spot" on Siesta Key and enjoy its "romantic atmosphere" and "views galore", plus an "exciting" Eclectic menu "presented in an appealing way" with "different choices" and "wonderful desserts"; it can get "pricey", but for "elegantly served, inspired cuisine", the majority agrees that this "A-one" place is "worth it."

## Oystercatchers S

| 26 | 26 | 25 | $35 |

*Hyatt Regency Westshore, 6200 Courtney Campbell Causeway
(Hwy. 60), Tampa, 813-281-9116*

■ "A beautiful water view" of Old Tampa Bay and "very good" seafood that some rate "best in the area" await at this Hyatt Regency Westshore fish palace, where the open kitchen is proudly on display; a "great brunch" and one of the "best breakfast buffets" around are more reasons why fans dub this "special-occasion" place simply "wonderful."

## Salt Rock Grill S

▽ | 26 | 28 | 23 | $33 |

*19325 Gulf Blvd. (¼ mi. north of Park Blvd.), Indian Shores,
727-593-7625*

■ Truly a "place to be seen", this "superb" surf 'n' turfer offers a "diverse", "interesting" menu from its open kitchen, a "great wine list" and stunning decor (including a cigar bar) that all merge to form the quintessential "yuppie hangout"; it's "good and noisy", but what else would you expect from one of Tampa Bay's most "popular" spots?

## Shula's Steak House S

| 26 | 23 | 25 | $45 |

*Wyndham Westshore, 4860 W. Kennedy Blvd. (Westshore Blvd.),
Tampa, 813-286-4366*

■ You can "eat like a football player" at this Westshore chophouse in the Wyndham Hotel serving "very, very good" food in immense portions that might be "too much" for the unathletic; decorated with memorabilia from Don Shula's coaching days with the Dolphins, this "men's club" delights the guys, who call the steaks "excellent" and the all-around experience "wonderful", even if it's "overpriced."

## SideBern's S

| – | – | – | M |

*2208 Morrison Ave. (S. Howard Ave.), Tampa, 813-258-2233*

This SoHo offspring of Bern's Steak House has recently revamped its menu and now offers a fusion medley that draws inspiration from both Asia and the Mediterranean, with the former represented by some stellar dim sum; though the wine list is not as encyclopedic as its parent's, the pared-down choices still impress, and its redesigned interior includes an 18-seat communal table that's a good spot to make new friends.

## Trattoria Primadonna S

| – | – | – | E |

*915 S. Howard Ave. (W. Morrison Ave.), Tampa, 813-258-3358*

Trendy SoHo Restaurant Row villa known for its expertly prepared Italian fare presented in a softy lit, rustic space with vine-covered walls; its open kitchen delivers signature dishes including a *cozze alla marinara* that takes mussels to delicious new heights as well as a melt-in-your-mouth osso buco.

# Tucson

## TOP 10 FOOD RANKING

| | Restaurant | Cuisine Type |
|---|---|---|
| **28** | Ventana Room | American/Eclectic |
| **27** | Janos | French/Southwestern |
| | Vivace | N/S Italian |
| | Le Rendez-Vous | French |
| **25** | Gold Room | Southwestern |
| | Cafe Poca Cosa | Mexican |
| | Rancher's Club of Arizona | Steakhouse |
| | Tack Room | Traditional American |
| **24** | Sachiko Sushi | Japanese |
| | Mi Nidito | Mexican |

## OTHER IMPORTANT PLACES

| | |
|---|---|
| Anthony's | Continental |
| Arizona Inn | New American |
| Cafe Terra Cotta | Southwestern |
| Daniel's | Northern Italian |
| ¡Fuego! | Southwestern |
| Kingfisher | American/Seafood |
| Le Bistro | French Bistro |
| Nonie | Cajun |
| Oven's | New American |
| Pastiche Modern Eatery | New American |
| Presidio Grill | New American |
| Wildflower | New American |

| F | D | S | C |
|---|---|---|---|

### Anthony's 🈂
| 24 | 27 | 24 | $36 |

*6440 N. Campbell Ave. (Skyline Dr.), 520-299-1771*
☑ This foothills Continental is a "gracious room with magnificent views" – "mountains out one window, city lights out the other"; admirers say the "views do not surpass the food" and praise the "notable wine cellar", but foes find the cooking "tired" and claim sporadic "threadbare linen" belies its "elite" intents.

### Arizona Inn 🈂
| 23 | 26 | 24 | $27 |

*Arizona Inn, 2200 E. Elm St. (bet. Campbell Ave. & Tucson Blvd.), 520-325-1541*
☑ Dine alfresco at this "elegant", "vintage" in-town oasis with a "top-notch" New American menu – "great" for power breakfast and lunch; however, some note that the "serene setting with "charming" gardens and fireplaces can "eclipse" the food.

### Cafe Poca Cosa
| 25 | 22 | 22 | $18 |

*88 E. Broadway Blvd. (bet. Scott & 6th Aves.), 520-622-6400*
### Little Cafe Poca Cosa ⊘
*20 S. Scott Ave. (Congress St.), 520-622-6400*
■ "Changed the course of Mexican food in Tucson forever" declare Cafe Poca Cosa fans who plead "don't tell anyone"; but word of the "fresh", artful platters "bursting" with "brassy" flavors has spread so far that nonlocals say it's "worth a special trip" here to sample the "changing menu", especially the "chef's choice *al día* of three superb entrees" – best enjoyed with a 'rita on the "magical patio"; N.B. the casual Little Cafe is breakfast and lunch only.

## Cafe Terra Cotta S  24 | 22 | 22 | $24
*St. Philip's Plaza, 4310 N. Campbell Ave. (River Rd.), 520-577-8100*
■ "Outstanding" and "still trendy after all these years", with a "clever" menu that leads in "defining SW gourmet" eats; the "great smells" from brick-oven pizzas "make spirits rise", as do "marvelous tortilla soup" and "wow desserts"; here you can "dine well at a variety of price points", catch "great people-watching" on the shaded patio, and on jazz nights, it's "nirvana."

## Daniel's Restaurant & Trattoria S  24 | 24 | 22 | $33
*St. Philip's Plaza, 4340 N. Campbell Ave. (River Rd.), 520-742-3200*
☑ Admirers consider this Northern Italian a "classic" and "one of the good 'finds' in Tucson", citing its "fabulous", "haute" menu, "great wines" and "attractive", "relaxing" setting, including a patio; detractors find the menu "overwrought" and note "uneven" service, but it's "much improved with a recent ownership change."

## ¡Fuego! Restaurant, Bar & Grill S  24 | 21 | 22 | $29
*6958 E. Tanque Verde Rd. (Sabino Canyon Rd.), 520-886-1745*
☑ Staking out culinary frontiers, this "noisy", "bright", clean-lined newcomer has an "excellent kitchen" "bordering on outstanding", turning out "innovative" Southwestern nouvelle cuisine, with special raves for chef Alan Zeman's signature dishes; but some find it "pricey", "pretentious" and "trying too hard for exotic combos."

## Gold Room S  25 | 26 | 25 | $34
*Westward Look Resort, 245 E. Ina Rd. (east of Oracle Rd.), 520-297-1151*
☑ Evocative SW-inspired fare and views of sunsets and city lights mark this "delightful mountain aerie" as a "Tucson classic", "recently redone to very nice result"; while most find the food "excellent" and laud a "lovely Sunday brunch", a few find service "patronizing" and "condescending."

## Janos  27 | 27 | 27 | $39
*3770 E. Sunrise Dr. (Via Palomita), 520-884-9426*
☑ Tucson's most famous chef, Janos Wilder, has recently moved his namesake gem – voted the Most Popular in the city – to roomier digs in the foothills, thus outdating the above decor rating; now, in a luxurious interior, diners can indulge in "accomplished" French-meets-Southwestern cuisine that "never misses"; try chile-rubbed beef tenderloin over spoon bread and you can boast that you've taken a walk on the Wilder side.

## Kingfisher ●S  23 | 19 | 22 | $26
*2564 E. Grant Rd. (Tucson Blvd.), 520-323-7739*
☑ "It may look like a converted bowling alley, but the food and wine are excellent" proclaim patrons of this American seafooder; the "pampering" service is enough to make most feel like big fish, but a few with eyes toward other waters say "trendy" and "overhyped."

## Le Bistro S  24 | 21 | 22 | $25
*2574 N. Campbell Ave. (bet. Glenn St. & Grant Rd.), 520-327-3086*
☑ This "first-rate French" is "friendly and relaxed" and serves some of the "best bistro food in Tucson": "marvelous mussels", surprising salads and "fantastic" chocolate towers that make it difficult to "leave without dessert"; but while some call the setting "small and romantic", others find it "cramped" and could do without the "concrete block" booths and "terrible chairs" that bite.

## Le Rendez-Vous 🗟
27 | 22 | 24 | $35 |

*3844 E. Fort Lowell Rd. (Alvernon Way), 520-323-7373*

■ Escape from the desert sun to the subdued light of this "intimate" bit of France in Tucson where diners "enjoy" "lovingly prepared" food that makes for "exceptional", "romantic" dining "à deux" that "never fails"; bien sûr, "don't miss the Grand Marnier soufflé" or you may hurt the owner's Gallic pride.

## Mi Nidito 🗟
24 | 17 | 20 | $13 |

*1813 S. Fourth Ave. (29th St.), 520-622-5081*

■ It's "my little nest" and a lot of others' as well ("still Tucson's most crowded Mexican"); the reason: reviewers unanimously (to the exclusion of any mention of decor or service) cite "large portions" of "excellent", "real" Mexican food; unfortunately, they've removed the "great jukebox."

## Nonie 🗟
– | – | – | M |

*2526 E. Grant Rd. (Tucson Blvd.), 520-319-1965*

This dark, bustling Cajun in Central Tucson is owned by writer Elmore Leonard's son, who named it after his grandmother; everybody loves the atmosphere and the great bar, but it's no mystery that the joint's real draws are the knock-your-socks-off oyster po' boy, crawfish étouffée and pecan pie.

## Oven's Restaurant 🗟
23 | 20 | 21 | $20 |

*4280 N. Campbell Ave. (bet. Limberlost Dr. & River Rd.), 520-577-9001*

■ Leave the jacket and tie at home because this American bistro ("Cafe Terra Cotta clone") with a terrific patio is "supercasual"; the "friendly staff" serves "ample portions" of "outstanding" and "unusual" seafood and pasta to a "trendy", "yuppie" crowd.

## Pastiche Modern Eatery ●🗟
– | – | – | M |

*3025 N. Campbell Ave. (Ft. Lowell Rd.), 520-325-3333*

Upscale but casual, intimate but fun – that's Pastiche, a Tucson New American bistro that's almost as famous for its artwork as its food; local artist David Adix makes fabulous wall hangings from 'found art' and like the place itself, the menu is eclectic, so expect the unexpected: jerk-spiced chicken with prickly-pear yogurt sauce and thyme-crusted sea bass with citrus beurre blanc.

## Presidio Grill 🗟
23 | 20 | 21 | $22 |

*3352 E. Speedway Blvd. (bet. Alvernon Rd. & Country Club Rd.), 520-327-4667*

☑ You feel like "you're back in TriBeCa" say displaced NYers of this "slick", "noisy", "big city" "bar hangout" serving "urban" New American fare; while some metropophiles thirst to sip the martinis, sample "sleek, imaginative food" (try the "roasted garlic and brie") and check out the "'in'-crowd", others say the "iffy service" and "overpriced" menu are why they left NYC in the first place.

## Rancher's Club of Arizona
25 | 24 | 25 | $37 |

*Sheraton Hotel & Suites, 5151 E. Grant Rd. (bet. Craycroft & Swan Rds.), 520-321-7621*

■ "Forget the cowboy steaks" – this "gem" "hidden" in a business hotel is where diners sit beneath steer-horn chandeliers in soft leather chairs and receive "white-glove"-and-cloche service along with "fine steaks cooked over a variety of hardwoods" with "adventurous sauces"; there are veggies cooked right and perfect crème brûlée too.

## Sachiko Sushi S     24 | 16 | 21 | $19

*1101 N. Wilmot Rd. (Speedway Blvd.), 520-886-7000*

◪ Fish and sushi fans flock to this "top" "neighborhood" sushi bar that also offers artful udon and tempura, making it our surveyors' pick for Tucson's "best Japanese"; "bright lights" and "lots of tables" don't win stellar decor scores, and some feel service could be improved, but the "excellent" food is "worth it."

## Tack Room S     25 | 25 | 25 | $46

*7300 E. Vactor Ranch Trail (Tanque Verde Rd.), 520-722-2800*

◪ Many still find this "lovely old ranch house" "close to perfect", with a "quiet elegance" that makes "you feel like a king"; its "superior" (albeit "pricey") SW-accented Traditional American menu, "outstanding service" and "strains of Chopin" from the piano make it a good place to take anyone from "your mother-in-law" to a "lover"; but with "more competition now", some say this "tack is not as sharp as it used to be" and "needs an infusion of pizazz."

## Ventana Room S     28 | 28 | 27 | $44

*Loews Ventana Canyon Resort, 7000 N. Resort Dr. (north of Kolb Rd. & Sunrise Dr.), 520-299-2020*

■ Nestled below granite peaks northeast of the city, this very "luxurious" American-Eclectic is acclaimed for its "spectacular" views (with shows of "summer lightning"), "gracious service" and, last but not least, "sumptuous", "savory" fare ("I learned to love caribou!") that earns Tucson's No. 1 rating for Food; it's a "top-notch" place for "gala dinners" that leaves just one regret: "wish we could afford it all the time."

## Vivace     27 | 21 | 24 | $27

*Crossroads Festival Plaza, 4811 E. Grant Rd. (Swan Rd.), 520-795-7221*

■ "Delightful in every way" sums up Tucson's top-rated Italian, which boasts a "stylish" "bistro atmosphere" and open kitchen that lets the high-energy crowd watch as chef Daniel Scordato ("terrific!") and his "enthusiastic" staff whip up creamy risotto, fabulous farfalle and other food that's consistently "excellent" and a "best buy"; a new, more intimate wine bar should satisfy those who find the wide open setting in need of "noise control."

## Wildflower S     – | – | – | M

*7037 N. Oracle Rd. (Iha Rd.), 520-219-4230*

Everybody says this elegant New American eatery – featuring fresh flowers, a fabulous trompe l'oeil blue sky ceiling and colorful art – looks too big-city to be in Tucson, but lucky you, it is; better still, the price for such an extravagance as warm Maine lobster salad dressed with white-truffle vinaigrette won't remind you of New York.

# Washington, DC

## TOP 20 FOOD RANKING

| | Restaurant | Cuisine Type |
|---|---|---|
| **29** | Inn at Little Washington | New American |
| **28** | Kinkead's | New American/Seafood |
| **27** | Makoto | Japanese |
| | L'Auberge Chez François | Classic French |
| | Obelisk | Northern Italian |
| | Gerard's Place | Classic/New French |
| | L'Auberge Provencale | Classic French |
| | Lespinasse | New French |
| **26** | 1789 | Regional American |
| | Galileo | Northern Italian |
| | Seasons | New American |
| | Prime Rib | Steakhouse |
| | Morrison-Clark Inn | New American |
| | Vidalia | American/Southern |
| | Four & Twenty Blackbirds | New American |
| | Melrose | New American |
| | Nora | New American |
| | Sushi-Ko | Japanese |
| | Morton's of Chicago | Steakhouse |
| **25** | Duangrat's | Thai |

## OTHER IMPORTANT PLACES

| | |
|---|---|
| Ardeo | New American |
| Bis | New French |
| Black's Bar & Kitchen | Seafood |
| Bombay Club | Indian |
| Bread Line | Bakery/International |
| Cashion's Eat Place | New American |
| Citronelle | Californian/French |
| DC Coast | New American |
| Equinox | New American |
| Georgia Brown's | Southern |
| Jaleo | Spanish/Tapas |
| Kaz Sushi Bistro | Japanese |
| Marcel's | Belgian/French |
| New Heights | New American |
| Old Ebbitt Grill | Traditional American |
| Pesce | Seafood |
| Pizzeria Paradiso | Pizza |
| Red Sage | Southwestern |
| Taberna del Alabardero | Spanish |
| Tahoga | New American |

**Ardeo [S]** — | — | — | M

*3311 Connecticut Ave., NW (Macomb St.), 202-244-6750*

The debut of this smashing art deco Contemporary American in a duplex on Cleveland Park's restaurant row is yet another indication that this neighborhood has come of culinary age; its founder, Ashok Bajaj (Bombay Club, 701, Oval Room), knows what DC wants: interestingly seasoned, light tasting fare served in sophisticated settings.

**Bis [S]** — | — | — | E

*Hotel George, 15 E St., NW (1st St.), 202-661-2700*

In his glowing New French bistro on Capitol Hill, James Beard award–winner Jeffrey Buben (Vidalia) refashions Paris-Lyons classics for what he terms the 'American sensibility' (escargot ragout, Provençale vegetable tart); while it's been celebrity central since day one, its gorgeous Gallic interior (by architects/interior designers Adamstein & Demetriou), with a spectacular zinc bar and roomy, leather-lined booths, appeals to every sensibility.

**Black's Bar & Kitchen [S]** — | — | — | M

(fka Gulf Coast Kitchen)

*7750 Woodmont Ave. (bet. Cheltenham Dr. & Old Georgetown Rd.), Bethesda, MD, 301-652-6278*

New chef-owners Barbara and Jeff Black (Addie's) add authority to this appealing Bethesda roadhouse's Gulf Coast kitchen with a new menu, reinvigorated staff and a sophisticated dining room redo; its rooftop deck and outdoor patio have always been a young-and-single scene, and now it's really cooking.

**Bombay Club [S]** 25 | 25 | 25 | $36

*815 Connecticut Ave., NW (bet. H & I Sts.), 202-659-3727*

■ Beltway insiders and "unknowns" alike are "treated like rajas" at this "plush and hushed" Anglo-Indian power-dining room near the White House, where the food is "elegant", "delicious" and impressive; in short, this place with "top-notch service" "gets everything right", causing one Republican to lament "too bad Clinton likes it."

**Bread Line** 21 | 13 | 14 | $11

*1751 Pennsylvania Ave., NW (bet. 17th & 18th Sts.), 202-822-8900*

■ Mark Furstenberg's "industrial chic" bakery/cafe near the White House raises "carryout to a new level" with Internationally inspired bread-based meals (empanadas, piadinas), "fabulous soups" and salads, plus "excellent" artisanal loaves; sure, you need "strong teeth" and high "tolerance" for lunchtime lines, but who else could make a "tuna sandwich remarkable?"

**Cashion's Eat Place [S]** 25 | 21 | 21 | $35

*1819 Columbia Rd., NW (bet. Biltmore & Mintwood Sts.), 202-797-1819*

■ At award-winning Ann Cashion's "refreshingly different" urban American bistro in Adams Morgan, you "don't have to dress up for great food" and "cosmopolitan" surroundings; they make everyone – from the President and parents with "teenagers in grunge clothes" to solo diners seated at the "happening" bar or sidewalk cafe – feel like "moving right in."

---

## Citronelle [S] 24 23 23 $48

(aka Michel Richard's Citronelle)

*Latham Hotel, 3000 M St., NW (30th St.), 202-625-2150*

◪ This posh Georgetown dining room is the "place to see the who's who of DC", and now that superchef Michel Richard is permanently "at home" in its kitchen, it is equally a place for "exquisite food" and expense-account pampering; given its spectacular multimillion dollar new look and its cutting-edge Cal-French cuisine, its already excellent ratings (which predated the redo) should soar and win over doubters who dub it "overpriced."

## DC Coast – – – E

*1401 K St., NW (14th St.), 202-216-5988*

Airy, mirrored, polished and dramatically chic, this long-heralded Downtown destination looks every inch the power center it was designed to be; its art deco style matches its smooth personnel profile and, with the much-missed Jeff Tunks (ex River Club) turning out multiregional New American cuisine, it's also fulfilling its food destination destiny.

## Duangrat's [S] 25 21 22 $25

*5878 Leesburg Pike (Glen Forest Rd.), Falls Church, VA, 703-820-5775*

■ The *DC Survey*'s top Thai provides an "elegant" Northern Virginia backdrop for "skillfully seasoned" food; to say that its "brilliant" specials and "gracious" waitresses (in traditional dress) "make French food seem boring and Italian waiters seem rude" may overstate matters, but still, this place will "impress the boss" for a fraction of the cost of a comparable meal Downtown.

## Equinox – – – M

*818 Connecticut Ave., NW (I St.), 202-331-8118*

Todd Gray's (ex Galileo) Mid-Atlantic roots and his respect for fresh ingredients inform the seasonal New American menu at his attractively-appointed, just steps-from-the-White House spot; it didn't take long for an A-list of power lunchers and *bec fins* to discover its sunny atrium, well-orchestrated service and fine fare.

## Four & Twenty Blackbirds [S] 26 22 24 $35

*Rte. 522 (Rte. 647), Flint Hill, VA, 540-675-1111*

■ "Take the back roads" to this "gratifying" example of Virginia small-town rusticity for "superb country dining" and "attentive" hospitality; the setting may be "bucolic", but the "scrumptious" Contemporary American cooking, which relies on top-flight regional ingredients, and the power-couple clientele are all quite urbane.

## Galileo [S] 26 23 23 $52

*1110 21st St. (bet. L & M Sts.), 202-293-7191*

◪ "The Italian of choice" for "wonderful" food and wine in a star-studded setting; Roberto Donna, his "creative" executive chefs and a "knowledgeable" staff "maintain standards" that win this "classy" Downtown spot national acclaim; go for a "fantastic" chef's tasting meal in the *Laboratorio* (his trendsetting restaurant within a restaurant) to understand why, even with "occasional lapses" and "pricey" tabs, it's "the most fun in town."

| F | D | S | C |
|---|---|---|---|

**Georgia Brown's [S]** 23 | 23 | 21 | $32

*950 15th St., NW (bet. I & K Sts.), 202-393-4499*

◪ "Stunning" spot lined with "lawyers and pols" who revel in its "huge portions" of "nouvelle" Southern cooking and "boisterous" bonhomie, this Downtown crowd-pleaser feels "truly" DC; sure, it's "too noisy for conversation" and sometimes serves "heavy" food that requires a "nap after lunch", but it's a surefire bet for spotting "dignitaries" and has a "spectacular" Sunday gospel brunch.

**Gerard's Place** 27 | 22 | 24 | $55

*915 15th St., NW (bet. I & K Sts.), 202-737-4445*

■ With star chefs Jean-Louis Palladin (of the Watergate) and Jean-Pierre Goyenvalle (Le Lion D'Or) gone from the DC scene, attention is focused on Gerard Pangaud's "subtle" but "stellar" and "worth every dime" French on McPherson Square; his cooking is showcased in this "small, intimate dining room", with the "elegant" touches and "impeccable" service that make a "power lunch or romantic meal"; the closing of his Georgetown bistro, Vintage, means he'll be spending more time here.

**Inn at Little Washington [S]** 29 | 29 | 29 | $96

*Inn at Little Washington, Main & Middle Sts., Washington, VA, 540-675-3800*

■ "Nearly perfect" scores make this the *DC Survey*'s No. 1 rated restaurant across-the-board, as well as the "ultimate" VA country destination; chef/co-owner Patrick O'Connell's "spectacular" Contemporary American food, "opulent" appointments and the staff's constant "attention to detail" leave surveyors sighing "nirvana" that's "worth every penny"; N.B. try to reserve a chef's table in the state-of-the-art, multimillion dollar kitchen.

**Jaleo [S]** 23 | 21 | 19 | $26

*480 Seventh St., NW (E St.), 202-628-7949*

■ The "atmosphere is electric" at this pioneering Penn Quarter trendsetter that "despite popularity, crowding" and "waits" just "keeps getting better"; most find it "impossible to get bored" with its Spanish tapas concept, which allows for the "pleasure" of sharing "great food" and offers "flexible" dining before or after MCI Center events.

**Kaz Sushi Bistro [S]** – | – | – | M

*1915 I St., NW (bet. 18th & 20th Sts.), 202-530-5500*

Kaz Okochi's (ex Sushi-Ko) distinctive East-West cuisine (ginger-cured duck confit, short ribs in soy sauce) and sparkling sushi have found a serene and stylish setting near the World Bank on I Street; here, novitiates can take advantage of the sushi tastings, bento boxes and Japanese specialties on the moderately priced menu to learn why this is a mecca for mega-chefs and food mavens.

**Kinkead's [S]** 28 | 23 | 25 | $44

*Red Lion Row, 2000 Pennsylvania Ave., NW (I St., bet. 20th & 21st Sts.), 202-296-7700*

■ Nearly 1,500 respondents rate Bob Kinkead's very '90s American bistro No. 2 for Food and Popularity in the *DC Survey*; his "brilliant innovation" – serving a "spectacular" seafood-oriented menu with "awesome choices" in handsome, "not too formal" settings – revolutionized DC "power" dining; "knowledgeable" service, an "excellent wine list" and "great jazz" are other reasons why most people feel "lucky" to "get in."

## L'Auberge Chez François 🅂    27   28   27   $50

*332 Springvale Rd. (2 mi. north of Georgetown Pike), Great Falls, VA, 703-759-3800*

■ There is "no more enjoyable place for a celebration" than this rustic French farmhouse in Great Falls, our DC surveyors' perennial Most Popular restaurant; lovingly managed by the Haeringer family in the "European" manner, its "hearty" Alsatian food is "plentiful, delicious" and gives "full value"; the "unique setting" down a "winding" country road is "less formal than you'd expect", with an utterly "magical" garden.

## L'Auberge Provencale 🅂    27   27   26   $64

*L'Auberge Provencale, Rte. 340 (Rte. 50), White Post, VA, 540-837-1375*

■ This "romantic getaway" near VA's horse country featuring a "creative, herb-enhanced [five-course] menu" and an "interesting wine list" makes "you think you're in a French Provençal hotel"; most find the effect "charming" and say "it's up there with the best."

## Lespinasse    27   28   26   $75

*Sheraton Carlton Hotel, 923 16th St., NW (K St.), 202-879-6900*

■ "Elegance personified", this "exquisite", "impeccable" New French showpiece in a hotel near the White House is the ultimate indulgence when someone else "pays" and the site of DC's most "dazzling" (some say "ostentatious") "VIP business" lunch; but given its NY prices, many expect it to "walk on water" – and it merely glides; N.B. it now boasts a new French chef, Sandro Gamba (who trained with France's Alain Ducasse), and a lower tab.

## Makoto 🅂    27   24   27   $44

*4822 MacArthur Blvd., NW (Reservoir Rd.), 202-298-6866*

■ "Exquisite little things just keep coming" during a "stunning set dinner" at this "sauna-sized" (four tables and 10 sushi bar seats) Palisades Japanese; one of the *DC Survey's* top-rated spots, a meal here is an "aesthetically pleasing experience" that's reputedly "as good as all but the best in Japan" and for "one quarter of the price."

## Marcel's    –   –   –   E

*2401 Pennsylvania Ave., NW (24th St.), 202-296-1166*

What a combo – Robert Wiedmaier's (ex Aquarelle, Cafe on M) Belgian-French cooking is showcased in what was Provence's Mediterranean-looking West End space; at this born-again venue (named after the chef's infant son), the flavorful menu, impressive wines, special-occasion setting and presence of front-of-the-house pros auger well.

## Melrose 🅂    26   25   25   $47

*Park Hyatt Hotel, M & 24th Sts., NW, 202-955-3899*

■ One of DC's top "creative" Contemporary Americans, this hotel dining room has an "understated elegance" that makes it a "quiet oasis" in the heart of the West End; with "excellent" food, "gracious" service and luxurious appointments like a "cascading fountain" on the "romantic" terrace, it's a "little pricey but perfect for a special occasion."

## Morrison-Clark Inn §

26 | 26 | 25 | $43

*Morrison-Clark Inn, 1015 L St., NW (bet. 11th St. & Massachusetts Ave.), 202-898-1200*

■ "A lovely restaurant with class, charm and the wonderful cooking" of Susan Lindeborg, one of the area's top chefs, who "imaginatively" "updates" "everyday" American food; while the "setting is elegant and refined", its "very professional" staff puts boldface names, "foreign visitors" and just-folks at ease; now that the nearby MCI Center is revitalizing what was an "out-of-the-way" neighborhood, its only "negative" becomes another plus.

## Morton's of Chicago §

26 | 22 | 23 | $49

*3251 Prospect St., NW (Wisconsin Ave.), 202-342-6258*
*Washington Sq., 1050 Connecticut Ave., NW (L St.), 202-955-5997*
*Fairfax Sq., 8075 Leesburg Pike (Aline Rd.), Tysons Corner, VA, 703-883-0800*

■ "Check your belt at the door" of these "macho" beefhouses and dig into a "steak as big as a house cat" and a baked potato that's the "size of Idaho"; sure, the "cigar smoke", the "hustle", the "chatty waiters" and the bill are all "a bit much", but isn't that the point? N.B. they serve lobster and veggie platters too.

## New Heights §

25 | 23 | 23 | $43

*2317 Calvert St., NW (Connecticut Ave.), 202-234-4110*

■ "Wonderfully seductive" and "original", this Contemporary American "pushes the creative envelope" with "gorgeous presentations", drawing a clientele that "never tires of trying something new"; its second-story space, overlooking Rock Creek Park, is awash with art and "when the trees are in bloom" is "magical", but service, while "phenomenally nice", is a bit "slow."

## Nora

26 | 24 | 24 | $47

*2132 Florida Ave., NW (bet. Connecticut & Massachusetts Aves.), 202-462-5143*

■ "DC's best combo of romance, fine food and unstuffy elegance", spiked with "guaranteed celebrity" sightings, is found at this "original" New American set in a "charming" carriage house near Dupont Circle; chef-owner Nora Pouillon practically invented market-driven menus featuring "natural" ingredients and her staff is "knowledgeable" too.

## Obelisk

27 | 23 | 25 | $53

*2029 P St., NW (bet. 20th & 21st Sts.), 202-872-1180*

■ "Refined and excellent" food makes Peter Pastan's "delightful little jewel box" off Dupont Circle the *DC Survey*'s top Italian; though the "prix fixe menu is limited", everything's "pure, simple, handmade" and hence "close to perfection"; since some say it's the "best high-end value in town", it's a "favorite for spoiling friends."

## Old Ebbitt Grill ❷§

19 | 22 | 20 | $28

*675 15th St., NW (bet. F & G Sts.), 202-347-4801*

■ "Deservedly mobbed", this handsome Downtown "institution" is virtually a White House "annex" filled with a "who's who" of "journalists" and "wide-eyed out-of-towners" who find that its "celebratory" mood, "polished" manners, long hours and "serious" all-American food fit any occasion; it's "quintessentially DC" and "considering the quality", "you get your money's worth."

## Pesce S

25 | 15 | 20 | $33

*2016 P St., NW (bet. Dupont Circle & 20th St.), 202-466-3474*

■ One of the town's top seafooders, this "lively" urban bistro off Dupont Circle boasts an "original", "skillfully" executed, daily-changing menu featuring "fish that doesn't get better than this", a "wine list of wonders" and "attentive" help (when not "rushed"); the whitewashed "fish store" setting is in keeping with the "exquisite simplicity" of the concept; the only gripe is too bad it's so "small."

## Pizzeria Paradiso S

25 | 17 | 18 | $18

*2029 P St., NW (bet. 20th & 21st Sts.), 202-223-1245*

■ "The epitome of pizza", "best anywhere", "no rivals" – once again, the *DC Survey's* top pizza honors go to this whimsically decorated Dupont Circle denizen and its "perfect" pies, which are distinguished by "delicious, fresh toppings" and a "smoky", crispy crust; other pluses include sandwiches, salads and a staff that doesn't panic "even when it's packed", i.e. at peak hours.

## Prime Rib

26 | 24 | 25 | $48

*2020 K St., NW (bet. 20th & 21st Sts.), 202-466-8811*

■ The "retro supper club appeal" of "blonds, booze", crab imperial, "exceptional" prime rib and getting "dressed up" for a "great evening out" keep this Downtown "art deco classic" steakhouse filled with distinguished-looking types, "trophy wives" and late-night revelers; run by real pros who "treat you right", it's been a "quiet place to do [the nation's] business" for years.

## Red Sage S

22 | 25 | 20 | $36

*605 14th St., NW (F St.), 202-638-4444*

☑ Mark Miller's "Southwestern circus" is enjoying a long run; located near big-name law and lobby palaces, the White House and the Mall, its "upstairs chile bar" "serves the masses", not to mention "celebs and pols", casual bites of "exciting" regional cuisine in "electric" surroundings – even more "spectacular" is the "tumbleweeds-on-acid decor" in the down-under dining room; "if you can handle the spice", the downstairs price and having your waiter occasionally "disappear", by all means, go.

## Seasons S

26 | 26 | 26 | $52

*Four Seasons Hotel, 2800 Pennsylvania Ave., NW (28th St.), 202-944-2000*

☑ An "opulent" and "tranquil" "dream world" setting "overlooking lots of green", and equally "elegant" New American cooking, are the reasons respondents rate this "luxurious" hotel one of DC's "best" dining sites for all seasons; it's a "great place for business meetings", "getting engaged" and "impressing your aunt", plus its Sunday brunch "buffet blitz" will bliss you out.

## 1789 S

26 | 27 | 26 | $51

*1226 36th St., NW (Prospect St.), 202-965-1789*

■ "Great everything" – "warm, inviting surroundings", "first-class" American Regional food and "special guest" treatment for all; its chef, Ris Lacoste (ex Kinkead's), sparked a "renaissance" at this "historic", "romantic" Georgetown residence, putting it in the Top 10 for Food, Decor and Service and causing hundreds of devotees to declare if you "have something to celebrate, do it here!"

### Sushi-Ko 🅂

26 | 15 | 20 | $29

*2307 Wisconsin Ave., NW (south of Calvert St.), 202-333-4187*
■ A post-*Survey* total transformation of DC's "drab" and "dated" "original sushi bar" into a sleek and tasteful retreat, together with the return of Japanese master chef Tetsuro Takanashi, who first made it the local "gold standard for sushi", can only increase the above food and decor ratings.

### Taberna del Alabardero

25 | 26 | 24 | $46

*1776 I St., NW (18th St.), 202-429-2200*
■ Diplomats and internationals in-the-know are utterly at home in this "beautiful" Downtown Iberian, as is anyone who delights in "refined" yet gutsy Spanish food, "lots of privacy" and "artful" service; a branch of one of Madrid's "world-class" restaurants, it lends a "sense of occasion" to a "wonderful" business meal or evening event.

### Tahoga 🅂

23 | 21 | 21 | $40

*2815 M St., NW (bet. 28th & 29th Sts.), 202-338-5380*
■ "Great beginnings" made its "minimalist" Georgetown digs a stage set for the stylish, yet this New American "keeps working on getting it right"; despite a chef change, its "generally good" food is becoming "even better"; one of the "best new restaurants" in the area, it has a "hidden courtyard" that's the most romantic place in town.

### Vidalia 🅂

26 | 23 | 24 | $43

*1990 M St., NW (bet. 19th & 20th Sts.), 202-659-1990*
■ It's not just the "namesake [Vidalia] onions" that chef-owner Jeffrey Buben transforms into "downright glamorous" fare – his "imaginative" renditions of Southern classics have made his "sunny basement dining room" ("looks like Van Gogh by way of Valdosta") a "premier" M Street site for "expense-account comfort food"; be sure to ask about his "fine wines."

## CITY ABBREVIATIONS

| | | | |
|---|---|---|---|
| AC | Atlantic City | MI | Miami/Miami Beach |
| AT | Atlanta | MN | Minneapolis/St. Paul |
| BA | Baltimore/Annapolis | NJ | New Jersey |
| BO | Boston | NO | New Orleans |
| CH | Chicago | NY | New York City |
| CI | Cincinnati | OC | Orange County, CA |
| CL | Cleveland | OR | Orlando |
| CO | Columbus | PB | Palm Beach |
| DA | Dallas | PH | Philadelphia |
| DC | Washington, DC | PO | Portland, OR |
| DE | Denver Area | PS | Phoenix/Scottsdale |
| DT | Detroit | SA | Santa Fe |
| FL | Fort Lauderdale | SC | Salt Lake City Area |
| FW | Fort Worth | SD | San Diego |
| HO | Honolulu | SE | Seattle |
| HS | Houston | SF | San Francisco |
| KC | Kansas City | SL | St. Louis |
| LA | Los Angeles | TB | Tampa Bay/Sarasota |
| LV | Las Vegas | TC | Tucson |

# CUISINES

**Afghan**
Helmand, BA

**American (New)**
American Rest., KC
Anago, BO
Angeluna, FW
Aqua, SF
Ardeo, DC
Arizona Inn, TC
Atwater's, PO
Aujourd'hui, BO
Aureole, LV
Aureole, NY
Bacchanalia, AT
Bayona, NO
Beach Bistro, TB
Beehive, DE
Bernards Inn, NJ
Biba, BO
Bijou Café, TB
Bistango, OC
Bistro Mezzaluna, FL
Boca, CI
Boulevard, SF
Buckhead Diner, AT
Buffet at the Kimbell, FW
By Word of Mouth, FL
Cafe Allegro, KC
Cafe Aspen, FW
Cafe Balaban, SL
Cafe Chardonnay, PB
Cafe Mira, SL
Cafe Sebastienne, KC
Canoe, AT
Cardwell's, SL
Cashion's Eat Place, DC
Chaparral, PS
Charles Court, DE

Charlie Trotter's, CH
Convivo, PS
Courtright's, CH
Cousins Heritage Inn, DT
Crofton on Wells, CH
Crossing, SL
DC Coast, DC
dick & harry's, AT
Dilworthtown Inn, PH
Ebbitt Room, NJ
11 Madison Park, NY
Equinox, DC
Evermay on the Delaware, PH
Fahrenheit, CH
Faust's, SL
Five Lakes Grill, DT
510 Rest., MN
Flagstaff House, DE
Flying Fig, CL
Food Studio, AT
Fork, PH
4 & 20 Blackbirds, DC
French Laundry, SF
Frog & the Peach, NJ
Gary Danko, SF
Gautreau's, NO
George's at the Cove, SD
Glitretind, SC
Globe, SF
Goodfellow's, MN
Gordon, CH
Gotham B&G, NY
Grace, CH
Gramercy Tavern, NY
Grand Finale, CI
Green Room, DA
Grille on Broadway, KC
Hamersley's, BO
Hampton's, BA

Handke's, CO
Harvest Moon Inn, NJ
Harvest on Huron, CH
Harvest, SL
Harvey's Bistro, OR
Hedgerose, AT
Herbfarm, SE
Highlands Garden Cafe, DE
Icarus, BO
Inn at Little Washington, DC
Iron Horse, CI
Jake's, PH
Jeffrey's, NJ
Kevin Taylor, DE
Keystone Ranch, DE
Kingfisher, TC
Kinkead's, DC
Kosta's, CL
La Bettola, BO
Le Parvenu, NO
Lindey's, CO
Little Nell, DE
Log Haven, SC
Lon's at the Hermosa, PS
Loring Cafe, MN
Lucia's, MN
Mainland Inn, PH
Manuel's on the 28th, OR
March, NY
Mariposa, SC
Maritana Grille, TB
Market Sq. Bistro, CL
Mark's, HS
Mark's Las Olas, FL
Martine, SC
Mary Elaine's, PS
Max's Grille, PB
Meetinghouse, SF
Melrose, DC
Mercer Kitchen, NY
Metropolis, KC
Metropolitan, SC
Michael's on East, TB
Mise en Place, TB
Morel, TB
Morrison-Clark Inn, DC
Moveable Feast, DT
Mumbo Jumbo, AT
Nana Grill, DA
New Heights, DC
Nora, DC
one sixtyblue, CH
Opus One, DT
Opus 251, PH
Palace, CI
Pano's & Paul's, AT
Park Avenue Cafe, CH
Park Avenue Cafe, NY
Park 75, AT
Pastiche, TC
Pebbles, OR

Peppercorn Duck, KC
Phoenix, CI
Pierpoint, BA
Plaza 600, CI
Potager, DE
Presidio Grill, TC
Printer's Row, CH
Radex, DE
Ramos Hse. Cafe, OC
Rattlesnake Club, DT
Redwood Grill, HS
Reflections, FW
Renaissance, DE
Restaurant Hapa, PS
Ritz-Carlton Grill, SL
River Cafe, NY
Riverview Room, CL
Rococo, PH
Rosemary & Sage, NJ
Rouge 99, PH
Rudys' 2900, BA
Saddle Peak Lodge, LA
Saddle River Inn, NJ
Seasons, CH
Seasons, DC
Seeger's, AT
Sevy's Grill, DA
Sidney St. Cafe, SL
Sierra Grill, HS
Spago, LV
Splendido, DE
Starker's Reserve, KC
Stolen Grill, KC
Strings, DE
Sturkey's, CI
Sundance Tree Room, SC
Swann Lounge, PH
Sweet Basil, DE
Syzygy, DE
Tabla, NY
Tahoga, DC
Tarbell's, PS
Tasca, HS
Tavern on the Green, NY
32 East, PB
302 West, CH
Too Chez, DT
Tremont 647, BO
Tribute, DT
Trio, CI
TRU, CH
240 Union, DE
208 Talbot, BA
Union Pacific, NY
Union Sq. Cafe, NY
Van Gogh's, AT
Ventana Room, TC
Veritas, NY
Washington Inn, NJ
Waters Edge, NJ
White Dog Cafe, PH

Whitney, DT
Wildflower, DE
Wildflower, TC
Windows on the World, NY
Woodward's Garden, SF
York St., DA
Zinnia, SL

## American (Regional)

Alpenglow Stube, DE
Artist Point, OR
Braddock's Grandview, CO
Cafe Alpine, DE
Cameron's, CO
Caprial's, PO
Charleston, BA
Dakota, NO
Dakota B&G, MN
Entre Nous, CH
Flying Biscuit Cafe, AT
Four Seasons, PB
Frazer's, SL
Greyhound Tavern, CI
Grouse Mtn. Grill, DE
Himmarshee B&G, FL
Kennedyville Inn, BA
Latilla Room, PS
Lola, CL
Mariposa, HO
Matt's No Place, DA
Milton Inn, BA
Orchids, CI
Oregon Grille, BA
Pierpoint, BA
Piñons, DE
Rainbow Lodge, HS
Roaring Fork, PS
Rowes Wharf, BO
1789, DC
Table of Contents, MN
Tina's, PO
Vidalia, DC
Watershed, AT
Wildwood, PO

## American (Traditional)

Bang!, DE
Briarwood Inn, DE
Cafe Bohemia, DE
Cap City Fine Diner, CO
Chez Betty, SC
First Floor Grill, LV
Goldener Hirsch, SC
Harvest, BO
Lark Creek Inn, SF
Local, MN
Marconi's, BA
Michael's, LV
Moxie, CL
New Yorker Club, SC
Old Ebbitt Grill, DC
Oven's, TC

Palace Arms, DE
Paris Coffee Shop, FW
Pike Street, DT
Ram's Head Inn, AC
Rib Room, NO
Ritz-Carlton Grill, DT
Rotisserie/Beef & Bird, HS
Shaw's, CO
Spencer's, SC
Stephenson's, KC
St. Paul Grill, MN
Stroud's, KC
Tack Room, TC
'21' Club, NY
Victoria & Albert's, OR
Watershed, AT
Worthington Inn, CO

## Asian

Ambrosia, BO
Belvedere, LA
Blue Ginger, BO
Buddakan, PH
Cafe Blanc, LA
Cafe Japengo, SD
Chaya Brasserie, LA
Chinois on Main, LA
EOS, SF
Five Feet, OC
Fusebox, AT
Liberty, DA
Mon Jin Lau, DT
Pacific Moon, CI
Pacific Time, MI
Painted Table, SE
Phnom Penh, CL
Restaurant Hapa, PS
Salamander, BO
Saucebox, PO
Scott Chen's, HS
Second St. Grill, LV
Shiro, LA
SideBern's, TB
Susanna Foo, PH
Taka, SD
Wild Ginger, SE

## Bakeries

BonBonerie, CI
Bread Garden, AT
Bread Line, DC
Vera's Bakery, BA

## Bar-B-Q

Angelo's, FW
East Coast Grill, BO
Fiorella's Jack Stack, KC
Goode Co., HS
Johnny Rivers', OR
Kennedyville Inn, BA
Montgomery Inn, CI
Railhead Smokehse., FW
Sonny Bryan's, DA

## Belgian

Belgian Lion, SD
Marcel's, DC

## Brazilian

Café Brazil, DE
Fogo de Chao, DA
Porcao, MI
Sergio's, CL
Vera's Bakery, BA

## Cajun/Creole

Antoine's, NO
Arnaud's, NO
Brennan's, HS
Brennan's, NO
Brigtsen's, NO
Christian's, NO
Clancy's, NO
Commander's Palace, NO
Dee Felice Cafe, CI
Delmonico, NO
Emeril's, LV
Emeril's, OR
410 Bank St., NJ
Galatoire's, NO
Harold's Cajun Glory, CO
Lafitte's Landing, NO
Le Parvenu, NO
Mr. B's Bistro, NO
Nonie, TC

## Californian

Aubergine, OC
Azzura Point, SD
Bel-Air Hotel, LA
Belvedere, LA
Bistro 45, LA
California Grill, OR
Campanile, LA
Charles Nob Hill, SF
Chaya Brasserie, LA
Cheesecake Factory, BA
Chez Panisse, SF
Chez Panisse Cafe, SF
Citronelle, DC
Citrus, LA
Delicias, SD
Devon, LA
Domaine Chandon, SF
Erna's Elderberry, SF
Forte, DT
Grand Cafe, SF
Hawthorne Lane, SF
JiRaffe, LA
Joe's, LA
Jozu, LA
Linwood's, BA
Michael's, LA
Moose's, SF

Pacific's Edge, SF
Pamplemousse Grille, SD
Parkway Grill, LA
Patina, LA
Pavilion, OC
Pebbles, OR
Pinot Bistro, LA
Pinot Brasserie, LV
Postrio, SF
Rancho Valencia, SD
Röckenwagner, LA
Rubicon, SF
Sage, BO
Shiro, LA
Spago, CH
Spago Bev. Hills, LA
Spago Hollywood, LA
Spago Palo Alto, SF
Strings, DE
Terra, SF

## Cambodian

Elephant Walk, BO

## Caribbean

Bahama Breeze, OR
410 Bank St., NJ
Ortanique, MI

## Chinese

Arc-en-Ciel, DA
Chopstix, AT
Ciao Mein, HO
Golden Dragon, HO
Golden Room, HS
Hunan, HS
Hunan Lion, CO
Legend Seafood, HO
Mandarin, SC
P.F. Chang's, LV
Shanghai 1930, SF
Shun Lee Palace, NY
Tropical Chinese, MI
Winnie's, OR
Yujean Kang's, LA

## Coffeehouses/Desserts

Patisserie Descours, HS

## Contemporary Louisiana

Dakota, NO
Emeril's, NO
Gabrielle, NO
NOLA, NO
Pelican Club, NO
Peristyle, NO

## Continental

Anthony's, HS
Anthony's, TC
Bijou Café, TB
Black Orchid Cafe, FL
Briarwood Inn, DE
Brooks, FL

Café L'Europe, TB
Canoe, AT
Charles Court, DE
Chatham's Place, OR
Chez Betty, SC
Christo's, PS
Crystal Cafe, MI
Darrel & Oliver's/Grill, FL
Five Crowns, OC
Flagstaff House, DE
Forge, MI
Fountain, PH
Four Seasons, NY
Goldener Hirsch, SC
Golden Mushroom, DT
Grapevine, SC
Gustaf Anders, OC
Hôtel St. Germain, DA
Inn at Perry Cabin, BA
Johnny's Bar/Fulton, CL
Johnny's Downtown, CL
Kathy's Gazebo, PB
La Réserve, HS
L'Ermitage, LA
Maison et Jardin, OR
Moveable Feast, DT
New Yorker Club, SC
Nikolai's Roof, AT
Old House, SA
100 South Ocean, PB
103 West, AT
Palace Arms, DE
Palm Court, PS
Pano's & Paul's, AT
Park Plaza Gardens, OR
Peter Scott's, OR
Pink Adobe, SA
Polo Grill, BA
Pyramid Room, DA
Rancho Valencia, SD
Rib Room, NO
Ritz, OC
Ritz-Carlton Buck. Cafe, AT
Rouge 99, PH
Rudys' 2900, BA
Swan at Inverness, DE
Swann Lounge, PH
Swiss Inn, HO
Tio Pepe, BA
Tony's, HS
Tosoni's, SE

## Crab Houses
Cantler's Riverside, BA

## Cuban
Chez Henri, BO
Rolando's, OR
Versailles, MI

## Delis/Sandwich Shops
Bread Garden, AT
Brent's Deli, LA

Carlos' Gospel Cafe, SA
Carnegie Deli, NY
Patisserie Descours, HS
White House, AC
Wolfie's, MI
Zingerman's Deli, DT

## Dim Sum
Tropical Chinese, MI

## Eclectic/International
Astor Place, MI
Bayona, NO
Bayport Cookery, MN
Bexley's Monk, CO
Blue Ginger, BO
Blue Heron, TB
Blue Room, BO
Boca, CI
Bread Line, DC
Buddakan, PH
Café Boulud, NY
Cafe Japengo, SD
Cafe L'Europe, PB
Chaparral, PS
Chef Reto's, PB
China Grill, LV
China Grill, MI
Clancy's, NO
Darrel & Oliver's/Grill, FL
EatZi's, DA
EOS, SF
Euphemia Haye, TB
Grand St. Cafe, KC
Grape, DA
Grape Escape, FW
Grill Room, NO
Handke's, CO
Higgins, PO
Hoku's, HO
Hot Chocolates, FL
Lark, DT
Laurels, DA
Lockkeeper's Inn, CL
Log Haven, SC
Manuel's on the 28th, OR
Mary Elaine's, PS
Michael's at the Citadel, PS
Mixx, SD
Morel, TB
Moshulu, PH
Nemo, MI
Ophelia's, TB
Park Plaza Gardens, OR
Randall's Gourmet, FW
Rigsby's, CO
Röckenwagner, LA
RoxSand, PS
Salamander, BO
Santacafe, SA
Savaradio, AC
SideBern's, TB

Taka, SD
Trio, CH
Upperline, NO
Ventana Room, TC
Yia Yia's, KC

## Eurasian
Bali-By-The-Sea, HO
Indigo, HO
Roy's, HO

## Floridian
Astor Place, MI
Maritana Grille, TB

## French Bistro
Aquitaine, BO
Aubergine Cafe, DE
Babette's Cafe, AT
Bistro at Maison de Ville, NO
Bistro Banlieue, CH
Bistro 45, LA
Bistro Jeanty, SF
Bistro St. Tropez, PH
Bouchon, SF
Brasserie Le Coze, AT
Cafe Bizou, LA
Cafe Bohemia, DE
Cafe Campagne, SE
Cafe des Amis, PO
Cafe Provençal, SL
Chaya Brasserie, LA
Chez Gerard, DA
Chez Henri, BO
Chez Nous, HS
Christopher's Fermier, PS
Floataway Cafe, AT
Fringale, SF
Hamersley's, BO
Hannah's Bistro, KC
Harvey's Bistro, OR
Julienne, LA
La Petite Maison, PB
Lavendou, DA
Le Bar Lyonnais, PH
Le Bistro, TC
Le Bouchon, CH
Le Coq au Vin, OR
Le Fou Frog, KC
Left Bank, FL
Metro Bistro, NO
Mise en Place Mkt. Bistro, TB
Montrachet, NY
Padovani's, HO
Pinot Bistro, LA
Pinot Brasserie, LV
Pinot Provence, OC
Saint-Emilion, FW
Soupçon, DE
Tapenade, SD
Truc, BO

## French (Classic)
Andre's, LV
Antoine's, NO
Arnaud's, NO
Aubergine, OC
Baricelli Inn, CL
Belgian Lion, SD
Café Boulud, NY
Café de France, SL
Café des Artistes, NY
Cafe 36, CH
Campton Place, SF
Castagna, PO
Chez Alphonse, CI
Chez François, CL
Chez Madeleine, NJ
Chez Vincent, OR
Christian's, NO
Citronelle, DC
Citrus, LA
Coventry Forge Inn, PH
Crozier's, NO
Daniel, NY
Deux Cheminées, PH
Diaghilev, LA
Dilworthtown Inn, PH
Drai's, LV
Earle, DT
Eiffel Tower, LV
El Bizcocho, SD
Emile's, SF
Fio's La Fourchette, SL
Five Feet, OC
510 Rest., MN
Fond de la Tour, CH
French Room, DA
Galatoire's, NO
Gerard's Downtown, NO
Gerard's Place, DC
Grand Finale, CI
Hôtel St. Germain, DA
Janos, TC
Kathy's Gazebo, PB
La Belle Vie, MN
La Caille, SC
La Caravelle, NY
La Colombe d'Or, HS
La Côte Basque, NY
La Grenouille, NY
La Mer, HO
L'Antibes, CO
La Palme d'Or, MI
La Petite France, CI
La Petite Maison, DE
La Provence, NO
Lark, DT
La Tour D'Argent, HS
L'Auberge Chez François, DC
L'Auberge Provencale, DC
Le Bec-Fin, PH
Le Cirque, LV

Le Cirque 2000, NY
Left Bank, DE
Le Gourmand, SE
Le Rendez-Vous, TC
Lespinasse, NY
Le Titi de Paris, CH
L'Orangerie, LA
Louis XVI, NO
Maisonette, CI
Maison Robert, BO
Malmaison, SL
Marcel's, DC
Michel's, HO
Mistral, BO
Montparnasse, CH
Palace Court, LV
Pascal, OC
Picasso, DE
Pyramid Room, DA
Refectory, CO
Ritz-Carlton, OC
Ritz-Carlton Buck. Cafe, AT
Ritz-Carlton Din. Rm., BO
Rover's, SE
Saddle River Inn, NJ
Savarin, CH
Suzette's, LV
Tante Louise, DE
Tatsu's, KC
Thee Bungalow, SD
Twins, SD
231 Ellsworth, SF

## French (New)

Ambria, CH
Ambrosia, BO
Aubriot, CH
Bel-Air Hotel, LA
Belvedere, LA
Bis, DC
Blue Door, MI
Bouley Bakery, NY
Brasserie Perrier, PH
Cacharel, FW
Cafe Blanc, LA
Cafe Bon Homme, DT
Cafe Panache, NJ
Campagne, SE
Carlos', CH
Cello, NY
Chanterelle, NY
Charles Nob Hill, SF
Chez Alphonse, CI
Chez Jean-Pierre, PB
Chinois on Main, LA
Ciboulette, PH
Clio, BO
Couvron, PO
DeVille, HS
Domaine Chandon, SF
El Bizcocho, SD
Elephant Walk, BO

Erna's Elderberry, SF
Everest, CH
Fleur de Lys, SF
Forte, DT
Fountain, PH
French Laundry, SF
Gabriel's, CH
Gautreau's, NO
Gerard's Place, DC
Grand Cafe, SF
Heathman, PO
Jardinière, SF
Jean Georges, NY
Julien, BO
La Cachette, LA
La Folie, SF
Laurel, SD
La Vieille Maison, PB
Le Bernardin, NY
Le Français, CH
Le Palais, AC
Le Provence, OR
Les Nomades, CH
L'Espalier, BO
Lespinasse, DC
Le Vichyssois, CH
Lumière, BO
Lutèce, NY
Maison Janeiro, PB
Masa's, SF
Mercer Kitchen, NY
Michael's, LA
Mille Fleurs, SD
Monte Carlo, LV
Nan, PH
103 West, AT
Pamplemousse Grille, SD
Papillon Café, DE
Parker's, CL
Patina, LA
Picasso, LV
Radius, BO
Renoir, LV
Ritz-Carlton Din. Rm., CH
Ritz-Carlton Din. Rm., SF
Riviera, DA
Rubicon, SF
Ryland Inn, NJ
Sent Sovi, SF
Serenäde, NJ
Silks, BO
Spago Bev. Hills, LA
Stage House Inn, NJ
Susanna Foo, PH
Tallgrass, CH
Terra, SF
Troquet, OC
Twins, SD
Vignola, SD
Vong, CH
WineSellar, SD

## Greek

Black Olive, BA
Milos, NY
Periyali, NY

## Hamburgers

Kincaid's, FW

## Hawaiian Regional

Alan Wong's, HO
Bali-By-The-Sea, HO
Chef Mavro's, HO
Ono Hawaiian Foods, HO
Padovani's, HO
Sam Choy's Diamond, HO

## Indian

Bombay Club, DC
Bombay Grille, CO
India Palace, SA
Taj Palace, CO

## Irish

Local, MN

## Italian

Abruzzi, AT (N&S)
Antonello, OC (N)
Antonio's La Fiamma, OR (N&S)
Armani's, TB (N)
Babbo, NY (N&S)
Baricelli Inn, CL (N&S)
Bar Italia, SL (N)
Barolo Grill, DE (N)
Barresi's, CI (N&S)
Boccaccio, BA (N)
Buca di Beppo, MN (N&S)
Cafe Italia/Mission, KC (N)
Cafe Juanita, SE (N)
Cafe Lago, SE (N&S)
Café Louis, BO (N)
Cafe Martorano, FL (N&S)
Caffé Abbracci, MI (N&S)
Caffe Mingo, PO (N&S)
Castagna, PO (N&S)
Chef Vola's, AC (N&S)
Christo's, PS (N)
Ciao Mein, HO (N)
Circo, LV (N)
Coco Pazzo, CH (N)
Cousin's, AC (N&S)
Damian's, HS (N&S)
D'Amico Cucina, MN (N&S)
Daniel's, TC (N)
DiPalma, PH (N)
Dominic's, SL (N&S)
Earle, DT (N&S)
Enzo's on the Lake, OR (N)
Escopazzo, MI (N&S)
Floataway Cafe, AT (N&S)
Fratello's, CL (N&S)
Fresco, SC (N)
Full Moon Grill, DE (N)

Gabriel's, CH (N&S)
Gabriel's, DE (N)
Galileo, DC (N)
Garozzo's Rist. Due, KC (N&S)
Genoa, PO (N)
Germano's, CI (N&S)
Giovanni's, CL (N)
Giovanni's, SL (N&S)
Girasole, AC (S)
Giuseppe's, CO (S)
Grappa, SC (N&S)
Il Capriccio, BO (N&S)
Il Mulino, NY (N)
Il Posto, DT (N)
Il Terr. Carmine, SE (N)
Il Tulipano, MI (N)
Irene's Cuisine, NO (N&S)
Johnny's Bar/Fulton, CL (N)
Johnny's Downtown, CL (N)
La Campania, BO (N&S)
La Famiglia, PH (N&S)
La Finestra, PB (N)
La Griglia, HS (N&S)
La Grotta, AT (N&S)
La Mora, HS (N&S)
La Piazza, FW (N&S)
La Riviera, NO (N&S)
La Tavola, CO (N)
La Veranda, PH (N&S)
Lidia's, KC (N&S)
Locanda Veneta, LA (N)
Lombardi Mare, DA (N&S)
Lupo, LV (N&S)
Maurizio's, BO (N&S)
Mia Francesca, CH (N)
Mi Piaci, DA (N)
Monte Carlo Liv. Rm., PH (N&S)
Moro's Dining, DT (N)
Nicola's, CI (N)
Nino's, HS (N&S)
Obelisk, DC (N)
Oliveto, SF (N)
Onda, LV (N&S)
Osteria del Teatro, MI (N)
Portofino, LV (N&S)
Pranzo Italian Grill, SA (N&S)
Primavera, FL (N&S)
Primavista, CI (N&S)
Rao's, NY (S)
Rist. di Modesta, DT (N)
Rist. Luci, MN (N&S)
Rose Pistola, SF (N)
Sage, BO (N&S)
Salumi, SE (N&S)
Salvatore's, SD (N)
Saporito's, BO (N&S)
Scalea's, CI (N&S)
Scalini Fedeli, NJ (N)
Sergio's, OR (N&S)
Simposio, HS (N)
Spiaggia, CH (N&S)

T. Cook's, PS (N&S)
Terramia, BO (N&S)
3 Doors Down, PO (N&S)
Tony's, HS (N&S)
Tony's, SL (N&S)
Trattoria Marcella, SL (N&S)
Trattoria Primadonna, TB (N&S)
Trattoria Roma, CO (N&S)
Tra Vigne, SF (N&S)
Tre Figlio, AC (N&S)
Tuscan Steak, MI (N)
Tuscany, SC (N)
Valentino, LA (N&S)
Valentino, LV (N)
Va Pensiero, CH (N&S)
Veni Vidi Vici, AT (N)
Vetri, PH (N&S)
Vivace, SD (N)
Vivace, TC (N&S)
Vivande, SF (N&S)
Zelo, MN (N)

## Japanese

Domo, DE
Ginza, BO
Hirosuke, LA
Ichiban Sushi, SC
JoAn, CI
Jun's, KC
Kacho, HO
Kamogawa, AT
Kaz Sushi Bistro, DC
Kyo-Ya, HO
Makoto, DC
Matsuhisa, LA
NINJA, NO
Nishino, SE
Nobu, LV
Nobu, Next Door, NY
Nobu, NY
Origami, MN
Restaurant Japan, CO
Restaurant Murata, PO
R-23, LA
Sachiko Sushi, TC
Sagami, NJ
Sapporo Wind, CO
Shiro's Sushi, SE
Shuhei, CL
Soto, AT
Sushi Den, DE
Sushi Huku, AT
Sushi-Ko, DC
Sushi Nozawa, LA
Sushi Ota, SD
Sushisay, NY
Tomoe Sushi, NY
Toni's, MI
Yohei Sushi, HO

## Latin American

Latin Rooster, CO
Tierra, AT

## Mediterranean

Acquario, PB
Aubergine Cafe, DE
Audrey Claire, PH
Azul, HO
Azzura Point, SD
Beach Bistro, TB
Beehive, DE
Bistro A, DA
Bistro Louise, FW
Brasa, SE
Caffe Bella, BO
Campanile, LA
Cascada, HO
Chez Panisse Cafe, SF
Chez Panisse, SF
Citricos, OR
Dmitri's, PH
La Belle Vie, MN
La Petite Maison, PB
Lucy's Table, PO
Martine, SC
Maurizio's, BO
Mediterraneo, DA
Moose's, SF
Olives, BO
Olives, LV
Overtures, PH
Palomino, DA
Palomino, HO
Palomino, MN
Pavilion, OC
Picholine, NY
PlumpJack Cafe, SF
Remy's Kitchen, SL
Renaissance, DE
Rialto, BO
Rigsby's, CO
Ritz-Carlton Buck. Din. Rm., AT
Ritz-Carlton, OC
Riviera, DA
Riviera Grill, HS
Sans Souci, CL
Splashes, OC
Strings, DE
T. Cook's, PS
Zov's Bistro/Bakery, OC
Zuni Cafe, SF

## Mexican/Tex-Mex

Cafe Azul, PO
Cafe Poca Cosa, TC
Eduardo de San Angel, FL
El Farol, SA
Frontera Grill, CH
Ixcapuzalco, CH
Javier's, DA
Joe T. Garcia's, FW
La Montaña, DE
Los Dos Molinos, PS
Luchita's, CL

Mi Nidito, TC
Old Mexico Grill, SA
Pappasito's Cantina, HS
Pueblo Solis, SL
Red Iguana, SC
Topolobampo, CH

## Middle Eastern
Steve's Backroom, DT

## New Mexican
La Casa Sena, SA
La Choza, SA
Rancho de Chimayo, SA
Shed, The, SA

## New World
Chef Allen's, MI
Darrel & Oliver's Cafe, FL
La Coquina, OR
Norman's, MI

## Northwestern
Artist Point, OR
Canlis, SE
Caprial's, PO
Cascadia, SE
Dahlia Lounge, SE
Fullers, SE
Georgian Room, SE
Heathman, PO
Inn at Langley, SE
Lampreia, SE
Lucy's Table, PO
Painted Table, SE
Paley's Place, PO
Szmania's, SE
Tina's, PO
Wildwood, PO

## Nuevo Latino
Yuca, MI

## Pacific New Wave
Chinois on Main, LA
Jozu, LA

## Pacific Rim
Anzu, DA
A Pacific Cafe, HO
Cascada, HO
Japengo, KC
Liberty, DA
Pacific Time, MI
Prince Court, HO
Roy's, HO
Roy's, PS
Second St. Grill, LV
Shiitake, SL
3660 on the Rise, HO

## Pan-Asian
Second St. Grill, LV
Yujean Kang's, LA

## Pizza
Figlio, CO
Pizzeria Bianco, PS
Pizzeria Paradiso, DC
Rotolo's, CO
Tacconelli's, PH

## Russian
Diaghilev, LA
Nikolai's Roof, AT
Russian Tea Room, NY

## Scandinavian
Aquavit, MN
Aquavit, NY

## Seafood
Al Biernat's, DA
AquaKnox, DA
Aqua, LV
Aqua, SF
Baleen, MI
Black Olive, BA
Black's, DC
Bristol B&G, KC
Cafe Pacifica, SD
Cafe Pacific, DA
Cantler's Riverside, BA
Capital Grille, DA
Cello, NY
Dmitri's, PH
Doris & Ed's, NJ
East Coast Grill, BO
Etta's Seafood, SE
Farallon, SF
Fishermans Wharf, CO
Flying Fish Cafe, OR
Flying Fish, SE
Fulton's Crab House, OR
Hobo's Fish Joint, FL
JJ's, KC
Joe's Stone Crab, MI
J's Fresh Seafood, CI
Kincaid's, MN
Kingfisher, TC
Kinkead's, DC
La Veranda, PH
Le Bernardin, NY
Legal Sea Foods, BO
Legend Seafood, HO
Lombardi Mare, DA
Mainstream Fish Hse., DA
Manhattan Ocean Club, NY
Market St. Grill, SC
Matsuhisa, LA
McCormick & Schmick's, BA
McCormick & Schmick's, HS
Milos, NY
Oceanaire, MN
Oceana, NY
Orchids, HO
Oyster Bar, NY

Oystercatchers, TB
Palm, AT
Pesce, DC
Prime, AT
Restaurant Oceana, PS
Rose Pistola, SF
Salt Rock Grill, TB
Savoy Grill, KC
Sea Grill, DA
Shiro, LA
Star of the Sea, SD
Striped Bass, PH
Sunfish Grill, FL
Water Grill, LA

## South American
Américas, HS
Churrascos, HS
Pasion!, PH

## Southern/Soul
Charleston, BA
Flying Biscuit Cafe, AT
Georgia Brown's, DC
Kingfish Café, SE
South City Kitchen, AT
Sylvia's, NY
Vidalia, DC

## Southwestern
Arizona Kitchen, PS
Armadillo Cafe, FL
Arroyo Grille, PH
Cafe Annie, HS
Cafe Diablo, SC
Cafe Pasqual's, SA
Cafe Terra Cotta, TC
Coyote Cafe, SA
¡Fuego!, TC
Geronimo, SA
Golden Swan, PS
Gold Room, TC
Inn of the Anasazi, SA
Janos, TC
La Casa Sena, SA
La Montaña, DE
Mansion on Turtle Creek, DA
Nava, AT
Old House, SA
Pink Adobe, SA
Reata, FW
Red Butte Cafe, SC
Red Sage, DC
Ruggles Grill, HS
Sierra Grill, HS
Star Canyon, DA
Star Canyon, LV
Vincent Guerithault, PS

## Spanish
Ceviche, TB
El Farol, SA
Emilio's Tapas Bar, CH

Harvest Vine, SE
Jaleo, DC
Marquesa, PS
Mesón Sabika, CH
Picasso, LV
Taberna del Alabardero, DC
Tapeo, PO
Tasca, HS
T. Cook's, PS
Tio Pepe, BA

## Steakhouses
Al Biernat's, DA
Al's, SL
Arnie Morton's, LA
Bern's, TB
Bob's Steak, DA
Bone's, AT
Brenner's, HS
Brighton Steak Hse., AC
C & H Steak Co., HS
Capital Grille, DA
Chamberlain's, DA
Chops, AT
Churrascos, HS
Citizen Kane's, SL
Del Frisco's, DA
Del Frisco's, DE
Del Frisco's, FW
Del Frisco's, OR
Eddie's Steak, SL
Fogo de Chao, DA
Gibsons, CH
Greystone, SD
Grill 23 & Bar, BO
Hyde Park Chop Hse., CL
Hyde Park Downtown, CL
Hyde Park Grille, CL
Hyde Park Grille, CO
Hy's Steak House, HO
JJ's, KC
Kincaid's, MN
Lawry's, LA
Lewnes', BA
Lynn's, HS
Manny's, MN
Morton's of Chicago, AT
Morton's of Chicago, CH
Morton's of Chicago, CI
Morton's of Chicago, CL
Morton's of Chicago, CO
Morton's of Chicago, DA
Morton's of Chicago, DC
Morton's of Chicago, DT
Morton's of Chicago, MI
Morton's of Chicago, OR
Morton's of Chicago, PB
Morton's of Chicago, PH
Morton's of Chicago, PS
Morton's of Chicago, SD
Palm, AT
Palm, LA

Palm, LV
Palm, MI
Palm, NY
Pappas Bros., HS
Peter Luger, NY
Plaza III, KC
Porcao, MI
Precinct, CI
Prime, AT
Prime, LV
Prime Rib, BA
Prime Rib, DC
Prime Rib, PH
Rainwater's, SD
Rancher's Club, TC
Ruth's Chris, BA
Ruth's Chris, CL
Ruth's Chris, HO
Ruth's Chris, KC
Ruth's Chris, LA
Ruth's Chris, NO
Ruth's Chris, PS
Salt Rock Grill, TB
Savoy Grill, KC
Shula's, TB
Smith & Wollensky, NY
Spencer's, SC
Steak Hse., LV
Sullivan's, DA
Young's, NO

## Swedish

Gustaf Anders, OC

## Swiss

Fio's La Fourchette, SL

## Tapas

Ceviche, TB
Emilio's Tapas Bar, CH
Harvest Vine, SE
Jaleo, DC
Mesón Sabika, CH
Tapeo, PO

## Tearooms

BonBonerie, CI

## Thai

Arun's, CH
Duangrat's, DC
Golden Room, HS
Nan, PH
Tamarind, AT
Typhoon!, PO
Vong, CH

## Vegetarian

Bluebird Cafe, KC
Flying Biscuit Cafe, AT

## Vietnamese

Arc-en-Ciel, DA
Cafe Trang, SC
Kim Son, NO
La Tre Vietnamese, PB
Lemon Grass Cafe, NO
Little Saigon, AC
Miss Saigon, MI
New Saigon, DE
Nine Roses, NO
Pasteur, CH
Slanted Door, SF

# ALPHABETICAL PAGE INDEX

**NOTES**

# NOTES

**NOTES**

# NOTES

# Wine Vintage Chart 1985-1998

This chart is designed to help you select wine to go with your meal. It is based on the same 0 to 30 scale used throughout this *Survey*. The ratings (prepared by our friend **Howard Stravitz**, a law professor at the University of South Carolina) reflect both the quality of the vintage and the wine's readiness for present consumption. Thus, if a wine is not fully mature or is over the hill, its rating has been reduced. We do not include 1987, 1991 or 1993 vintages because, with the exception of cabernets, '91 Northern Rhônes and '93 red Burgundies and Southern Rhônes, those vintages are not especially recommended.

| | '85 | '86 | '88 | '89 | '90 | '92 | '94 | '95 | '96 | '97 | '98 |
|---|---|---|---|---|---|---|---|---|---|---|---|
| **WHITES** | | | | | | | | | | | |
| **French:** | | | | | | | | | | | |
| Alsace | 25 | 20 | 23 | 28 | 28 | 24 | 28 | 26 | 24 | 25 | 24 |
| Burgundy | 24 | 25 | 19 | 27 | 22 | 23 | 22 | 27 | 28 | 25 | 24 |
| Loire Valley | – | – | – | 26 | 25 | 18 | 22 | 24 | 26 | 23 | 22 |
| Champagne | 28 | 25 | 24 | 26 | 28 | – | – | 24 | 26 | 24 | – |
| Sauternes | 22 | 28 | 29 | 25 | 26 | – | 18 | 22 | 23 | 24 | – |
| **California:** | | | | | | | | | | | |
| Chardonnay | – | – | – | – | – | 24 | 22 | 26 | 22 | 26 | 26 |
| **REDS** | | | | | | | | | | | |
| **French:** | | | | | | | | | | | |
| Bordeaux | 26 | 27 | 25 | 28 | 29 | 18 | 24 | 25 | 24 | 23 | 23 |
| Burgundy | 24 | – | 23 | 27 | 29 | 23 | 23 | 25 | 26 | 24 | 24 |
| Rhône | 26 | 20 | 26 | 28 | 27 | 15 | 23 | 24 | 22 | 24 | 26 |
| Beaujolais | – | – | – | – | – | – | 21 | 24 | 22 | 24 | 23 |
| **California:** | | | | | | | | | | | |
| Cab./Merlot | 26 | 26 | – | 21 | 28 | 26 | 27 | 25 | 24 | 25 | 26 |
| Zinfandel | – | – | – | – | – | 21 | 23 | 21 | 22 | 24 | 25 |
| **Italian:** | | | | | | | | | | | |
| Tuscany | 27 | – | 24 | – | 26 | – | – | 25 | 19 | 28 | 25 |
| Piedmont | 25 | – | 25 | 27 | 27 | – | – | 23 | 25 | 28 | 25 |

Bargain sippers take note: Some wines are reliable year in, year out, and are reasonably priced as well. They include: Alsatian Pinot Blancs, Côtes du Rhône, Muscadet, Bardolino, Valpolicella and inexpensive Spanish Rioja and California Zinfandel and are best bought in the most recent vintages.